Recovered Legacies

In the series

Asian American History and Culture

Edited by Sucheng Chan, David Palumbo-Liu, Michael Omi, and K. Scott Wong

Recovered Legacies

Authority and Identity in
Early Asian American Literature

Edited by

KEITH LAWRENCE AND
FLOYD CHEUNG

TEMPLE UNIVERSITY PRESS
Philadelphia

PS
153
. A 8 4
R 4 4
2005

Temple University Press
1601 North Broad Street
Philadelphia PA 19122
www.temple.edu/tempress

Library of Congress Cataloging-in-Publication Data

Recovered Legacies : authority and identity in early Asian American literature /
 edited by A. Keith Lawrence and Floyd D. Cheung.
  p. cm.—(Asian American history and culture)
 Includes bibliographical references and index.
 ISBN 1-59213-118-2 (alk. paper)
 ISBN 1-59213-119-0 (pbk. : alk. paper)
  1. American literature—Asian American authors—History and criticism. 2. Asian Americans—Intellectual life. 3. Identity (Psychology) in literature. 4. Asian Americans in literature. 5. Group identity in literature. 6. Authority in literature.
 I. Lawrence, A. Keith, 1954– II. Cheung, Floyd D., 1969– III. Series.
 PS153.A84R44 2005
 810.9′895—dc22

                                                    2004062557

2 4 6 8 9 7 5 3 1

Contents

Preface

As PROFESSORS of Asian American literature, we quite naturally find satisfaction and purpose in Asian American literary scholarship: our own research projects engage and motivate us; we are revitalized through our scholarly dialogues and interactions with colleagues. But each of us, in our respective university and college assignments, is first and foremost a teacher. Our first thoughts are always for our students; and in the way we structure our courses, in the texts and authors we choose, and in the discussions and activities we build our classes around, we seek to engage our students, to challenge them, and to develop in them significant and lasting skills that will help them to negotiate literature and life.

In our Asian American literature courses, and especially in our survey courses, we have often lamented the dearth of approaches to or "ways of reading" the pioneer texts of Asian American literature—virtually all texts published before the late 1960s. We have also been troubled by the fact that insofar as theoretical approaches to early texts and authors do exist, they tend to polarize their subjects into "good" and "bad" or "real" and "fake" camps, sometimes quite casually dismissing a text or author for exhibiting the wrong politics, the wrong aesthetic, or the wrong tone. We have longed for approaches to early texts and authors that, through careful and clearheaded analysis, would not only define and explain fractures and flaws but would also engage texts and authors on their own terms and in ways that would fairly and logically reveal their strengths and contributions. This book, in large measure, represents an attempt to satisfy such longings.

To be sure, this book is directed to fellow scholars. But Asian American literature students, together with those who teach them, constitute our primary audience. Given our pedagogical aims, we have required contributors not only to maintain high standards of scholarship, originality, and sophistication, but also to write clearly and directly to our intended audience, avoiding unnecessary jargon and convoluted language. In our initial formulation of this project, in our selection of pre-1960s authors, and in our own editing of each article, we have had our student audience in mind. We hope that through the perspectives and analyses afforded by this book, our fellow scholars—students as well as teachers—will discover new ways of looking at favorite texts and that, in some cases, they might adopt "neglected" texts as new favorites.

Certainly, there are omissions in our project. Difficult content decisions were made in line with our desire to put forward lesser known writers and texts. Satisfied that most of our readers would bring with them an appreciation of Sui Sin Far and Hisaye Yamamoto, for example, we elected not to "recover" such writers here. Otherwise, we have tried to represent major Asian American authors and texts before the 1960s, although constraints of space and time meant that deserving texts and writers would be left out and that some analyses would be curtailed. However, the analyses of texts and authors considered in this book also suggest approaches to works and writers we have been unable to include; and we trust our audience to find not only new applications for our ideas and those of our contributors, but other wonderful and productive ways of reading a large body of too-long-neglected works.

To our contributors, we owe our deepest gratitude for their generosity, intellect, loyalty, and patience. We would also like to thank our colleagues—known and anonymous—who have reviewed and nurtured our text through its various stages of development. We acknowledge the unflagging support of our editors at Temple University Press, especially David Palumbo-Liu, Janet Francendese, and William Hammell: they have improved the project with their incisive criticism and sustained us with their encouragement. Many of the articles in this collection began as papers sponsored by the Circle for Asian American Literary Studies (CAALS) and presented at annual conferences of the American Literature Association (ALA). We recognize the executive officers of the ALA—particularly Gloria Cronin and Alfred Bendixen—who helped lay the groundwork for this collection by supporting CAALS as a fledgling organization and by warmly encouraging our scholarly endeavors. We appreciate undergraduate and graduate research assistants who have assisted us with word processing and proofreading responsibilities—especially Cameron Pipkin, whose expert editorial guidance was all the more appreciated because it was voluntary. We are grateful for grants from our respective departments and colleges at Brigham Young University and Smith College and from the Woodrow Wilson National Fellowship Foundation: these enabled us to do research, to write, to participate in conference activities related to this project, and to create and then sustain CAALS through its first years.

For their care and devotion, we thank our friends and families—all of whom we can acknowledge properly only by returning their love. We owe our fondest gratitude and our hearts to our respective best friends and companions Tracy and Sheri, who have sacrificed much so that *Recovered Legacies* could be compiled. To our students, we dedicate this volume.

Keith Lawrence and Floyd Cheung
May 2005

Chronology of Works Discussed

Date Published	Title	Author
1887	*When I Was a Boy in China*	Yan Phou Lee (1861–1938?)
1909	*My Life in China and America*	Yung Wing (1828–1912)
1912	*Mrs. Spring Fragrance*	Edith Eaton/Sui Sin Far (1865–1914)
1915	*Me, A Book of Remembrance*	Onoto Watanna/ Winnifred Eaton (1879–1954)
1925	*A Daughter of the Samurai*	Etsu Inagaki Sugimoto (1874–1950)
1937	*And China Has Hands*	H.T. Tsiang (1899–1971)
1937	*East Goes West*	Younghill Kang (1903–1972)
1937–55	*College Plays*	Various playwrights, including Ling-Ai Li, Wai Chee Chun, and Charlotte Lum
1942–45	Various poems in *Trek*	Toyo Suyemoto (1916–2003)
1943	"The Travelers"	Toshio Mori (1910–1980)
1945	*Fifth Chinese Daughter*	Jade Snow Wong (1922–2002)
1946	*America Is in the Heart*	Carlos Bulosan (1911–1956)
1947	"Unfinished Message"	Toshio Mori (1910–1980)
1949	*Yokohama, California*	Toshio Mori (1910–1980)
1953	*Nisei Daughter*	Monica Itoi Sone (1919–)
1957	*No-No Boy*	John Okada (1923–1971)
1958	"Bread of Salt"	N.V.M. Gonzalez (1915–1999)
1959	"The Long Journey and the Short Ride"	Toshio Mori (1910–1980)

1964	*The Martyred*	Richard E. Kim (1932–)
1968	*The Innocent*	Richard E. Kim (1932–)
1986	*Clay Walls*	Ronyoung Kim (1926–1987)
1995 (written 1955)	*The Cry and the Dedication*	Carlos Bulosan (1911–1956)
2000 (written 1944)	*The Brothers Murata*	Toshio Mori (1910–1980)

Introduction

KEITH LAWRENCE AND FLOYD CHEUNG

FOR MORE than a century, immigrants from various Asian countries and their descendants have made America their home. Throughout
this time, writers whom we could call Asian American have expressed
their joys, lamented their losses, crafted new forms, and imagined new
worlds in their poetry, stories, novels, and plays. *Recovered Legacies:
Authority and Identity in Early Asian American Literature*, which focuses
on the period of Asian American literary history between roughly 1880
and 1965, assists in the recovery of the rich, diverse, and complicated
writings of Asian American literary pioneers. We acknowledge, as Cary
Nelson reminds us, that "literary history is never an innocent process of
recovery. We recover what we are culturally and psychologically prepared to recover, and what we 'recover' we necessarily rewrite, giving
it meanings that are inescapably contemporary, giving it a new discursive life" (1989, 11). Working at the dawn of the twenty-first century, our
contributors and we recover and reassess many texts that have been
ignored or denigrated by previous critics of Asian American literature.
We have found that by approaching early texts with a wider range of
expectations, paying close attention to the circumstances of their composition (including their original historical, social, and sometimes archival
contexts) while applying traditional and recent critical theories to our
readings of them, we have been able to rediscover what was valuable
about the texts for their initial audiences as we infuse them with new
discursive life for contemporary readers.

The subtitle of our volume would suggest that, from our perspective,
affording new life to early Asian American literature is synonymous
with establishing its authority and identity. We appreciate that *author* is
the root of *authority*—and that both words derive from the Latin *auctor*,
or "creator." We wish to restore, in measure, the authority of (and for)
early Asian American literary texts to the respective authors of these
texts. One of our fundamental assumptions here is that every literary

text is engendered by unique circumstances—that, more precisely, these circumstances dictate how the author of a given text will shape it and what he or she will include in it. If the authority of (or for) this text is to be restored to its author—especially if the text is historically removed from us—we are thus obliged, as a point of departure, to re-create and understand the text's engendering circumstances. The *identity* of a literary text, given connections of the word itself to the Latin *idem* ("same," "consistent") and *essentitas* ("being"), will derive, certainly, from these "engendering circumstances" as well as from the text's self-contained structure and content. In this sense, the identity of a late nineteenth-century Asian American text should not depend (to put it bluntly) on the agenda of an early twenty-first-century reader. In emphasizing literary authority and identity, this volume contributes to the study of the "early" period of Asian American literary history in two ways: first, as a corrective to the presentist trend in existing scholarship, and second, as part of an effort to rethink why multicultural—in this case, Asian American—perspectives from the period matter.

Transcending Presentism

As the recent publication of *Re/collecting Early Asian America* (Lee, Lim, and Matsukawa 2002) signals, the time has come to reconsider how we "recollect"—that is, how we select and remember—early Asian American cultural productions. One key historical marker for the work of Lee et al. is the same for us: the significance of 1965 as the year of the Hart-Celler Act, which mandated changes in the immigration quota system and consequently allowed for many more immigrants from Asian countries to enter the United States, thereby fundamentally changing the demographic composition of Asian America. Another date of importance for us is 1968, when students at San Francisco State University (joined by their peers at many other institutions) called for an end to U.S. military intervention in Vietnam as well as for reforms to an educational system that did not address their needs. Finally, the late 1960s saw the invention of the terms "Asian American" and "Asian American literature"; during this period, concerted efforts were made by Asian American writers and scholars, especially in California, to define, codify, and stimulate appreciation for Asian American literary production. These events help to make the late 1960s a watershed moment for Asian American literary studies. And as David Palumbo-Liu (1995) has pointed out, most scholarship has focused on literature following this moment—and indeed on literature *of* the moment, a phenomenon he calls the "fetishization of the present" (qtd. in Chang 1996, xv). Overcoming or transcending such presentism depends on successfully meeting at least three challenges: to dismantle the resistance/accommodation model of the Asian American experience, to resist prescription while embracing dialogue, and to perceive America as (in Rémi Brague's words [2002]) an "eccentric culture."

Challenge 1: Dismantling the Resistance/Accommodation Model

We have been inspired by scholars of other ethnic American literatures as they have moved beyond the necessary and important work of canonizing so-called representative writers and texts to consider American multicultural production from new and more broadly developed perspectives on diversity and interconnectedness. We acknowledge, for example, the work of Kirsten Silva Gruesz (2001) on late nineteenth-century Latino writing, where she adeptly demonstrates how hitherto unknown Latino authors creatively engage not only the historical shifts in U.S.-Latin American relations but also such writers of the mainstream tradition as Whitman, Longfellow, and Bryant. While she pays careful attention to historical and materialist concerns, Gruesz works among a growing body of scholars who no longer choose to view their field solely through the binary lenses of resistance and accommodation, lenses worn by many late twentieth-century critics of ethnic American literature. Indeed, the resistance/accommodation model of Asian American experience is closely attached to present-centered Asian American literary and social theory. As one of our contributors, Viet Thanh Nguyen, argues in *Race and Resistance: Literature and Politics in Asian America*, "Resistance and accommodation are actually limited, polarizing options that do not sufficiently demonstrate the *flexible strategies* often chosen by authors and characters to navigate their political and ethical situations" (2002, 4; emphasis in original).

Collectively (and we are both oversimplifying and extrapolating Nguyen's argument here), Gruesz (2001) and fellow scholars like Geneviàve Fabre and Michel Feith (2002) and Craig Womack (1999) remind us that the resistance/accommodation model is problematic in two ways. First, it is clearly the product of its own era, measuring both "resistance" and "accommodation" by codified standards of the late twentieth century. Second, and more crucially, it measures (and again, only in codified ways) little more than how politically, emotionally, or socially active one is as an "American" or, in contradistinction to it, an "ethnic American" of a particular type. Larger issues of one's materialism, ideology, spirituality, aesthetics, biology, morality, culture, or sociality—of one's identity and humanity—are thus misrepresented or altogether ignored. Take, for instance, the case of Edith and Winnifred Eaton, who wrote under the names of Sui Sin Far and Onoto Watanna at the beginning of the twentieth century.

A review of Sui Sin Far's and Onoto Watanna's differing receptions—past and present—provides insights into trends in Asian American literary criticism, especially a sense of how changing political priorities have affected the ways in which scholars interpret and evaluate the work of early figures. As one of the first authors to be recovered after the birth of the field in the 1960s, Sui Sin Far consistently has attracted scholarly attention, thus making her a particularly good case for our consideration. Writing for a range of newspapers and literary journals during the turn of the twentieth century, she published her only book-length work, a collection of short stories titled *Mrs. Spring Fragrance*, in 1912. After her death in 1914, her literary reputation remained dormant until about 1970, when scholars in the field of Asian American studies began recovering her work. Initially, scholars celebrated her stories and other writings for reasons that made sense in the critical climate of the 1970s. Half English and half Chinese, Sui Sin Far, née Edith Eaton, chose to write under a Chinese pseudonym. Scholars interpreted this choice as brave, proud, and confident during an age when Sinophobia was dominant in America. Accordingly, they historicized Sui Sin Far as an early exemplar of the values they themselves advocated through the Asian American movement: greater ethnic pride and increased social accountability. In particular, they emphasized how Sui Fin Far's protagonists—who were invariably likable and complex human individuals—countered negative stereotypes of Chinese as inhuman hordes. Following the success of *The Woman Warrior* in 1975, feminist critics searched for Maxine Hong Kingston's (1975) antecedents to recover an Asian American women writers' tradition; and not surprisingly, they identified Sui Sin Far as one of Kingston's "literary grandmothers" (Ammons 1992, 60). Routinely throughout the 1970s and 1980s, critics and teachers compared her favorably with her sister, Winnifred Eaton, who chose to write under the pseudo-Japanese penname of Onoto Watanna at a time when Japan and things Japanese were positively viewed by most Americans. Thus, the narrative forwarded by such scholar-teachers posits that while Edith heroically emphasized her Chinese identity, Winnifred chose a much easier and more lucrative path, one that appeared to support stereotypical notions of a problematically exotic and devious Japanese character. During the first period of recovery, in short, early authors were measured—and embraced or denounced—according to their apparent ethnic pride and ostensible resistance to negative stereotypes of Asians and Asian Americans.

In the past ten years, a body of criticism by a new generation of critics—including Yuko Matsukawa (1994), Min Song (1998), Dominka Ferens (2002), and our contributor David Shih—asks a different set of questions of both Sui Sin Far's and Onoto Watanna's writings: To what degree did these writers act as trickster figures? How do new theories of gender and sexuality afford fresh lenses through which to interpret their work? Does it matter that early writers sometimes positioned themselves as insiders when, in contrast to the Asian and Asian American communities about which they wrote, they were indeed outsiders by virtue of their class and mixed-race identities? In what ways did the demands of their publishers affect what they could write? What other constraints—and opportunities—attended their idiosyncratic careers?

As the example of the Eaton sisters' reception demonstrates, scholars in the field of Asian American literature have begun to move from a compensatory to a transformative mode. During the first phase of recovery, Asian American literary critics tended to read early literature as either supportive or unsupportive of present-day political goals—and to advocate individual texts according to such readings. In a sense, these politically conscious, committed, and well-intentioned critics asked not what they could do for early Asian American literature but what early Asian American literature could do for them. More to the point, they asked which early figures anticipated the compensatory cultural work that they themselves sought to perform through their own criticism and teaching. While exceptions exist, only in the past decade have critics in the main begun to ask different and more open questions, approaching literature of the past with greater attention to original circumstances of production. For Sui Sin Far and Onoto Wantanna, especially, this work is well under way, but for many other early figures—some of whom are discussed in this volume—the work of transformative reassessment has just begun.

Challenge 2: Resisting Prescription and Embracing Dialogue

In *The City of Man* (1998), Pierre Manent satirically observes that relying on accepted scientific methodology, the scholar has virtually boundless freedom in setting up and developing arguments—especially given that "he is methodologically exempt from connecting to other facts, which is to say from the whole of the human phenomenon," so that he is "spared the sole true difficulty of knowledge." Such scholars, Manent continues, tend to rely on interdisciplinary research, "as if the sum of the biases they profess could ever yield the unity of an impartial examination." Indeed, such reliance stems in large part from a complicit understanding among disciplines about which rules may, with impunity, be broken—to the end that " 'interdisciplinary research' is to scientific rigor what routing is to military discipline or a stampede to horsemanship" (111, 112). For Manent, there is an attendant scholarly problem, one centered in "the contrast found in the spirit of modern democracies between reforming activism under the banner of universal rights and scientific passivity in the name of cultural diversity." The problem is not simply that the tension between scholarly passivity and action is finally unresolvable, but that asserting man as a cultural being in measure contradicts and is contradicted by asserting man as a being with rights (148, 149). Put differently, the doctrine of rights leads sociologists quite naturally to the doctrine of cultural diversity—but paradoxically makes full or genuine diversity impossible. Either this or a championed diversity begins to impinge upon an unfettered possession or exercise of rights.

Manent's argument should give any body of scholars pause. It has, it seems to us, a number of important ramifications for Asian American literary studies; but we focus on only one here. We began our discussion with an indictment of presentism—which as a matter of course champions both *rights* and *diversity* as Manent uses the terms. The presentist model prefers to ignore tensions or schisms between the two; at best, it makes only cursory efforts to reconcile or arbitrate such tensions. Somewhat ironically, however, it rewards the fervor with which moral convictions or prescriptions are drawn from analyses of diversity or rights (or both together)—perhaps to call attention away from the logically flawed processes whereby such morality is deduced. More problematic still is the possibility that in employing the presentist model, one begins a textual analysis with a moral judgment or prescription already in mind, so that the resulting study is more parable than analysis, exemplifying (to collapse Manent's terms) all the rigor of a stampede.

Admittedly, aesthetic criticism is and must be, in important ways, prescriptive. But even a casual analysis of the critical tradition tells us that prescription is a double-edged sword—and that, for every legitimate or healthy prescription, there are probably dozens that, because they invoke censorship or abuse, only compound ignorance, bigotry, isolation, and suffering. That our own discipline of Asian American literature has a tradition of prescriptive criticism (especially as our field has developed over the past half century) should, then, be reason for introspection—as should the fact that our prescriptiveness may be compounded by justifiable changes in the umbrella field over our discipline, Asian American studies, wherein the field itself has become less isolationist and theoretical and increasingly activist and utilitarian.

Tendencies toward prescriptiveness sometimes lead us to gauge self-worth or, more problematic still, the worth of "real" and "textual" others by dents made in literary canons, university course offerings, or the American social condition. In so doing, we open ourselves not only to judging falsely but to perpetuating the very separatism—the divisiveness—we wish to eradicate from our classrooms, campuses, and larger communities. And when our scholarly business is reduced, as it sometimes is, to valuating a text according to its relative "fakery" or legitimacy—or according to our measure of the politics of its author— we may find ourselves on the shady side of Mars' Hill, scrabbling at the foundations of the tribunal stand of the Areopagus with our picks. Indeed, such thinking is not merely divisive or separatist, but at the very root of what Philip Curtin has called the ghettoization of ethnic studies in the American academy (1993, A44).

In a recent *Heath Anthology of American Literature Newsletter* article, Robert Jackson (2003) recounts experiences teaching *To Kill a Mockingbird* at a historically black college in Alabama. Suggesting that we question not only *what* but *why* we read, Jackson admits surprise in discovering that his students seemed less inclined to read Lee's novel for "political, historical, racial, or other agendas" than for a single aesthetic or emotional agenda: the "desire for a good story." While certainly not discounting what he might call "non-aesthetic" ways of reading, Jackson nevertheless argues that his students' story-centered engagement with Lee's novel should "remind professional scholars" precisely "what got them into the business in the first place"—that is, presumably, formative reading experiences where one's identification with a favorite narrator or narrative "temporarily, ecstatically suspends everything outside the story." Such reading, Jackson argues, is "transcendent," leading readers to recognize of favorite authors what one of his students wrote of Lee: "The woman had skills" (10).

As editors of the present volume, then, what is at issue for us is the extent to which one's own prescriptive baggage (or that of one's field) intrudes upon one's capacity to perceive the "skills" of the early authors or texts one engages. But as we attempt to set aside our prescriptions, we may discover the uncomfortably fine line between tolerance and accommodation, between empathy and emotionality, and between respect and self-deprecation. We must not leave ourselves open to what Renato Rosaldo (1989) has labeled, in an essay of the same title, "imperialist nostalgia"—the inadvertent though nonetheless insidious colonizing and memorializing of the other through corrupt ideology. While Rosaldo's deconstructionist framework dates his essay, and while his glib dismissal of all ideologies as corrupt is troubling, a core assumption remains provocative and incisive: that the social anthropologist's mistake is to merely name and "demystify" false ideologies when in fact nothing short of "dismantling" them will do. Such dismantling is effected, says Rosaldo, by "giving voice to the ideologies"—by letting them assume character and expression, as it were, and then allowing them to talk themselves to death. As they reveal themselves "at once [to] be compelling, contradictory, and pernicious," Rosaldo argues, they "fall under their own weight," the "inconsistencies within and between voices becoming apparent" (Rosaldo 1989, see 110 ff.). Speaking for ourselves and our contributors, our collective desire is (to borrow Rosaldo's metaphor) to give voice to the ideologies, both the corrupt and the worthwhile, that surround the authors and texts of early Asian American literary history. As the corrupt voices talk themselves to death and the worthwhile voices gain in authority and clarity, the works which the voices foreground are brought into sharp relief. Seen in new ways, the works—to put it most simply—become more significant, complex, and compelling than we previously imagined them to be.

This is one way we have attempted to embrace dialogue as a means of counterbalancing prescription. Another is a more straightforward process: we have attempted to meet Asian American authors on their own grounds, reading a particular text against re-creations of the world in which it was originally produced and, insofar as judgments are applied to the text, allowing the standards of the author's world (rather than always those of our own) to mediate our assignments of value or merit to the author's writing. In the present volume, we and our contributors have espoused literary rather than other forms of scholarship, making concerted efforts to write useful, historically grounded criticism. To the extent that we have closely and carefully delineated the texts we write about, we have indeed adhered to what might be termed, in the broadest sense, a "formalist" approach. But careful readers of our volume will see that it is also grounded in a variety of other approaches—New Historical, feminist, neo-Marxist, neo-Freudian, postcolonial, ethnohistorical—that balance and contextualize "close readings" (by affording them immediacy and cultural currency) without de-emphasizing or displacing the literary analysis itself (or the corresponding primary texts). We remain convinced that such an approach eschews unwarranted prescriptiveness and encourages significant dialogue with the texts we engage. It is in this light that we briefly consider Jade Snow Wong's autobiographical novel *Fifth Chinese Daughter*.

Written at the height of World War II and published as the war was drawing to a close, Wong's best-selling *Fifth Chinese Daughter* (1945) was the most widely read work of an Asian American writer during the late 1940s and early 1950s; its popularity among white audiences has justifiably invited, over the intervening decades, an intense scrutiny by Asian American literary critics of Wong's politics, ideologies, themes, style, and characterizations, together with her use of Chinese and Chinese American cultural material. The upshot is that Wong has emerged as the designated persona non grata of Asian American letters; her very name (in the forms "a Jade Snow" or the punning "Snow job") has come to signify an Asian American text that, in its false and Anglophilic representations of Asian or Asian American cultures, prostitutes itself to white Orientalist tastes. Likely the most damning epithet attached to Wong is the infamous noun string of the anonymous male writer cited by Merle Woo in her "Letter to Ma," a string that, in its linguistic versatility, works adjectivally as well as nominally: "Jade Snow Wong Pocahontas yellow" (Woo 1994, 163).

While it is virtually impossible to imagine an entirely positive contemporary review of Wong, current appraisals run a fairly broad gamut—from the perfervid condemnation of a scholar like Karen Su (1994) to the dispassionate analysis and muted praise of Leslie Bow (2001). Su argues, finally, "for an interpretive strategy that can subvert attempts to read [Wong's] texts as 'model minority' narratives" and that show "Wong's 'badge of distinction'" to be in "the way in which her texts reveal her own submission to the dominant American ideologies that oppress her." Bow's thesis, in contrast, is that while Wong's "ethnic commodification fed white appetite for difference," her text, as feminist discourse, "provides a normalizing counterpoint to ethnic differentiation"; accordingly, *Daughter* itself proves that "narratives of gender oppression often assume an air of timelessness, particularly in cases where thwarted self-actualization is situated within a narrative of parent/child conflict" (Bow 2001, 91).

While Bow (2001) and, to a lesser extent, Su (1994) quite brilliantly explain what Wong was subconsciously or inadvertently about in *Daughter*, both could more effectually explain what Wong knowingly accomplished in her history. If, in our approach to Wong's first book, we delay asking questions about "fakery" and "autobiography," and if, for the moment, we leave politics out of the mix, we might be more sensitive to Wong's stance and purpose as a modernist author steeped in formalism. We might recognize, for example, that while the anonymous male writer cited by Merle Woo effectually links Wong to the American narrative/myth of John Smith and Pocahontas, he has possibly focused on the wrong character. Arguably, in other words, Wong's *Daughter* has much more to do with Smith than Pocahontas. Despite Wong's rather coy explanation in her original author's note that "although a 'first person singular' book, this story is written in the third person from Chinese habit" (xiii), it is possible that she deliberately constructs herself as a "stranger in a strange land"—and that she co-opts Smith's own linguistic and emotional method of confronting the unfamiliar landscape in third person. Perhaps Wong, like many other high school students in the 1930s, read the following description of John Smith in the popular high school anthology *American Literature* edited by Briggs, Herzberg, and Bolenius:

> In spite of dissension and privation, the two years of Smith's stay [in the Virginia colony] were in many respects the happiest period the colony knew for many years. He understood the Indians and was able to gain their friendship; moreover, he could command and govern the colonists. He had quite probably no intention of remaining in Virginia for any great length of time. No one place would ever have been able to satisfy his insatiable thirst for new risks. The new world was something he had wanted to see; colonization, an adventure he longed to add to the list of his experiences. (1933, 619)

If Wong's exposure to John Smith possibly occurred under such circumstances, one might then consider the rhetorical or political significance of Wong's creating herself as "colonizer"—and the sort of rhetorical, psychological, or sociological control afforded by the third-person voice that mocks humility by evoking a kind of immutability. One might also consider the textual layering that occurs in *Daughter* when Wong assumes Smith's role (a decidedly masculine one in his own era) of "adventurer/historian." Such considerations lead to questions about the ethnic irony in Wong's narrative, especially the irony deriving from the fact that the indigenous population with which Wong must be ingratiated or with whom she must contend are descendants, figuratively, of Smith himself. While history now marks Smith as a naive if not inept interpreter of the events in which he participated, Wong (in contrast) may be not merely a fully conscious but a *manipulating* participant.

A close reading of virtually any chapter in the book gives rise to subsidiary questions. Take, for example, chapter 7, which is entitled "Learning to be a Chinese Housewife." True enough, the core of the chapter tells how the protagonist learns her mother's role and assumes partial responsibility for domestic matters. But, given its title, a reader naturally wonders why the chapter begins with a lengthy description of Wong's father's successfully transforming an unattractive basement into a thriving business location and place of residence for his family. One wonders, too, about the long digression later in the chapter describing "Uncle Jan," the attentive and unusually successful Chinatown butcher. And one asks why, particularly in this chapter, the only detailed method of food preparation recounted by the protagonist (the traditional method of cooking rice familiar to virtually every Asian or Asian American) is a method taught her not by her mother but by her father. One begins to consider, in short, how the narrative works to subvert gender and ethnic roles and thus to enable or empower its protagonist/author, along nontraditional lines, to assume a hybrid Asian American identity.

Challenge 3: Viewing America as an Eccentric Culture

In *Eccentric Culture: A Theory of Western Civilization* (2002), Rémi Brague defines Europe as an "eccentric" (as opposed to a "concentric") entity— that is, as an entity centered outside itself. As the origin of what we now know as Western civilization, Europe is (according to Brague) definable as a *container* rather than in terms of specific *contents*; or, more precisely, "the content of Europe" is "just to be a container, to be open to the universal." In this sense, says Brague, the idea of *Eurocentrism* is not merely "a misnomer," but "the contrary of the truth" (134, 146). Furthermore, that America is "founded on transplantation and on the idea of establishing a *novus ordo seclorum*" proves "the profoundly European legitimacy of the United States" (35).

Brague's argument is important to our purposes here. It reminds us to see America as evolving, decentered, and even fragmented rather than as static, definable, and monolithic. Too often, ethnic American sociological or aesthetic criticism assumes a rigidly uniform "America" existing in juxtaposition with—or opposition to—the ethnic body in question.

Pushed to extremes, this assumption simultaneously (and somewhat paradoxically) victimizes, objectifies, and orphans the relevant ethnic body. For the ethnic American literary critic engaged in historical or cultural analysis, this assumption has an additional consequence: collapsing history and culture into clichéd metanarratives of manipulation and loss, it blindsides the social and personal exceptions, aberrations or justifications that constitute, in many cases, the historical or aesthetic heart of the text in question.

Narrowing our discussion to the Asian American literary critic, we might consider, for example, how he or she responds to the year 1882, a date that will have enormous—and particularized—resonance. While the critic likely will not see "America," much less all Americans, embodied in the passage of the Chinese Exclusion Act, he or she may nevertheless contextualize 1880s America as ethically and culturally fixed, and as fixated on issues of race, rights, and identity. True enough, the late nineteenth and early twentieth centuries were indeed marked by what can only be termed ethnocentric, cruelly delimiting, and finally unconstitutional policies of immigration, settlement, and citizenship; this was also the grand period of Orientalism, with its attendant objectification, exoticism, condescension, and oppression. But these decades are also marked by such phenomena as Lafcadio Hearn's renouncing America for Japan—where he settled permanently as a Japanese citizen—and then by his enjoying an increased popularity in America as he published balanced essays on Japanese culture and English editions of Japanese ghost stories. Or Mark Twain's writing incisive journalistic "filler" for the *Sacramento Union* and other papers wherein he satirized whites' hypocrisy, insularity, and inhumanity in their dealings with Chinese Americans. Or the appearance of numerous stories and articles sympathetic to Asia and Asians (some written by Asian Americans) in mainstream periodicals like the *Youth's Companion, Harper's Monthly,* and *Century Magazine.* While it is certainly not our purpose to suggest that such historical details somehow soften or compensate for American immigration/naturalization policies or for American Orientalism, we nevertheless argue that an Asian American text of the late nineteenth or early twentieth century must be situated in the eccentric and complex culture that bore and fed it—and not in the artificially concentric culture in which we might choose to display it.

We must also take care not to construct Asia or its separate cultures or nations in monolithic ways. Sometimes early critics quite notoriously did precisely this, constructing Asian Americans as those with Chinese,

Japanese, or Korean ancestry and excluding all others, for example, or positing as studied and universal facts such notions as that autobiography is a white Christian and non-Asian (or even anti-Asian) form or that for most early writers, both their writing and their lives give evidence of their personal politics having been malformed or corrupted by (white) American racism.

Simply avoiding monolithic constructions is not enough. We also need to reformulate the very questions we ask of texts we read; we may need to modify such questions for each author—or even each text—we seek to understand. There are general questions we might put forward, beginning with the extent, ethically speaking, to which we may *demand* that early writers mirror our own values or perspectives. As we take measure of an early writer or text, we should give consideration to the racial/ethnic attitudes of the larger American community in which the writer worked, as well as to the social, economic, or educational status of the writer. We should also weigh the writer's need to "fit in" to the larger society in order to survive—as both writer and citizen. Such thoughtful exploration will point us away from the tendency to measure the full stretch of Asian American literary history against the concentric and presentist model of the post-1960s. It will point us instead toward a richer appreciation of Asian American history, so that crucial moments or points of origin—such as when three Chinese sailors aboard the *Pallas* were left stranded in Baltimore in 1785, or when "John" Manjiro Nakahama disembarked from the *John Howland* in May 1843, or when the first Chinese laborers arrived at "Gold Mountain" in early 1848—will be understood as comprising part of the "contents" (to return to Brague's analogy) of *America*, and not just of Asian America. This brings us to the second purpose of this volume: to rethink the significance of multicultural perspectives on early Asian American literary history.

RETHINKING MULTICULTURAL PERSPECTIVES

Thanks to theorists like Aihwa Ong and David Palumbo-Liu, we are starting to understand the significance of early twentieth-century developments in the dynamic shaping not only of the modern United States of America but also of the circum-Pacific region. During this period, as Palumbo-Liu puts it, literature imagined the "discursive space of Asian America, . . . both delineat[ing] its boundaries and envision[ing] particular modes of crossing them" (1999, 43). That is, authors of this period lived and worked during a time when cultural, political, and economic connections between Asia and America were being formed in their modern incarnation; moreover, through their works these early authors participated in the process of critique and imagination that led eventually—albeit unevenly and not inevitably—to the Asian American Movement of the 1960s itself.

Questions we are now prepared to ask—and to pose answers to—are centered in the following issues:

- the response of Asian American writers to the Chinese Exclusion Act of 1882, the National Origins Act of 1924, and World War II;
- the ways in which early Asian American writers were global, multinational, or transnational, even before jet planes and the Internet;
- the extent to which early Asian American writers are *American* writers, *Asian* writers, or *modernist* writers;
- the meaning of being "Asian American" (if anything) before the term itself was invented; and
- the existence of an Asian American Renaissance akin to the Harlem Renaissance.

Essays in this volume suggest answers to these and other questions, making it more possible for us to engage productively with a group of writers that, only now perhaps, we are "culturally and psychologically prepared" to rediscover (Nelson 1989, 11).

Our capacity to consider Asian American literary history as a multicultural phenomenon has also been changed—and invigorated by—international recognition and analysis of Asian American literary discourse. For example, since 1996 several workshops at conferences of the European Association of American Studies (EAAS) have been devoted to such topics as Asian American identities, writings, and social ceremonies. Partly an outgrowth of a pioneering EAAS workshop was a special issue of UC Berkeley's *Hitting Critical Mass*, "European Perspectives on Asian American Literature" (1996). In *Asian American Literature in the International Context: Readings on Fiction, Poetry and Performance* (2002), editors Rocío G. Davis and Sämi Ludwig recognize "the remarkable imaginative and narrative contributions of Asian American literature . . . outside the boundaries of the United States" (10). Davis and Ludwig perceive their book as the first in a series of volumes that will not "merely theorize transcultural issues and the internationalization of research"—which they say only "endorses the already hegemonic position of powerful United States academic institutions"—but will instead *"be* international rather than talk about it" while "presenting the research of scholars who are both inside *and* outside of the established discourse of Asian American studies" (12).

As scholars outside the United States have explored distinctions between and conflations of "Asian" and "American," have unpacked American and Asian American cultural production, and have engaged in transnational considerations of ethnic differentiation, gender, and identity among Asian Americans, possibilities for discussing the whole of Asian American literary history have increased. That is, multinational and multicultural criticism have helped create a liminal space where early Asian American authors and texts may be considered not only as "Asian" and "American" but as simultaneously international, multicultural, and *individual* as well. At this point, before proceeding to an overview of the essays in this volume, it would be well to consider briefly the multicultural quality—the demographics—of Asian America between 1880 and 1965.

A Word on the Demographics of Early Asian American Literature

A consultation of King-Kok Cheung and Stan Yogi's standard bibliography of Asian American literature, which was published in 1988, builds on two foundational assumptions: first, that Asian American literature, for better or worse, can be subcategorized into ethnic groups; and second, that up until the 1960s, literature by Chinese Americans and Japanese Americans—and to a lesser extent, of Filipino Americans and Korean Americans—dominates the comprehensive listing of works. Patterns of immigration before the 1960s account for the preponderance of Chinese American and Japanese American texts in Cheung and Yogi's bibliography, as well as in this volume. As historians have recounted, immigration from China flowed relatively freely from the mid–nineteenth century until the Chinese Exclusion Act of 1882. U.S.-based capitalists requiring new sources of labor after the passage of this act arranged for workers from Japan and, for a short time thereafter, Korea and India. In 1924, however, the National Origins Act placed quotas and restrictions on immigration from all Asian nations. The only major exception during the 1920s and 1930s was the Philippines, which was, at the time, a U.S. colony whose denizens qualified as U.S. nationals; the Tydings-McDuffie Act of 1934, however, soon excluded even Filipino laborers.

Thus, members of more diverse ethnic and national groups did not immigrate to or settle in the continental United States in significantly large numbers until after the 1960s, when the Hart-Celler Act lifted quotas restricting immigration from Asian nations. Furthermore, immigration from Southeast Asia did not rise significantly until after the United States retreated from Vietnam in 1975, and after the Refugee Act was passed in 1980. Literary critics in Asian American studies have responded to the increasing diversity of post-1960s Asian American immigration and settlement patterns mainly by including more recent writing by South Asian Americans, Southeast Asian Americans, and Pacific Islander Americans in their scholarship and syllabi. Early works by members of these groups are only now being recovered. For instance, South Asian American writer Dhan Gopal Mukerji's 1923 autobiography, *Caste and Outcast,* was reprinted by Stanford University Press in 2002. In future years, we expect that many more once rare yet significant works will reemerge—and that incisive critical assessments will follow.

A Critical Overview of the Present Volume

In establishing the authority and identities of the early authors and texts they examine, contributors to the present volume have successfully named and refuted false cultural expectations, seductive brands of prescription-making, and bewitching displays of cultural "nonwhiteness." As we have previously stated, the overriding objective of our volume is to provide richer, broader, and—in some cases—more accurate readings of early Asian American works, readings that don't merely assert "how far we've come" but that allow us to see the dignity of early writers and the genuine merit of what they wrote. To accomplish this objective, contributors have, as appropriate, deliberately stepped outside current ideologies, models, and values and have, as new historians, ethnohistorians, and postcolonial revisionists, tried to show how early works were produced and received in their own time periods and how we might most fairly and profitably read them today.

In "Early Chinese American Autobiography: Reconsidering the Works of Yan Phou Lee and Yung Wing," Floyd Cheung argues that Lee's autoethnography, *When I Was a Boy in China*, relies on Lee's authority as a privileged Chinese and a well educated American—"his unique socioeconomic and racialized position"—to fight Chinese exclusion by contesting "what he perceived to be inauthentic and unflattering ethnographies of the Chinese." Yung similarly capitalized on his authority as a "financially successful, U.S.-educated Chinese American man" to "fashion a version of himself"—in his writing and his private life—that, in its embodiment of male respectability and accomplishment, quietly undermined the masculine Eurocentrism promulgated by Theodore

Roosevelt. Both Yung and Lee teach us, Cheung argues, that "authenticity itself is contingent upon individual circumstances, personal motives, and historical context."

David Shih argues in "The Self and Generic Convention: Winnifred Eaton's *Me, A Book of Remembrance*" that "as a Chinese Eurasian living in Canada and the United States during the Exclusion era, Eaton turned to writing as the most direct way to manage her situation as racialized subject." But "far from providing her with the means to recover an authentic self," Shih argues, "her autobiographical act only confirmed that the articulation of any sense of individuality must always be mediated by the forms and structures available to the autobiographer." In this sense, *Me* poignantly records the emergence of a "self still in transition, a woman ready to alter the course of her life but not at the expense of her livelihood."

In "Diasporic Literature and Identity in *A Daughter of the Samurai*," Georgina Dodge discusses the unquestionable influence of Sugimoto's novel on Lydia Minatoya's *Strangeness of Beauty*—partly to show how *Daughter* is to be read and partly to demonstrate its continuing topical and aesthetic relevance. Read accurately, says Dodge, Sugimoto's narrative (like Minatoya's more recent one) "skillfully blends diverse identities in order to challenge the boundaries of gender, class, and nationality"—and questions "cultural models based on traditional values," models which "can serve as templates for behavior but must change with the times."

In "The Capitalist and Imperialist Critique in H. T. Tsiang's *And China Has Hands*," Julia H. Lee decries the current tendency to read Tsiang's text "as merely a historical artifact," as an "authentic" recounting of "a reactionary time in America." Doing so, she suggests, has blinded us to "how capitalist and imperialist enterprises racialize or sexually objectify their victims . . . in order to maintain power" and to how Marxism is inscribed "as the foundational principle of the novel." In the end, despite its determined presentation of a "transcendent vision of a . . . political state" at the expense of "addressing the troubling issues of sexuality, race, and gender," which fuel "the oppressive machinations of capitalism and imperialism," the novel "provocatively insists that racial intolerance and gender oppression" are at the heart of all exploitative systems.

In his "Unacquiring Negrophobia: Younghill Kang and the Cosmopolitan Resistance to the Back and White Logic of Naturalization," Stephen Knadler measures *East Goes West* against the "logic of naturalization" represented by *Ozawa v. the United States* (1922), thus reading Kang's novel as a "parody of twentieth-century narratives of whiteness—and of the negrophobia such logic invoked in Asian immigrants." The novel's purpose—according to Knadler—"is to devalue whiteness as a prize property that must be protected" and to endorse "an affiliative or cosmopolitan consciousness, a consciousness that is most accurately defined as 'post-ethnic.'"

Josephine Lee, in "Asian American (Im)mobility: Perspectives on the College Plays, 1937–1955," considers representative authors/texts from "the ten-volume set of plays written for the classes of English professor Willard Wilson at the University of Hawai'i." Lee argues that the plays—all by women—should be read as "depictions of and contradictions to the social relationships and issues of ethnic identity that were being redefined both in Hawai'i and on the mainland during the crucial period before, during, and following World War II." Contrasting Kathryn L. Bond's *We'll Go See the World* and Clara Kubojiri's *Country Pie*, Lee shows how the two plays delineate a "paradigmatic opposition between 'old' and 'new' forms of Asianness, as marked by obsolescence or incorporation into modernization and Americanization."

The premise of John Streamas's "Toyo Suyemoto, Ansel Adams, and the Landscape of Justice" is that—contrary to Susan Schweik's argument that the overtly appropriate nature of Suyemoto's poetry renders it passive and apolitical—Suyemoto's criticism of the internment was "particularly relevant to the imprisoned *nikei* community," in large part because the language of her poetry was "the simple language of landscape" and because it clearly signified oppression, thus recalling the "racial geographies of plantations, reservations, and concentrations camps."

Two post–World War II male writers are the focus of Viet Nguyen's "Wounded Bodies and the Cold War: Freedom, Materialism, and Revolution in Asian American Literature, 1946–1957." These are Carlos Bulosan and John Okada, whose primary works attempt to "recuperate the wounded bodies of Asian American men" by "speaking to American society in terms that it could understand: freedom and materialism." Bulosan and Okada strategically sought to "construct a usable manhood" within "the political and cultural regime of the United States as it transformed itself" in ways "justified by its own sense of democratic exceptionalism." Because, in *America Is in the Heart* (1946) and *No-No Boy* (1957), Bulosan and Okada, respectively, were writing from a "moment of racial equilibrium" that depended on an apparent conformity to white American norms, they "relied on an authorial irony about racial relations and racial identities" that subverted such conformity.

In *The Cry and the Dedication* (MS completed 1955; published posthumously 1995), Bulosan attempts the "recuperation of a wounded manhood, healed through a virile sexuality that enables and is enabled by a violent revolution."

Suzanne Arakawa's "Suffering Male Bodies: Representations of Dissent and Displacement in the Internment-Themed Narratives of John Okada and Toshio Mori" is concerned with how "the role of Japanese American dissenters in postwar American politics and culture" is subsumed in the fiction of Mori, Okada, and their contemporaries. Most simply put, writes Arakawa, *No-No Boy* "emphasizes the tensions involved in the desire to assimilate and one's perceived inability to do so," while Mori's camp stories "not only point up the complexity of returning Japanese American bodies to a pre-World War II home, but question the advisability of attempting such a venture."

In "Toshio Mori, Richard Kim, and the Masculine Ideal," Keith Lawrence argues that in his "allegories of masculine place," Mori's *Yokohama, California* effactually "collapses 'masculine' and 'feminine' perspectives into a Taoist...paradigm for masculine *being*"—so that "through the dismantling or reworking of polarized assumptions and tradition, life is not merely possible for the Asian American male but potentially good, edifying, joyous." Kim's *The Martyred* and *The Innocent* dictate, in contrast, a masculine responsibility "to effect meaningful social change" by remaining "physically within one's culture while emotionally or spiritually separating oneself from it, silently gathering strength to reach out to others," knowing that "in such fruitful withdrawal there is enormous opportunity for self-understanding."

Warren D. Hoffman reminds us in "Home, Memory, and Narrative in Monica Sone's *Nisei Daughter*" that as *Nisei Daughter* both "interrogates and operates as a site of 'home,'" Sone "details the search of a fixed and tangible personal space (indicative of one's place in society) and argues that finding such a space is both essential and possible." The memoir is "both courageous and subversive," given that Sone "functioned not only as autobiographer, but as social historian, creating a narrative that, while not replacing 'official history,' quite directly calls it into question."

In "The 'Pre-History' of an 'Asian American' Writer: N. V. M. Gonzalez' Allegory of Decolonization," Augusto Espiritu refers to the "pre-1960s period" of what we now call *Asian American literature* as "pre-history" and argues that Gonzalez is one of several important "pre-history" writers to "trouble both the periodization of 'Asian American literary studies' and its inherent meanings or implications" through simultaneously "expanding and conflating the imagined geography of 'Asian America,' thereby forcing the label itself to account for works and themes that contradict or even subvert it or its prevailing paradigms."

We conclude with an essay that initially doesn't seem to fit with the dates and intentions of our project, an essay by Pamela Thoma entitled "Representing Korean American Female Subjects, Negotiating Multiple Americas, and Reading Beyond the Ending in Ronyoung Kim's *Clay Walls*." Kim's novel, which she began in 1976 and published in 1987, is, in sensibility, language, and subject, very much a novel of an earlier time in Asian America. In fact, Kim's objective was to write her mother's story—and hence cast her mind back to her mother's life in Los Angeles of the 1920s through the midcentury (Hahn 1999). Also tying the novel to pre-1960s Asian American texts is its pioneering exploration of the Asian female immigrant experience—and its duplicating the rigorous scrutiny with which Younghill Kang and Carlos Bulosan describe the immigrant experience of the Asian male. Yet the novel's rich structure and thematic impulses point away from those of pre-1960s texts and toward those of texts appearing in the late 1970s through the early 1990s: Asian American generational distinctions, female identity formation, mother-daughter bonding, "role playing," dissimilation.

We believe, in short, that *Clay Walls* is a crucial bridge between "early" and "later" Asian American literature—that while the novel's subjects and attitudes recall the texts of pre-1960s writers, its nuanced representations of Asian American life anticipate post-1960s literature's sensitivities to what Lisa Lowe has so famously called "heterogeneity, hybridity, and multiplicity" (Lowe 1996, chap. 3). The narrative structure of *Clay Walls*, which moves from the viewpoint of one generation to another, borrows a technique of early twentieth-century canonical writers like William Faulkner and Sherwood Anderson but perhaps also serves as an Asian American model for Amy Tan's mother-daughter narratives in *The Joy Luck Club* (1989) or *The Kitchen God's Wife* (1991), or for the dual female protagonists of Bharati Mukherjee's *The Holder of the World* (1993). Thus we find that *Clay Walls*, perhaps not unlike the novels of Jane Austen, glances backward at themes raised by predecessors while at the same time anticipating experimental points of view and narrative techniques that characterize literature of later periods.

More apropos to our purposes here, we also believe that Thoma's essay incisively demonstrates how the "ways of reading" advocated by the present volume may be applied appropriately and well to post-1960s Asian American texts. Thoma relies on close readings combined with feminist and ethnohistorical perspectives to argue that Kim's characterizations of Haesu Chun and her daughter Faye (the mother-daughter protagonists of *Clay Walls*) construct "women's representations not as static depictions of national subjects but as dynamic formations that uneasily intersect with national structures and struggles." Thoma thus asserts that the novel's central female characters "negotiate multiple discourses in self-formation"— and that while their narratives are deliberately constructed as counter to the "well-married" female *bildung* paradigm, the two women are themselves defined by their "valuable political and cultural labor" and by their successfully negotiating the "various discourses that contribute to their articulations of subjectivity." We are honored, then, to give Pamela Thoma the "final word" in this collection.

Early Asian American Literature and the Question of Renaissance

The study of Asian American literature is a relatively new endeavor. Only after 1968, when college students demanded and won an expansion of their curriculum, did the study of Asian American letters begin. By the early 1990s, scholars of the new field remarked with wonder at the quality and quantity of work by authors such as Maxine Hong Kingston, Gish Jen, Amy Tan, David Henry Hwang, and Jessica Hagedorn, to name just a few. Indeed, influential scholar Amy Ling labeled this burgeoning nothing less than a literary "renaissance" (1991, 192). But what tradition, if any, preceded this renaissance of the last quarter of the twentieth century? From what was Asian American literature *reborn*? For partial answers to these questions, we offer *Recovered Legacies: Authority and Identity in Early Asian American Literature*.

WORKS CITED

Ammons, Elizabeth. 1992. *Conflicting Stories: American Women Writers at the Turn into the Twentieth Century*. New York: Oxford University Press.

Bow, Leslie. 2001. *Betrayal and Other Acts of Subversion: Feminism, Sexual Politics, Asian American Women's Literature*. Princeton: Princeton University Press.

Brague, Rémi. 2002. *Eccentric Culture: A Theory of Western Civilization*. Trans. Samuel Lester. South Bend, IN: St. Augustine's Press.

Briggs, Thomas H., Max J. Herzberg, and Emma Miller Bolenius. 1933. *American Literature*. Boston: Houghton Mifflin.

Chang, Juliana, ed. 1996. *Quiet Fire: A Historical Anthology of Asian American Poetry, 1892–1970*. New York: Asian American Writers' Workshop.

Cheung, King-Kok, and Stan Yogi. 1988. *Asian American Literature: An Annotated Bibliography.* New York: Modern Language Association.

Chung, L. A. 1991. "Asian Writers Clash Over How to Portray Chinese Americans." *San Francisco Chronicle*, Sept. 1, p. G1.

Curtin, Philip D. 1993. "Ghettoizing African History." *Chronicle of Higher Education*, March 7, p. A44.

Davis, Rocío G., and Sämi Ludwig, eds. 2002. *Asian American Literature in the International Context: Readings on Fiction, Poetry and Performance.* Münster: Lit Verlag.

Fabre, Geneviàve, and Michel Feith, eds. 2002. *Temples for Tomorrow: Looking Back at the Harlem Renaissance.* Bloomington: Indiana University Press.

Ferens, Dominika. 2002. *Edith and Winnifred Eaton: Chinatown Missions and Japanese Romances.* Urbana: University of Illinois Press.

Gruesz, Kirsten Silva. 2001. *Ambassadors of Culture: The Transamerican Origins of Latino Writing.* Princeton: Princeton University Press.

Hahn, Kim. 1999. "The Korean American Novel: Kim Ronyoung." In *The Asian Pacific American Heritage: A Companion to Literature and the Arts*, ed. George J. Leonard, 527–33. New York: Garland.

Jackson, Robert. 2003. "A Vital Crossroads: On Teaching *The Heath Anthology* at an Historically Black College." *Heath Anthology of American Literature Newsletter* 26 (Fall): 9–11.

Kingston, Maxine Hong. 1975. *The Woman Warrior: Memoirs of a Girlhood among Ghosts.* New York: Knopf.

Lee, Josephine, Imogene L. Lim, and Yuko Matsukawa, eds. 2002. *Re/collecting Early Asian America: Essays in Cultural History.* Philadelphia: Temple University Press.

Ling, Amy. 1991. " 'Emerging Canons' of Asian American Literature and Art." In *Asian Americans: Comparative and Global Perspectives*, ed. Shirley Hune et al, 191–97. Pullman: Washington State University Press.

Lowe, Lisa. 1996. *Immigrant Acts: On Asian American Cultural Politics.* Durham and London: Duke University Press.

Manent, Pierre. 1998. *The City of Man.* Trans. Marc A. LePain. Princeton: Princeton University Press.

Matsukawa, Yuko. 1994. "Cross-Dressing and Cross-Naming: Decoding Onoto Watanna." In *Tricksterism in Turn-of-the-Century American Literature*, ed. Elizabeth Ammons and Annette White-Parks, 106–25. Hanover: New England University Press.

Mukerji, Dhan Gopal. 2002. *Caste and Outcast.* Ed. Gordon H. Chang. Stanford: Stanford University Press. (Orig. pub. 1923.)

Mukherji, Bharati. 1993. *The Holder of the World.* New York: Knopf.

Nguyen, Viet Thanh. 2002. *Race and Resistance: Literature and Politics in Asian America.* Oxford: Oxford University Press.

Nelson, Cary. 1989. *Repression and Recovery: Modern American Poetry and the Politics of Cultural Memory, 1910–1945.* Madison: University of Wisconsin Press.

Palumbo-Liu, David, ed. 1995. *The Ethnic Canon: Histories, Institutions, and Interventions.* Minneapolis: University of Minnesota Press.

Introduction 23

———. 1999. *Asian/American: Historical Crossings of a Racial Frontier*. Stanford: Stanford University Press.

Rosaldo, Renato. 1989. "Imperialist Nostalgia." In *Culture and Truth: The Remaking of Social Analysis*, 68–87. Boston: Beacon Press.

Song, Min. 1998. "The Unknowable and Sui Sin Far: The Epistemological Limits of 'Oriental' Sexuality." In *Q&A: Queer in Asian America*, ed. David Eng and Alice Hom, 304–22. Philadelphia: Temple University Press.

Su, Karen. 1994. "Jade Snow Wong's Badge of Distinction in the 1990s." *Hitting Critical Mass: A Journal of Asian American Cultural Criticism* 2 (1) [unpaginated Web journal].

Sui Sin Far. 1912. *Mrs. Spring Fragrance*. Chicago: McClurg.

Tan, Amy. 1989. *The Joy Luck Club*. New York: Putnam.

———. 1991. *The Kitchen God's Wife*. New York: Putnam.

Womack, Craig S. 1999. *Red on Red: Native American Literary Separatism*. Minneapolis: University of Minnesota Press.

Wong, Jade Snow. 1945. *Fifth Chinese Daughter*. New York: Harper.

Woo, Merle. 1994. "Letter to Ma." In *New Worlds of Literature*, ed. Jerome Beaty and J. Paul Hunter, 159–65. 2nd ed. New York: Norton.

1 Early Chinese American Autobiography: Reconsidering the Works of Yan Phou Lee and Yung Wing

Floyd Cheung

IMPORTANT CRITICAL debates over Asian American autobiographical writing have centered on the question of authenticity. For over two decades now, influential critics such as Frank Chin and Amy Ling have been delimiting the criteria necessary for works to qualify as authentic or inauthentic, "real" or "fake."[1] With characteristically Manichean logic, Chin argues that "real" writers heroically defend "yellow fact and truth," while "fake" writers succumb to "high assimilation" and "Christian stereotype" (1985, 109–10). In a similarly comparative mode but with different results, Ling contends that Asian American women writers, in fact, have been "more authentic" than men, since the former advance more "significant" and "more personal" experiences (1990, 15–16). Evidently, Chin and Ling measure authenticity not only in the word's usual sense of factual or experiential verifiability but also in terms of what facts or experiences count as valuable or dismissible, thereby associating value with ideology—be it cultural nationalist or feminist. Consequently, Chin's and Ling's deployments of authenticity as seemingly objective "mechanisms of cultural selection" lend authority to their ideologically interested judgments (Smith 1988, 47).

So authorized, judgments of insufficient authenticity have all but deselected two of the earliest book-length works by Chinese Americans published in English: Yan Phou Lee's *When I Was a Boy in China* (1887) and Yung Wing's *My Life in China and America* (1909).[2] These works lack value to Chin and Ling precisely because they do not appear to speak to their particular canon-building goals of the 1970s through the 1980s. As Elaine Kim puts it, critics during this era celebrate defiant Chinatown cowboys and warrior women (1983, 173). To such critics' ears, sensitized by the strident tones of the Third World, Black Power, Asian American, and women's rights movements, Lee's and Yung's relatively unobtrusive writing styles and inoffensive content sound too meek, too stereotypically docile and accomodationist. "Nothing," in either author's works, according to Ling, "gives the slightest indication of their awareness of or concern about how others perceived them . . . despite the fact that this period was one of virulent sinophobia. For the men, this facet of life in the United States seemed to be beneath their notice" (1994, 83–84). Ling deems Lee's work as that of a "tourist guide" who merely provides "titillation by his exotic and quaint revelations" (1990, 16). Chin calls Yung's work the story of a "mission-schoolboy-makes-good Gunga Din licking up white fantasy" (1991, 11).

Interestingly, Ling's and Chin's comments also indicate resentment at their subjects' class position. As students who immigrated to America under the auspices of the Chinese and U.S. governments, Lee and Yung seem to share little with the much more numerous and disadvantaged working-class Chinese laborers discussed in most scholarship. Critics typically qualify Lee's and Yung's socioeconomic station as "elite" and therefore less authentic a position from which to experience and write about being Asian American at the turn of the twentieth century (Zhang 1998, 43).[3] Instead of only emphasizing how these authors' unique circumstances restricted their literary response to anti-Chinese racism, this essay examines the opportunities that their privilege allowed them to exploit in terms of their choice of genre, style, and subject. Rather than derive their authority from late-twentieth-century notions of authenticity, Lee's and Yung's works authorize themselves, albeit problematically, through discourses and conventions appropriate to their class position and historical situations.[4] Via autoethnography Lee responds to degrading descriptions of Chinese culture popular during the 1880s, while via autobiography Yung defends against assaults on Chinese character made by Theodore Roosevelt and others during the late 1890s and early 1900s.

YAN PHOU LEE: AUTHORITY VIA AUTOETHNOGRAPHY

A contemporary book review printed in the British journal *Academy and Literature* specifies a crucial element of the context of *When I Was a Boy in China* that most present-day critics have ignored: "Its appearance was most opportune, while the Americans were, and are, endeavoring to prevent the Chinese altogether from entering their territories." In fact, just five years before the publication of Lee's book, Congress had passed the Chinese Exclusion Act of 1882; however, as a contemporary essayist noted, this "bill was only a provisional disposition of the question" since it restricted Chinese immigration for the finite period of ten years (Durst 1884, 256). By 1887, when Lee's autobiography was published, President Grover Cleveland's administration was in the midst of trying to convince Congress, the Chinese government, and the U.S. public to extend Chinese exclusion for another thirty years (Tsai 1986, 72).[5]

Yan Phou Lee, who published an essay in the *North American Review* titled "The Chinese Must Stay" (1889) against those arguing that the "Chinese must go," played an active role in the contemporary debate over Chinese exclusion. It should not be surprising, then, that while *When I Was a Boy in China* at first may appear to be safely apolitical, it also possesses a polemical edge. With authority drawn from a U.S. education, which culminated in a degree from Yale College in 1887, and with authority drawn from his childhood in China, Lee strategically intervened in the debate over the Chinese question by publishing an autoethnography with the Lothrop Company of Boston. Thus does Lee use his unique socioeconomic and racialized position to contest what he perceived to be inauthentic and unflattering ethnographies of the Chinese, which were often used by politicians and the press to advocate for Chinese exclusion. Autoethnography differs from ethnography, as Mary Louise Pratt explains, in the following way: "I use these terms [*autoethnography* and *autoethnographic expression*] to refer to instances in which colonized subjects undertake to represent themselves in ways which engage with the colonizer's own terms. If ethnographic texts are a means in which Europeans represent to themselves their (usually subjugated) others, autoethnographic texts are those the others construct in response to or in dialogue with those metropolitan representations" (1992, 6–7). To make a case against ethnographies cited by politicians like Denis Kearney and produced by anthropologists like John Barrow (1972), Lee's autoethnography resorts to several tactics including positioning an essentialized Chinese identity against equally essentialized African American and Japanese identities; employing a rhetoric of cross-cultural simile vis-à-vis Greek, Roman, and British cultures; and embedding a critique of mainstream U.S. civilization in his storytelling. The first two of these tactics are understandably problematic for many critics; such tactics nevertheless demonstrate that Lee armed himself with the "tourist guide" role not merely to "titillate" but rather to do battle with the "virulent sinophobia" of his day.

During the second half of the nineteenth century, one of the major arguments against Chinese immigration rested on the fear that so-called coolie labor would lead to another "race problem" and another civil war (Rowell 1909, 230; Miller 1969, 152).[6] Anti-Chinese activists commonly made the accusation that Chinese immigrants came to the United States as slaves and hence, like African Americans, were a potential source of violent resistance. For example, the *San Francisco Chronicle* reported, "When the coolie arrives here he is as rigidly under the control of the contractor who brought him as ever an African slave was under his master in South Carolina or Louisiana" (qtd. in Takaki 1979, 217). As another contemporary polemicist put it, "The copper of the Pacific [could] yet become as great a subject of discord and dissension as the ebony of the Atlantic" (Helper 1855, 96). Some pseudoscientific viewpoints authorized these fears. For instance, ethnographers claimed that Chinese and Africans shared genetic kinship (Miller 1969, 235n44). Barrow's book offers portraits of a Chinese and a Hottentot "drawn from the life" as hard evidence for his thesis regarding their genetic commonality (1972, 50).[7] In short, Chinese Americans underwent what one historian has called a process of "negroization" (Caldwell 1971, 127).

Within the context of this pseudoscientific and alarmist discourse, Lee found it logical and necessary to distance Chinese American identity from African American identity, however unfair such a distancing might have been toward either group. Lee's description of San Francisco as "the paradise of *self*-exiled Chinese" serves as a refutation against those who claimed that all Chinese laborers are slaves (1887, 106; emphasis added). Without dwelling on this point, Lee gently reminds his readers that most Chinese chose to leave their birthplace to make a living in the United States and were not forced here by coolie or slave traders.

Moreover, Lee distances Chinese American laborers from African American slaves by laying out reasons for trusting the former as unobtrusive and obedient members of the community. In an account of his childhood, he relates stories of how he, like all Chinese, learned to respect authority, explaining that discipline was maintained "by customs handed down from one generation to another. Fathers and teachers have undergone the same training. The customs of their ancestors enjoin it, the teachings of Confucius prescribe it, and the laws of the empire arm it with authority" (20). Lee admits, however, that members of lower classes may not exercise equal self-discipline, but he emphasizes, "The family regulations in China are such that so soon as a child begins to understand, he is not only taught to obey, but also loses freedom of action" (17). In this case, Lee reinforces the problematic stereotype of Chinese docility, but he does so for tactical advantage. During this tense time between 1882 and 1887, while the extension of Chinese exclusion was being discussed, Lee found it more expedient to accent the characteristics of essentialized Chinese identity that the American public would find least threatening and most self-serving, rather than to sue stridently for Chinese rights. Thus, he framed the Chinese as voluntarily coming to America and as culturally conditioned to follow rules. Lee sought to draw a contrast between stereotypical Chinese American docility and stereotypical African American rebelliousness.

But while Lee found it necessary to distance Chinese Americans from African Americans, he also found it tactically advantageous to highlight similarities between the Chinese and the Japanese. During the late nineteenth century and early twentieth century, the U.S. public generally held Japanese immigrants in much higher regard than their Chinese counterparts. Historian Roger Daniels quotes from newspaper articles printed in 1869 and 1888 that declared, "The objections raised against the Chinese . . . cannot be alleged against the Japanese" (1962, 3). Even schoolbooks taught that the Japanese were more progressive and assimilable.[8] This impression is due at least in part to the fact that the Japanese government "screened" its emigrants more carefully than did the Chinese government (Takaki 1989, 46). Furthermore, the Japanese government consciously used the 1876 and 1893 world's fairs—hosted by Philadelphia and Chicago, respectively—as ways to stage versions of its culture in a flattering light (Rydell 1984; 30, 48); thus did the Japanese government perform autoethnography. For these and other reasons too numerous and complex to explore here, Japanese immigrants were not excluded from the United States as the Chinese were during the 1880s and 1890s.[9]

Lee recognized this difference in treatment and perception as a curious inconsistency in European American racism. Like Lee, Hubert Howe Bancroft observed, "Anything black or white was proper material for American citizenship; yellow was the only off-color. But even the yellow race, with sage discrimination, is now divided, the Japanese being admitted, while . . . Chinese are excluded" (1904, 265). Consequently, *When I Was a Boy in China* challenges the absurdity of this contradiction with the equally absurd—and risky—argument that since Japanese people and culture originated from China, both the Chinese and the Japanese deserve equal treatment.[10]

Lee couches this argument within a narrative of his and his class-mates' boat trip from China to the United States via Japan. He writes, "After a stormy voyage of one week, with the usual accompaniment of seasickness, we landed at Yokohama, in the Country of the Rising Sun. For Japan means 'sun-origin'"; but then with a satirical undertone, he adds, "The Japanese claim to be descendants of the sun, instead of being an off-shoot of the Chinese race" (105). Next, Lee modulates back to the more charming tone of a young student who, with his fellows, was "delighted to learn that the Japanese studied the same books as we and worshipped our Confucius, and that we could converse with them in writing.... We learned that the way they lived and dressed was like that in vogue in the time of Confucius. Their mode of dressing hair and their custom of sitting on mats laid on the floor is identical with ancient Chinese usage" (106). Thus the Japanese are not only genetic and cultural "off-shoots" of the Chinese, but they are also—contrary to American perceptions—less progressive since they still practice "ancient Chinese" behaviors. Certainly, Lee's critique can be faulted in many ways, but it nevertheless raises the reader's consciousness of the disparity between U.S.-Japan and U.S.-China relations, in addition to the problematics of racism itself.

Comparisons of Chinese Americans with Japanese and African Americans serve certain purposes, but these tactics alone might imply that the Chinese, no matter what their qualities, still exist as aliens, unassimilable with dominant European American culture. In the late 1870s, Workingmen's Party leader Denis Kearney, among many others, made the essentialist argument that race equals culture, that the Chinese can never acculturate and become truly American, because as Justice John Marshall Harlan later would write, the Chinese are of "a race so different from our own" (Thomas 1997, 58).[11] In order to counter this notion, Lee disturbs and perhaps alters his readers' expectations by describing Chinese culture with pointedly Western images. Through a rhetoric of cross-cultural simile, Lee makes reference to many elements of Chinese and Chinese American culture with language that alludes to Greek, Roman, and British cultures, thereby suggesting a symmetry between them. For example, he says of Chinese discipline: "The bamboo rod hung over my head like the sword of Damocles"; and he compares a Chinese skylight to "the *compluvium* in the dwellings of the Romans" (1887, 21–22). With regard to British culture, he compares the Chinese practice of celebrating the first month of a baby's life to "christening-day ... in England" and likens a Cantonese spectacle to a Shakespearean play (8, 76).[12] Nineteenth-century readers were used to portrayals that considered the Chinese and Chinese Americans as wholly other. With this rhetoric of cross-cultural simile, Lee encourages them to reconsider.

Lee turns his reader's attention much closer to home in the final chapter, titled "First Experiences in America." While describing his train ride from California to Massachusetts, Lee cleverly critiques American civilization through an entertaining yet subversive Western adventure story. The conventions of such stories invariably call for Chinese characters to play the role of cowards for comic relief, and Lee fulfills this expectation.[13] As Lee's train makes its way eastward, men riding horses bring it to a halt and rob it. After shots are fired, Lee reports, "Our teachers told us to crouch down for our lives. We obeyed with trembling and fear"; furthermore, he overheard one of his teachers "calling upon all the gods of the Chinese Pantheon" (108). Undoubtedly, Lee relates this particular moment in this comical fashion to play up to the reader's expectations, but the robbery itself seriously critiques U.S. civilization itself by reminding readers that chaos and destruction already coexist with progress in the American West, contrary to the view that a pristine, virginal frontier lay exposed to the dangerous incursion of the Chinese "yellow peril."[14] Moreover, in this case, the source of the chaos is not alien: a few "ruffianly" European American men are responsible. Lee concludes the narrative by dryly stating, "One phase of American civilization was thus indelibly fixed upon our minds" (108).

Next, Lee shifts to a description of his hostess, "a most motherly lady in Springfield" (109). Before attending Yale, Lee studied at the Chinese Educational Mission, which relied upon families in Massachusetts and Connecticut to provide room, board, and other services. In his brief chapter about his first days in Springfield, he recounts a humorous story about going to church and a description of his informal education in language acquisition: "We learned English by object-lessons. At table we were always told the names of certain dishes, and then assured that if we could not remember the name we were not to partake of that article of food. Taught by this method, our progress was rapid and surprising" (111). With these words Lee's work ends abruptly, not only because it was designed to focus on his childhood in China, but also quite possibly as a result of tampering during the publication process. As Ling points out, the illustrations that seem not to correspond with Lee's text support the suspicion that the publisher had considerable control over the presentation of the book (1994, 82). I would add that the publisher may have chosen to limit Lee's scope and cut short his description of life in America because his treatments of the latter levied criticism most European Americans were not ready to accept from a Chinese American perspective—however authorized by class or education. A contemporary review of *When I Was a Boy in China* published in the *Dial* reads: "With ingenious simplicity, it details the influential details in the author's child life, and in so doing presents instructive pictures of the domestic habits of the Chinese ... ; we read its statements with confidence, although they correct, in some important particulars, beliefs that we have long cherished regarding the character and manners of that interesting and much misunderstood nation." This reviewer suggests, then, that while Lee's autoethnographic project concerning Chinese culture was successful, it did not strike a self-reflexive critical chord. Though valiant, neither of Lee's publications, *When I Was a Boy in China* and "The Chinese Must Stay," prevented the renewal of the Chinese Exclusion Act in 1892 and 1902. After Congress extended the period of Chinese exclusion indefinitely in 1904, Lee's mentor, Yung Wing turned to a different strategy to change European American attitudes regarding the Chinese, emphasizing a valorization of character over an explanation of culture, autobiography rather than autoethnography.

YUNG WING: AUTHORITY VIA AUTOBIOGRAPHY

Having immigrated to America in 1847 to pursue an education in New England grammar schools and being the first person of Chinese descent to graduate from an American college—Yale—in 1854, Yung Wing was uniquely positioned to communicate about Chinese character to a U.S. audience. Early in his life, Yung surmised that China suffered from imperialist incursions at the hands of its neighbors like Japan and distant countries like Britain, because it possessed neither modern technologies nor economic and political systems sophisticated enough to prosper in an increasingly globalized world. Later in his life, he concluded that his country's weak stature negatively affected how Chinese immigrants were treated in America. The Chinese who were held, questioned, sometimes admitted, and sometimes processed for deportation at the Angel Island U.S. immigration center between 1910 and 1940 came to the same conclusion as Yung did. Relatively poor and powerless, however, those who resided at Angel Island for periods as long as two years expressed

themselves by carving Chinese-language poems into the wooden walls
of their cells. One prisoner etched:

> Our country's wealth is being drained by
>   foreigners, causing us to suffer national humiliations.
> My fellow countrymen, have foresight, plan
>   to be resolute,
> And vow to conquer the U.S. and avenge
>   previous wrongs!
>
> (qtd. in Lai, Lim, and Yung 92)

In contrast to this strident message that was cloaked in obscurity until translators and preservationists intervened, Yung capitalized on his
authority as a financially successful, U.S.-educated, Chinese American
man to defend his country of birth and his fellow countrymen by publishing with the Holt Company of New York. That he chose the medium
of autobiography to do so was a result of his individual circumstances,
his racialized identity, the early-twentieth-century popularity of the
genre, and the discourse that connected national and individual manliness promoted by Theodore Roosevelt.

In an 1899 speech titled "The Strenuous Life," to an audience of men
whom he wished to badger into supporting U.S. imperialism in the
Philippines and elsewhere, Roosevelt positioned China as a strawman:
"We cannot, if we would, play the part of China, and be content to
rot by inches in ignoble ease within our borders, taking no interest in
what goes on beyond them...heedless of the higher life, the life of
aspiration, of toil and risk...; what China has already found, that in
this world the nation that has trained itself to a career of unwarlike
and isolated ease is bound, in the end, to go down before other nations
which have not lost the manly and adventurous qualities" (1926, 13:322).
China and the Chinese, he claimed, did not live "the strenuous life"—the
life of aspiration, toil, and risk—and now were facing the consequences
(13:319). Of course "manly" is a highly problematic term, but during his
time, Roosevelt persuasively generalized that manly men make manly
nations and manly nations make manly men. According to this logic,
America was the product and the producer of manly American men, and
China suffered an unmanly fate precisely because it was full of unmanly
men. "As it is with the individual, so it is with the nation," he intoned
to his listeners at the Hamilton Club of Chicago, who published the
speech immediately (13:321).[15] On the one hand, Roosevelt's essentialist
thinking privileged national spirit, but on the other, the importance
of the individual as an agent of change held much sway. Roosevelt

harangued his listeners to support his colonial designs in order to be manly, or, he warned, America would degrade into a China.

Yung, strawman to no one, seized the opportunity opened by Roosevelt's logic to present his individual character as proof that China could be a manly nation. As naïve as his plan might appear today, in the 1900s it seemed to Yung that a valorization of one Chinese man's life via autobiography might improve how European Americans viewed all those who hailed from his nation of birth. As a diplomat and concerned Chinese American, Yung would have been aware of Roosevelt's positions on China and the Chinese. Furthermore, Yung's diary provides evidence that he had a subscription to the periodical *Outlook* in which Roosevelt frequently published his speeches and other essays (24 Nov. 1902).

In *My Life in China and America*, Yung echoes Roosevelt's very words but to serve his own purposes. For instance, Yung declares, "In a strenuous life one needs to be a dreamer in order to accomplish possibilities" (1909, 65). His dreams, however, include revitalizing the military, economic, and political systems of China and winning respect for the Chinese wherever they reside. As Ling rightly notes, Yung "revels in all his public accomplishments" (1994, 76), but he does so not merely for selfish reasons. Although he details his success-story rise from poor rice gleaner to wealthy businessman to educational reformer with obvious pride, his ability to live the strenuous life demonstrates that most Chinese also could do so—under the right conditions. Yung spent his life working alongside the proponents of the Chinese Self-Strengthening Movement to realize those conditions (Leung 1988, 394). The movement, which rose to prominence in the 1860s, maintained the following dictum: "Chinese learning for the foundation, Western learning for practical use" (qtd. in Leung 1988, 392). Yung promoted the latter half of the dictum by establishing the Chinese Educational Mission, which brought more than one hundred Chinese students, including Yan Phou Lee, to study in America so that they could return to, reform, and empower their nation of birth.[16] Significantly, Yung's public stature in China and America enabled him to accomplish such nationalistic goals.

His stature as a man, in particular, reinforced his own character and that of his countrymen. Yung's manly performances, which he relates with zest in the autobiography, contest stereotypes of Chinese emasculation popular during the turn of the century. Xiao-huang Yin, an authority on early Chinese American literature, notes Yung's valiant engagement with a Scot who assaulted him in Shanghai and

Yung's offer of his services to the Union during the Civil War. Besides illustrating Yung's "courage in taking the law into his own hands" and his "patriotism" (Yin 2000, 73), these actions attest to his manliness. Moreover, Yung's individual accomplishments in this arena reflect well on not only himself but also his countrymen. Referring to the latter, Yung makes the following comment directly after describing his victory over the rude Scot: "Their meek and mild disposition had allowed personal insults and affronts to pass unresented and unchallenged, which naturally had the tendency to encourage arrogance and insolence on the part of ignorant foreigners. The time will soon come, however, when the people of China will be so educated and enlightened as to know what their rights are, public and private, and to have the moral courage to assert and defend them whenever they are invaded" (1909, 72–73). With the success of the Chinese Educational Mission, "the people of China" would indeed eventually become more enlightened and better able to assert and defend their rights. Therefore, this passage brings together his public plans for reform with his personal life of strenuosity. Although his modesty might be questioned, his sincere intent to defend Chinese character through his own life story in passages like this one cannot be challenged.

In fact, throughout his later years, Yung had intervened on behalf of his Chinese American counterparts. On March 9, 1880, for example, he wrote to the U.S. Secretary of State William Evarts (Notes from the Chinese Legation to the Department of State) to argue that "tens of thousands of my countrymen are by law deprived of shelter and prohibited from earning a livelihood and are in hourly expectation of being driven from their homes to starve in the streets. Under such circumstances I could not acquit myself of my duty if I did not protest earnestly, but most respectfully, against the wrong in which they have been subjected." Also, Yung worked covertly with figures such as Homer Lea and Charles Boothe in an effort to overthrow what he believed was a corrupt government in China, a government incapable of defending Chinese at home or abroad. On 4 January 1909, he wrote to Boothe saying, "This is the time to strike when the whole world is against the Manchu Regime" (Charles Boothe Papers). He worried that England and France might hinder their planned revolution in an effort to defend what Yung called their "ill gotten colonies" (Charles Boothe Papers, 16 Jan. 1909); but he rallied his allies, promising to help fund their military expenses, provide intelligence gleaned from his U.S. sources, dispatch his son Bartlett as his representative, and serve "in a civil capacity" himself (Charles

Boothe Papers, 14 Dec. 1908, 16 Jan. 1909, and 14 Sep. 1909).[17] While these plans never came to fruition, Sun Yat-sen, who led a successful revolution in China in 1911, recognized Yung's potential and invited him to join his new government. Unfortunately, by this time, Yung's health had deteriorated, forcing him to decline Sun's offer.

That Yung's autobiography does not discuss his work as a diplomat arguing for better treatment of Chinese laborers in the American West or his work as an underground revolutionary in China raises several questions. Did Yung's publisher excise passages? Did Yung choose to keep quiet on these matters because he was embarrassed about them? Regarding his silence on his diplomatic work, was he avoiding the subject of "racist exploitation" in order to maintain a "polite and restrained" tone palatable to his audience (Ling 1994, 75–76)? Did he avoid discussing his underground activities, as Peter Wan disapprovingly claims, because he wanted "to project an image" of being an honorable man "or create an effect" of trustworthiness? (1997, 14). Although all of these possibilities have some veracity, Ling's and Wan's disapproving assessments obscure a more complicated picture.

In the early 1900s, Yung, like his contemporary Booker T. Washington, projected one image for the public while pursuing an alternative program behind the scenes. Washington may have practiced tactical accommodation in his 1901 autobiography, *Up from Slavery*, but this work operated as only one part of his broader strategy. Representing himself as a hard-working, education-valuing, and law-abiding young African American man in the success-story mode helped him to attract and persuade donors for the development of the Tuskegee Normal and Industrial Institute. This fund-raising plan supported by his autobiography worked simultaneously with what Louis R. Harlan calls Washington's "secret methods to undermine the system of racial discrimination that he publicly acquiesced in" (1986, xvii).

Similarly, Yung fashioned a version of himself that, while certainly addressing racism in a subtle way, primarily concentrates on deploying his authority in a manner designed to change European American attitudes toward China and the Chinese. In addition, Yung's autobiography reinforced his reputation as a scholar and businessman, which helped him to be taken seriously when arguing for various reforms in China and America. Yet, even as he was "quite busy being engaged in finishing my autobiography," Yung plotted secretly to change radically the Chinese government (Letter to Boothe, 6 Dec. 1908). In this manner, Yung worked for reform both above and below the public's consciousness. Like Washington, he "never tried to reconcile his secret machinations with his public life, perhaps because, being secret, they did not pragmatically require justification" (Harlan 1986, xviii). As Sidonie Smith makes clear, the genre of autobiography does not simply convey a "self-identity [that] emerges from a psychic interiority, located somewhere 'inside' the narrating subject"; rather, "the autobiographical speaker becomes a performative subject" (1995, 17). Yung-the-man held contradictory views and carried on various careers with mixed success, but Yung-the-subject of *My Life in China and America* performs a version of Chinese American character meant to dramatize that China and the Chinese are able to live the strenuous life and are worthy of respect.

With a vocabulary that echoes that of African American racial uplift, one contemporary reviewer of Yung's work notes, "The autobiographical details of this most interesting volume illuminate the *upbuilding* of the oldest of the nations" (Churchill 1910, 383; emphasis added). To some extent, then, Yung's individual narrative succeeds in spurring a reevaluation of his communal origin, but as in the African American case, the degree to which the Chinese and Chinese Americans can be accepted as equals with European Americans is qualified. As David Palumbo-Liu explains, "Even when the minority subject acquires the cultural capital of the Other it may not be enough. In the cultural politics that leverages a racist national subjectivity even as it presumes upon universal value, entrance can be constantly deferred" (1999, 427n6). Both Yan Phou Lee and Yung Wing succeeded in acquiring the cultural capital of the Other. Through this cultural capital, they authorized works that at once gained them entry into U.S. systems of value and enabled them to contest negative views that they thought sabotaged "universal" respect and, hence, respectful treatment for China and the Chinese. That Lee's and Yung's works were contained by a cultural politics that acknowledged their authority while also denying their critique of racism is clear. Their status as authentic—that is, valued—writers in the Asian American canon, however, is in question unless we recognize that authenticity itself is contingent upon individual circumstances, personal motives, and historical context.

NOTES

Acknowledgments: An earlier version of this essay was published in *a/b: Auto/biography Studies*, whose editors I thank for granting me permission to reprint here. I also thank Mary Ann Janda, Keith Lawrence, Rebecca Mark,

Felipe Smith, Maaja Stewart, and Xiaojing Zhou for their comments on earlier drafts; and Stefanie Grindle for research assistance.

1. Other writers such as Amy Tan question the usefulness of these debates altogether, offering instead a call for artistic freedom and renewed attention to artistic quality over moral correctness. In a recent essay, Tan laments readings that "dwell more on [a work's] historical relevance and accuracy . . . than on its literary merits—for instance, the language, the characters, [and] the imagery" (1996, 7). She rejects the cooptative gazes of ethnic studies departments and other "factions" in order to concentrate on writing "to startle my mind, to churn my heart, to tingle my spine, [and] to knock the blinders off my eyes," as if such purposes remove her work from the worldly political to the transcendent universal (7, 9).

2. On their title pages, Lee follows European American convention by listing his family name last; Yung follows Chinese convention by listing his family name first.

3. For a critique of how Asian American studies courses tend to overemphasize the working-class experience to the exclusion of considering socioeconomic advancement, see Yanagisako (1996).

4. For historically conscious assessments of Lee's and Yung's work, see Wong (1998, 3–40), Kim (1982, 25), Yin (2000, 55–62), and Yin (69–77). I supplement Wong's historical approach by examining the writers' rhetorical strategies. I expand upon Kim's insight that Lee's "book is a conscious attempt to correct these [stereotypical] distortions" (1982, 25). And I build upon Yin's literary history by emphasizing the writers' deployment of authority.

5. See Hune (1982, 5–6) for a review of the scholarship on the Chinese Exclusion Act of 1882. For an extensive bibliography of English-language material on the Chinese Question, see Cowan and Dunlap (1909). See Tsai (1983) for an analysis based on Chinese-language sources.

6. See Takaki (I1979, 216–29) for a fuller discussion of this fear. He brings together several pertinent sources, including the *San Francisco Alta*, whose editor wrote in 1853, "Every reason that exists against the toleration of free blacks in Illinois may be argued against that of the Chinese here" (217).

7. Miller notes that Barrow's *Travels in China* was extremely popular in the United States, and Barrow was the first to propose that Chinese are genetically related to Hottentots (1969, 43).

8. Miller notes that a "study of nineteenth-century school books by Professor Ruth Miller Elson [1964] reveals a . . . preference for the Japanese as 'the most progressive people of the mongolian race'" (1969, 150).

9. For a fuller comparison of the treatment and perception of Chinese and Japanese immigrants, see Daniels (1988), especially chapters 2 and 4; and see Miller (1969), chapter 7.

10. As it turns out, anti-Chinese groups such as the American Federation of Labor eventually made the argument that the Japanese, like the Chinese, were both "Asiatic," thus deserving of the same discriminatory treatment. In 1924, Congress passed a bill that prohibited all immigrants from Asian countries, except for the Philippines, which was a U.S. protectorate.

11. On the Workingmen's Party and Kearney's anti-Chinese rhetoric, see Saxton (1971).

12. Again, Lee's solutions do not come without their own problems. Even as he describes Chinese music with an allusion to English drama, he associates it with the otherworldliness of witches: "The shrill fiddles may be distinguished in the din like the witches' voices above the storm in *Macbeth*" (76).

13. See Fenn (1933) and Oliver (1958) for studies of Chinese characterization in American literature.

14. See Whitney (1880, 86–87), for example.

15. The full text of the speech was first published as part of the Hamilton Club of Chicago's record of festivities held at its Appomattox Day Banquet in 1899. Roosevelt republished the speech with related essays in 1900 with the Century Company.

16. See LaFargue (1942) for an account of what Yung's students accomplished. While some like Yan Phou Lee remained in the United States, most returned to China, taking posts in government, communications, medicine, and the military.

17. I offer my sincerest thanks to Elena S. Danielson, archivist of the Hoover Institution, for her help in obtaining access to these papers.

WORKS CITED

Academy and Literature. 1888. Review of *When I Was a Boy in China*, by Yan Phou Lee. 34: 318.

Bancroft, Hubert Howe. 1904. "The Folly of Chinese Exclusion." *North American Review* 179:263–68.

Barrow, John. 1972. *Travels in China*. 2nd ed. Taipei: Ch'eng Wen. (Orig. pub. 1806.)

Caldwell, Dan. 1971. "The Negroization of the Chinese Stereotype in California." *Southern California Quarterly* 53:123–32.

Charles Boothe Papers. Hoover Institution on War, Revolution, and Peace. Stanford University.

Chin, Frank. 1985. "This Is Not an Autobiography." *Genre* 18:109–30.

———. 1991. "Come All Ye Asian American Writers of the Real and the Fake." In *The Big Aiiieeeee!: An Anthology of Chinese American and Japanese American Literature*, ed. Jeffery Paul Chan, Frank Chin, Lawson Fusao Inada, and Shawn Wong, 1–92. New York: Meridian.

Churchill, William. 1910. Review of *My Life in China and America*, by Yung Wing. *Bulletin of the American Geographical Society* 42:383–84.

Cowan, Robert Ernest, and Boutwell Dunlap. 1909. *Bibliography of the Chinese Question in the United States*. San Francisco: Robertson.

Daniels, Roger. 1962. *The Politics of Prejudice: The Anti-Japanese Movement in California and the Struggle for Japanese Exclusion*. Berkeley: University of California Press.

———. 1988. *Asian America: Chinese and Japanese in the United States since 1850*. Seattle: University of Washington Press.

Dial. 1887. Review of *When I Was a Boy in China*, by Yan Phou Lee. 8:85.

Durst, John. 1884. "The Exclusion of the Chinese." *North American Review* 139:256–73.

Elson, Ruth Miller. 1964. *Guardians of Tradition*. Lincoln: University of Nebraska Press.

Fenn, William Purviance. 1933. *Ah Sin and His Brethren in American Literature*. Peking: College of Chinese Studies.

Harlan, Louis R. 1986. Introduction to *Up from Slavery*, by Booker T. Washington. New York: Penguin.

Helper, Hinton Rowan. 1855. *The Land of Gold: Reality Versus Fiction*. Baltimore.

Hune, Shirley. 1982. "Politics of Chinese Exclusion: Legislative Conflict, 1876–1882." *Amerasia* 9:5–27.

Kim, Elaine. 1982. *Asian American Literature: An Introduction to the Writings and Their Social Context*. Philadelphia: Temple University Press.

LaFargue, Thomas E. 1942. *China's First Hundred*. Pullman: State College of Washington.

Lai, Him Mark, Genny Lim, and Judy Yung, eds. 1991. *Island: Poetry and History of Chinese Immigrants on Angel Island, 1910–1940*. Seattle: University of Washington Press.

Lee, Yan Phou. 1887. "The Chinese Must Stay." *North American Review* 148:476–83.

———. 1887. *When I Was a Boy in China*. Boston: Lothrop.

Leung, Edwin Pak-wah. 1988. "China's Decision to Send Students to the West: The Making of a 'Revolutionary' Policy." *Asian Profile* 16:391–400.

Ling, Amy. 1990. *Between Worlds: Women Writers of Chinese Ancestry*. New York: Pergamon.

———. "Reading Her/stories against His/stories in Early Chinese American Literature."In *American Realism and the Canon*, ed. Tom Quirk and Gary Scharnhorst, 69–86. Newark: University of Delaware Press.

Miller, Stuart Creighton. 1969. *The Unwelcome Immigrant: The American Image of the Chinese, 1785–1882*. Berkeley: University of California Press.

Notes from the Chinese Legation to the Department of State. National Archives, Record Group 98.

Oliver, Egbert S. 1958. "The Pig-Tailed China Boys Out West." *Western Humanities Review* 12:159–78.

Palumbo-Liu, David. 1999. *Asian/American: Historical Crossings of a Racial Frontier*. Stanford: Stanford University Press.

Pratt, Mary Louise. 1992. *Under Imperial Eyes: Travel Writing and Transculuration*. New York: Routledge.

Roosevelt, Theodore. 1926. *The Works of Theodore Roosevelt*. 20 vols. New York: Scribner.

Rowell, Chester H. 1909. "Chinese and Japanese Immigrants: A Comparison." *Annals of the American Academy of Political and Social Science* 34:223–30.

Rydell, Robert W. 1984. *All the World's a Fair*. Chicago: University of Chicago Press.

Saxton, Alexander. 1971. *The Indispensable Enemy: Labor and the Anti-Chinese Movement in California*. Berkeley: University of California Press.

Smith, Barbara Herrnstein. 1988. *Contingencies of Value*. Cambridge: Harvard University Press.

Smith, Sidonie. 1995. "Performativity, Autobiographical Practice, Resistance." *a/b: Auto/Biography Studies* 10:17–33.

Takaki, Ronald. 1979. *Iron Cages*. New York: Knopf.

———. 1989. *Strangers from a Different Shore: A History of Asian Americans*. Boston: Little, Brown.

Tan, Amy. 1996. "Required Reading and Other Dangerous Subjects." *Threepenny Review* 17 (Fall): 5–9.

Thomas, Brook, ed. 1997. *Plessy v. Ferguson: A Brief History with Documents*. Boston: Bedford.

Tsai, Shih-Shan Henry. 1983. *China and the Overseas Chinese in the United States, 1868–1911*. Fayetteville: University of Arkansas Press.

———. 1986. *The Chinese Experience in America*. Bloomington: Indiana University Press.

Wan, Peter Pei-de. 1997. "Yung Wing, 1828–1912: A Critical Portrait." PhD diss., Harvard University.

Washington, Booker T. 1986. *Up from Slavery*. New York: Penguin. (Orig. pub. 1901.)

Whitney, James A. 1880. *The Chinese and the Chinese Question*. New York: Thompson.

Wong, K. Scott. 1998. "Cultural Defenders and Brokers: Chinese Responses to the Anti-Chinese Movement." In *Claiming America: Constructing Chinese American Identities During the Exclusion Era*, ed. K. Scott Wong and Sucheng Chan, 3–40. Philadelphia: Temple University Press.

Yanagisako, Sylvia. 1996. "Transforming Orientalism: Gender, Nationality, and Class in Asian American Studies." In *Naturalizing Power: Essays in Feminist Cultural Analysis*, ed. Sylvia Yanagisako and Carol Delaney, 275–98. New York: Routledge.

Yin, Xiao-huang. 2000. *Chinese American Literature since the 1850s*. Urbana: University of Illinois Press.

Yung Wing. 1902. Diary of Yung Wing. Manuscript. Connecticut State Library Archives, Hartford.

———. 1909. *My Life in China and America*. New York: Holt.

Zhang, Qingsong. 1998. "The Origins of the Chinese Americanization Movement: Wong Chin Foo and the Chinese Equal Rights League." In *Claiming America: Constructing Chinese American Identities during the Exclusion Era*, ed. K. Scott Wong and Sucheng Chan, 41–63. Philadelphia: Temple University Press.

2   The Self and Generic Convention: Winnifred Eaton's *Me, A Book of Remembrance*

David Shih

IN 1914, in the four weeks between Thanksgiving and New Year, Winnifred Eaton completed what would become her autobiography, a work she published anonymously the following year under the title *Me, A Book of Remembrance*. In the eyes of her friend Jean Webster, Eaton's achievement was especially remarkable because she had drafted the book while in the hospital, recovering from an operation of such gravity that it required her to remain in bed for two weeks. This productive stage made perfect sense to Eaton, however, for according to her, "these two weeks I have just passed in the hospital have been the first time in which I have had a chance to think in thirteen years. As I lay on my back and looked at the ceiling, the events of my girlhood came before me, rushed back with such overwhelming vividness that I picked up a pencil and began to write" (Watanna 1915). What about Eaton's circumstances of the time inspired her to recollect the events of her "girlhood" and set them to paper? Thirteen years earlier, a novel titled *A Japanese Nightingale* (1901) had catapulted to fame a writer named Onoto Watanna, who, we know now, was none other than Winnifred Eaton. Like her older sister Edith, Eaton was a Chinese Eurasian, the daughter of a Chinese mother and an English father, but she had adopted a Japanese-sounding pseudonym in order to "pass" as a writer of authentic Japanese tales. As Onoto Watanna, Eaton proved to be a commercial success by satisfying a literary marketplace eager to consume stories of an "exotic" Japan. Only later did a series of public and personal events move Eaton to despair over her masquerade, precipitating a state of depression that coincided with her stay in the hospital. Just as her convalescence was to heal her body, Eaton decided, so too was writing to be part of her self-recovery. Language had invented a false identity for her, and language would in turn reveal and recuperate a "true" self that had been eclipsed by the figure of Onoto Watanna. For Eaton, the autobiographical act went beyond the usual transcriptive practice of the memoirist to become a conscious attempt to change, if not to save, her life.

Eaton had written a string of best-sellers during her career as Onoto Watanna, and her first novel, *Miss Numè of Japan* (1899), can also be considered the first to be published in the United States by a person of Chinese ancestry. Today, her fiction readily falls into the genre of historical romance, a popular form in the United States at the fin de siècle, but one often neglected by literary historians in favor of realist, naturalist, or modernist experiments. As both Amy Kaplan (1990) and Nancy Glazener (1989) have suggested, the revival of historical romance was largely in response to public anxiety over the emergence of the nation as a world power following the Spanish American War. The novels of Onoto Watanna referenced the much-publicized relationship between the United States and Japan, a nation that for the last third of the nineteenth century had been regarded as a kind of American protégé. By the turn of the century, both nations had emerged as imperial powers whose spheres of influence in the Pacific were sufficiently close to arouse American interest in Japanese people and culture. Eaton traded on these tensions by fashioning romances set in feudal Japan involving native Japanese or Eurasian women and British or American men. Rather than realistically treat the conditions of Japan during the Meiji period (1868–1912), however, books such as *Miss Numè of Japan* and *A Japanese Nightingale* depicted the encounter between Japan and the West in a highly stylized, romantic fashion.[1] This device proved to be quite successful for Eaton, who, according to Amy Ling, "received as much as $15,000 advance royalty before publication, with 50% over-riding royalty after publication" (1990, 29). At the height of her career, Eaton was something of a literary phenomenon: she was already the author of ten novels, had seen *A Japanese Nightingale* adapted for the stage (to enjoy a run on Broadway alongside David Belasco's *Madame Butterfly*), and was a regular in literary circles that included such luminaries as Edith Wharton and Mark Twain. A book of memoirs hardly seemed out of order given these accomplishments. Yet when *Me, A Book of Remembrance* appeared in 1915, it not only avoided any mention of Onoto Watanna but failed even to disclose the name of its author.

It is clear now that the stake Winnifred Eaton had in the reception of her writing went beyond money and fame to touch her on a psychological level. Her novels worked to promote a positive image of the Japanese for an American audience at the same time they consolidated her identity as Onoto Watanna. These motivations went hand-in-hand: if the Japanese were held in high esteem by the public, then Onoto Watanna, as their cultural representative, would share in any feelings of goodwill. Accordingly, one cannot fully appreciate Eaton's work without considering the history of racialization of groups such as the Chinese and Japanese as a key factor in her creative process. As a Chinese Eurasian living in Canada and the United States during the Exclusion Era, Eaton turned to writing as the most direct way to manage her situation as a racialized subject. As a tacitly pro-imperial and white-supremacist discourse, the historical romance reflected and reinforced the idea of race as a biological phenomenon with social and cultural consequences. The cumulative effect of the production of these romances (books with such gender- and racially coded titles as *The Wooing of Wistaria* [1902] and *The Heart of Hyacinth* [1903]) on Winnifred Eaton was the graduation of "Onoto Watanna" from pseudonym to alternate self—a persona that she and her publishers protected and cultivated and whose reach ultimately extended beyond the text to govern her life and the lives of her family. Eventually, an understanding of the exploitative nature of the historical romance inspired Eaton to abandon her pseudonym and write autobiography with the hope that she was at last free to practice her craft independent of generic conventions. Far from providing her with the means to recover an authentic self, however, her autobiographical act only confirmed that the articulation of any sense of individuality must always be mediated by the forms and structures available to the autobiographer.

Between 1894 and 1902, half of the top best-sellers in the United States were novels of high romance. These historical romances follow the ideological trajectory of earlier romances by writers such as Lydia Maria Child, James Fenimore Cooper, and Catherine Maria Sedgwick in their efforts to reconcile the relationship between an emergent American nation and various peoples of color, whose presence complicated efforts of national territorial expansion. Just as works such as *Hobomok* (1824), *The Last of the Mohicans* (1826), and *Hope Leslie* (1827) lyricized the disappearance of the Indian in anticipation of the 1830 Indian Removal Act, the new historical romances of the late-nineteenth and early-twentieth centuries demonstrated a marked interest in the place of the United States and Americans vis-à-vis other nations and peoples, this only a few years after the official closing of the frontier. In 1947, Frank Luther Mott recognized that the appeal of these romances lay in their "falling in with the great American expansionist ideology of the turn of the century. Although these books did not deal directly with the Spanish-American War or Funston in the Philippines or the white man's burden or McKinley's imperialist policy, they did sublimate the fighting and the politics in easy emotional satisfactions. They suited the moods of the times" (207). The signal accomplishment of the new historical romance was its ability to cater to an incipient imperial imagination without overtly admitting to imperial ambitions. Writers of these books managed this feat by temporally or spatially relocating Americans into realms that either belonged to the past or did not exist at all, or by disassociating the protagonist from national allegiance altogether (Kaplan 1990, 669–70). "Fantasies indeed," writes Kaplan, "these novels enact the desire for infinite rule, the disembodiment of national power from geographical boundaries" (671). Notable examples of this genre include Richard Harding Davis' *Soldiers of Fortune* (1897), Mary Johnston's *To Have and to Hold* (1900), and George Barr McCutcheon's *Graustark* (1901). Such narratives explored alternative ways to assert a powerful American presence, one of the most popular being the embodiment of national potency in the figure of the young man abroad.

In the novels of Onoto Watanna, the romantic success of an American (man) in Japan is representative of American prowess in this newly expanded world. *A Japanese Nightingale* (1901), Onoto Watanna's second novel and first for Harpers, is in many respects a paradigm for her early romances. In it, a wealthy American man, Bigelow, pursues a young Eurasian woman, Yuki, throughout Japan only to lose her temporarily to mysterious circumstances before reuniting. The novel's pleasing aesthetic design, exotic setting, and uncomplicated plot and character motivation all help to explain its mass appeal. Feminized and infantilized, Japan poses no threat to the United States for, in Yuki's words, "Japan liddle bit country. America, perhaps, grade big place, big as half the whole worl—" (1901, 101). Thus, part of the allure of Onoto Watanna's Japan was its distance—temporal and spatial—from turn-of-the-century America. The feudal settings of *The Wooing of Wistaria* and *Daughters of Nijo* (1904) recall the harmlessness of Japan's isolationist policy, while the American presence in the restoration settings of *The Love of Azalea* and *Tama* (1910) is a reminder of the military means that ended this policy.[2] In terms of sales, these motifs succeeded famously for Onoto Watanna, whose popular *Miss Numè of Japan* and *Daughters of Nijo* were marketed as "a Japanese-American Romance" and "a Romance of Japan," respectively.

Along with the immense popularity of the genre came its share of criticism. In his column in the *North American Review*, William Dean Howells took time to lament the popularity of the new historical romance, "whose din of arms, the horrid tumult of the swashbuckler swashing on his buckler" unhappily drowned out the more serious literary efforts of the realist and naturalist schools. "Characters?" he scoffed. "Are they characters, any of those figments which pass for such in the new historical romances? They are hardly so by any test of comparison with people we know in life or in the great fictions" (Howells 1900, 942). The problem with the new historical romance, it seemed, was its formulaic reduction of the complexity of the human condition to the basest passions and motivations. In short, it was insufficiently mimetic. Yet the romances of Onoto Watanna evoked altogether different reactions from American reviewers. The *New York Times*, for instance, found her novel *Tama* to hold "the very spirit of Japan, a spirit fragrant, dainty, elusive" (1911, 16). Clearly unaware that Eaton was born in Montreal, a reviewer for the *Literary Digest* gushed that the "fascination of Japan . . . could not be in better hands than those of Onoto Watanna, a native by birth" (1912, 795). Indeed, only a year after his editorial on the new historical romances, even Howells came to similar conclusions in his review of *A Japanese Nightingale*. So convinced was he of the "justly Japanese" character of the heroine Yuki that he decided, "Nothing but the irresistible charm of the American girl could, I think, keep the young men who read Mrs. Watana's [*sic*] book from going out and marrying Japanese girls" (Howells 1901, 881). Howells' statement is especially remarkable for its description of how Americans were apt to regard other regions and peoples of the world (as frontiers for masculine assertion), especially the Japanese, with whom intermarriage was not entirely unmentionable. One might say that the romances of Onoto Watanna so convincingly satisfied an American psychological and ideological need for empire because their milieu derived from a sensibility that was itself colonized.

In a late interview Eaton explained that she had chosen to write about the Japanese because her sister, Sui Sin Far, had already claimed the Chinese as the subject of her own writing (Doyle 1994, 54). It appears more likely, however, that the novels of Onoto Watanna featured Japanese Eurasian heroines who eventually marry white men and are accepted into Western society because that was how Eaton imagined her life in the ideal. A Chinese Eurasian, she chose to identify with the Japanese mainly because of the high esteem granted to them by the dominant society, and also because of the ease with which she could do so.[3] The works of Onoto Watanna capitalized on the popular belief that there existed a meaningful difference between the Chinese and the Japanese—that is to say, a distinct *racial* difference reflected in the state of their respective nations.[4] Next to a weak and degraded China—whose citizens had been excluded from American shores since 1882 and whose nativist Boxer Rebellion in 1900 had been put down by a coalition of European and Japanese forces—Japan was a shining example of the benefits of Western influence upon a "heathen" nation. Onoto Watanna's novels implicitly distinguished the Japanese as a race different from other Asian races and, by the rite of intermarriage, hierarchized them on a level equivalent to the Anglo-Saxons.[5] "I myself was dark and foreign-looking, but the blond type I adored," admits the narrator of *Me*. "In all my most fanciful imaginings and dreams I had always been golden-haired and blue-eyed" (1915, 41). If Eaton saw blonde hair and blue eyes as an impossible fantasy, she also found that passing as what might have been the next best thing required only an unwavering conviction and an uncritical public.

For a while Winnifred Eaton and Harpers did everything in their power to guard Eaton's reputation as an authentic Japanese writer. Eaton used her pen name for all publicity while insisting upon a Japanese heritage in her interviews. James Doyle notes that in "these interviews, her ethnic origins tended to shift: her father was sometimes Japanese and sometimes English; her mother was usually Japanese, but occasionally part Japanese and part Chinese" (1994, 55). A remarkable example of their joint commitment is the frontispiece of *The Wooing of Wistaria*, which displays a photograph of an obviously posed Onoto Watanna dressed in a Japanese kimono, reading a book and standing before an Oriental screen. Japanese calligraphy runs down the lower right-hand margin while the caption reads: "Fac-simile of the author's autograph in Japanese" (fig. 1). Two textual modes commonly associated with the authentic—the photograph and the autograph—cooperate to legitimate her masquerade. Additionally, Eaton placed other texts to corroborate the fiction of her Japanese heritage, including her entry in *Who's Who in America*; indeed, the latest edition of *Who Was Who in America* continues to list the birthplace of "Winnifred Eaton Babcock" as Nagasaki, Japan (1976, 15). Even the obituary she had written for her sister Edith proved to be self-serving in its insistence that their father had "married a Japanese noblewoman who had been adopted by Sir Hugh Matheson as a child and educated in England" (*New York Times* 1914, 11). It is clear that, like her character Yuki in *A Japanese*

Nightingale, Eaton hoped that she would be perceived as "Japanese despite the hair and eyes," and that her audience would conclude, as Bigelow had, that "[t]here was no other country she could belong to" (1901, 24–25).

By 1912, Eaton had published ten novels as Onoto Watanna and continued to claim the biography she had invented for her alter ego as her own. Not long afterward, however, her commitment began to show signs of wavering. The *New York Times* obituary for Edith, for instance, ends rather incongruously by telling us that "one of Miss Eaton's sisters, Mrs. Bertram W. Babcock of New York, is an author, writing under the pen name of Onoto Watanna" (1914, 11). Although Eaton was not ready to admit her Chinese heritage, she went so far as to reveal, in a very public forum no less, that Onoto Watanna was nothing more than a pseudonym. Moreover, she had seemingly taken a break from writing her romances, and in 1914 she coauthored a cookbook, *Chinese-Japanese Cook Book*, with her sister, Sara Bosse. If these two texts—the obituary and the cookbook—appear somewhat inconsistent with the persona Eaton had so meticulously crafted for herself, we might assume that she had, to an extent, become dissatisfied with her association with Onoto Watanna. On one hand, there was her disenchantment with historical romance, whose popularity, some speculated, had been on the wane as early as 1900. Even as he decried the public's infatuation with the genre, William Dean Howells went on to suggest that "there are clear signs that its immense favor is abating; there are sullen whispers in the Trade that the historical romance, as a 'seller,' has had its day" (1900, 944). More importantly, Eaton faced another change in public opinion that would have an even more profound effect upon her—the growing distrust of Japan and the Japanese.

By the turn of the century, as more and more Japanese laborers arrived to take the place of the excluded Chinese, white American nativist and working-class groups began to lobby for similar checks against *all* Asian immigrants. Adding to this anti-Asian sentiment was the unease many Americans felt as a result of Japan's emergence as a world-class military and imperial power. In 1905, Japan's victory in the Russo-Japanese War marked the first time that an Asian nation had defeated a European nation—itself a colonial power—in modern warfare. The war was the first modern conflict to be covered by international press corps, and not long after its close a jingoistic American press all but predicted war between the United States and Japan over their respective interests in the Pacific. Although Theodore Roosevelt managed to defuse a volatile diplomatic situation stemming from the exclusion of Japanese children from California public schools, the relationship between the two nations suffered. Especially after the Gentlemen's Agreement of 1908, relations noticeably cooled, growing into a mutual distrust that would explode most dramatically thirty years later at Pearl Harbor. Indeed, not long after the Allied nations declared war on Japan in 1941, Eaton at last came forward to express regret over the handling of her career. "Actually I am ashamed of having written about the Japanese," she revealed in an interview after Canada had joined the war effort. She went on to assert her great pride in being Chinese on her mother's side (qtd. in Doyle 1994, 57). It is clear that the crisis of Canadian involvement in World War II forced Winnifred Eaton to make public the sentiments that she had held in check for so long; yet many of the same feelings of regret that she had revealed to the press had surfaced a generation earlier in her autobiography, *Me, A Book of Remembrance*.[6]

In her introduction to *Me, A Book of Remembrance*, the writer Jean Webster suggests that the reason the book was completed in so short a time was that it was "pure reporting," and that "the author has not branched out into any byways of style, but has merely told in the simplest language possible what she actually remembered." Eaton likewise denied the entrance of imagination into her autobiographical enterprise by claiming that an irrepressible memory had structured the narrative: "As I lay on my back and looked at the ceiling, the events of my girlhood came before me, rushed back with such overwhelming vividness that I picked up a pencil and began to write" (Watanna 1915). The idea that the autobiographical act represents nothing more than the simple transcription of events has met, predictably, with much resistance among theorists of the genre. Roy Pascal, for example, makes the important observation in *Design and Truth in Autobiography* that autobiography actually has more relevance to the present situation of the writer than to the events of the past (1960, 11). The nature of autobiography is not in its faithful reconstruction of historical experience, adds Paul John Eakin, but in the play "of the autobiographical act itself, in which the materials of the past are shaped by memory and imagination to serve the needs of present consciousness" (1985, 5). In *The Examined Self*, Robert Sayre suggests that Henry James's departure from the house of fiction in his autobiographies *A Small Boy and Others* (1913) and *Notes of a Son and Brother* (1914) responded in part to a need to commemorate his family after the death of his brother William in 1910. At the same time, James was troubled over the public reception of his writing, especially after his failure as a dramatist with *Guy Domville* and the poor sales of the New York Edition of his works. Although ostensibly concerned with the events of his youth, *A Small Boy* and *Notes* also bore reference to the present state of their author. For James, the "effort to remember the events of early youth was thus also an effort to regain his creative powers by reviving the hopes and freshness of youth" (Sayre 1964, 144–45).

Me, A Book of Remembrance might fruitfully be approached in a similar manner, so that the production of the text is not read as "pure reporting" but as a biographical moment, that is, as important an event in the definition of the self as the events narrated in the text itself. Only then can we apprehend the import of Eaton's "girlhood" memories beyond their significance as verifiable fact. Because Webster situates the book in the picaresque tradition of autobiography,[7] she can only conceive of the present as a "time of well-merited repose, of seeing oneself finally a winner, of finding a place in the social order" (Starobinski 1909, 83). And when Webster proclaims at the end of her introduction that "the aspirations of the little girl of seventeen have been realized!" she assumes that the present self (particularly one that "has written a number of books that have had a wide circulation") is the logical—and desirable—culmination of past events. If, on the other hand, the present is marked with self-doubt or despair, as it was for Eaton, the past might be reconstructed as a time of authenticity or confidence from which the autobiographer has gradually deviated. To be sure, Eaton's personal and professional lives in 1914 are remarkably similar to those of James: her older siblings Edward Charles and Edith had both passed away within the past few years, and although her own writing remained popular, she had become dissatisfied with its direction. Moreover, she was on the path to divorcing her abusive husband, Bertrand Babcock. At thirty-nine, Winnifred Eaton was by no means a writer at the close of her career, but she spoke as though she no longer had the desire to write—at least the kind of material for which she had become famous. "You perceive I had an excellent opinion of my ability at this time [seventeen]," says the narrator of *Me*. "I wish I had it now. It was more a conviction then—a conviction that I was destined to do something worth while as a writer" (1915, 115). Sometime between the end of the period of her life detailed in *Me* and the period of its composition, Eaton had lost whatever conviction she had had that she would become a serious writer. If she desired to return to her state of mind as a young woman, then the autobiographical act could provide her with the means to do so. In other words, *Me* does not simply revisit Eaton's happier days as a young woman, but it demonstrates an active effort to discard an unwanted self and reinvent another—one more worthy of respect—in its place.

One might rightly question the depth of Eaton's determination to distance herself from Onoto Watanna given that her autobiography was published anonymously, with only the introductory words of Jean Webster to vouch for its authenticity. Although some have suggested that Eaton's anonymity was intended to keep her reputation as a writer of Japanese stories intact, the fact that she even entertained the idea of the autobiographical project—when it would potentially reveal her previous work to be inauthentic—only underscores the importance of its undertaking.[8] In an unpublished document titled "You Can't Run Away from Yourself," Eaton describes her need for a change:

> I dreamed of the day when I could escape from the treadmill of writing about a subject I did not love. . . . [V]ogues are transient things and my readers probably were as tired of reading about little Japanese women as I was of writing about them. . . . Came a day when publishers no longer made me tempting offers of large advance royalties; when editors ceased to solicit stories by me. I said to myself: "I can write another type of story. This is my opportunity to get away from Japanese tales." So I wrote three anonymous stories. (qtd. in Birchall 2001, 140)

It is perhaps least useful to gauge Eaton's level of authority in *Me* through its correlation with biographical and historical fact, the strategy of an anonymous reviewer in the *New York Times* in 1915.[9] Rather, in analyzing Eaton's claim to selfhood, we are better served by a Bakhtinian dialogical approach as outlined by G. Thomas Couser, who suggests that "[a]uthority is located neither in correspondence to an extratextual reality nor in the self-determining agency of language; rather it is negotiated in the engagement of contending parties and voices in the world" (Couser 1995, 42). The authority of autobiography, Couser continues, "is proportional to the narrator's recognition and disarming of threats to it" (47). As we will see, Eaton experimented with a number of rhetorical modes, to varying degrees of success, in order to regain control over her identity.

For Eaton, the choice of seventeen-year-old Nora Ascough as the protagonist of *Me* signals not only a tacit rejection of Onoto Watanna but also a desire to *reclaim* some part of that earlier sense of self for the present.[10] In this way, *Me* disrupts the effects of Eaton's past novels, each of which successively alienated her from an uncorrupted or "authentic" self. In *Fictions in Autobiography*, Paul John Eakin explains that

> the act of composition may be conceived as a mediating term in the auto-biographical enterprise, reaching back into the past not merely to recapture but to repeat the psychological rhythms of identity formation, and reaching forward into the future to fix the structure of this identity in a permanent self-made existence as literary text. This is to understand the writing of autobiography not merely as the passive, transparent record of an already completed self but rather as an integral and often decisive phase of the drama of self-definition. (1985, 226)

The primary narrative of *Me* covers the short period between Ascough's departure from her family in Montreal to her move to Chicago to begin her literary career. The book begins with a sketchy, one-page history of her mother and father. We learn that her father, like Edward Eaton, is "an English-Irishman," but only that her mother is "a native of a far-distant land" (3). "This story is frankly of myself," explains Ascough, "and I mention these few facts merely in the possibility of their proving of some psychological interest later" (4). The dismissal of her heritage as a crucial component of her subjectivity exemplifies how Ascough privileges the autonomous self over historical determination, even to the point of denying any kind of connection with reality: "I had always secretly believed there were the strains of genius somewhere hidden in me; I had always lived in a little dream world of my own, wherein, beautiful and courted, I moved among the elect of the earth" (4). To the extent that Eaton in the present held a low opinion of herself, she imbued the young Ascough with a supreme self-confidence: "Down in my heart there was the deep-rooted conviction, which nothing in the world could shake, that I was one of the exceptional human beings of the world, and that I was destined to do things worth while. People were going to hear of *me* some day. I was not one of the commonplace creatures of the earth, and I intended to prove that vividly to the world" (76). If Ascough were to succeed in her professional and romantic ventures, she would do so on the basis of her own merit and not because of any mediating forces. Her decision to leave her mother's nationality open-ended and, moreover, to ascribe to it a fairy-tale aspect ("a far-distant land") signals a conscious intent to avoid introducing race as a meaningful signifier. The singular trait that had defined the heroines of Onoto Watanna is conspicuously muted in the character of Nora Ascough.

This is not to suggest that Eaton desired an uncritical return to her psychological state as a teenager. Like many of Eaton's novels, *Me* is a version of the female *bildungsroman* and must necessarily foreground the naïveté of its protagonist in order to track her development throughout the narrative. Indeed, one of the defining features of the bildungsroman, according to Rita Felski, is "an ironic distance between the perspectives of narrator and protagonist" (1989, 136). The narrator of *Me* is a mature Nora Ascough, whose sensibility we might read as being that of Winnifred Eaton at thirty-nine, and who functions as an interpreter of events for the reader. Although we are supposed to witness the convergence of both perspectives by the end of the narrative, the narrator is often quite critical of the innocent attitude of the protagonist. Thus, at the same time Eaton expressed a desire to reach back and recapture the optimism and conviction of her youth, she also recognized the pitfalls of such thinking. "I realized that what as an ignorant little girl I had thought was fame was something entirely different," she admits, in sharp contradiction to Webster's triumphant introduction. "What then I ardently believed to be the divine sparks of genius, I now perceived as a mediocre talent that could never carry me far. My success was founded on a cheap and popular device" (1915, 153–54). The device to which she refers is nothing other than the genre of historical romance, Eaton's variety of which depended greatly upon perceived differences in race for dramatic effect. A timely combination of ethnic difference and generic convention had substituted, in Eaton's mind, for singular "talent." How this tension enters into and is resolved within the narrative is, ironically, through the conventions of the bildungsroman: Ascough must mature as a protagonist by overcoming the challenges of the social world. For Eaton, then, creating Ascough offered something more than a chance to revel in the hubris of youth: it was an opportunity to return to a moment in her life when she successfully resisted the efforts of those whose interest in her evolved out of her racialization.

Ascough, like Eaton at her age, is an aspiring writer, and much of the narrative tension develops out of her efforts to balance her professional and personal lives. The central drama of *Me* revolves around Ascough's relationship with an older man, a multimillionaire by the name of Roger Avery Hamilton. A member of the cultural elite and "of one of the greatest families in America" (183), Hamilton never admits his love for Ascough, maintaining that he is merely "interested" in her as his "discovery" (241). Discouraged by his offers to keep but not to marry her, Ascough at one point accuses him of being interested in her only as a "sort of curiosity," an understanding that eventually makes her "sick at heart" (241). Here, both protagonist and narrator apprehend that their appeal to others derived not from any inherent uniqueness, but from the reputation of Asian women as "curiosities": objects to be enjoyed and forgotten but not taken seriously. It is in this way that the figure of Hamilton comes to stand in for all of the impersonal forces responsible for the making of Onoto Watanna and, consequently, for the crisis of identity in which Eaton now found herself. In order to affirm her own sense of integrity, Eaton needed to fashion a self-reliant Ascough: "Now, although poor and working, I was a free woman. What I had, I honestly earned. I was no doll or parasite who needed to be carried by others. No! *To retain my belief in my own powers, I must prove that they actually existed.* . . . I had the youthful conviction that *I* was one of the exceptional souls of the world, and could carry myself" (244; emphasis added). In the same way that Ascough understood that she could not pursue her literary career under the protection of Hamilton's patronage, Eaton hoped that her abandonment of Onoto Watanna and historical romance would set her on a path "to do things worth while." The significance that Ascough placed on her first literary attempts, Eaton likewise invested in *Me*, a foray away from an earlier aesthetic that was now seen as immature and disappointing. Eaton turned to the autobiographical act as the first step toward faithfully representing herself—for the work to begin showing the effect of a mature life—but by wedding her self-validation to her ability to produce "serious" writing, she risked disillusionment in the event that her art failed to measure up to the standards of canonicity.

To the extent that the bildungsroman afforded Eaton a model through which to reconcile her anxieties of race and writing, it also delimited the boundaries of her autobiographical self. In *Touching the World*, Paul John Eakin reminds us "that the tension between the experiential reality of subjectivity on the one hand and the available, cultural forms for its expression on the other always structures any engagement in autobiography" (1992, 88).[11] One of the characteristics of the bildungsroman, for instance, is the protagonist's gradual coming to terms with the limitations of individual will. Ascough, who began the narrative as a free spirit, eventually comes to appreciate and endorse the customs of the extant social order. The essentially conservative designs of the bildungsroman help to determine an equally conservative subject: "It was slowly dawning upon me that, after all, this thing we call convention, which I had previously so scouted, is in fact a necessary and blessed thing, and that the code which governs one's conduct through life is controlled by certain laws we cannot wilfully break" (1915, 296). Such a conservative turn only allows the narrator to articulate her situation in terms of personal limitation and failure. Literary convention restricted her ability to name the forces responsible for her present state of malaise, forcing her to turn inward to explain her failings. Rather than reprove her publishers who exploited the topicality of her subject,[12] Ascough instead blames herself for the transience of her fame: "Such fame (if fame I may call it) as came to me later was not of a solid or enduring kind. My work showed always the effect of my life—my lack of training, my poor preparation for the business of writing, my dense ignorance. I can truly say of my novels that they are strangely like myself, unfulfilled promises" (318–19). Complex historical play is reduced to simple lack—of talent, of will—on her part, thereby casting her in the long line of the disenfranchised who see their plight as the consequence of personal deficiency, of not "working hard enough" to rise to the level of respectable social participation.[13] "We arrive at a stage of philosophic despair when we calmly recognize our limitations," cautions the narrator (154).

For Ascough, the failure of individual will as a suitable life-governing myth is mitigated by the possibility of communal identity. The most enigmatic testimony to this new sensibility comes when she exclaims, "Oh, I had sold my birthright for a mess of potage [*sic*]!" (153–54). The mention of a "birthright" is highly ambiguous, referring perhaps to her destiny to be a serious writer had she not enlisted in the ranks of the writers of the "cheap and popular" historical romance. If, on the other hand, we consider it to be Eaton's cautious first attempt to reckon with her Chinese heritage, then *Me* takes on a new significance. The reference is better understood in light of certain personal events that moved Eaton to reevaluate the direction of her life. Her older sister Edith, who had published under the pseudonym Sui Sin Far, died less than eight months before Eaton began work on her autobiography. In *Me*, Eaton seemingly alludes to her death when the narrator thinks of her sisters, including "the eldest, a girl with more real talent than I—who had been a pitiful invalid all her days. She is dead now, that dear big sister of mine, and a monument marks her grave in commemoration of work she did for my mother's country" (194). The monument to which she alludes is a gravestone placed in gratitude by the Chinese community of Montreal and Boston and inscribed with Chinese characters that read, "The righteous or loyal one does not forget China" (Ling 1990, 32). Although Eaton continues to be vague about her mother's race, her tone suggests a new appreciation for the importance of community—familial and racial. Race, which in the past had been viewed as a means to iso-late and exploit people like Ascough, now enabled the imagination of a supportive community. Indeed, Ascough laments that it "seemed a great pity that I was not, after all, to be the savior of the family, and that my dreams of the fame and fortune that not alone should lift me up, but all my people, were built upon a substance as shifting as sand and as shadowy as mist" (194). This "substance," of course, is nothing more than the literary taste of a fickle and unsympathetic public. Incredibly, the same autobiography that began with a seventeen-year-old Ascough asserting her desire to stand apart from others concludes with a mature self hopeful of standing alongside her "people."

Me ends as it had begun, with Ascough in transit, alone, leaving be-hind the exhausted prospects of one city for the promise of another. This time it is New York and its publishing houses that draw her from the Midwest. One cannot help but respond to this decision with pause, knowing from Ascough's own words that the culture of literary pro-duction in New York would in time destroy her sense of self-worth. Yet Eaton chose not to end the book with a cynical affirmation of her past and future inadequacy. *Me* was meant to be a text with regenerative po-tential, and thus even Hamilton's duplicity is a necessary step toward her renewal: "He had destroyed something precious and fine; he had crushed my beautiful faith, my ideals, my dreams, my spirit. . . . Worse, he had ruthlessly destroyed Me! I was dead. This was another person who stood there in the snow staring at the waters of Lake Michigan" (351). Given that this version of the self was in many ways a false one, its demise serves as a fitting climax to a narrative of self-redefinition, allowing Ascough to conclude the final chapter hopefully: "I lay awake in my berth and stared out at a black night; but in the sky above I saw a single star. It was bright, alive; and suddenly I thought of the Star of Bethlehem, and for the first time in many days, like a child, I said my prayers" (356). Eaton appropriates the icons of Christianity to mark a watershed moment of her own, and one finishes her book sensing that it too is a kind of prayer, in that it is most meaningful in a private con-text. Regardless of the actual events to follow, this scene ushers in a new present for Eaton. Like Ascough, who returns to the familiarity of prayer she had practiced as a child, Eaton tempers the inspiration drawn from the best and uncorrupted aspects of her youth with an honest estimation of her ability. Her hope is for this moment of optimism to be as much prophecy as history, and for the debut of *Me* in the literary circles of New York to be the debut of a changed Winnifred Eaton. How the book fared critically—reviews were mixed—was probably not as important to her as its value as the proof of her transformation.

Eaton's quest to narrate an authentic self in *Me* responded to those who would deny her the possibility and means of determining her own identity. She is most successful when her narrative is able to break free of generic conventions, especially those governing the production of the autonomous "individual" of autobiography (à la Rousseau) or the heroine of sentimental romance. Although she continued to write in the autobiographical vein as Nora Ascough in her next book, *Marion, The Story of an Artist's Model* (1916), also published anonymously, Eaton returned to the formulaic romance with *Sunny-San* in 1922, perhaps spurred on by the financial problems of her second husband, Frank Reeve (Birchall 2001, 136). Nora Ascough is, finally, representative only of a self still in transition—ready to alter the course of her life but not at the expense of her livelihood. This understandable but wholly unromantic corollary to the publication history of *Me* reveals a side of the author only too well aware of the pressures of reality and the limits of fiction.

Notes

1. As in the description of the city of Sendai in *The Heart of Hyacinth*, even when aware of the Meiji Restoration—a social phenomenon that elevated the industrial and military capacity of Japan at the expense of its peasants—Eaton conspicuously avoids a realistic treatment of its effects. "Not even the shock of the Restoration had brought this region's people into that prophetic regard for the future which pervaded all other parts of the empire," states the narrator (Watanna 1903, 3).

2. Japan's transformation into a modern state came in response to its humiliation at the hands of Matthew Perry, the American commodore who sailed into Edo (later Tokyo) Bay with a fleet of warships in 1853 with orders of establishing trade and diplomatic relations with the historically isolationist nation.

3. When Sui Sin Far speaks of those "unfortunate Chinese Eurasians" forced to "cringe" behind the mask of a Japanese identity in order to advance themselves (1909, 131), she clearly has her sister Winnifred in mind.

4. International respect for Japan was largely synonymous with respect for its military, which in the space of ten years had won impressive victories over China and, more significantly, Russia. The editor of the *New York Times* lauded Japan for "fielding troops in uniform" in command of "breech loaders" and "well equipped men of war," and held off recognizing China's status as a civilized nation until "she demonstrates her ability to kill men in a scientific manner." James Gordon Bennett of the *Herald* predicted that "Japan through the United States" would "regenerate Asia" (qtd. in Miller 1969, 149–50).

5. See Lee 260–66, for a reading of Onoto Watanna's *Tama* in which she elaborates on the Japanese–Anglo-American racial economy.

6. An appreciation of the cast of the 1941 invasion of Hong Kong—Canadian, Japanese, Chinese, British—must have had particular resonance for Eaton, who throughout her life attempted to manage a confluence of racial and national subject positions. Canada entered the Pacific theater in defense of the colony's garrison, where 557 Canadians (of 1,975) died before surrendering to the Japanese on Christmas Day.

7. Jean Starobinski notes that "the picaresque narrative is attributed to a character who has arrived at a certain stage of ease and 'respectability' and who retraces, through an adventurous past, his humble beginnings at the fringes of society" (1909, 82).

8. Indeed, only two months after *Me* was published, the *New York Times Book Review* correctly identified its author as "Mrs. Winnifred Eaton Babcock, whose pen name is Onoto Watanna" (qtd. in Moser 1997, 365).

9. Birchall describes the peculiar deductive method of the article's author, hinting that he was most likely an acquaintance of Eaton (2001, 116–17).

10. By naming her protagonist "Nora Ascough," Eaton maintains her ostensible anonymity. However, Diana Birchall, Winnifred Eaton's granddaughter, suggests that Eaton may have named her protagonist after Hannah Ayscough, the mother of Sir Isaac Newton, to whom Eaton claimed relation (2001, 7). In this way, Eaton departs from her alter ego Onoto Watanna by embracing a more credible genealogy.

11. As evidence, Eakin cites the tradition of "as told to" autobiographies, namely the example of collaborative slave narratives, whose form—a personal narrative prefaced by an introduction by a reputable white acquaintance of the author—*Me* notably resembles.

12. A.L. Burt & Co., which published two of Eaton's romances, conspicuously traded in Orientalist material, including the novels of Sax Rohmer, the creator of Dr. Fu Manchu.

13. The melancholy in her voice becomes more poignant when juxtaposed with the optimism of the autobiographical "success" stories of Eaton's better-known contemporaries, Mary Antin and Edward Bok, whose ethnicities (Russian Jew and Dutch) did not generate the same sense of inassimilable difference—within themselves and others—as did "race" for Eaton.

WORKS CITED

Babcock, Winnifred Eaton [Onoto Watanna]. 1976. *Who Was Who in America with World Notables, Volume VI, 1974–1976*. Chicago: Marquis Who's Who.

Birchall, Diana. 2001. *Onoto Watanna: The Story of Winnifred Eaton*. Urbana: University of Illinois Press.

Couser, G. Thomas. 1995. "Authority." *a/b: Auto/biography Studies* 10 (1): 34–49.

Doyle, James. 1994. "Sui Sin Far and Onoto Watanna: Two Early Chinese-Canadian Authors." *Canadian Literature* 140 (Spring): 50–58.

Eakin, Paul J. 1985. *Fictions in Autobiography: Studies in the Art of Self-Invention.* Princeton: Princeton University Press.

———. 1992. *Touching the World: Reference in Autobiography.* Princeton: Princeton University Press.

Felski, Rita. 1989. *Beyond Feminist Aesthetics: Feminist Literature and Social Change.* Cambridge: Harvard University Press.

Glazener, Nancy. 1989. "Romances for 'Big and Little Boys': The U.S. Romantic Revival of the 1890s and James's *The Turn of the Screw.*" In *Cultural Institutions of the Novel,* ed. Deidre Lynch and William Warner, 369–98. Durham: Duke University Press.

Howells, William D. 1901. "Psychological Counter-Current in Recent Fiction." Review of *A Japanese Nightingale,* by Onoto Watanna. *North American Review* 173:880–81.

———. 1900. "The New Historical Romance." *North American Review* 171:935–48.

Kaplan, Amy. 1990. "Romancing the Empire: The Embodiment of American Masculinity in the Popular Historical Novel of the 1890s." *American Literary History* 2:659–90.

Lee, Rachel C. 1997. "Journalistic Representations of Asian Americans and Literary Responses, 1910–1920." In *An Interethnic Companion to Asian American Literature,* ed. King-kok Cheung, 249–73. Cambridge: Cambridge University Press.

Ling, Amy. 1990. *Between Worlds: Women Writers of Chinese Ancestry.* New York: Pergamon.

Literary Digest. 1912. "The Honorable Miss Moonlight." Review of *The Honorable Miss Moonlight,* by Onoto Watanna. Nov. 2, p. 795.

Miller, Stuart C. 1969. *The Unwelcome Immigrant: The American Image of the Chinese: 1785–1882.* Berkeley: University of California Press.

Moser, Linda T. 1997. Afterword to *Me, A Book of Remembrance* (1915), by Winnifred Eaton. Jackson, MS: Banner Books.

Mott, Frank L. 1947. *Golden Multitudes: The Story of Best Sellers in the United States.* New York: Macmillan.

New York Times. 1914. "Edith Eaton Dead: Author of Chinese Stories under the Name of Sui Sin Far." Apr. 9, p. 11.

New York Times Book Review. 1911. "Tama." Review of *Tama,* by Onoto Watanna. Jan. 14, p. 16.

New York Times Book Review. 1915. "Is Onoto Watanna Author of the Anonymous Novel *Me*?" Oct. 10, p. 869.

New York Times Book Review. 1915. "Me." Review of *Me, A Book of Remembrance,* by Anonymous [Onoto Watanna]. Aug. 22, p. 302.

Pascal, Roy. 1960. *Design and Truth in Autobiography.* Cambridge: Harvard University Press.

Sayre, Robert F. 1964. *The Examined Self: Benjamin Franklin, Henry Adams, Henry James.* Princeton: Princeton University Press.

Starobinski, Jean. 1980. "The Style of Autobiography." In *Autobiography: Essays Theoretical and Critical,* ed. James Olney. Princeton: Princeton University Press, 73–83.

Sui Sin Far. 1909. "Leaves from the Mental Portfolio of an Eurasian." *Independent*, Jan. 21, pp. 125–32.

Watanna, Onoto. 1899. *Miss Numèof Japan: A Japanese-American Romance.* Chicago: Rand McNally.

———. 1901. *A Japanese Nightingale.* New York: Harpers.

———. 1902. *The Wooing of Wistaria.* New York: Harpers.

———. 1903. *The Heart of Hyacinth.* New York: Harpers.

———. 1904. *Daughters of Nijo: A Romance of Japan.* New York: Macmillan.

———. 1904. *The Love of Azalea.* New York: Dodd, Mead.

———. 1910. *Tama.* New York: Harpers.

———. [Anonymous]. 1915. *Me, A Book of Remembrance.* New York: Century .

———. [Anonymous]. 1916. *Marion: The Story of an Artist's Model.* New York: W.J. Watt.

3   Diasporic Literature and Identity: Autobiography and the I-Novel in Etsu Sugimoto's *Daughter of the Samurai*

Georgina Dodge

Etsu Inagaki Sugimoto's autobiography, *A Daughter of the Samurai*, was published in book form in 1925 after much of it had been serialized in *Asia* magazine the previous year.[1] By 1935 over 80,000 copies of the book had been sold. The autobiography was reissued in 1966, and more recently, a paperback edition appeared in 1990. The initial popularity of Sugimoto's narrative and its persistence in print make it one of the best selling and most widely read Japanese American autobiographies ever published. Sugimoto's influence on her contemporaries was large. An excerpt from Sugimoto's narrative is included in a 1931 anthology of women's autobiography that credits *A Daughter of the Samurai* for having "done more to further the friendship between Japan and the United States than any other single volume." In Ruth Benedict's influential 1946 anthropological study of Japan, *The Chrysanthemum and the Sword*, some of Sugimoto's recollections of her childhood in Japan are cited as examples of the Japanese lifestyle. And in a 1948 philosophical study of pioneering individuals that includes sections devoted to such august figures as Jesus of Nazareth, Abraham Lincoln, and Ralph Waldo Emerson, Sugimoto merits her own chapter in which she is referred to as a "world citizen" who is emotionally and politically bound to her native country even though she was once described as a "loyal citizen of America."[2]

Yet *A Daughter of the Samurai* is seldom taught in Asian American literature courses and has not been the subject of significant literary scholarship.[3] Recent critics have dismissed the text for many of the same reasons that it was once lauded: the author's reputed loyalty to America, her alleged conversion to Christianity, and, perhaps most importantly, her upper-class status. This current focus on the author's "illegitimate" qualifications not only overshadows a beautifully crafted and lyrically written book but has led to the text's categorization as assimilationist autobiography—and to its subsequent dismissal as "inauthentic" Asian American literature. This much said, my purpose here is not to negotiate between recent tendencies to ignore the text and earlier inclinations to extol it. Instead, I wish to provide a transnational interpretation of the autobiography more accurately reflective of its value as a hybrid narrative—that is, a narrative which, like the immigrant Sugimoto herself, crosses borders and, rather than assimilating with the adopted culture, molds it to her indigenous expectations and values.

As she herself effectually commuted between two different societies, Sugimoto creates a protagonist whose diasporic identity is reflected in the literary form of the text. *A Daughter of the Samurai* brings the Japanese "I-novel" (*watakushi shōsetsu* or *shi-shōsetsu*) together with the American immigrant autobiography, linking Eastern and Western narrative patterns even as it emphasizes or makes connections to significant social issues of late nineteenth- and early twentieth-century Japan and the United States. This confluence of form and substance is difficult to perceive (much less to assess) exclusively from American literary paradigms. An expanded approach to the autobiography, one that accounts for diasporic (that is, both Japanese and American) elements of the text, is necessary to perceive the play of both Asian and American elements in Sugimoto's narrative—and to evaluate the significance of Asian literary types within this distinctively Asian American narrative.

Perhaps because of the book's classification as an American immigrant autobiography, critics and teachers have ignored the influence of Japanese literary tradition on its composition. Like the narratives of writers from Eastern Europe who came to the United States during the "second wave" of immigration in the late nineteenth and early twentieth centuries, *A Daughter of the Samurai* features the all-too-familiar "cultural discoveries" and "gaffes" of the immigrant protagonist as she learns the social codes of her new home. But in Sugimoto's case an understanding of the American way does not necessarily imply acceptance of it; and a close reading of Sugimoto's narrative, coupled with biographical information, shows that the assimilation pattern contained within most American immigrant autobiographies is markedly absent from hers. Her eventual and permanent return to Japan, along with the theme of Japanese sovereignty within her final novel, *Grandmother O Kyo* (1940), suggests that if Sugimoto did indeed consider herself to be

an American, this national affiliation was only temporary. In her autobiography, Sugimoto herself makes no claim to an American identity.
Although she recognizes the impact that Western culture has had upon
her, she never suggests that she is anything but Japanese. In fact, the self-
conscious Japaneseness prevalent throughout the text appealed to her
first American readers—who accepted Sugimoto as an unquestionable
representative of that country. At the same time, true enough, they perceived her as acknowledging the superiority of certain Western ways,
as evidenced by her conversion from Buddhism to Christianity and her
critique of some Japanese customs. It is this latter point of embracing
the West that is problematic from a twenty-first-century perspective:
acquiescence is now seen as the denial and corruption of ethnic origin.
In fact, Sugimoto's preoccupations with America and the West directly
reflect those of her natal country during the latter nineteenth and early
twentieth centuries, when many Japanese became dissatisfied with the
indigenous culture and (especially among the educated elite) turned
to Christianity. In this sense, Sugimoto's so-called Western preoccupations are, both paradoxically and ironically, among the most "Japanese"
elements of the narrative.

After nearly seven centuries of rule by the samurai class, Japan underwent significant social and spiritual changes with the overthrow of
the Tokugawa shogunate and the restoration of the Emperor Meiji in
1868. Of course, Japan did not transform itself overnight; prior to the
Meiji Restoration, a growing civil strife was caused in part by increased
contact with—and pressure from—the West. During the first phase of
the Meiji period, which extended from 1868 to 1912, Japan looked to
the West as a model of national identity, given that all things Western
were considered necessary to modernization. Signs of modernity ranged
from technological adaptations—such as railroads, a national postal service and, gas-burning streetlights—to fads involving clothing and food
(Varley 1977, 162–65). Although the cultural impact of the Meiji Restoration was felt primarily in large cities, Sugimoto asserts that the Western
craze influenced her childhood home in the remote province of Echigo.
At one point, her father returns home from one of his trips to the capital
with Western clothes for her. All admire the young girl as she struts about
in her costume even though, unbeknownst to the family, the clothes were
intended for a boy (Sugimoto 1990, 123). And while eating beef is contrary to Buddhist tradition, beef is incorporated into the family diet at
the insistence of Sugimoto's father, to the end that each may become
' "as strong [and clever] as a Westerner" ' (27).[4]

Meiji Japan not only borrowed superficial trappings of Western culture, it adopted certain Western ideals. Chief among these were the concepts of "equality and individualism" that provided the basis for the 1874 Freedom and People's Rights Movement (*Jiyūminken undō*), which agitated against the authoritarian Meiji regime and petitioned for an elective assembly (Hall 1970, 290–295; Suzuki 1996, 26–27). Not that the government fully opposed calls for popular representation and participation in the political process: such ideas provided a way to dismantle localized systems of government in favor of a centralized national one. According to Tomi Suzuki, "Indeed, the Meiji government embraced Western Enlightenment notions of natural rights, freedom, and individual equality in order to introduce and justify the new systems of centralization, which emphasized the duty of citizens to their nation" (1996, 27). Standards of Western individualism contained in such texts as John Stewart Mill's *On Liberty*, translated in 1872, and Samuel Smiles's *Self-Help*, translated in 1870–71, were used to promote the "homogenization of citizens" as equal beings or at least as "equal subjects" to the emperor (Suzuki 1996; 27, 33). The notion of an individual "self" weakened the rigid caste system of Japan's feudal past and provided the basis for developing loyalty to the nation-state rather than to regional clans.

The concept of "self" quickly spread from the political realm to other realms of Japanese life. For many Meiji intellectuals, capturing the full spirit of Western democracy could not be accomplished without also accepting Western philosophical thought, including religion. The ban against Christian missionaries was lifted in 1873; and by 1880 approximately 30,000 Japanese became Christians (primarily Protestants), a number that tripled by 1890. Among the converts were many former samurai retainers who transferred their allegiance to the "new God of the enlightened West" (Hall 1970, 291). Sons of supporters of the former Tokugawa shogunate who were now disenfranchised by the Meiji government turned to Christianity both as a means to disregard governmental authority in light of a higher one and to "transcend" the increasing impact of Western nations on Japan's politics and economy: "Christianity satisfied, in an ironically inverted form, the 'will to power' of those young people who felt both powerless and resentful" (Suzuki 1996, 34–35).

Like many samurai families, Sugimoto's family lost both money and social status after the restoration. Her own Christian "conversion" occurred when she attended a Methodist school for girls in Tokyo. Although she writes that "I do not know exactly how I became a

Christian," the ideals of Christianity that she embraces, particularly freedom and cheerfulness, are embodied by the Western women who teach
at the school (1990, 145). Initially shocked by the teachers' behavior,
which violates her conservative ideas of the teacher–student relationship, Sugimoto soon finds herself drawn to the extroverted women:

> The more I saw of my teachers, the more I admired them. I had lost my
> feeling of repulsion at their lack of ceremony when I learned to understand
> the hidden dignity that lay beneath their individual differences, and finally
> it began to dawn upon me that the honourable position of instructor was
> not inconsistent with being merry and gay. My Japanese teachers had been
> pleasantly courteous, but always lofty and distant in manner; while these
> smiling, swift-moving creatures ran with us in the gymnasium, played
> battledore and shuttlecock with us, and took turns in eating with us in
> our own dining room where Japanese food was served on trays as it was
> on our small tables at home. (123)

Sugimoto's conflation of Christianity, freedom, happiness, and equality was common among young people during this period. According to Suzuki, "For these Western-educated youths, who turned to
Christianity in the late 1880's and early 1890's, Christianity was inextricably linked to the Enlightenment, liberal political ideals of freedom
and independence—both individual and national—and to Western ro-
manticism" (36). The Western texts that Sugimoto and her classmates
read in school encouraged a romanticized freedom that shaped all aspects of life from religiosity to gender roles. According to Sugimoto,
"Enoch Arden was our hero. We were familiar with loyalty and sacrifice on the part of a wife . . . but the unselfishness of the faithful Enoch
was so rare as to be much appreciated" (131). Poems like Tennyson's
"Enoch Arden" led to "exaggerated ideas that we had of the dominant
spirit of American women and the submissive attitude of American
men" (161). When she later learns that American men traditionally propose marriage to women, Sugimoto is "somewhat surprised; for I, with
most Japanese people of that day, so interpreted the constant references
in books and papers to the American custom of 'women choosing their
own husbands'" (161).

The perceived independence of Western women inspired a small
number of Japanese women to participate in the Freedom and People's
Rights Movement; they believed the organization would help secure
better positions for women in Japan's changing society. But they
quickly discovered that the men in control of the movement were
more interested in obtaining power for themselves than in insuring

"freedom" for their followers, male or female (Thomas 1996, 197). By 1890, the Freedom and People's Rights Movement dissolved under increased governmental pressure and the adoption of a national constitution in 1889. Infatuation with the West began to wane, and Japanese conservatives called for a return to traditional values. Nonetheless, Japanese culture had been indelibly marked by Western influences, and the concept of an individual self—which was vital to Japan's political and social development during the Meiji era—became an intrinsic feature within Japanese literature as well.

In the late 1800s and early 1900s Japanese literati held up the Western novel as the ideal novel form, the "true *shōsetsu*" (Suzuki 1996, 19). Critics contended that the traditionally didactic emphasis within Japanese novels should be replaced with the "'truth of human nature' . . . an imagined reality, whose model was thought to exist in the West but had yet to be achieved in Japan" (Suzuki 1996, 36). In order to convey the "truth" of life, writers turned to their own lives as subjects about which they possessed accurate knowledge that they could convey honestly to their readers. The publication of Katai Tayama's *Futon* [*The Quilt*] (1907), is commonly seen as the genesis of the Japanese I-novel, a term that was created retroactively in the mid-1920s. As with many literary forms, there is some slippage between designation and definition, but the *shi-shōsetsu* is generally seen as an "autobiographical narrative in w゛ ゛1 the author is thought to recount faithfully the details of his or her ɟ ⸗rsonal life in the thin guise of fiction" (Suzuki 1996, 1). As Edward Fowler notes, however, Japanese critics are not entirely comfortable referring to the I-novel as fiction; nor are they comfortable calling it autobiography (1988, xxii). The I-novel instead becomes its own genre and narrative type peculiar to Japanese literature. True, the term *shi-shōsetsu* was originally applied to autobiographical sketches written by Meiji authors for their contemporaries. But it soon took on a more amorphous meaning. While some critics have defined the I-novel according to thematic paradigms, others have focused on authorial intention or the relative factuality of recorded events. Suzuki argues:

> [T]he term *watakushi shōsetsu* circulated as a powerful and uncanny signifier without a fixed, identifiable signified, generating a critical discourse that informed not only the nature of literature but also views of Japanese selfhood, society, and tradition. This critical discourse, which I refer to as "I-novel discourse" or the "I-novel meta-narrative," is not a descriptive representation of a particular body of pre-existing texts. Rather, the characteristics of the so-called I-novel texts were largely defined by and within

this I-novel meta-narrative and then projected back on certain texts. . . .
[T]he uncanny ability of *watakushi shōsetsu* as a signifier to generate such
a powerful literary and cultural meta-narrative derived from the special mystique of the notion of *watakushi*, the "I" or "self," and from the
privileged status of the novel, both of which emerged under the cultural
hegemony of Western modernity. (1996, 2)

Regardless of other features of the I-novel, its central concern with
"self"—particularly in the context of Western influences—is a critical element of *A Daughter of the Samurai*. Throughout her narrative, Sugimoto
attempts to define herself through newly learned ideas of selfhood that
she encounters at the Tokyo school and in the United States. Typical of
the I-novel form, the concept of the individual self within Sugimoto's
narrative does not simply reflect Western notions of selfhood, nor is this
self derived exclusively or even largely from Western thought. Traditional Japanese views profoundly influence the development and actions of Sugimoto's protagonist, whose unique position well illustrates
the convergence of both Western and Japanese concepts of the individual. Even though she embraces Western ideas of equality, particularly in
regard to women's rights, Sugimoto never questions the circumstances
that bring her to Tokyo to learn English and that ultimately take her to
the United States to marry a man she has never met. Her marriage to
Matsuo Sugimoto is arranged—in traditional Japanese fashion—by her
family in order to recognize and repay Matsuo for helping Sugimoto's
elder brother, who, after having been victimized in a fraudulent business transaction, had been left stranded in America, penniless and in
ill-health. When she is summoned before the family council and told
of her betrothal, Sugimoto "had no thought of asking, 'Who is it?'" She
continues, "I did not think of my engagement as a personal matter at
all. It was a family affair" (1990, 89).

The concept of self that Sugimoto displays here is alien to the Western
notion of autonomous individuality but consistent with her belief that
the "devout Buddhist is absolutely submissive to Fate" (40). Coupled
with religious tradition is the Japanese concept of duty that Sugimoto
subscribes to throughout her text: "If duty lies behind, undone, nothing,
while life lasts, can break the heart pull, the brain planning, the soul
prayer to reach, even partially, the lost goal. Such is the deep-hidden
soul of Japan" (85). This combination of *giri* (duty or obligation) and *gudō*
(pursuit of the Way) is central to a distinctly Japanese sense of self that
defines and shapes the Japanese I-novel. Obviously, such an ideology of
self is not Western; it must be attributed to and assessed or understood

from a specifically Japanese cultural perspective. According to Fowler, "It is ironic that the so-called 'I-novel,' treated by many Japanese critics as the showcase of the 'modern self' (*kindai jiga*), actually questions what it ostensibly champions" (1988, 14). Fowler cites Japanese critic Hideo Takahashi, who "urges that we revise our notions of the [modern] self in Japan" to take into account the influences of traditional Japanese culture in shaping it:

> Rather than equate it with modern Western society's individuated self, which has been largely weaned from nature and tradition, he [Takahashi] concludes that it is more properly conceived of as a premodern "element" of man that aspires to fusion with its surroundings. The *shishōsetsu*'s *watakushi* has brought new meaning to the "self," Takahashi argues, not by an assertion of individuality but by its reversion to self*less*ness, as exhibited in the protagonist's return to the comforting embrace of nature, family, and tradition—to which we might add, in the case of those politically motivated writers in the 1930s who underwent ritual "conversion" (*tenkō*), the state. (Fowler 1988, 14–15; emphasis Fowler's)[5]

Sugimoto's eventual return to tradition and the state in *Grandmother O Kyo* is prefigured throughout *A Daughter of the Samurai* as Sugimoto-as-protagonist struggles "to keep my memories of beautiful old customs and ideals from completely overshadowing the new, progressive path that I was striving to follow" (1990, 292). Both the old and the new are interwoven throughout the text in a narrative display of what Stuart Hall refers to as *diaspora identity*, a term defined

> not by essence or purity, but by the recognition of a necessary heterogeneity and diversity; by a conception of "identity" which lives with and through, not despite, difference; by *hybridity*. Diaspora identities are those which are constantly producing and reproducing themselves anew, through transformation and difference. (1997, 119–20; emphasis Hall's)

While the idea and application of the word *hybridity* has been contested within postcolonial studies, Hall's invocation of the term implies a mixing of diverse elements that concurrently impact identity, a concept that certainly has relevance to the American immigrant. In Sugimoto's case, diaspora identity cuts across temporal boundaries as well as cultural and geographical ones. Ancient codes of behavior that she herself feels bound to observe have little significance within modern Japan except as nostalgic emblems of the past; they are even more foreign within contemporary American culture. As Hall stresses, there is no historically "authentic" identity to be found in precolonial or precontact cultures. Thus, while Sugimoto bemoans the loss of certain traditions, she does not fail to see how many of those customs placed limits upon individual potential, particularly that of women. Her gradual coming to terms with the shifts and amalgamations resulting from changing times and places illustrates an emergent formulation of the diaspora identity among Japanese American women.

Sidonie Smith applies the concept of diasporic identity specifically to women's autobiography when she examines one of the most elusive autobiographical subjects in American women's literature, Zora Neale Hurston's in *Dust Tracks on a Road* (1942). According to Smith, Hurston engages in a "jazzed-up performance of diasporan subjectivity" that enables her to "resist her reader's attempt to fix her in the identity of the exceptional black woman by undermining the bases upon which that identity is founded" (1993, 105). By inverting the chronology of her narrative, inserting tales and folklore into it, presenting her childhood self as a tomboy, and speaking in different cultures and tongues—all characteristics of Sugimoto's autobiography as well—Hurston unfixes her subject from the single, socially assigned identity of "black woman." Hurston's role as both participant and observer in the writing of *Dust Tracks* results in a "personal space of both appreciation and critique" that situates her simultaneously as insider and outsider so that the "diasporan subject of Hurston's text moves by incorporation rather than exclusions" (Smith 1993, 124).

Like Hurston, Sugimoto occupies a space that continually crisscrosses borders of identity and culture, incorporating diverse social elements. While the self she displays in her autobiography is not as playful or sardonic as that created by Hurston, it is an equally complex example of a self with a diasporic identity. Situated within both Japan's feudal past and its modernity and dictated by the cultures of East and West, Sugimoto's textual self or "identity" incorporates or encompasses the various persons, places, events, and phenomena she encounters and inherits. Hence, as Stuart Hall suggests, "Identities are the names we give to the different ways we are positioned by, and position ourselves within, the narratives of the past" (1997, 112). Just as this identity is not pure, it is also not constant. The Sugimoto who writes *A Daughter of the Samurai* is in many ways different from the author who appeals to Japanese nationalism fifteen years later in *Grandmother O Kyo*. It is possible to see her position at the outset of World War II (WWII) as more congruent with Hall's concept of a "cultural identity" that "reflect[s] the common historical experiences and shared cultural codes which provide us, as 'one people,' with stable, unchanging and continuous frames of reference and meaning, beneath the shifting divisions and vicissitudes of our actual history" (Hall 1997, 111). If, as Hall argues, cultural identity is produced through a retelling of the past, Sugimoto's return to Japan and to a Japanese cultural identity can be seen as the inevitable outcome of her literary production: in this sense, her return is the necessary result of her having grounded her writing in a recollected past—in a recollected sense of her own origins.

While the strong links that can be made between historical and modern Japan and Sugimoto's Japanese identity strengthen the connections between her autobiography and the Japanese I-novel, it would be a mistake to see the text simply as an English-language manifestation of that somewhat nebulous literary form. As mentioned earlier, the parallel approaches taken by Sugimoto and Hurston allude to common strategies undertaken by women of color in the United States to formulate autobiographical subjectivity, which is often at odds with reader expectations. Just as Hurston undermines attempts to identify herself as the prototypical—much less the "exceptional"—black woman, Sugimoto also challenges attempts to fix her identity as that of the representative Asian woman. Writing against the stereotypes of Asian women's passivity (stereotypes that persist today), Sugimoto emphasizes her own tomboy behavior and her admiration of women's courage. One of Sugimoto's American neighbors, Mrs. Newton, is a delicate and timid woman who initially met with Sugimoto's disapproval because she "allowed her husband to be too attentive to her. He carried her cloak and umbrella for her; and once, in the carriage, I saw him lean over and fasten her slipper strap" (Sugimoto 1990, 204). Sugimoto later learns, however, that her shy, frail neighbor shot a snake that threatened one of several birdhouses that she had built and hung from trees in the yard. On discovering that Mrs. Newton once lived on a western ranch where she overcame hardships and deprivation, Sugimoto concedes that Mrs. Newton is, after all, like a Japanese woman because her timid manner conceals a steely interior. Each of the American women Sugimoto admires is granted the honorary classification of being "like a Japanese woman."

Sugimoto portrays Japanese women themselves as possessing the confidence and courage befitting the daughters of a country that originated as a matriarchal society.[6] When another neighbor challenges her to present a "specimen of a Japanese genuine woman's-rights woman [*sic*]," Sugimoto tells her about the island of Hachijo, where for centuries men performed traditional housekeeping chores such as cooking and child care while women tended the profitable silkworms and governed the island. She ends her story of Hachijo by stating that "the social life there is more strictly moral than it is in any other community of equal intelligence in Japan" (1990, 202–203). Through her evaluation Sugimoto brings together two of the main focal points within her autobiography, the value of tradition and the capabilities of women, to illustrate that the near-perfect society is one where women rule according to ancient tradition.

The value that Sugimoto places on social mores of the past makes it tempting to position her as an "authentic" Japanese who persists into and beyond the Meiji Restoration and who survives Western corruption—but the critic who did so would end up in problematic territory. According to Rey Chow, "[A]ttempts to salvage the other often turn into attempts to uphold the other as the non-duped—the site of authenticity and true knowledge. Critics who do this can also imply that, having absorbed the primal wisdoms, they are the non-duped themselves" (1994, 145). In other words, to read Sugimoto as a purist (or a "non-duped" Japanese) who courageously upholds a venerable past is not only to *mis*read her but also to place oneself—as critic— within a privileged category of knowledge-holders having full access to an unpolluted, uncolonized past. Reading Sugimoto as purist is, in this sense, synonymous with reading her narrative strictly as a critique of the West—in that it permits the critic an affiliation with the authentic native who sees through the fog of modern capitalism (or other postcolonial institutions) and to maintain or recapture an untouched purity. As Chow notes, such a position says much about our own quest for power: "Our fascination with the native, the oppressed, the savage, and all such figures is therefore a desire to hold onto an unchanging certainty somewhere outside our own 'fake' experience. It is a desire for being 'non-duped,' which is a not-too-innocent desire to seize control" (1994, 145).

Read closely, Sugimoto's narrative is most appealing in its considered "non-control." That the protagonist of *Daughter* may be seen as an authentic Japanese native on one hand and as a loyal American citizen on the other—and that either reading is in measure supportable through the text—is a fact that should give the impulsive critic pause. More significant still is the fact that neither reading accurately reflects the protagonist's status as *either* Japanese or American. And positioning the protagonist as somehow caught between two cultures is equally problematic: she is not drawn as a victim, much less an imprisoned one.

Nor is seeing her as a detached observer the answer. Such a critic, much like Sugimoto's American contemporaries who praised her work as an appropriate challenge to the "cold, hard, and feudal code" of premodern Japan as well as to the "strange and violent ways" of modern America,[7] runs the risk of reducing Sugimoto's narrative to reportage, to a neutral description of the world by an objective outsider who has no other agenda than to inform dispassionately. Placing Sugimoto into cultural limbo as neither Asian nor (Asian) American precludes needs for further classification and provides yet another avenue through which to dismiss her narrative.

Nor does the autobiographical form of Sugimoto's *Daughter* make it any easier to classify. Because the Japanese I-novel is as much the portrait of a cultural sensibility as it is a defined narrative genre, its characteristics are—as we have already seen—difficult to pinpoint and assess, particularly from Western perspectives. One contemporary Asian American author who has tried to delineate its characteristics is Lydia Minatoya, who wrote *The Strangeness of Beauty* (1999) as an I-novel supposedly penned by her fictional protagonist, drawing (quite intriguingly) characters and events from *A Daughter of the Samurai*. Minatoya even includes a bibliography at the end of her novel—and lists *Daughter* within it; she does not detail her obvious borrowings from Sugimoto, but these are easily identified by the reader. The protagonist of *The Strangeness of Beauty* is named Etsuko Sone; Sugimoto was often called Etsuko as a child. In Minatoya's novel, the protagonist's niece is named Hanae (blossoming flower); Sugimoto's eldest daughter is named Hana (flower). Like Sugimoto, Minatoya's protagonist is born into an upper-class samurai family. Historical events in *The Strangeness of Beauty* mirror those found in Sugimoto's autobiography; for example, in *Beauty* a female ancestor is instructed to set fire to the family home in the event that her husband is captured during the Restoration. We are told in *Daughter* that, after her husband is imprisoned, Sugimoto's mother actually burns the family mansion to keep it from being occupied by enemy forces.

More important than similar content is Minatoya's engagement with the I-novel form that gives Sugimoto's autobiography its structure. At the outset, Minatoya's first-person narrator states, "This, of course, is my I-story" (1990, 16); and throughout the novel, she muses on the origins and functions of the *shi-shōsetsu* as she reflects upon her own identity. This conflation of literary form and personal and national identity quite accurately mirrors the self-assessment with which Sugimoto's autobiography is concerned. *Beauty* "translates" the I-novel through self-conscious references to uniquely Japanese literary ideals, to the advantages of reflection over action, and to the symbiosis of social upheaval and individual change—all attributes of *Daughter*.

Set primarily in Japan during the first half of the twentieth century, but focusing primarily on a circle of Japanese American and "westernized" Japanese characters, *The Strangeness of Beauty* considers contemporary roots of both personal and Japanese national identity while simultaneously demonstrating the relevance of Sugimoto's diasporic elements (especially those of *Daughter*) to present-day Japanese American writers' explorations of ethnic selfhood. For Minatoya, in other words, *Daughter* provides an appropriate template for literary contemplation of Japanese American heritage and identity. Although *Beauty* is quite obviously an original novel, its connections to *Daughter* point up the generational capacity and vitality of early Asian American texts—which continue to impact contemporary Asian American writing and which live on through new artistic interpretations. While both *A Daughter of the Samurai* and *The Strangeness of Beauty* must be considered and evaluated within their respective cultural contexts, their close relationship suggests that a sophisticated understanding of the pioneering text is crucial to a full appreciation of the later incarnation.

Because *Daughter* may accurately be described as an American immigrant narrative, one expects to find within it the ordered event pattern characteristic of the genre that flourished during the early years of the twentieth century, the pattern of *arrival*, *confusion*, and *eventual acculturation* that identifies immigrant authors as newly formed Americans. Just as the Japanese I-novel responds to a particular cultural moment, the American immigrant narrative alludes to a specific set of events. But even though Sugimoto adopts Western ideas and beliefs, she continues to define herself as Japanese and to situate herself as an outsider, a visiting student of American culture. Thus, given that the Japanese I-novel responds to a particular cultural moment from the vantage point of Japanese traditionalism, the I-novel form is particularly suited to Sugimoto's purposes. Throughout her autobiography, Sugimoto approaches the United States and its culture as a tourist who is "shopping" for cultural exports that can benefit Japan. She is pleased, for example, by the autonomy enjoyed by American women, especially in marriage, where they are not expected to consume only those foods that their husbands enjoy or to sleep only when their husbands do. The ability of individual women to step outside narrowly defined social boundaries amazes and delights Sugimoto. She generally praises her new home and its inhabitants, but she criticizes Americans in general as a people who are "both admirable *and faulty* in a giant way" (1990, 155–56; emphasis mine).

This is not to imply that Sugimoto's autobiography may be described primarily as a cultural critique. In the first place, cultural assessment is only one of the tasks Sugimoto undertakes in *Daughter*. In the second, her commentary on American culture and society is not finally precise *or* groundbreaking so much as it is good-humored and even humorous.[8] To the limited extent that Sugimoto positions herself as an arbiter of cultures, however, her kind-spirited documentation of quirky American customs provides opportunities to showcase the more reasonable or worthy counterpart customs from the Japanese cultural tradition; these explanations of Japanese culture position her as a knowing but gracious representative of Japan to her American audience. As Elaine Kim notes, early Asian immigrant writers were well aware of the West's limited and often negative views of Asia and served as Asian "ambassadors of goodwill" to the American people, seeking "to win friends" by teaching Western readers about Asian cultures (1982, 24–25). Primarily from the upper classes in Asia, these writers produced texts

> marked by dissociation from the Asian common people, whether in Asia or in the West, and even their pleas for racial tolerance are made primarily on behalf of members of their own privileged class. They tended to accept discrimination against the poor and uneducated members of their own race as reasonable, questioning instead the logic of discrimination against the educated elite. For this reason, their explanations of Asia to the West were usually focused on high culture, and the indignation they express at American race policies is often tentative and apologetic. (Kim 1982, 24–25)

Kim's description of early Asian American writers is certainly applicable to Sugimoto, who was a member of the upper class in both Japan and the United States. For some current critics, this fact potentially complicates Sugimoto's status as an "authentic" Asian American representative; for, as Sylvia Yanagisako has observed, "The past that constitutes Asian American subjectivity—the collective conscience and sense of being and acting in the world—is deemed a working-class one" (1995, 283). That is, Sugimoto's experiences were nothing like those of the majority of the 27,000 Japanese who came to the United States during the last decade of the nineteenth century and who resided primarily on the West Coast, working in agriculture.[9] Her familial lineage and social position marked her as one of the Japanese elite, even though (at least in *Daughter*) she attempts to mitigate her privileged status by exposing her family's declining financial circumstances after the Meiji Restoration. Still, even in *Daughter*, she shows a clear awareness of the advantages her class provides. She writes appreciatively of the material comforts she enjoys in America, knowing from the earlier experiences of her brother—who spent difficult time in San Francisco—that she has been much less the victim of racial and social prejudice.

While in America, Sugimoto lives in the College Hill suburb of Cincinnati in isolation from other Japanese Americans except for her merchant husband, Matsuo, who owns an import business. An affluent neighborhood characterized by sweeping lawns and stately homes with grand porches, College Hill is nothing like Sugimoto's rural home province in Japan, and yet the living conditions in most of the houses are in some ways similar. There are servants to do the bulk of the housework, and each home has beautiful furnishings and well-tended gardens. In this idyllic setting, Sugimoto associates primarily with upperclass European American women who treat her as a uniquely exotic addition to their neighborhood. One in fact declares that Sugimoto is the "only Japanese woman that I ever saw—except at the exposition" (1990, 202). Despite the obvious condescension in their bearing toward her, in other words, these neighborhood women encircle Sugimoto with goodwill and the trappings of privilege. They will eventually constitute Sugimoto's target audience when she begins writing her autobiography: like her, they are women of refinement and sensibility who have the money and leisure to contemplate cultural differences. Their assessments of such differences are, of course, largely confined to the domestic realm. Although Sugimoto admires the freedoms enjoyed by American women, she is—and they are— regardless of the settings in which they find themselves, necessarily limited by the social customs of the educated elite.

And yet Sugimoto's American experience is neither so confined nor so predictable as it may first appear. Before she began writing *A Daughter of the Samurai*, Sugimoto's husband died, and she was left a widow with two young daughters. Her children were, as is Japanese custom, under the legal and formal custody of her late husband's family. But the fact that Sugimoto lived in the United States, away from her Japanese in-laws, allowed her to exert parental control over her children, to guide their education, and to prevent their entering marriages arranged by her husband's family. In order to gain at least a degree of financial independence for herself and her daughters, she taught courses in Japanese language and literature at Columbia University and wrote autobiographical sketches of Japan, sketches that become the basis for *Daughter*. Her writing was meant to be marketable, particularly to her target audience of European American women. To this end, she quite deliberately chose topics that would appeal to her American readers' interest in Japan while also presenting herself as "not too foreign" for American acceptance. She fulfills this latter goal in part by showing that her concerns are congruent with those of women in the United States, whose struggles for civil rights were of great interest to progressive women in Japan.

Identity politics have undergone substantial changes since Sugimoto's autobiographical writings first appeared; and contemporary expectations are that Asian American writing, like much of ethnic American literature, will feature condemnation of, resistance to, or victimization by American dominant culture—none of which characterizes Sugimoto's autobiography. The shifting critical evaluation of the text between the first and the second halves of the twentieth century reveals much about the changing nature of (Asian American) literary criticism as well as (Asian) American political identities. The social contacts and audience that made it possible for Sugimoto to publish her narrative are now considered liabilities. Although the purveyors of Asian American culture continue to hail primarily from the middle and upper classes, the concept of the "authentic" Asian American has undergone enormous shifts in the wake of WWII and postcolonial theory. In the prewar era of Sugimoto's autobiography, Japan perceived itself as a nation of colonizers rather than of the colonized. Writing from a subtle but recognizable position of nationalist superiority, Sugimoto does not comply with contemporary ideas of the victimized Japanese American forced into a relocation camp, leaving behind land and possessions. Instead, she continually asserts a moral code of behavior practiced in premodern Japan that valued honor and duty more than life or property. That this moral code is the basis on which Japan justified attacks on China, Korea, and other Asian nations in its quest to expand helps to explain, in part, the current difficulty involved in claiming as "Asian American" the writings of the daughter of a violent and warlike past who is neither victim nor apologist. Dismissing Sugimoto because of her class status keeps postmodern critics from having to situate a highly ambiguous or even contentious figure whose position within both Japanese and Japanese American cultures cannot be defined simply.

Just as Sugimoto herself is hard to classify, so is her narrative. The similarities between the Japanese I-novel and Western autobiographical forms make it difficult to identify distinct characteristics of either within the narrative. Nevertheless, acknowledging the multifaceted dimensions of identity permits a more accurate evaluation of Sugimoto's text. In particular, an understanding of her shifting diasporic identity—her fluid concept of self within both modern Japanese and modern American cultural contexts—provides access to Sugimoto as a transnational rather than as a delimited "Asian" or "Asian American" subject. Accordingly, *Daughter* can then be read as a transnational text whose integrity is not solely dependent on its conformance to Asian or Asian American identity politics. Yanagisako writes in a 1995 essay that

> Asian American studies has responded to dilemmas of national allegiance and class alliance by confining "Asian American experience"—in other words, the collective experiences that constitute Asian American ethnic subjectivity—to locations within the borders of the nation rather than viewing it as a transnational process involving individuals, families, communities, events, and sociopolitical structures that crosscut these borders. (291)[10]

As Yanagisako suggests, we must begin to consider the impact of diasporic identity, in all of its culturally and historically specific manifestations, on textual form and content. Approaches to Asian American literature must move beyond debates about factuality and distortion, authenticity and inauthenticity, to more nuanced discussions of politics, aesthetics, and "ethnic integrity" that appropriately account for all cultural influences that shape textual identities—and that do not ignore the particular circumstances of autobiographical production.

The conflicts surrounding gender roles and self-realization central to Sugimoto's autobiography result in a narrative tension that mirrors debates within the United States as well as in Japan at the turn of the century. Rather than being dismissed as yet another story of an American immigrant's successful assimilation, *A Daughter of the Samurai* needs to be reevaluated as a text that skillfully blends diverse identities in order to challenge the boundaries of gender, class, and nationality. Particularly when read in conjunction with Sugimoto's three later novels, which all feature Japanese women as protagonists, the autobiography calls into question cultural models based on traditional values—models that, according to Sugimoto, can serve as templates for behavior but must change with the times. That the change Sugimoto most insistently calls for is the expansion of women's rights lends even more urgency to a recovery of her written voice. Sugimoto articulates the needs and feelings of women who seek to live with honor in their specific societies while also pursuing individual interests and needs. Reassessing the cultural and literary identity of Sugimoto's *Daughter* will appropriately challenge the borders currently delineating the Asian American literary canon, allowing for a more genuine appreciation of women whose concerns and identities have been dismissed as inauthentically Asian American.[11] Through transnational paradigms that allow greater appreciation of the continued influence and importance of early Asian American texts, the voices of all our ancestors can reverberate more richly in our shared literary heritage.

NOTES

1. Throughout this article, Japanese names are Americanized, with a given name preceding the surname. Although Sugimoto retains her maiden name of Inagaki on the book's cover, the practice of doing so is not common in Japan unless a son-in-law of lower caste is "adopted" by a titled family.

2. See, in order, Helen Ferris, ed., *When I Was a Girl: The Stories of Five Famous Women as Told by Themselves* (New York: McMillan, 1931), 224; Ruth Benedict, *The Chrysanthemum and the Sword: Patterns of Japanese Culture* (New York: World Publishing, 1946) 268, 280–82, 294–95; and George Henry Gilbert, *Pioneers in Self-Government: Informal Studies in the Natural Philosophy of Self-Government* (Segreganset, MA: Builders of America Publishing Co., 1948), 128. The term "citizen" is used rather loosely here; Sugimoto did not become an official citizen of the United States.

3. Students of Asian American literature may now receive some exposure to *A Daughter of the Samurai* with the recent appearance of Shirley Geok-lin Lim's anthology, *Asian American Literature* (Lincolnwood, IL: NTC Publishing, 2000). Lim includes a short excerpt from the autobiography as the first selection in the anthology, under the section appropriately titled "The Immigration Experience."

4. According to H. Paul Varley, eating beef was "symbolic of the humorous side of foreign borrowing" (1977, 164). In *Japan* (New York: Facts on File Publications, 1988), Peter Spry-Leverton and Peter Kornicki cite an 1871 satire that features a Japanese dandy eating beef while expounding upon the glories of the West (55).

5. Hideo Takahashi, *Genso to shite no "watakushi": Watakushi shōsetsu sakka ron* [The "self" as an element: On writers of watakushi shōsetsu] (Tokyo: Kodansha, 1976.) According to Fowler's footnote, "See the introductory and concluding essays, esp. pp. 23–23 and 288–89" (15).

It is important to recognize that the communal nature of individuality in Japan is not simply an element of the past but still exists today. When Japanese American anthropologist Dorinne Kondo lived in Japan to study the "self," she "was never allowed to be an autonomous freely operating 'individual'" (26). Kondo's study, *Crafting Selves: Power, Gender, and Discourses of Identity in a Japanese Workplace* (Chicago: University of Chicago Press, 1990), moves beyond the simple binary of individual versus group to show a more nuanced sense of self in relation to various power structures that exist in Japan.

6. Early Japanese society was matriarchal, with female shamans governing. Shinto, Japan's native religion, holds a female deity—Amaterasu Omikami, the sun goddess—as the central religious figure. See Peter Tasker, *The Japanese: A Major Exploration of Modern Japan* (New York: E.P. Dutton, 1987) 105.

7. See Christopher Morley's introduction to *A Daughter of the Samurai*, xviii–xix.

8. Befitting, for better or worse, her class status and gender. See Georgina Dodge, "Laughter of the Samurai: Humor in the Autobiography of Etsu Sugimoto," *MELUS* 21, no. 4 (1996): 57–69.

9. Roger Daniels, *The Politics of Prejudice: The Anti-Japanese Movement in California and the Struggle for Japanese Exclusion* (New York: Antheneum, 1977), 1–2. Daniels points out that immigration statistics from this period are suspect as they often include native-born Japanese Americans as well as immigrants who, like Sugimoto, return to Japan.

10. Among recent titles helping to shift this paradigm is *Immigrant Subjectivities in Asian American and Asian Diaspora Literatures* by Sheng-mei Ma (Albany: SUNY, 1998), which investigates "overseas student literature" written by student immigrants from Taiwan and published in Taipei. See also *Orientations: Mapping Studies in the Asian Diaspora*, edited by Kandice Chuh and Karen Shimakawa (Durham: Duke University Press, 2001), especially Sau-Ling Wong's essay, "The Stakes of Textual Border-Crossing: Hualing Nieh's *Mulberry and Peach* in Sinocentric, Asian American, and Feminist Critical Practices."

11. According to Sylvia Yanagisako, privileging men's experiences within Asian American history courses is done in part "to challenge the metonymic equation of Asian with the feminine" (287).

Works Cited

Benedict, Ruth. 1946. *The Chrysanthemum and the Sword: Patterns of Japanese Culture*. New York: World.

Chow, Rey. 1994. "Where Have All the Natives Gone?" In *Displacements: Cultural Identities in Question*, ed. Angelika Bammer, 125–51. Bloomington: Indiana University Press.

Ferris, Helen, ed. 1931. *When I Was a Girl: The Stories of Five Famous Women as Told by Themselves*. New York: Macmillan.

Fowler, Edward. 1988. *The Rhetoric of Confession: Shishōsetsu in Early Twentieth-Century Japanese Fiction*. Berkeley: University of California Press.

Gilbert, George Henry. 1948. *Pioneers in Self-Government: Informal Studies in the Natural Philosophy of Self-Government*. Segreganset, Mass: Builders of America.

Hall, John Whitney. 1970. *Japan: From Prehistory to Modern Times*. New York: Dell.

Hall, Stuart. 1997. "Cultural Identity and Diaspora." In *Contemporary Postcolonial Theory: A Reader*, ed. Padmini Mongia, 110–21. London: Arnold.

Kim, Elaine H. 1982. *Asian American Literature: An Introduction to the Writings and Their Social Context*. Philadelphia: Temple University Press.

Minatoya, Lydia. 1999. *The Strangeness of Beauty*. New York: Simon and Schuster.

Smith, Sidonie. 1993. *Subjectivity, Identity, and the Body: Women's Autobiographical Practices in the Twentieth Century*. Bloomington: Indiana University Press.

Sugimoto, Etsu Inagaki. 1932. *A Daughter of the Narakin*. New York: Doubleday.

———. 1935. *A Daughter of the Nohfu*. New York: Doubleday.

———. 1940. *Grandmother O Kyo*. New York: Doubleday.

———. 1990. *A Daughter of the Samurai*. Rutland, VT: Charles E. Tuttle. (Orig. pub. 1925.)

Suzuki, Tomi. 1996. *Narrating the Self: Fictions of Japanese Modernity*. Stanford: Stanford University Press.

Thomas, J. E. 1996. *Modern Japan: A Social History since 1868*. New York: Addison Wesley Longman.

Varley, H. Paul. 1977. *Japanese Culture: A Short History*. 2nd ed. New York: Praeger.

Yanagisako, Sylvia. 1995. "Transforming Orientalism: Gender, Nationality, and Class in Asian American Studies." In *Naturalizing Power: Essays in Feminist Cultural Analysis*, ed. Sylvia Yanagisako and Carol Delaney, 275–98. New York: Routledge.

4   The Capitalist and Imperialist Critique in H. T. Tsiang's *And China Has Hands*

JULIA H. LEE

AND CHINA Has Hands (1937) by H. T. Tsiang presents difficulties to the reader on many interpretive levels. A polemical text that makes clear its commitment to communist revolution, *And China Has Hands* relies on a notion of representation that is inextricable from politics: characters symbolize various ideological positions, and the novel decides their fates on the basis of their relationship to an emerging class revolution. The novel has two explicit purposes: first, to call attention to the dire situation of the Chinese in America (specifically, in New York's Chinatown), a situation marked by their economic exploitation and social isolation; and second, to raise world consciousness of Chinese resistance to Japan's invasion of China. Additionally, Tsiang's life experiences make a reading of his novel seem fairly straightforward. Tsiang first came to the United States to study in 1926, but quickly turned to political activism. He was forced out of the Kuomintang (KMT), the Chinese nationalist organization headed by Chiang Kai-shek, because of his revolutionary beliefs, and eventually wrote for the communist periodicals *Daily Worker* and *New Masses*. The nationalist KMT and the American government were suspicious of Tsiang because of his leftist leanings, while the Communist Party thought him politically unreliable because of his tendency in his novels to celebrate liberal notions of individual heroism. Harassed by both American authorities and the right-wing of the KMT throughout the 1930s, Tsiang managed to publish several English-language novels with revolutionary themes: *China Red* and *The Hanging on Union Square*, both in 1931, and *And China Has Hands* in 1937. After attempting unsuccessfully to join the Communist Party of America several times, Tsiang changed course and became a bit actor in Hollywood.

Yet the supposed transparency of the novel's leftist politics is undermined by the novel's presentation of the relationship between triangulated interracial dynamics in a local, American scene and Western-inspired, imperial encroachment on a global scale. What little critical work done on *And China Has Hands* has tended to ignore these particular literary or political elements of the text, analyzing instead the cultural milieu from which it arose. The text's dogmatic political moorings invite a reading of it as an authentic history of a reactionary time in America. Elaine Kim devotes one paragraph to *And China Has Hands* in her landmark work *Asian American Literature: An Introduction to the Writings and Their Social Context*, judging Tsiang's novel exclusively on the authenticity of its depiction of New York's Chinatown in the 1930s.[1] While Kim praises the novel for its portrayal of "the laundryman's daily life and his experiences in American society" and for its depictions of "the Chinatown tourists from the laundryman's point of view" and of "the underside of American society as experienced by the waiters and laundrymen who comprised the majority of Chinese in the United States before 1950" (1982, 109), she does not mention Tsiang's revolutionary aims or anti-Japanese message. Him Mark Lai (1992) also focuses on the historical context of the novel and does not allude to the novel's plot or characters in his article "To Bring Forth a New China, To Build a Better America." Lai's interest resides in Chinese American radical movements of the 1930s, and he mentions *And China Has Hands* in order to prove Tsiang's commitment to those movements.

My concern, in contrast, is with how Tsiang uses race and gender to ground his critiques of American capitalism and Japanese imperialism. *And China Has Hands* portrays how capitalist and imperialist enterprises racialize and sexually objectify their victims (in this case, the Chinese) in order to maintain power. Throughout the novel, Tsiang critiques the ways in which capitalism and imperialism relate to and enable each other as hegemonic systems of domination through racialized and gendered discourses. In other words, *And China Has Hands* complicates its vision of class revolution by figuring its critiques of Western capitalism and Japanese imperialism through the representational paradigms of race and gender. Within this context, it is the highly racialized and sexualized body of Pearl Chang—who is half Chinese, half African American—that most fully dictates the political stance of the novel. Thus, while Wong Wan-Lee is the novel's protagonist, it is

Pearl, his potential love interest and fellow revolutionary, who actually encodes the codependent relationship in the text between imperialism and capitalism. Furthermore, the discourses of both imperialism and capitalism manipulate the "natural" identity markers of race and gender in the novel to doubly marginalize Pearl as a racial mongrel and a sexual oddity. While the double marginalization of Pearl is the textual moment most fully embodying the intertwined powers of imperialism and capitalism, it is also the moment which most completely exposes their vulnerabilities. Indeed, it is the very quality of Pearl's "unnatural" racial and "exotic" sexual identity that threatens capitalist or nationalist discourse and makes her dangerous to its categorical imperatives.[2] That is, despite the problematic nature of Pearl's racial and sexual identities and despite her being the most troubled symbol of a revolutionary state, *And China Has Hands* nevertheless invests her with a tremendous power signifying the nature of the class revolution that will overturn capitalist and imperialist discourses.

And China Has Hands depicts the "American life" of Wong Wan-Lee, a character who arrives in the United States as a paper son with dreams of fortune and success.[3] Wong operates a laundry in New York City's Chinatown but eventually falls victim to a series of swindles and economic reverses. As already suggested, the most important figure in his life is Pearl, who initially dreams only of movie stardom and economic success. Forced to abandon his business, Wong becomes a waiter at a successful Chinese café where Pearl is also employed. While working together at the café, both Wong and Pearl experience a political awakening. Wong is a strong vocal supporter of Chinese American rights, achieving a certain prominence in union activities and labor demonstrations; Pearl is increasingly aware of the falsity of her original dreams. At a pro-labor rally, Wong is assassinated by a Japanese agent and dies in Pearl's arms; Pearl vows to carry on his work.

The central plot of *And China Has Hands* revolves more obviously around the local economic injustices faced by Chinese laborers in New York City than it does around the momentous contemporary events in China or Japan. But as David Palumbo-Liu (1999) argues in *Asian/American: Historical Crossings of a Racial Frontier*, the multiple ways in which Asian American identity has been constituted and reconstituted throughout this century necessitates a reading of both Wong Wan-Lee and Pearl in terms of their evolving and imagined relationships to distinctive and "authentic" Chinese and American identities, whatever these might be. Like Palumbo-Liu, I argue that *And China Has Hands* is as deeply invested in negotiating a Chinese identity and critiquing Japanese imperial aggression as it is in condemning American economic oppression.[4] The novel's dedication and its final scene (Wong's death in Pearl's arms, as mentioned earlier) provide the most sustained anti-imperialist rhetoric, with language that is both poetic and epic. At the end of this essay I will discuss Wong's death, but I wish to begin with an analysis of the novel's dedication—and to thus show the centrality of the novel's anti-imperialist stance to its critique of capitalism.

The dedication stands out, not only because of its position at the head of the text, but also because it differs so radically from the rest of the novel in terms of its syntax and vocabulary and sentence complexity.[5] Titled "To the Death of the Japanese Empire," the dedication describes how twice as many Chinese as Japanese people died in the opening weeks of the Sino-Japanese War, "by which rate of killing . . . when one hundred and twenty million Chinese—little more than one-fourth of the Chinese population—should be killed, there would be sixty million Japanese—the whole Japanese population—killed, and thus no more Japanese left, and thus no more Japanese Empire" (Tsiang 1937, 7). The dedication exhibits a patriarchal vision of martial honor; militaristic strength and bravura constitute the most effective and privileged modes of resisting imperial aggression. Jingoistic in tone, this dedicatory passage does not seem to subvert imperialist discourse but rather to advocate the annihilation of its Japanese occupiers by means of violent warfare. Tsiang's gruesome yet triumphant portrayal of a Japan finally defeated at the cost of one-quarter of the Chinese population horrifies the reader, but the tone of the dedication clearly indicates that such a sacrifice will ensure the ultimate victory of the Chinese people and, more importantly, the end of Western-style imperialism in east Asia.[6] Even the westernized efficiency of the Japanese in "the art of killing" cannot stand up to the sheer numbers of the Chinese.

The relationship between Wong and Pearl constitutes the spring that sets the novel's political appraisal in motion. Pearl's entrance in the middle of the story highlights the gendered nature of capitalism's ideological work. From the beginning, the text makes clear that Wong and immigrants like him are unequipped to deal with life in a capitalist society. To Wong, the laundry represents a pathway to freedom and success, and yet this success is not figured in terms of personal happiness or fulfillment. Rather, Wong fantasizes about how he will use his wealth to avenge himself on his past employers and coworkers:

> [Wong Wan-Lee] would order a few expensive dishes in a very leisurely manner.
> Then he would ask the waiter to bring him two packages of cigarettes; one for himself and the other for the waiter.
> When he finished the dinner, he would . . . go right to the cashier to pay his bill and would hand the remaining change to the cashier and ask him to give it to the waiter: so he would pay one man's tip and two men would know about it.
> Then he would buy two fine cigars. (13)

Tsiang suggests that, at least in the popular mind, capitalism figures success as the ability to purchase commodities that others will envy. His text posits that the definitions of terms such as "success" and "freedom" have been so utterly transformed that Wong (and others like him) have no way of comprehending, much less achieving, the "American Dream" on its own terms. Although Wong subscribes completely to the idea that he can make a fortune in America, he has no way of understanding that the system, by its very nature, is not meant to advance the prospects of Chinese or other marginalized groups. In fact, the opposite is true: workers of color are permitted to exist in America only to fill a production void; they are "allowed" to service a system designed to enrich only the most privileged.[7]

The ideology informing *And China Has Hands* requires that Wong Wan-Lee fulfill the role of a naive dreamer who initially does not understand why he cannot acquire the fortune that he wholeheartedly believes he can earn—why the very existence of "Gold Mountain" depends upon cheap workers like him. In other words, the novel portrays how the American myth of success seduces people like Wong and Pearl (who have no capacity to understand how money—or "value"—circulate in the American system), persuading them to absorb and practice capitalist tenets in order to exploit them and their labor. That Wong Wan-Lee's name, which translates from the Chinese into "Out of one investment, there will be ten thousand fortunes drawn," ironically plays on America's motto, "E Pluribus Unum" ("Out of Many, One"), to reinforce the notion that Wong is doomed to fail precisely because he can never convert his name, character, identity, or "Chinese" understanding of himself (which is dictated by China's land-based culture) into American capitalist terms. In fact, American capital inverts the meaning of Wong's name: that is, rather than promising that one man's investment will make the fortunes of many, the logic of American capital can insure only that the investments of many will secure a single fortune. Wong is completely handicapped at every turn by a culture that is relentless in its pursuit of individual wealth at the cost of communal good.

The laundry space itself is described in minute detail in order to underscore the marginalized position occupied by workers like Wong. His home is one with his workplace: a basement apartment on the fringes of an urban ethnic ghetto created to control the movements, lives, and productivity of the Chinese sojourners. The work and lifestyle are dehumanizing and isolating, turning men into mechanisms ("His hand was not a machine, but he had to move his hand as fast as a machine" [20]).[8] The decentered, mechanical quality of Wong's life is underscored by the novel's episodic structure. Although some readers justifiably argue that such a structure weakens the narrative focus of the novel, each incident acts as a miniature fable warning of the dangers of adhering to the myths perpetuated by capitalism. Each character that Wong encounters is a symbol of some aspect of Western capitalism: its seductiveness, its duplicity, its treachery. The Chinese overcoat salesman, for example, is a Ph.D. student whose dissertation topic is "selling China more profitably" (109); he clearly embodies the capitalist ethic of commodity fetishism when he pronounces that "no matter how much money you had you could not change your face, but with money, you could change your manner"—or that "the overcoat was the very thing to show outsiders what you were and what you had in your pocket and what you had in your head" (38–39). The object signifies the worth of the owner, signaling the kind of false identity and alienation that a capitalist system perpetrates on its adherents. Wong's decision to buy an expensive and useless coat—imagining it will allow him to win over Pearl and become a successful businessman—reveals the extent to which, in embracing material objects as signifiers of his own worth, he has participated in his own capitalistic objectification and commodification. Here again, Tsiang shows how mutually dependent capitalist ideology and imperialist aggression are. We later learn that the overcoat salesman leaves America to help the Japanese manage their occupation of China. Presumably (and under the auspices of the Japanese government) his trade there will be similar to the one he was plying in New York: subduing a rebellious Chinese population by indoctrinating them into a system that alters their sense of themselves and the goods and services they produce.

As Wong Wan-Lee vainly attempts to keep his laundry going, he is slowly exploited by America's inexorable cultural landscape, including the Chinatown community itself. Nevertheless, Tsiang's castigation of American capitalist practices is in no sense a concurrent nostalgia for the agrarian life that Wong knew in China; in fact, Tsiang implies that the "old" way of life in China is just as worthy of censure. At one point, Wong feeds and talks to an old man who is dying, a man whose life is intended to be a cautionary tale—not simply for Wong, but for the reader as well:

> Had [the old man] died as a revolutionist, he would have been remembered as a hero forever.
> "Beware, while you are still young!" he warned Wong Wan-Lee. "America is an evil land and once you sink in you can never get out....Don't let the destiny that was mine be a shadow of your own!" (49)

Here, the "old" China of Wong's time is not elevated as the ideal, but the revolutionary China of the future; further, the only genuine or lasting hero is the revolutionist. Eventually, Wong heeds the old man's advice, but only after he has lost everything through robberies, protection rackets, and gambling—through misplaced faith in the corrupt (and corrupting) Western ideals.

If Wong Wan-Lee's character reveals the extent to which the capitalist exploitation of workers is a racialized construct, then Pearl most completely embodies the effects of this exploitation. Pearl's very name conjures up images of exchange and value; the connotations of her name reinforce the fact that she, unlike Wong, possesses a savvy knowledge of the capitalist and commodity culture that Tsiang so harshly criticizes. When Wong throws lichee nuts at the neighborhood boys to try and stop them from screaming insults at him, Pearl rescues him by effectively using American street English ("The kids heard her smart English and saw her terrible look and they understood that she was not fooling" [23]) and invoking street applications of American laws ("'You rascals, I'll call the cop or I may break your neck myself!'" [23]). Pearl then casually offers Wong the crucial tenet to success in America: "You are not an American. When they call you names, you lose nothing. If you throw away nuts just like that, you will never become rich. With one penny you could start a savings-account and draw interest from it" (25). Pearl's matter-of-fact statement about Wong's identity ("'You are not an American'") is legally incorrect (Wong is an American citizen because he is a paper-son) but substantially accurate. That is, Wong is completely unattuned to the "business" (both literal and figurative) of possessing an American identity, which Tsiang reduces to a blind acceptance of capitalist values: to be

American, Wong believes, he must be rich. Wong notes that giving away lichee nuts worked in China to make him popular, but he cannot understand that this same act—a symbolic sharing of cultural property—does not translate into the American context of consumerism.

Despite her superior practical knowledge, Pearl, as a woman of mixed color, is particularly vulnerable to the racism and sexism that operate in a consumer society. Pearl, like Wong, desperately seeks the American myth of wealth and happiness that she sees propagated in Hollywood films. Pearl is convinced that race, and especially racial ambiguity, potentially stand in the way of that happiness; if she is to have any chance of "American success," Pearl believes, she must "choose" the racial identity that best enables her social and economic advancement. Blacks clearly face greater economic and social obstacles than do Chinese, and so Pearl emphasizes the Chinese part of her racial makeup. Thus, Pearl's decision to "pass for pure Chinese" is based wholly on economic circumstances, especially those embodied in the hierarchy of race in the American South: "In the South, Negroes are not allowed to ride in the same streetcar with whites, but Chinese are. Black children are not allowed to go to school with white children, but Chinese children are" (26). The American South in particular and the United States in general assume a binaristic conception of race: one is either white or black. Pearl's very body upsets this binary; her deviant status is heightened by the fact that she is a woman of black and Chinese ancestry, that she has no white "blood" in her body. As a Southern woman, Pearl is clearly convinced that her social and economic mobility depends on how others construct her racially; and given the social stigma surrounding her hybridized racial identity, Pearl attempts to obliterate all traces of her African American self:

> Pearl Chang was every inch a Chinese.
> The trouble, it seemed to her, was that she had curly hair. When she went out she had to use a large hat to cover the hair up.
> The second trouble was that she had heavy lips. She had to use lipstick and dark powder to make them look smaller.
> In spite of her skillful make-up she had frequently met the same persecution as other Negresses had met. So Pearl Chang packed up and came to New York. (28)

The statement "Pearl Chang was every inch a Chinese" is ambiguous in its tone: is the narrator uncritically affirming Pearl's choice of racial identity or is the pronouncement laced with authorial irony? Certainly, Pearl's failed attempt to physically mask her "blackness" points up the impossible nature of her naive quest for a "pure" identity. Pearl's attempt to construct such an identity constitutes the book's most radical critique of the racial and gender normalization perpetrated by capitalism and imperialism. That is, in a nation that bars African Americans from the very principles it holds up to the world, the logic of socioeconomic necessity forces Pearl to consider her identity in additive, binary terms—and then to reject her African American ancestry as a liability. Condemning capitalist hierarchies for the racism and the racializing processes that undergird them, Tsiang suggests that those very racialized bodies enable antiestablishment alliances across geographic, class, and racial lines, potentially fueling a proletarian revolution necessary for the creation of an ethnically transcendent society.

Pearl's drive for "authentic" Chinese experience leads her to Wong. Even though she is clearly not familiar with many of the traditions and habits of Chinese or Chinese Americans, she continually insists that she is a genuine Chinese, sometimes with comical results. When Pearl queries Wong about the absence of chow mein and chop suey in the meal that he serves her, he informs her that these dishes are not Chinese at all. Pearl's response ("You see how easily Americans get fooled! I am glad I am a Chinese!" [58]) is ridiculous precisely because she, too, had been fooled until just that moment. Predictably, Pearl's attempts to be "Chinese" are ridiculed by Wong who disparagingly calls her a "Mo-No," an insult reserved for obviously Americanized Chinese—but a term that Pearl herself does not understand. Wong's dismissal of Pearl as a "Mo-No" implies that she can never be a "true" Chinese subject. But because Wong uses the insult despite his being physically attracted to Pearl, the scene also suggests, rather ironically, that he is little different from other "Americans" in judging Pearl according to notions of racial and ethnic purity.

Pearl's experience working at the Chinese restaurant signifies the extent to which capitalism inculcates notions of racial "purity" into workers. While Pearl's ethnic self-classification has heretofore gone unquestioned, her opportunistic Chinese boss has gradually become convinced that Pearl is not purely Chinese and fires her. "Your mother didn't do a good job on you," he declares. "We Chinese are dark enough and don't want to become any darker. As I am a member of the Chinese Nationalist Party, I have to respect the national race-purity" (127). Despite his desire to claim ethnic "purity" for himself and other Chinese, the owner's statement that Chinese "are dark enough" implies that they are dangerously close to being *too* dark. Here, Tsiang pointedly condemns how the Chinese Nationalists mimic the racial and economic oppression of America and the West. The owner is concerned about the racial purity of his "people," but he is more worried that the presence of Pearl will drive away his customers. His objection to Pearl's racial hybridity is inextricable from his fear that she will ruin his business. By emphasizing the owner's position within the Chinese Nationalist Party, Tsiang links the racism of Western capitalists and Chinese Nationalists: in both cases, a naturalized understanding of "race" justifies profiteering.

In the case of the restaurateur, Chinese Nationalism is more or less equated with white capitalism in the American South—to the end that the restaurateur worries that a "black" waitress will drive his white (and Chinese) customers away. "Don't fool me," he commands. "I don't want the reputation of my restaurant spoiled and my place made cheap!" Following his outburst, we are told that Pearl, "like a caught thief, could not say anything. She pulled her hat down to cover her hair. She bit her lips to make them look smaller. She put powder on her face to make it whiter" (127). Suspicion of impurity is enough to convict Pearl; one drop of non-Chinese blood insures her ejection from this restaurant, which is figured to symbolize the most privileged aspects of Chinese life in America. Her boss's discovery of her biracial heritage arouses feelings of shame in Pearl; most crucially, this shame figures itself in terms of theft, as if Pearl were stealing a racial identity. The moral implications of thievery are important here: theft, of course, ideally "advances" the thief, and it invariably occurs at the expense of others.

As a woman of mixed racial heritage, Pearl must find ways to combine or accommodate her ethnicity and gender if she is to survive in a capitalist society—if she is to "commodify" herself successfully. The corollary is also true: Pearl's racial hybridity is inextricably enmeshed with her gender, and a discussion of one must inevitably lead to an analysis of the other. Her ethnicity and gender are not just potentially "problematic" qualities leading to incrementally more serious instances of marginalization; rather, they are damning absolutes that disrupt, in exponential ways, Pearl's navigation of a racist and sexist sphere. The novel quite clearly implies that Wong would not objectify Pearl as he does if she were a "real" Chinese or a "real" white woman; it is her liminal racial status that makes her sexually available to him. Ironically, however, Wong's objectification depends upon Pearl's hiding the physical traces of her "blackness" by hyperfeminizing herself—according to Chinese or, perhaps more accurately, white standards of beauty— through the use of makeup and dress. That is, if Pearl "appeared" black, she would be as unavailable to him as if she were "true Chinese" or white.

Put somewhat differently, the identity markers of race and gender doubly marginalize Pearl: her ethnic hybridity excludes her from Chinese, black, and white communities; her position as a woman caught between male-dominated cultures means that she is at the sexual mercy of the men around her, regardless of their ethnicity. And, most important for the book's ideology, her gender and racial status make her economic situation all the more tenuous. Despite Pearl's initial faith in the American myth of economic success and personal satisfaction (she hopes to become a movie star and carries around pictures of stars in her purse), she begins to realize that a person's ability to fulfill these goals depends very much on racial identity. Wong's treatment of Pearl as an unworthy Chinese subject and Pearl's own belief that she can gain an authentic Chinese identity by watching Chinese films and eating Chinese food point to a familiar impasse of identity politics—that is, authentic identity is naturalized and marked by the subject's ability to manipulate certain "ethnic" material signifiers. In much the same way that she believes that she can acquire a "pure Chinese identity"—that identity itself is a commodity—Pearl also believes in a step-by-step approach to the mythology of American success, an approach built upon the studious application of certain racial and gender paradigms. Within such a racial discourse, a Chinese identity in this case becomes a commodity to be acquired, just like the movie-star status that Pearl so desperately covets.

Pearl's marginalized status also reveals crucial flaws in the American system: she embodies the consequences of the enthronement of racial and sexual imperatives. If we see Pearl as the intersection of a racialized and gendered critique of imperialist aggression, we can more accurately understand the book's finale. As Wong bleeds to death in Pearl's arms, her dress becomes red with his blood, an image that is foreshadowed earlier in the book when an angel appears to Wong dressed in red promising to save him. Pearl is, of course, that angel, transformed from starstruck shopgirl to proto-revolutionary. The words at the conclusion of the novel seem to figure Pearl (and workers like her) as the savior of all of China: "Now she laughed little, talked little and moved her hands little; but she thought more. . . . And now her youth had passed away and she had reached her maturity" (131). As he dies, Wong realizes that Pearl's independence and honesty should be valued, abandoning his previous judgment of her as a "Mo-No." Indeed, as Pearl's inherent independence and candor are joined by her newly developing political awareness, Pearl becomes symbolic of a reborn China and of an emergent and empowered Chinese American community.

In part, Tsiang makes Pearl a potent symbol for revolution precisely because she embodies all of the anxieties of a capitalist society. But such an investiture is a vexed one. In the first place, it begs an important question: to what extent is Pearl's new consciousness or authority the product of the very systems that Tsiang impugns? In the second, Pearl's authority or power arguably derives from her ultimate position as symbol or icon. Essentially Pearl is handed the quintessentially feminine role of muse: she acts as the inspiration for someone else's revolution; her own ability to effect change, to act as a political subject, is severely restricted—at least in the novel itself. In the third, Pearl's authority as the symbol of a New China depends on her status as a marginalized individual. Tsiang's vision of history robs her of the capacity to act politically until after the revolution has arrived; until that moment, she cannot hope to effect economic or social progress for other marginalized persons. Finally, Pearl's eventual role as revolutionary icon precludes her emergence as a sexual being; accordingly, the sexual dimension of Pearl and Wong's relationship is not merely left unresolved but rendered infantile.

There are problems, then, in the ways that *And China Has Hands* signifies or constructs race and sexuality to serve an imperialist and capitalist critique. Most obviously, the text's transcendent vision of a political state seems to allow the novel to ignore the troubling implications of sexuality, race, and gender that it invokes in order to show the oppressive machinations of capitalism and imperialism. In other words, Tsiang's novel does not ultimately question—much less justify—the troubling representations of Wong and Pearl that it sets forward. Although Tsiang clearly intends that the reader feel outrage over Wong's treatment, Wong's portrayal is far from sympathetic. In fact, Wong's rather bumbling life, replete with childish observations and miscalculated actions, seems the very antithesis of the life of a revolutionary—especially when the text itself withholds comment (explicit or implicit) on Wong's behavior and views. And although Wong is briefly drawn as a relatively mature and even admirable character at the novel's end, even here he uncritically replicates many stereotypes of Asian masculinity—he is passive, asexual, and (as he is through vast expanses of the book) pitiable. Wong experiences a political awakening, true enough, but he never articulates a critique of the injustices he faces. Even as Tsiang shows how capitalism and imperialism disempower or emasculate Wong, he rarely imbues Wong with any genuine sense of consciousness or agency;

and the allegorical power he might otherwise hold for the reader is diminished.

The novel's approach to Pearl's sexuality is perhaps more problematic still: is Tsiang critiquing sexual stereotypes or merely propagating them? Tsiang's depiction of Pearl's sexuality is often bizarre and at times highly misogynistic. In reporting that Pearl's ethnic identity marks her as "unnatural" to others, the text is not critical of such constructions of deformity. Engaged in the task of attempting to normalize Pearl's multiracial female body, the novel shows Pearl learning from casual observation of the naked bodies of white female models that her own body is no different from theirs—a sameness she considers in terms that manage to deform *all* female bodies: "When she had been in high school, the white girls very often had asked her, speaking of her sex, 'Which way does it go?' Now she took a look at the white girls, naked. She nodded her head and said to herself: 'The same way!'" (30). Here, the ambiguous use of the term "sex" (does the text mean the clitoris *or* the vagina?) and the vaguely phallic implication of the phrase "Which way does it go?" function to shroud the Asian female body in a cloud of exotic mystery and, simultaneously, to naturalize the white male body as the discursive norm for descriptions of sexuality. The text encourages the reader to feel relief along with Pearl that her body does go "the same way," but it does so by enforcing a normative sexuality that is both white and masculine. Despite Pearl's seeming physical similarity to all of the other girls, *And China Has Hands* reifies the white patriarchal notion that nonwhite female bodies are somehow sexually deviant.

This problematic moment is complicated by the way Tsiang recounts the objectification of Pearl's body. As she models, Pearl realizes (with a misplaced sense of elation) that "those evil-minded artists seemed more interested in what was going on the canvas than in looking at her" (30). Pearl's relief that the artists are not "looking at her" does not allow her to see how the artists are more concerned with their own construction of Chinese womanhood than with an actual Chinese woman. Pearl's work as a model—an attempt on her part to make herself a marketable, desirable "star"—highlights how race is commodified for the easy consumption of the public. Tsiang seems to be indicting the artists, as he does the overcoat salesman, for their willingness to package China and Chinese identities into manageable (albeit exotic) and consumable bits. But this critique not only sidesteps Pearl's packaging of her own sexuality, it also constructs Asian female sexuality in binary terms: in the eyes of others, Pearl is either "enshrouded" or "naked." If the former, she is, potentially, a sexual monstrosity ("it" might not go the right way); if the latter, she is, in her sameness to all other objectified or eroticized female bodies, rendered virtually invisible.

Nowhere is Pearl's vulnerable position as woman more evident than in her solitary sexual encounter with Wong, a strange scene occurring rather late in the novel. The scene opens with a conversation between Pearl and Wong, a conversation about Wong's vegetarianism. As the conversation unfolds, it quite clearly suggests questions that Wong has about his own masculinity; he seems to interpret Pearl's questions about his eating habits as a direct assault on his sexual identity or prowess. In the abortive act of lovemaking that follows this conversation, Wong (who is obviously threatened by Pearl's greater linguistic and physical competence) clumsily objectifies Pearl by effectually reducing her body and personality to her breasts, and then by metaphorically apostrophizing them as tennis balls and lichee nuts. As Wong pinches Pearl's nipple, just as he would a lichee nut, he reveals both his sexual incompetence and his chauvinism. Thus, Pearl can no longer maintain her fantasy wherein Wong is a Chinese prince and she his Chinese princess. Humiliated, she tries to clear Wong's fogged mental state by asserting her individuality, by declaring that Wong is touching *her breasts*, and *not* tennis balls.

And yet Tsiang's tone toward this extraordinary incident seems to be one of objective indifference, as if incidents like these should be expected between people from different cultures. The lack of direct or indirect commentary at this juncture indicates the problematic construction of sexuality in *And China Has Hands*: the sexual humiliation of the novel's two primary characters is completely detached from the book's political commentary. While the text deliberately constructs both characters as sexual beings, even calling attention to their sexuality, Wong is portrayed as sexually naive if not impotent, and Pearl is objectified and physically degraded. And particularly in Pearl's case, the text works to block the full expression of her sexuality. In significant ways, Pearl's characterization underscores the linkage of ethnicity and gender to class status or social standing—a linkage that, according to Tsiang, American capitalism would like to ignore. Pearl's status as woman and ethnic hybrid not only relegates her to a more marginalized position than that occupied by Wong but emphasizes her extremely precarious position as an American. This much said, her status also invests her with a potentially grand subversive agency. Pearl is the book's most powerful symbol of revolutionary ideals; thus, her emblematic and disruptive function does not detract from the urgent politics of the text. Instead, it underscores Tsiang's efforts to unmask the racist assumptions of American capitalism and supports his agenda to situate Chinese laborers at the forefront of local and global socialist movements.

The novel's conclusion reveals how tightly knit are the anticapitalist and anti-imperialist campaigns of the revolutionary movement. The nationalistic rhetoric and images of martial power, which, following the dedication, are absent from most of the rest of the book, resurface in the final tableau of the novel, when Wong Wan-Lee's death by an assassin's bullet occasions a reprise of the anti-imperialist sentiment of the dedication. Initially, the reader believes that Wong has been shot by an employer who opposes the strike in which Wong has participated, but we discover later that Wong has been killed by a Japanese agent who targets Wong for his active criticism of the Japanese invasion of China. Curiously, we are not informed of Wong's anti-Japanese activities until *after* he has been shot. This omission renders the final section of the novel somewhat unconvincing: we are simply required to accept that Wong has been more active in political activities since losing his laundry business than anyone—including us as readers—has suspected. Structurally and thematically, however, the sudden revelation that a Japanese agent has killed Wong in an act of political vengeance has a crucial significance, shifting the novel's critique away from the domestic, economic injustices suffered by one immigrant man in one American city and back to the international stage, with a pointed jab at the way in which imperialist aggression can leap international boundaries. It is equally important that by not immediately divulging the identity or motive of the assassin, Tsiang suggests that Wong could have been killed by either a pro-Japanese imperialist or a pro-capitalist businessman: he constitutes a danger to both systems.

Wong's final moral victory over imperial Japanese also represents a victory over capitalist oppression. "[T]he Chinese Reds now have one-fifth of the whole Chinese population and one-sixth of the whole Chinese territory," he declares. "In the years to come they shall have more, more and endlessly more and as I'm the one who works for my own rice and I'm a Chinese, so I'm the boss and I'm the owner!" (163). Here, Wong triumphantly prophesies the rise of the Chinese Communists, not the Chinese Nationalists (the Kuomintang, or KMT, lead by Chiang Kai-shek) in reestablishing order once the Japanese have been expelled. Tsiang recognizes that the war over Chinese sovereignty is also a struggle between two different visions of community; the expulsion of the Japanese invaders is a required step in the reclamation of China into the communist fold. *And China Has Hands* implies, then, that successful opposition to imperialist ventures goes hand-in-hand with the emergence of a communist state.

Tsiang morally equates the overtly imperialist agenda of the Japanese with the overtly capitalist agenda of the United States; in either case, powerless characters are entrapped by an authoritarian and oppressive system. Indeed, Tsiang adopts the position that military dominance and economic hegemony are opposing sides of the same coin. The two work in complicity—to the end that, in the context of the novel, Chinese workers in America are no less the subjugated victims of the prevailing order than Chinese workers in Japanese-controlled Manchuria. Every indictment that the novel levels against capitalism stands as indictment of imperialism as well.

And China Has Hands makes clear that capitalist society is inherently racist, that it employs a "race-based" socioeconomic hierarchy to perpetuate its system of exploitative labor. This theme is most strongly developed through the character of Pearl, who, despite the fact that she hungrily embraces the capitalistic American Dream, eventually learns that the combination of her female body and hybrid ethnicity excludes her from virtually all privileges of white American males—and even from the few privileges accorded to ethnic American males like Wong. As the text takes pains to stress, the capitalist enterprise is not unique amongst hegemonic systems; the imperialist machinations of Japan echo the marginalizing and dominating system of capital. Indeed, Tsiang posits that the relationship between capitalism and imperialism must be acknowledged and fully theorized before true social change can be effected. In this way, *And China Has Hands* negotiates the ideological connections between capitalism and imperialism, provocatively insisting that racial intolerance and gender oppression are integral to the workings of both movements.

NOTES

1. For more information on the economic and social conditions of Chinese waiters and laundrymen during the first half of the twentieth century, see Paul Siu (1987) and Renqiu Yu (1998).

2. In her study *The Americas of Asian American Literature* (1999), Rachel Lee argues that gender and sexuality disrupt nationalist narratives (3).

3. Paper sons were those Chinese men who immigrated to the United States, claiming to the be the sons of Chinese Americans. The passage of the Chinese [Exclusion Act] in 1882 meant the end of legal migration to the United States for most Chinese. Chinese men who had somehow obtained citizenship, either through birth or naturalization, would claim to have sons still residing in China. They would then return to China, sell those slots to young Chinese men wanting to immigrate, and then return to the United States with their "paper sons."

4. Palumbo-Liu argues in *Asian/American: Historical Crossings of a Racial Frontier* (1999) that *And China Has Hands* exemplifies the ways in which definitions of "Asian American" shifted as American geopolitical engagement with Asia changed. Thus the relationship between "Asian" and "American" loses its monolithic status and instead becomes configured as "both the distinction installed between 'Asian' and 'American' and a dynamic, unsettled, inclusive movement" (1). Palumbo-Liu asserts that the two central characters of Tsiang's novel, Wong Wan-Lee and Pearl, must face "the disappearance of "China" as an idealized point of national identification, with particular reference to a political as well as cultural attachment to an Asia undergoing profound political and cultural change" (49).

5. Perhaps part of the reason why *And China Has Hands* has been so steadily ignored in Asian American literary studies can be explained by its lack of stylistic polish. Alan Wald conjectures that "[Tsiang's] use of brief chapters, short paragraphs..., genre mixing, blurring of history and fiction, and his overall episodic construction may well be a consequence of his background in Chinese literary forms, as well as the difficulty of writing in a second language, or perhaps translating mentally as he wrote" (1996, 344). As Wald implies, the novel's lack of stylistic grace reemphasizes the very critique that Tsiang makes in *And China Has Hands*: that novels, just like any other product, emerge from the material conditions under which their creators operate. My point in focusing momentarily on the book's formalistic inadequacies is not to privilege a realm of pure aesthetics that only certain canonical works can presume to enter; rather, it is to encourage scholars to consider how the social circumstances under which Tsiang was operating further elucidates our understanding of the text as a whole.

6. Japan claimed the right of imperial power because of its ability to adapt Western modes of government, capital, and organization. Throughout the late nineteenth and early twentieth centuries, Japan positioned itself as the protector of Asian nations who were too backward to understand a modern geopolitical order. As the United States did with Native Americans at home and Filipinos abroad, Japan engaged in a "civilizing" discourse with Formosa and Korea in order to justify its takeover of those nations. It is perhaps for this reason that the Japanese were often called the "energetic little Yankees of the Orient" (Christ 2000, 684). For more information on Japanese attempts to legitimize its colonization of China, see Carol Christ's "The Sole Guardians of the Art Inheritance of Asia: Japan and China at the 1904 St. Louis World's Fair," *positions* 8.3 (2000): 675–709.

7. Lisa Lowe (1996) tackles the relationship between labor capital and nationalism in *Immigrant Acts*. Tsiang's characters seem to exemplify Lowe's assertion

that Asian workers – economically exploited, racially differentiated, and politically marginalized – resolve the contradictions between capital's need for a stratified labor force and nationalism's prerequisite of a unified and homogeneous population.

8. As Floyd Cheung (2000) has noted, *And China Has Hands* emphasizes the quotidian details of laundry life in order to create "laundry work" as demeaning manual labor, thereby challenging the romantic notion that operating a laundry embodies the American entrepreneurial spirit.

WORKS CITED

Cheung, Floyd. 2000. "Race, Class, and Revolution in *And China Has Hands* by H. T. Tsiang." Unpublished essay.

Christ, Carol Ann. 2000. "The Sole Guardians of the Art Inheritance of Asia: Japan and China at the 1904 St. Louis World's Fair." *Positions* 8 (3): 675–709.

Kim, Elaine. 1982. *Asian American Literature: An Introduction to the Writings and Their Social Context*. Philadelphia: Temple University Press.

Lai, Him Mark. 1992. "To Bring Forth a New China, To Build a Better America: The Chinese Marxist Left in America to the 1960s." *Chinese America: History and Perspectives*, 3–82.

Lee, Rachel. 1999. *The Americas of Asian American Literature*. Princeton: Princeton University Press.

Lowe, Lisa. 1996. *Immigrant Acts: On Asian American Cultural Politics*. Durham: Duke University Press.

Palumbo-Liu, David. 1999. *Asian/American: Historical Crossings of a Racial Frontier*. Stanford: Stanford University Press.

Siu, Paul C. P. 1987. *The Chinese Laundryman: A Study of Social Isolation*, ed. John Kuo Wei Tchen. New York: New York University Press.

Tsiang, H. T. 1937. *And China Has Hands*. New York: Robert Speller.

Wald, Alan. 1996. Introduction to *Into the Fire: Asian American Prose*, by H. T. Tsiang. Ed. Sylvia Watanabe and Carol Bruchac. Greenfield: Greenfield Review Press.

Yu, Renqiu. 1998. "'Exercise Your Sacred Rights': The Experience of New York's Chinese Laundrymen in Practicing Democracy." In *Claiming America: Constructing Chinese American Identities During the Exclusion Era*, ed. K. Scott Wong and Sucheng Chan, 64–91. Philadelphia: Temple University Press.

5   Unacquiring Negrophobia: Younghill Kang and Cosmopolitan Resistance to the Black and White Logic of Naturalization

STEPHEN KNADLER

DURING HIS picaresque wanderings across 1920s America, the Korean immigrant narrator of Younghill Kang's novel, *East Goes West* (1937), encounters a Negro student—Wagstaff—who works as a "yes-suh" elevator man in Boston while putting himself through college. This black Falstaffian wag counsels the exiled Shakespearean scholar Chung-pa Han to "learn the language of gyp, learn to gyp too. Confess honestly that right is not might, but might is right, always since the world began. That's the perspective that only a Negro gets" (Kang 1937, 274). Throughout his fictionalized memoir, wherein he writes as one of the "drifting" Korean resident aliens in America cut off from his homeland following the Japanese annexation of Korea in 1910, Kang inserts the "perspective of the Negro" and implies a common colonial oppression and displacement. Resorting to a dream vision at the novel's close to voice the protest hidden behind barriers of polite respect, Chung-pa imagines that he is trapped in a "dark and cryptlike cellar" in the company of some "frightened looking Negroes" as a "red-faced" lynch mob storms their prison, or fortress, intent on burning them all to death (369).

In thus disclosing the shared hope and disillusionment of African and Korean Americans, Kang turns his fictional autobiography into a "coalitional" memory. Yet it is a problematic memory: even as Kang's protagonist tries to open up political ties of affiliation among Asians and African Americans, he discovers differences among their respective lived experiences of racial discrimination. Specifically, during the course of his social initiation, he is told by the cynical Wagstaff that the Asian American exists "outside the two sharp worlds of color in the American environment." Forced to admit that this "was in a way true,"

Chung-pa then recognizes that "through Wagstaff I was having my first introduction to a crystallized caste system, comparable only to India, here in the greatest democratic country in the world" (273).

Chung-pa's exchange with Wagstaff situates Kang's *East Goes West* as a story of a particular kind of affiliation: not (as might be expected) one marking ethnic distinctions or, on the other hand, advocating a union with "whiteness." Instead, the novel advocates an identification with the black other to challenge white affiliation. Although later Asian American writers such as Frank Chin undergo what Susan Gubar calls a "racechange" by mimicking an exaggeratedly masculine blackness (1997, 5–6), Kang raises the Negro question in the autobiography of the Korean American immigrant in order to replace the language of racial consciousness (even in its various postmodernist forms of strategic essentialism) with an alternative set of assumptions that work to repair multiracial civility and to challenge America's biracial "crystallized caste system."

To the postcolonial or cultural studies critic who reads it only casually, Kang's fictional autobiography may seem insufficiently resistant to western European and Anglo-American civilization. Yet, as Jinqi Ling observes, current readings of early Asian American literature are often flawed because they ignore the particular forms of social power and oppression faced by Asian American authors within their respective historical eras or situations (1998, 18). Such critical imperialism is marked by impatience with former writers or texts that fail to take the proper stand—that is, the ideologically "subversive" or "oppositional" stand of contemporary identity politics. Some current readings of *East Goes West* are marked by precisely this kind of impatience. Read knowingly, however, Kang's novel supports its own subversive paradigm: a variety of civil and racial disobedience that challenges the *legal* property of whiteness (along with its complementary "negrophobia"), which other Asian Americans sought to acquire. Written against the grain of racial nationalism, Kang's *East Goes West* satirizes notions of whiteness and blackness to trace an affiliative or cosmopolitan identity that might best be defined as postethnic. That is, if Kang eschews staking out a non-Western cultural space for the diasporic Korean Americans, he does so in order to avoid a countercultural practice that assimilates the foundational logic of twentieth-century whiteness. And he thereby anticipates what Lisa Lowe describes in *Immigrant Acts* as the most difficult challenge faced by the minority writer: to demarcate a cultural identity independent of the old Anglo-European logic of race and nationalism (1996, 70).

Historical Cosmopolitanism, Whiteness/Blackness, and Assimilation in *East Goes West*

To underscore Kang's parody of twentieth-century narratives of whiteness in *East Goes West*—and of the negrophobia such logic invoked in Asian immigrants—I wish to provide two historical contexts. First, I will consider how Kang's novel squares with twentieth-century American cosmopolitanism, a theory of identity based on affiliation rather than distinction. Second, to emphasize Kang's perspectives on race and nationality, I will set the "affiliative identities" of *East Goes West* against the logic of naturalization evident in the landmark legal case *Ozawa v. the United States* (1922).

While cosmopolitanism was resuscitated in the late 1990s as a neopolitical alternative to ethnocentric nationalism and multicultural pluralism, its history dates back to the Greeks, particularly to the Stoic philosopher Zeno. The term was resurrected in the modern era by Emmanuel Kant as a central component of his "Idea for a Universal History with Cosmopolitan Intent" (1991). In their historical overview of cosmopolitanism, Robert Fine and Robin Cohen (2002) argue that it should be perceived less as a single coherent philosophy than as a vision or practice that has resurfaced—with slightly different definitions and uses—at specific historical moments throughout the long early modernist era. The years following WWI, as Timothy Brennan argues, saw the emergence of twentieth-century American perspectives of cosmopolitanism as a political tool useful to such projects as building transnational communities and establishing crosscultural and racial identification. Such perspectives of cosmopolitanism challenged conventional ideas of belonging, identity, and citizenship; these perspectives (as Brennan again argues) spread rapidly in the 1920s and intensified in the 1950s (1997, 122).

In the syndicated column he wrote between 1931 and 1967, American political journalist and philosopher Walter Lippman especially became a vocal advocate of cosmopolitanism. Writing in the 1930s against rigid constructions of democratic theory, Lippman urged U.S. citizens to become more fully aware of the complex interdependencies of modern mass societies and to welcome the personal and social enrichment deriving from exposure to ideas and practices outside confined everyday experience (Blum 1984, 13). Also during the 1930s, Stalinists in Russia and fascists in Germany and Italy linked cosmopolitanism and Semitism as twin threats to national purity (Brennan 1997, 21). In contrast to a socialist internationalism between the wars, cosmopolitanism emerged among some U.S. public intellectuals of the 1950s and 1960s as a way of seeing the world and other people that would foster disarmament and usher in a new globalism. Later still, in the 1980s, early postcolonial theorists repudiated cosmopolitanism as a detached bourgeois aesthetics deriving from an elitist perspective of global cultures as tourist commodities.

In his essay "The Cosmopolitical—Today," Pheng Cheah (1998) has argued the need to revisit early twentieth-century ideas of cosmopolitanism—and to restore to the term a sense of the liminal or the liberating, which has been lost from it. To its detractors, cosmopolitanism suggests a noncommittal or uninterested stance toward the particular needs and often painful social striving of the localized other. In contrast, Cheah believes that early twentieth-century cosmopolitanism nurtured diversity—that the intellectual outlook of its adherents fostered appropriate communal responses to questions of political or social identity. In *East Goes West*, Younghill Kang likewise endorses cosmopolitanism as a complex, nonterritorial, and postnational form of allegiance; accordingly, Kang's cosmopolitans battle discrimination through coalition and affiliation rather than through a collective retreat into (for example) Asian or African American separatism.

Kang's affiliative stance in *East Goes West* counters the deep-seated views of many early twentieth-century Asian Americans, especially those views represented by the well-known case *Ozawa v. the United States* (1922), wherein Japanese-born Takao Ozawa waged an eight-year battle (1914–22) for U.S. citizenship. The legal brief filed by the sixteen-year U.S. Army veteran defined national identity as a matter of the heart, not the skin: "In name, General Benedict Arnold was an American, but at heart he was a traitor. In name, I am not an American, but at heart I am a true American. I set forth the following facts which will sufficiently prove this" (qtd. in Ichioka 1994, 407). In setting up an opposition between physical features and sentimental loyalties, Ozawa attempted to separate national identity from the question of "race," arguing a spiritual proof of national identity—a proof dependent on heart and soul rather than on blood and genes. In awarding citizenship, then, the courts were encouraged by Ozawa to replace slippery morphological or race-based measurements with valuations of personal commitment to the nation's government and political ideals.

And yet to claim that America was in the heart meant that one's right to citizenship effactually arose from the "shared" cultural values actually determined and enforced by European Americans. Even though Ozawa insisted that nationality was not a "racial" entity, he construed citizenship as dependent on one's relative "whiteness." During his trial, as Ian F. Haney Lopez summarizes, Ozawa had pointed to the skin on his cheek to indicate the whiteness of his body and had brought in ethnological research to argue that the Japanese were often lighter skinned than many of the swarthier European groups accepted into American society (Lopez 1996; see also Ichioka 1994, 406–14). Arguing the case before the Supreme Court during the October term of 1922, Ozawa's lawyer, George Wickersham, marshaled ethnographic evidence to prove the "indeterminancy" of whiteness and to thereby challenge the meaning of the "uniform rule of naturalization" in the Naturalization Act of 1906. But Wickersham did so by attempting to persuade the Court to accept a specific meaning of race-based whiteness; that is, that a *"white person, as construed by the Court and by the state courts, means a person without Negro blood"* (*Ozawa v. the United States* [1922] 182). Insisting that when the first Congress passed the Naturalization Act of 26 March 1790, they intended—through using the phrase *free white citizen*—to exclude only "Negroes" from full rights, Wickersham asserted that "the only safe rule to adopt is to take the term as it undoubtedly was used when the naturalization law was first adopted, and construe it as embracing all persons not black." According to this rule, the "Japanese is 'white' in color and is of the Caucasian type and race" (*Ozawa v. the United States* [1922] 184–85).

In response to Ozawa's suit, the Court codified two intertwined racial assumptions: first, the twentieth-century notion of transparent and self-evident whiteness (Flagg 1998, 36); and second, the separateness of black culture and experience from "American" identity. Referring to *Ozawa* and similar landmark decisions involving ethnic American plaintiffs as "prerequisite cases," Lopez has shown how, in each, claimants turned to the courts to be declared white so as to be allowed to naturalize or otherwise avoid extradition. Between 1878 and 1952, the U.S. Supreme Court heard fifty-two prerequisite cases, and through their collective deliberations, the Court helped to redefine whiteness as less a matter of biology or culture than of "common sense." Put more simply still, whiteness was redefined as "not colored" or "non-black" (Lopez 1996, 80–86; Jacobson 1998, 236).

Kang's *East Goes West* is a satire whose intent is to devalue whiteness as a pure property that must be protected, thereby subverting the very premise on which the "prerequisite cases" were built: that whiteness must function as an ideological tool in the process of accepting (or rejecting) and assimilating (or not assimilating) American immigrants. Rather than acquire the negrophobia that could make a case for his inclusion within a broadened category of "Caucasian" or "white" Americans, Kang in *East Goes West* reimagines his "not-citizen" exile as the opportunity to forge a new transnational and transracial consciousness that oversteps traditional borders and ties African Americans and "Oriental Yankees" together in a cosmopolitan affiliation.

In her introduction to the collection of essays *Displacing Whiteness*, Ruth Frankenberg has argued that whiteness must be understood as a historically contingent racial identity or identifier that has shifted over time, varying according to such quantities as the gender, class, and nationality of its subject (1997, 20). Between the First and Second World Wars, as Matthew Frye Jacobson (1998) has noted, there occurred a significant reconceptualization of whiteness as the ideological center of a system of classification used to determine inclusion in (and the meaning of) an imagined or idealized American national community. While a number of social scientists began to question the naturalness of racial distinctions, especially as applied to ethnic groups, the nation's understanding of race was nonetheless refigured along black and white lines. In the expanding and increasingly dominant category of the "Caucasian," Jewish and Eastern European immigrants and their children (Jacobson argues) found themselves part of a normative "American" whiteness, but this inclusiveness depended upon renaming racial conflict as a "Negro problem" (1998, 103–10). And while Asian immigrants did not number among those generally assumed to be within the emerging category of the Caucasian, on arriving in the United States, Asian immigrants often acquired the concomitant negrophobia that functioned to acculturate the Asian immigrant into Caucasian mainstream society (Hellwig 1977, 103).

For a variety of reasons, this phenomenon was exacerbated within the Korean American community. Particularly following the Japanese invasion of Korea in 1894 and the formal annexation of Korea by Japan in 1910, first-generation Korean Americans found community, ethnic identity, and a means of protesting against imperialism by joining nationalist and race-based political organizations such as the Korean Nationalist Association (1909). Suffering acutely as men without a home to return to, the numerous *chong gak* (bachelors) in America developed, as Ronald Takaki notes, a profound sense of ethnic nationalism (1989, 277).

In forcing his readers to consider the "Negro question" within the localized history of (male) Korean America, Younghill Kang refuses to lock himself into simple oppositional ways of thinking that ignore the heterogeneity of American racial groups and their collective experience of oppression. Writing decidedly against the political grain, Kang criticizes the establishment of separatist ethnic organizations poised to do battle with a uniform Western or Japanese imperial culture, asserting that such mobilizing of exiles repeats in an alarming way the "removal" of African Americans in the prevailing fiction of a reputedly "white" or "European" American culture. In *East Goes West*, Kang avoids building upon racial assumptions of both colonials and anticolonials by questioning narratives that abandon the "Negro" (and other peoples of color) beyond the pale of the American scene. Kang thus sabotages the familiar ethnic studies paradigm built around the conflict between white and nonwhite, Western and non-Western, native and colonizer, or Asian and American—such that other minority Americans (here, specifically African Americans) are rendered invisible.

THE "LOGIC" OF NATURALIZATION

In 1939 Illinois Congressman Kent E. Keller introduced a bill to the U.S. House of Representatives (HR. 7127) proposing that Professor Younghill Kang of New York University be naturalized as a U.S. citizen (see Lee 1997, 136). Included within the bill was a collection of statements on Kang's behalf compiled by the Committee on Citizenship for Younghill Kang, a committee including such notable literary figures and civic leaders as Malcolm Cowley, Pearl S. Buck, Lewis Mumford, Maxwell Perkins, and Charles Scribner. The same year, a second bill was introduced before the Senate by Matthew M. Neely of West Virginia declaring Kang an "American." Neither bill passed. Were it not for its particular evidence of the legal fiction of "race," the failure of Younghill Kang's legislative bid for citizenship might be construed as just one more historical consequence of the 1924 Immigration Exclusion Law. In his essay for *Common Ground* magazine in 1941, Kang pointedly declared, "I am an American in all but the citizenship papers denied me by the present interpretation of the law of 1870 under which a Korean is not racially eligible for citizenship" (Lee 1997, 389). While Kang's comparatively restrained assertion suggests that he understood the role of racism in the judicial and legislative failures to secure his naturalization, it also indicates that he knew that his "race" was a matter of "present interpretation,"

where such terms as "citizen," "American," and "race" did not constitute stable entities. In preserving the link between American citizenship
and whiteness, Congress (it might be argued) was protecting a kind of
"acquired inheritance." As Cheryl Harris has noted in her groundbreaking article for the *Harvard Law Review* (1993), whiteness as an aspect of
identity had been translated within the nineteenth-century American
legal system into an external object of property and a sign of status
(104), and naturalization cases became arguments over the meaning of
and rights to "whiteness" itself. To be identified as or named "white"
was to share in a "possessive investment" in the American privileges of
opportunity, accumulation, and upward mobility (Lipsitz 1998, 8).

In *East Goes West*, Kang frames the story of his first years as a country-
less exile with brief but telling references to the Immigration Exclusion
Act and to his various legal bids for naturalization.[1] At the beginning
of his novel, Kang has Chung-pa remark that, arriving in America as
an eighteen-year-old, he "got in just in time before the law against Oriental immigration was passed" (1937, 5). More significantly, near the
end of the novel, as Chung-pa is hitchhiking around New England, he
relates his on-the-road encounter with the "eminent former Wisconsin
Senator" Kirby. As is true of many scenes in the novel, this scene is
grounded in satirical understatement, a form of what Homi Bhabha has
called "sly civility" (1994, 83). In response to the senator's nativist query
about Chung-pa's citizenship, Chung-pa quips, "Legally I am denied."
Unperturbed and not understanding, the senator trivializes Chung-pa's
objection by assuring him that "there are still ways and means of proving exceptions." Kang's memory—and anticipation—of his own futile
struggles to prove himself an "exception" to American race logic are
encoded in the senator's faithless invitation that concludes the scene:
"Next time I hold government office . . . write me and I will help you"
(1937, 383).

Much more important than Kang's self-reflexive irony is the insis-
tent questioning throughout the novel of the nature and legality of exclusionary "whiteness." In the language of the novel, Senator Kirby's
short-sighted patriotism is linked to the specific language of naturalization cases heard before Congress; these include the Ozawa case referred
to earlier, as well as Kang's own. In the context of such cases, Senator
Kirby's exhortation to Chung-pa to "believe in America with all your
heart," to think of himself as "one of us" because he has the same spirit of
"ambitious enterprise" (352), taps into the argument often made in naturalization and prerequisite cases: that national identity is not a matter of

skin color but of inner loyalties. Superficially, at least, such an equation of national allegiance with the dispositions of the heart seems transformative of race-based definitions of "American" identity.[2] In the end, however, if we fully understand the implications of Kirby's assertions, we will recognize that his particular dissent from racial nationalism actually perpetuates the negrophobia that the "doctrine of whiteness" inculcates in immigrants as the price of admission to the United States.

The racial logic of early twentieth-century America, as Gary Okihiro has shown, involved the contradictory identification of Asian Americans as both white *and* black (Okihiro 1994, 53). If the process of becoming a U.S. citizen involves acquiring both civic–political rights (the right of individual liberty, freedom of speech, association, and government influence) *and* a cultural identity encompassing a sense of belonging to a social community, Asian Americans could hope, at best, to be seen as culturally "white"—while remaining, incontrovertibly, politically "black." Thus, Asian Americans might be praised as exemplifying middle-class "American" values of self-help, hard work, and resourcefulness; but they were nevertheless relegated to the marginal political (and economic) status endured by African Americans.

In contrast to this way of thinking, Kang attempts to create in *East Goes West* a multiracial consciousness; that is, a recognition of the fact that, along with its unquestionable western European origins, American culture is also founded on the histories and cultures of African Americans—and, by extension, on those of Native Americans, Asian Americans, Hispanic Americans, and so on. Kang thereby challenges the enabling fiction that underlies Wickersham's defense in the Ozawa case—and, by extension, the entire "doctrine of whiteness" present in American social law: that the "American way of life" stands altogether independent of that of African Americans (or other ethnic Americans). Kang points to the omnipresence of jazz, for example, as revelatory of the instability of white American self-definitions: "It had caught up the rhythm of America—this Negro jazz—it had taken possession of the Western planet, working upon all hitherto known cultures and civilizations" (18). Kang inverts the "normal" direction of colonization to show the unnaturalness of a generally accepted standard of whiteness, an acceptance that hides from itself its own vibrant multicultural origins.

Despite the fact that *East Goes West* was written and marketed as a novel, it ostensibly follows many of the conventions of Western autobiography. But just as Homi Bhabha argues that the native's resistance to the dominant language of colonialism often arises through an imperfect imitation that gives a different accent to the master's speech (1994, 245), so Kang reveals—through his apparently slavish imitation of the lyric subjectivism of the late romantic American modernists (Strange 1994, 37)—that he is invoking and repeating the Western "I" only to reinvent it. Specifically, he "contaminates" the American notion of romantic (white) individualism by speaking the story of his protagonist through a polyglot of ethnic tongues and perspectives. Mimicking both the language of Thomas Wolfe and the gyp of the Negro, Kang exposes the alien within the supposedly "pure" white national identity and releases the prohibited anger of nonwhite peoples.

THE SPACE AND TIME OF AFFILIATION

Like his fictional alter ego, Chung-pa Han, Younghill Kang immigrated to the United States in 1921 as one of a privileged few "refugee students" issued passports by the Japanese government of occupied Korea (Lee 1991, 64). Although Kang (and other refugee students) came from the *yangban* or aristocrat class in Korea—which alone had the privilege of education—he quickly learned, once in America, that he and his fellows would be forced into manual labor despite their extensive study. Working as farm hands, houseboys, cooks, waiters, railroad porters, and miners, these students may not have been representative of the typical Korean American immigrant laborers brought to the United States as work teams or *sip-changs,* as Elaine Kim argues (1982, 34); the rather intriguing consequence, however, was that in their underemployment and "segregated integration," they could better identify with the situation of the Negro in America. At one point in *East Goes West,* Chung-pa is told by the Schmitts' cook Laurenzo that one can be "chockfull of education" but remain "still a niggerman" (1937, 262). Later, in his own revisionist history of civilization, Chung-pa's mentor Kim reiterates this shared marginalization by telling a fable about the survival of "African cats" and "Asian rats" in Europe and America; and although the cat and the rat might be considered natural enemies, in Kim's tale they cohabit peacefully in the slums of America, surviving together against the forces that would otherwise kill them (256).

One way to approach the question of Kang's coalitional or cosmopolitan frame of reference in *East Goes West* is through the trope of space as centered around descriptions of an autonomous world—Harlem or Chinatown or the Lower East Side—indifferent to mainstream white

American society and representative of an oppositional site of cultural identity. This oppositional site—the ethnic or racial neighborhood—enables distinct self-representation; and although some writers found such a ghetto claustrophobic or tyrannical, its communal life held forth the option of turning one's back on the history, ideals, and prejudices of white America and of writing a forceful, assertive "tale of the ghetto" in place of omnipresent white narratives. While Kang emphasizes exile and wandering as Chung-pa's American inheritance, and not ghetto life, one setting in the novel nevertheless emerges as an oppositional site for Chung-pa, and that is Harlem. As much as Chinatown or the Village, Kang's Harlem stands as a "city of refuge" for Chung-pa. Soon after he arrives in Harlem, Chung-pa begins to learn his close affiliation with the African American. Trying to get a job at the YMCA, Chung-pa is informed that he does not qualify since the position must "not be given to a Negro and Oriental" (19).[4] And when Chung-pa and other Asian students try to sell Hsun's tea, the only place they receive a civil welcome is in Harlem: "Harlem was a favorite selling ground. They did not get kicked out there" (64). The episodic structure of *East Goes West* underscores the absence of the idealized Korean American neighborhood, but surprisingly it is the black community that becomes most important to Chung-pa. Because he sees blacks as fellow victims of political and economic exclusion and discrimination, Chung-pa finds greater humanity among them than elsewhere, and Harlem becomes a home of altruism and justice.

While Chung-pa identifies blacks as fellow victims of American racism, he sees African American culture as the representative soul of modern New York—and thus as a key embodiment of a distinctive American identity. During his first trip to a cabaret show, Chung-pa observes that "the jolly rich, highly emotional atmosphere seemed to caricature New York" as he himself knew it, replete with "frank love, loose laughter, a lack of discipline" and with "vulgarity, good humor, sheepishness, plenty of smartness, too, and pavement cunning" (75). At first glance this passage may seem to repeat the rhetoric of primitivism popularized by modernist artists from Stephen Crane to Eugene O'Neill. Yet Chung-pa's equation of modern America with Harlem actually reverses the symbolic denial of the other's humanity on which primitivism depends. Not only do African Americans stand as displaced symbols for what efficient industrialized society has given up (heightened sexuality, emotionalism, and spontaneity), for Chung-pa and his friends they *are* "America." By equating America with its "exotic" other, Chung-pa thus collapses the assurance of separation that the "slummer" felt in knowing he was different from the primitive African.

We can see Kang's efforts not to repeat the primitivist caricatures of blacks when he describes residents of Harlem, but instead to "blacken" the culture of America so as to expose a repressed reverse acculturation within "white" American nationalism. This is especially evident in his descriptions of Greenwich Village life. At a speakeasy party, for example, Chung-pa satirizes the stereotyping of African Americans as "savage" others when he reports a brief exchange between an inebriated flapper named Sally and a "serious-looking young Negro." When the black man in question offends the revelers with his sobriety, Sally enjoins him to act more like a "Negro," telling him to "throw away all in-in-in-hibitions. D-dance and sing—and be-be a Negro" (163). In his ironic reflection on Sally's romantic racism (Frederickson 1988, 109), Kang takes care that his identification with the African American does not duplicate the Anglo-European's patronizing fantasies. Although the villagers seek an "inside" glimpse of the New Negro in order to escape sexual and social conventions that displaced unconscious desires onto African Americans, Kang strives to break the primacy of the Anglo-American perspective without simply repeating the villagers' colonial primitivism.

Indeed, what Chung-pa continually finds among the avant-garde is a fervent wish to be "black" (to undergo a race change) and yet to hide the heritage of Africa in "Americanness." In sharp contrast to the whites with whom he associates, Chung-pa himself celebrates jazz as the crooning spirit of modernism. In creating Chung-pa's sensitivities, Kang borrows the ideas of such New Negro writers as J. A. Rogers who, in "Jazz at Home" (printed in Locke's *Survey Graphic* anthology), glorifies jazz as a vehicle for democratization and racial amalgamation (1992, 220). While Langston Hughes saw jazz as the "eternal tom-tom beating in the Negro soul," Kang uses it as a motif for the *American* soul, the soul concealed behind the racial masquerade of whiteness.

Kang points up the standard immigrant conflict between "white" culture and "authentic" identity so that he can reformulate it as the tension between what might be called unicultural and multicultural paradigms of America itself. This reformulation is perhaps most evident in Kang's portrayal of George Jum, the "Americanized Pagan" who "had left all Asian culture behind as a thing of nought" (31). While George Jum (like Kim) acts as a foil to Chung-pa, it is significant that George, as a representative of the "Americanized Korean," is in love with

Harlem—or, more specifically, with the Harlem cabaret dancer, June (73). That June is not really "colored" but a white woman who wears dark makeup to appear in the chorus line only underscores Kang's points about the pervasive racism of "American" culture. By linking George's Americanization to his love for the Harlem dancer, Kang challenges the "white-face" of America's self-understanding, together with the formulaic process of immigrant Americanization. But Kang issues an even broader challenge to the American status quo as he questions the "need" not only to imitate white America but also to accept—as a matter of common sense, let alone of ethics—the racial constitution of white America implicit in the rhetoric of prerequisite naturalization cases.

WHITENESS AND THE "DENIAL OF DIFFERENCE"

Running counter to Kang's affiliative trope was a white denial of the multicultural or ethnic other, a somewhat paradoxical "denial of difference" necessary to the preservation of American whiteness. Recent "race traitors" like Noel Ignatiev (1996), George Lipsitz (1998), and David Roediger (1994) have examined "white racial identities" as constructs that arise at specific historical moments because of the political, economic, or psychological usefulness of the construct in question. But whiteness itself, as the Ozawa and Lum cases point out, has not only gone largely unexamined and unchallenged, it has also been posited as a homogeneous quantity pointing to a singular identity set against a variety of colored others (Chambers 1997, 145). To see ethnicity or "race" in such oppositional terms permits precisely the obfuscation of complex racial and cultural intermixing on which whiteness depends for its centrality and "purity."

Such obfuscation is dramatized in *East Goes West* through the disingenuous Chung-pa's response to the racial masquerades and minstrelsy of Cotton-Club Harlem. Chung-pa remembers his first encounter with June in these words: "Soon he [George] returned with June, who to our surprise was not black but white, white as chalk. So she must be a white girl unless behind that white mask lived a Negro soul. She still looked to us a strange thing and all the more for her simple dress" (1937, 76). In this semicomic scene Chung-pa discovers that the "black" cabaret dancer is really white, and not just white, but exaggeratedly pale—"chalk white." And in his musing that maybe June isn't really white, despite appearances, for she might have a "black soul," Kang interrupts the security of whites-in-blackface, questioning their "inalienable right" to the (racial) property of blackness. While the minstrel performer and the Harlem slummer assure themselves that their "love and theft" of black expressive style, to use Eric Lott's phrase, can end whenever they need or want to reclaim their "natural" identities (1993, 83), Kang suggests that the performance is never over, and possibly that the foundational mimicry offstage may be of the black soul insisting on its pure white face. Like the Asian American, the white American, too, has an ambivalent racial identity, assuming at times—when it is to his advantage or pleasure—a politically white, but culturally "colored," identity. In Chung-pa's encounters with June are brought together the ideas of identity and masquerade; Kang intimates that gender and race identities are often unconscious imitative performances, and, as a consequence, that there is no natural or unchanging essence behind one's "ethnic" identity (Butler 1993, 9–13).

In altering the process of "Americanization," Kang requires Chung-pa to become acclimated to an American society that is "black." This blackness is not indigenous to a separate African American culture but, as seen in June, is part of the very culture that whites claim or "perform." In *Immigrant Subjectivities*, Sheng-mei Ma argues that in the subconscious fantasy of the male Asian immigrant, America is personified as a "white woman." While such an association of America with white womanhood recurs throughout *East Goes West*, it would be wrong not to detect the irony underscoring George's displaced assimilationist desire for the "white woman," especially given that Kang creates her as not really white. Indeed, Kang thereby calls into question the racial body of the "white" erotic fantasy of the Asian male in order to complicate the "color" of America. In finding June to be a "strange thing," an ambiguous sign of American national identity—simultaneously a white actor in black face and a black soul under a white masquerade—Chung-pa pushes the reader toward a taboo suspension of clear racial differences, a suspension that *Ozawa* only superficially supported.

Cosmopolitan Identity

When the Reverend Bonheure, an African American preacher from Boston, invites Chung-pa to testify as part of his ministry, Kang's alter ego delivers a secular sermon, a Washingtonian or even Franklinian message of self-help and discipline. "Make something of yourselves. Be educated," he says. "Don't depend on your leaders. They can't help you. Nothing can, but your own will to make something of yourself'

(Kang 1937, 338). Telling his story before a black audience, Chung-pa at first reverts to the self-made immigrant story of the model minority; yet he eventually delivers less an accommodationist message than an indirect warning against trusting "good-time" con artists—even including ministers—inclined to abuse the vulnerability of their audiences. The people, however, do not *hear* his message: they only see the miracle of an articulate Korean who does not conform to their stereotyped views of the Oriental. Indeed, one woman cries out, "Chinaman can speak, too!!" (338). Interpreting the other according to simple race logic, such individuals cannot discern the genuine from the false messenger, just as they cannot discriminate between the real Asian and the Oriental stereotype, to say nothing of distinguishing between a Korean, for example, and a Chinese. Kang extends this association of authenticity with racial insularity in Chung-pa's conversation with Bonheure after the revival. Lauding Chung-pa for his "good speech," Bonheure then confides the need to correct the Korean immigrant's mispronunciations. For example, he notes, the correct way to say "genuine" is "genu-wine" (339).

Rather than trying to pen into his fictional autobiography a "genuine" or authentic Korean American group identity, Kang posits what might be called a cosmopolitan consciousness of multiple affiliations (including black, white, and Korean). Yet if Kang never names what is appropriately called a cosmopolitan or post-identity consciousness, he quite clearly points to the ironic sabotaging of whiteness as the first stage of its development. This undoing of whiteness is most clearly evident in the tragicomic romance of Kim, a self-proclaimed Asian philosopher, and Helen, the American daughter of a prosperous Boston family. As her symbolic name suggests, Helen is written into Kang's "third-world text" (to borrow Frederic Jameson's phrase) to deliberately add a "political dimension in the form of a national allegory" (Jameson 1986, 69). Read as a "national allegory," Kim and Helen's interracial romance—which, in 1937, would have been proscribed in many states as miscegenation— functions as a deterrent narrative, a narrative warning against an unbalanced "Oriental" obsession with the beauty of Euro-American or white civilization. Kim thinks that he has found in Helen the perfect complement to his exiled Asian self: "Her difference of ideas was a thrilling stimulation, yet his own innate simplicity of soul—an Eastern quality— found an echo in hers from New England" (222). Although it might seem that Kang is arguing here for a congruency of souls bespeaking the Korean's claims to naturalization despite his color, he implies instead that such complete "whitening" finally leads to Kim's diminution and death.

In Kim and Helen's romance Kang deliberately taps into nationalist paranoia, where anxiety about sexually imperiled white daughters of the empire was used to stoke racial violence against the ethnic males who allegedly threatened them (Sharpe 1993, 4–6). But he also employs the story as a connection to *Ozawa v. the United States*. In arguing his rights to citizenship, Takao Ozawa reasoned that the immigrant's internalization of the "heart" of nationalism could be witnessed in his love for American education, the English language, Western churches, and American (that is, white or appropriately Americanized) women. Clearly, in Ozawa's argument, assumptions about the natural body of the true American were overlaid on assumptions about gender; for to prove that America was "in the heart," Ozawa abrogated not only his culture but the "too-ethnic" body of women of color. Ozawa proudly reminded the judges that "I chose as my wife one educated in American schools … instead of one educated in Japan" (qtd. in Ichioka 1994, 407).[5] In proclaiming his devotion to the idealized Western female (Helen), Kim (like Ozawa) was drawing upon a long traditional use of feminine types to define racialized national identities.[6]

Kang thus links Helen to America's premodern New England cultural heritage. Chung-pa initially is struck by a peculiar quality in Helen that he can't name, but he later supposes that "it was that obviously she could never be Chinized! No more than a white meetinghouse.... She moved from the higher centers and she had the temperament if not the talent for the realm of higher ideas" (213). Through the metaphor of the white colonial meetinghouse, the site of Puritan religion and Revolutionary War meetings, Helen becomes an incarnation of America's spiritual and political ideals. Put another way, Kang's Helen is an ironic type of Henry Adams' virgin—the embodiment of a motivating Platonic love set against the modern world's utilitarian values.[7] Thus, while Kim adulates Helen as the idealized Western woman, she is more accurately the modernist descendent of imperial and racial "manifest destiny." In comparison to Kim, who acknowledges that his "sane pessimism" has driven him to a cultural relativism (227, 236), Helen believes in moral absolutes, the absolutes of her New England fathers. Through his typically dispassionate and satirically understated prose, Chung-pa reveals the prudish superficiality of Helen as idealized New England woman: "She was bred in an old-fashioned Christian home which forgot that Adam was ever naked with his wife and not ashamed in the Garden of Eden" (219). When Kim speaks to Helen about less-inhibited African responses to sexuality, Helen can only read such "immodesty" as a sign of American cultural superiority: "There! And you still argue we are not better off than to be in Africa?" (225). In order to exalt the noble Helen and to declare to her that it took "three centuries to make you what you are," to provide "just the right pattern" (223), Kim must be blind to Helen's rigidly puritanical white supremacism.

Kim's story is an allegory not simply about disillusioned (or delusional) object worship (either of Helen or America), but about the consequences of black and white reductionism. When Chung-pa naively exclaims that "Helen might save Kim if she only would," Kang connects Kim's story with Ozawa's story—and thus to the stories of many Asian immigrants to Gold Mountain. While Kim has "given up one world" and is searching for another (207), Kang clearly shows that Kim's restless exile need not end in his wedding the Anglo–New England tradition that Helen represents, a tradition often legitimizing colonialism and white nationalism. As Chung-pa remarks, "Kim had no defense against Helen's conservative background. It intensified the feeling he had had all along, that he was an unwanted guest in the house of Western culture" (244). Behind the Korean philosopher's "idealization" of the white Western woman is finally a self-hatred. Although Helen intensifies Kim's awareness of his difference, he persists in believing that marrying her will enable him to transcend his foreignness. Through his love for Helen, in other words, Kim believes he can secure (like Ozawa) America "in the heart," thus reconciling East and West.

Through the story of Kim and Helen, Kang exposes the inauthenticity, the nongenuine nature of the "white" soul—and, by extension, of the larger "American" consciousness. More crucially still, Kang refuses to fix any single racialized identity as the endpoint of his fictional autobiography. In this refusal, Kang opens up a space for what Ross Posnock in his own recent study of W.E.B. Du Bois calls a performative cosmopolitanism that anticipates the contemporary moment of post-identity thinking (1998, 9–10). As a diasporic postmodernist, Kang was aware that there was no premodern or precolonial American Eden to rediscover as "home." Nor, as he writes in *East Goes West* (composed during the period of Japanese and American expansionism in the Pacific), was there a Korean homeland to return to (341): politically, Korea had become a different and even a dangerous place; culturally, its ideologies and customs were disintegrating as they passed under the forces of modernization. Kang finally points to what Stuart Hall (1990) has also suggested in his essays on race and culture: identities are more a matter of becoming than of being or discovering; they are future oriented rather than backward looking (225). Beginning with his opening poetic meditation on time, Kang emphasizes the individual in "process," arguing that personal American identity is continually evolving, fed by black and white and yellow streams.[8]

Through the character of Lin, the Korean nationalist who assassinates Chinwan (the Japanese-educated Korean who "looked kindly" on all Asians regardless of their country of origin), Kang invites his fellow Asian American readers to reimagine their own exiles as starting points for cross-racial identification with other colonized peoples.[9] While Lin contends that he had to kill the "spy" Chinwan to prove that he himself was a "true Korean," Kang in the voice of Chung-pa calls instead for a greater sense of cosmopolitanism: "Here in this cosmopolitan city I saw Lin as living in a narrow world, a small world in a large. No message came back and forth from the large world to the little nor from the little world to the large" (69). Although equally displaced in "America" with Lin, his fellow Korean, Chung-pa condemns a narrow-minded ethnic exclusivity and invites readers to enter a new America of cosmopolitan affiliations.

Later, when Chung-pa hitchhikes across America, "repeating the life of his grandfather, the geomancer," he becomes a kind of paradigm of the "new American," living out "a roving life of ever new contacts and scenes" (344). Kang's own story, as told through the life of the fictional Chung-pa, is one of continual self-displacement, marked by the refusal to assimilate with "America" or to settle into or reside within any one tradition. In words that echo the resistance of earlier nineteenth-century American nonconformists such as Thoreau, Chung-pa remarks as he takes flight from Boston: "We left Boston behind; however, the accumulation of puritanic dirt made me uneasy. I would have liked to jump at once into the river, wash off all dirts and send them down to the sea, becoming a child again as I was in Korea" (235).

To remain static is, for Kang, to accumulate dirt, to lose one's receptivity to change and growth; stasis is for him a denial of what he calls in one moment of reflection "the new age of broad communication, cross-fertilization, and the shaking of boundaries" (268). In leaving Korea, in stopping by the Maritime Provinces in Canada, in traveling from Boston, in heading for New York, Kang displays a restless motivation that, he tells us, "craved a more cosmopolitan environment" (176). Rather than simply demystifying race or nation-based ideas of identity, Kang affiliates himself with many different and particularized ethnic communities, participating in their various points of view and thus opening up translocal affections and solidarities.

In both his lament over his exile and his transposing of it as a trope for a higher consciousness not answerable to national and racial borders, Kang anticipates the diasporic internationalism in the work of Salman Rushdie and V. S. Naipaul that Tim Brennan describes. His homelessness characterizes a frame of mind defined by its openness, its tolerance of uncertainty and contradictions, its freedom, its mixture of curiosity and skepticism, and its constant flux and change. As Kang travels the American West early in the novel, he confesses, "I was eager to feel its life in an unbroken stream pass through my heartblood." Yet he imagines this America as an evolving modernity rather than a historical essence, declaring, "Seen in this way, history becomes not history, but poetry and creative process" (190). Although it would be wrong to suggest that Kang ever stopped feeling the loneliness that accompanies alienation, he staunchly refuses in his story of Chung-pa Han to authenticate *any* single destination or to signal Chung-pa's arrival *anywhere*.

While many early critics of the novel read its conclusion as an intimation of Chung-pa's reunion with Trip, Chung-pa is (in an allegorical reading, at least) obsessed by the "trip" he has been on, by the roving desire itself. Perhaps it is to belabor the obvious in a novel that is so insistently episodic, but the absence of a single resting place or destination or "home"—especially as such a location might exist in opposition to Korea or America—is a narratological clue to the theme of the text. The "Oriental Yankee" subject of Kang's *East Goes West* is, unlike Ozawa, a citizen of many different places, regions, and points of view: a "genu-wine" cosmopolitan always unfolding in time—never fixed or static but always (as Kang notes in his closing image) being reborn in a "happier reincarnation." For Kang, ethnic and racial identity is a homeland that he has left behind for a life that constantly opens itself up to new additions, new affections for and affiliations with others. It is an exile's journey that has no end except the trip itself—and further opportunities for new incarnations.

Notes

1. As previously suggested, the immigration laws excluding Chinese (1882) and Asian Indians (1917) were extended in 1924 to include Koreans and Japanese as well. Not until the McCarran-Walter Act of 1952 and the later Immigration and

Nationality Act (1965) did the U.S. Government lift its interdicts against Asian-origin groups; even then, the entrance of Asian-origin groups into America was regulated according to the strategically based quotas of the Cold War era (Chan 1991, 140–42).

2. Indeed, a decade later, Carlos Bulosan, who credited Kang as his authorial role model, would name his postwar novel about Filipino migrant workers *America is in the Heart*.

3. Kang's peripatetic narrative form might be explained away on the level of genre (he is writing a comic picaresque adventure, a travelogue) or of biography (he is recounting his own homelessness), but neither explanation identifies his artistic aim. It is, after all, a bit myopic to see Kang as beholden to the literal facts of his own experience or even to sociological analysis.

4. The equivalence of Asian to black is underscored when Chung-pa later obtains a job as a domestic, and his employer says she hired him to replace her former Negro help.

5. Since the end of the nineteenth century, as Martha Banta (1987) has carefully documented, advocates of cultural exceptionalism have associated American society with its Daisy Millers and other New Women.

6. Kang was well aware of the American connection between gender and nationalism, for in one of his few documented speeches, he argued (as the *New York Times* reported in 1935) for the further economic emancipation of American women, asserting that gender equality would emphasize the advanced national culture of the United States. To take America to heart, the logic of the Ozawa case implied, was also to embrace the nativist woman.

7. An antimodernist idealism is the essence of Helen's Western beauty as Kim perceives it: after telling Helen the story of the plant that found a state of bliss in the land of nonexistence, he remarks that "this has been my philosophy, in utilitarian civilizations wherever I and my muse are not wanted" (216)—thus implying the nonutilitarian nature of Helen herself and his own ease in her company.

8. Throughout *East Goes West*, as a consequence, there is a tone of mourning, one that records the isolation, alienation, instability, and rootlessness that Kang felt as an exile. As Chung-pa remarks, describing the between-war period of the 1920s and 1930s, it was a "great age of disintegration and new combinations" (314). However, rather than falling into a postcolonial nostalgia, Kang turns mourning into an opportunity for new creative possibilities. Specifically, Kang refuses a backward glance toward the cultural cohesion of race—whether the logic of "whiteness," "yellowness," "blackness," or "redness"—and, instead, struggles to point to, though he is never able to name, a new Utopia. Kang's Utopia would be one (as he himself writes) of "new combinations"—that is, of cultural interplays and mergers among different races and ethnicities, of a reborn American society that finally triumphs over the "logic" of naturalization that would teach Korean immigrants an acquired negrophobia.

9. Kang's criticism of the insularity of Lin's anti-Japanese nationalism is loosely based on the murder of Durham Stevens (1908), the American employed by the Japanese to downplay for the U.S. Government and business community the Korean anger over Japan's invasion of its shores (Takaki 283). Yet in a telling

reversal of history, Kang refashions the Korean nationalist hero Chang In-hwan as his character Chinwan, the victim of a nationalist zealotry.

WORKS CITED

Banta, Martha. 1987. *Imagining American Women: Idea and Ideals in Cultural History*. New York: Columbia University Press.

Bhabha, Homi. 1994. *The Location of Culture*. New York: Routledge.

Blum, D. Steven. 1984. *Walter Lippmann: Cosmopolitanism in the Century of Total War*. Ithaca: Cornell University Press.

Brennan, Timothy. 1997. *At Home in the World: Cosmopolitanism Now*. Cambridge: Harvard University Press.

Butler, Judith. 1993. *Bodies that Matter: On the Discursive Limits of 'Sex'*. New York: Routledge.

Chambers, Ross. 1997. "The Unexamined." *Minnesota Review* 47 (May): 141–56.

Chan, Sucheng. 1991. *Asian American: An Interpretation*. Boston: Twayne.

Cheah, Pheng. 1998. "The Cosmopolitical—Today." In *Cosmopolitics: Thinking and Feeling beyond the Nation*, ed. Pheng Cheah and Bruce Robbins, 20–41. Minneapolis: University of Minnesota Press.

Fine, Robert, and Robin Cohen. 2002. "Four Cosmopolitanism Moments." In *Conceiving Cosmopolitanism: Theory, Context, and Practice*. New York: Oxford University Press.

Flagg, Barbara. 1998. *Was Blind But Now I See: White Race Consciousness and the Law*. New York: New York University Press.

Frankenberg, Ruth, ed. 1997. "Introduction: Local Whiteness, Localizing Whiteness." In *Displacing Whiteness: Essays in Social and Cultural Criticism*. Durham: Duke University Press

Fredrickson, George. 1988. *The Arrogance of Race: Historical Perspectives on Slavery, Racism, and Social Inequality*. Middletown: Wesleyan University Press.

Gubar, Susan. 1997. *Racechanges: White Skin, Black Face in American Culture*. New York: Oxford University Press.

Hall, Stuart. 1990. "Cultural Identity and Diaspora." *Identity, Community, Culture, and Difference*. Ed. Jonathan Rutherford. London: Lawrence & Wishart.

Harris, Cheryl. 1998. "Whiteness as Property." *Black on White: Black Writers on What It Means to Be White*. Ed. David R. Roediger. New York: Schocken. (First published 1993 in the *Harvard Law Review*.)

Hellwig, David. 1977. "Afro-American Reactions to the Japanese and the Anti-Japanese Movement, 1906–1924." *Phylon* (June): 93–104.

Ichioka, Yuji. 1994. "The Early Japanese Immigrant Quest for Citizenship: The Background of the 1922 Ozawa Case." In *Japanese Immigrants and American Law: The Alien Land Laws and Other Issues*, ed. Charles McClain, 397–418. New York: Garland.

Ignatiev, Noel, and John Garvey. 1996. *Race Traitor*. New York: Routledge.

Jacobson, Matthew Frye. 1998. *Whiteness of a Different Color: European Immigrants and the Alchemy of Race*. Cambridge: Harvard University Press.

Jameson, Frederic. 1986. "Third-World Literature in the Era of Multinational Capitalism." *Social Text* 15 (Fall): 65–88.

Kang, Younghill. 1931. "The Amateur Spirit and Korean Letters." *New York Times Book Review*, July 26, pp. 8, 19.

―――. 1931. "China is Different." *New Republic*, July 31, pp. 185–86.

―――. 1931. "Our Culture Likened to China's in 800 B.C., Or Kang Sees Economic State as Only Difference." *New York Times*, Oct. 11, p. A1.

―――. 1937. *East Goes West*. New York: Charles Scribner's Sons.

Kant, Emmanuel. 1991. "Idea for a Universal History with Cosmopolitan Intent." In *Political Writings*, ed. H. S. Reiss, 41–53. Cambridge: Cambridge University Press. (Orig. pub. 1784.)

Kim, Elaine. 1982. *Asian American Literature: An Introduction to the Writings and Their Social Context*. Philadelphia: Temple University Press.

Lee, Kyhan. 1991. "Younghill Kang and the Genesis of Korean-American Literature." *Korea Journal* 31 (4): 63–78.

Lee, Sunyoung, ed. 1997. "The Unmaking of an Oriental Yankee." Introduction to *East Goes West: The Making of an Oriental Yankee*, by Younghill Kang. New York: Kaya.

Ling, Jinqi. 1998. *Narrating Nationalisms: Ideology and Form in Asian American Literature*. New York: Oxford University Press.

Lipsitz, George. 1998. *The Possessive Investment in Whiteness: How White People Profit from Identity Politics*. Philadelphia: Temple University Press.

Lopez, Ian F. Haney. 1996. *White by Law: The Legal Construction of Race*. New York: New York University Press.

Lott, Eric. 1993. *Love and Theft: Blackface Minstrelsy and the American Working Class*. New York: Oxford University Press.

Lowe, Lisa. 1996. *Immigrant Acts: On Asian American Cultural Politics*. Durham: Duke University Press.

Ma, Sheng-mei. 1998. *Immigrant Subjectivities in Asian American and Asian Diaspora Literature*. Albany: State University of New York Press.

Okihiro, Gary. 1994. *Margins and Mainstreams*. Seattle: University of Washington Press.

Ozawa v. the United States, 260 U.S. 179 (1922).

Posnock, Ross. 1998. *Color and Culture: Black Writers and the Making of the Modern Intellectual*. Cambridge: Harvard University Press.

Roediger, David. 1994. *Towards the Abolition of Whiteness: Essays on Race, Politics, and Working Class History*. London: Verso.

Rogers, J. A. 1992. "Jazz at Home." In *The New Negro*, ed. Alain Locke. New York: Atheneum.

Sharpe, Jenny. 1993. *Allegories of Empire: The Figure of Woman in the Colonial Text*. Minneapolis: University of Minnesota Press.

Strange, David. 1994. "Thomas Wolfe's Korean Connection." *Thomas Wolfe Review* 18 (2): 36–41.

Takaki, Ronald. 1989. *Strangers from a Different Shore: A History of Asian Americans*. Boston: Little, Brown.

6 Asian American (Im)mobility: Perspectives on the *College Plays 1937–1955*

Josephine Lee

What the writing student is encouraged to do is to look around him, and without intense concentration upon the variations of Hawaiian life from that in other places—variations which to a student without travel are not always apparent anyhow—to attempt to present life as it has impinged upon him and as he sees it. The student is encouraged to write of real people like himself with very little attention being given to the theatrical devices of what has been called the "well made play." Exploration of character is represented as being much more important that [*sic*] stage trickery. Honesty and sincerity of purpose in saying something important to the student is rated much higher than imitation of Broadway or Hollywood technique.

Willard Wilson, Introduction to Volume II, *College Plays
1937–1955*

SELECTED WORKS from the student-authored collection of *College Plays 1937–1955*[1] have been hailed by some as the first "Asian American" writing for the theater, and recent interest in Asian American theater and performance has begun to renew interest in this largely forgotten set of works.[2] The ten-volume set of plays written for the classes of English professor Willard Wilson at the University of Hawai'i provides a unique perspective on what might be called "Asian American" playwriting.[3] Given Wilson's directive to the student "to write of real people like himself," these plays provide intriguing examples of dramatic writing seemingly free from commercial and aesthetic constraints on expression.[4] The plays significantly precede the Asian American theater work of the 1960s and 1970s, and they correct views of Asian American writing—particularly writing for the theater—as limited to the mainland.[5]

Yet, although the timing of this inquiry invites immediate comparisons between these plays and more recent works of drama by mainland

Asian Americans, we should be suspicious of any "kinship" that we assume. The lived experience and felt identities of Asian Americans must be distinguished from the political agendas and cultural imperatives set by the more recent Asian American movement; these plays exhibit little of the pan-ethnic solidarity, racial self-consciousness, or radical aspirations that many might see as defining more contemporary instances of Asian American theater.[6] Rather than attempting to read these plays as reflections of a nascent Asian American consciousness, in other words, one should see them as depictions of and contradictions to the social relationships and issues of ethnic identity that were being redefined both in Hawai'i and on the mainland during the crucial period before, during and following World War II.

The plays in Volume I from Wilson's class were written during the fall semester of 1936; Volume II begins with the postwar year of 1946–47; subsequent volumes pick up with subsequent years of the postwar era. Taken together, the ten volumes delineate a time when the social status of Asian Americans in Hawai'i was clearly in flux. In Hawai'i as on the mainland, Asian immigration in large part was spurred by economic hardships in Asia and the demand for cheap labor in the United States; immigrants and their descendants were systematically exploited and victimized by institutional discrimination, oppression, and prejudice. The years between 1937 and 1955 might be remembered in terms of the anti-Japanese paranoia inspired by the attack on Pearl Harbor, wartime martial law, and the internment of Japanese Americans—and in terms of the grim racism inspired by postwar anti-Communist fervor. At the same time, this period also saw significant gains by Asian Americans in Hawai'i, marked especially by the end of plantation feudalism and the political dominance of the largely haole Republican party. In the years following World War II, the status of certain Asian American groups in Hawai'i has changed to the extent that "in the minds of many in the local community, Asians are more central than marginal" (Morales 1998, 116).

The social status of Chinese, Japanese, and Korean Americans in Hawai'i, as measured in terms such as income, home ownership, education, and political visibility,[7] has clearly risen since the 1950s. However, at the present moment, social stratification in Hawai'i in terms of income level, land ownership, access to education, and political representation continue to belie the island's reputation as a multicultural paradise; Noel Kent argues that "the transformation of the old *kamaaina* [in this case, the traditional white elite] corporate complex in Hawai'i from local sugar agencies to medium-sized transnational corporations with far-reaching interests has *not*—contrary to prevailing wisdom—acted as a force for genuine economic development and political liberation in Hawaii" (1983, 121). This social inequality is still very much defined along ethnic and racial lines; such divisions, as Jonathan Okamura suggests, present an ethnic hierarchy: "An overall ranking of groups in the ethnic/racial stratification order would have Caucasians, Chinese, and Japanese holding dominant positions.... The midrange of the ethnic/racial stratification order is occupied by Koreans and, to some extent, by African Americans.... The lower levels of the ethnic/racial stratification order continue to be occupied by Filipinos, Native Hawaiians, and Samoans, a situation that appears unlikely to change in the next generation" (Okamura 1998, 200–201). Current concerns about native Hawaiian autonomy also complicate the perception of Asian American success and "progress."[8]

In this light, postwar changes in social status for Asian Americans might be interpreted as a perpetuation of economic inequality and social hierarchy—only this time with particular Asian ethnic groups, such as the Japanese, "on top." Rodney Morales describes the 1950s as "a time of sweeping change," which he describes in ways that suggest that "privileged" Asian American groups—especially Japanese and Chinese—perpetuate exploitative power structures at the expense of not only native Hawaiians but also other less economically successful Asian ethnic groups, such as Filipinos[9]:

> In 1954, a group of Democrats, mostly of Asian ancestry, many of them Japanese who had fought for America in World War II, came to power. As a result, the *haole*-dominated, mostly Republican Big Five lost the total dominance that they had held over Hawai'i's economy and people for more than half a century. The Japanese and Chinese citizens who came to political power, however, sought economic wealth.... By the 1980s, Japanese and Chinese, along with descendants of earlier boatloads of Koreans, were among the wealthiest groups in the Islands. (Morales 1998, 124)

As former Lieutenant Governor Thomas Gill reflected, "Making the old order over became less important than simply making it" (Wright 1972, 239).

Such charges allow us to turn to the *College Plays* with an even greater curiosity about what they reveal. If it is true that artists of Asian descent in Hawai'i do not articulate a unitary "minority voice" in a white-dominated state,[10] and if constructing theater history as "Asian American" cannot, as Stephen Sumida argues, simply celebrate "the process of forging a new national identity through politics, economic strides, and the raising of our own voices" (1997, 278), then how might we interpret the dramatic texts of *College Plays*? One way might be to concentrate on how Asian American social mobility (or the lack thereof) is depicted. In these plays, we can see not only the immediate economic and political effects of this transformative period—particularly how Hawaiian economic and military development opened up business, farming, and educational opportunities to Asian Americans— but also the ideological constructions that helped pressure such changes into being. The *College Plays* depict not only the evidence of Asian American social mobility, but also the fantasies that construct racial and ethnic identities in relation to economic success and technological progress.

The College Plays as Responses to Modernization

During and after the Second World War both the rhetoric and the technological apparatus of "progress" in Hawai'i took on a particular urgency. Hawai'i's strategic location gave it military importance for the United States; it also made it a prime target for material redevelopment as part of a U.S. "Pacific Rim" strategy. In the American postwar project of global transformation, the development of a Pacific Rim economic strategy was key; the United States targeted Japan and Southeast Asia as markets for American goods and as regions for the export of capital.[11] This economic strategy had a large impact on how Hawai'i would be imagined in public discourse: as being on the "fast track" of economic change and development that made its modernization (like its earlier annexation) an aspect of inevitable "progress" and manifest destiny.

Willard Wilson's introductions to the *College Plays* underscore such changes. In his introduction to the Volume I (1937–38), Wilson mentions events of local interest, including labor strikes by shipping, laundry, cane, and railroad workers. However, his focus quickly moves to "our comparative isolation in Hawaii" in contrast to "momentous changes going on in the outside world: a world trembling with power like a racing motor with a jammed accelerator." In Volume II, Wilson suggests that this isolation has been broken; he describes a celebration of the fortieth anniversary of the university, in which there was generated "considerable interest in the developing role of Hawaii and the University in the so-called Pacific Era." In later volumes, Wilson returns repeatedly to his observations of material changes in the daily lives of his students that affect the subject and nature of their playwriting:

> All the islands now have daily plane service. The ratio of car owners to [the general] population is supposed to be about 1–4; every third person has a radio; most remote rural communities are served by electric power and telephone companies; one can get fresh-frozen Alaska salmon or Oregon

peas at almost any little country store; the "movies" and "comics" provide
the matrix of thought for 90% of Hawaiian youngsters, just as they do for
their enlightened siblings in Los Angeles or New York. (Volume III)

In Volume V, he notes the conspicuous absence of "Hawaiian regional
flavor" and concludes that "this inability to seize local material and turn
it into grist for the dramatic mill may be unfortunate from a historical
point of view, but it seems to me a somewhat inevitable result of the cosmopolitan and almost international way in which the society of Hawaii
has been going for many years."

Many of the student plays also openly register this climate of change
and make it fundamental to their characterizations and dramatic purposes. Two such examples—Kathryn L. Bond's *We'll Go See the World*
(Volume I) and Clara Kubojiri's *Country Pie* (Volume VII)—exemplify
two different modes of figuring Asian and Asian American characters
with respect to Hawai'i's modernization. As we shall see, these two plays
present a paradigmatic opposition between "old" and "new" forms of
Asianness, as marked by obsolescence or incorporation into modernization and Americanization.

Bond's *We'll Go See the World* focuses on the antics of two old "China-
men," Lim Sui and Wing Bo, who saw logs, smoke their pipes, joke about
a friend ("John Pake") and his new "Pololican" (Portuguese) wife, and
banter with Mrs. Wall, their welfare case worker, who has come to get
them to apply for the Old Chinese Home in Honolulu. In her choice to
depict these former plantation workers, Bond hints at a more elaborate
history of the Chinese in Hawai'i: as Mrs. Wall fills out her forms, she
asks them for details of their lives. The two men tell of coming to the
island in order to work at Kohala Plantation during the time before au-
tomobiles and tractors: "Cow pull cane car." Wing Bo recalls how their
friend "John Pake" got his generic appellation: "Haole mans no can talk
'Wing Tduck Tzeh' Allee mans speak John Pake. Wing Tzeh no speak.
Allee time speak John Pake." However, a more rounded characterization is ultimately sacrificed in favor of making Lim Sui and Wing Bo
into comic types, to the end that Lim is described as a "short, shriv-
elled old Chinese with only two or three teeth left. High shrill cack-
ling laugh. Comparatively lively" and Wing as a "fat, bloated old man.
Low sepulchral grunt, which takes place of laughter. Phlegmatic old
man." The play constructs its caricatures not only through emphasizing comic mannerisms, but also by limiting its use of oral history. Even
when asked, Lim Sui cannot remember how old he is or when he came
to the island. Wing Bo is equally short on exact answers: "Some time

tallo patch hanna hanna, some time banana hanna hanna, sometime plantation."

Instead of constructing a realistic past for her characters, Bond uses her one-act to set up a different sense of "living in the past." The two men are depicted as lazy, isolated, and backward. Their ways of living (sawing logs, digging holes, cooking, and eating with chopsticks) are portrayed as obsolete and inefficient. The social worker, Mrs. Wall, chides them for eating rotten fish out of rusted tin cans and relying on Chinese medicine to treat Wing Bo's injured leg. Their ignorance of modern conveniences is both comic (asked why he did not call Mrs. Wall to report the death of their friend Yap Ng, Lim Sui replies, "No goo' telephone. Wha for telephone? Missee no can makee Yag Ng pau muckee") and life-threatening: Wing Bo's leg proves to be badly infected and ultimately must be treated by the government doctor.

However much a comic sketch, *We'll Go See the World* nonetheless highlights in some detail the modern technologies of travel and medicine as a means of emphasizing the backwardness of the older Chinese characters. Their isolation is depicted as both rural and cultural. While they are aware of the technologies of travel (Wing Bo comments on the daily evidence of airplanes: "Everyday look see bird go nisee place"), they cannot themselves use any of them until they are literally spirited away by Mrs. Wall, the haole social worker, in her automobile. It is this "goo' laily," as the two men call her, who allows them into the contemporary world; she in turn is the agent of government programs and doctors, by whose benevolence and science they will be protected and provided for while they are alive and after they are dead:

LIM SUI. They give box, that place?
MRS. W. Box? What kind of box?
LIM SUI. Muckee time box.
MRS. W. Yes, they will give you a nice coffin.
LIM SUI. You no lie? No box, no likee go.
WING BO. Too long time me give Tong Boxx nisee place tlentee fi' cen' one
   month for buy muckee time box.
MRS. W. Yes boys, I promise, you will have a good box when you die. But
   you have long time yet before you will need it. (*Old men greet this with
   cackles.*)
WING BO. No too long time. Goo' box got, no tlouble. Today muckee,
   tomollow, muckee, any time muckee, no tlouble—sappose nice box
   got.

As Mrs. Wall emphasizes, placing the two men in the Old Chinese Home is for their own protection. The play ends with Wing and Lim in awestruck anticipation of Mrs. Wall's promises—not only of a future airplane ride to Honolulu but also of an immediate trip in her automobile to Mahukona, ten miles away, to "see the boat"; in their excitement, they "chatter in Chinese." Mrs. Wall marvels, "Here fifty years and they've never been ten miles to Mahukona"; she offers them what will be their first ride in what they refer to as the "ollomobile," declaring, "Come along boys, we'll go see the world!"

We'll Go See the World is not alone among the *College Plays* in its preoccupation with defining Asian and Asian American characters through their response to modernization. Clara Kubojiri's domestic drama *Country Pie* (Volume VII) also relies on a background of a changing rural Hawai'i. Set in "an isolated farming district," the play considers the troubled marriage of the Japanese American couple George and Martha. Martha's mother and siblings, who arrive after George runs off to the movies, criticize him for ignoring Martha and their daughter Emi; Martha's mother (Okasan[12]) reminds Martha that she should have married "that Kuroda boy" instead of George. When George returns, Okasan confronts him angrily. George explodes in rage, tells his in-laws to leave, and yells at Martha to leave with them. Martha refuses, and her loyalty prompts an emotional reconciliation in which George realizes how much she loves him.

At first, it seems as though the play's plot centered on what might be seen as more "universal" character traits, such as George's self-centered, jealous, and impatient personality, and Martha's nagging and exhaustion. Later on, though, their mutual misunderstanding is resolved by assertions of love and loyalty. And the play's reminders of ethnic difference—for instance, through Okasan's use of Japanese phrases—are kept to a minimum. What eventually infiltrates the texture of the play much more emphatically is an emphasis on changing technologies. Martha's problems are located not just in her unappreciative husband, but also in a life of inefficient and obsolete labor, unrewarded by the pleasures of new housewares and the convenience of modern appliances. Working alongside George all day on the farm, she must save her household tasks for evening where she does them by the inadequate light of her kerosene lamp. Throughout the play, we see Martha employed in menial domestic tasks: sorting laundry, darning socks, ironing shirts, baking pies, and cleaning her home; she is forced to live with old curtains, a gas iron, a manual sewing machine. For Okasan, George's lack of concern for his wife is exemplified by his reluctance to buy her a washing machine.

The happy ending is bolstered by the promise of new devices that will materially change the nature of Martha and George's work. Without these new appliances, the play suggests, no domestic peace is possible; in the absence of household technologies such as refrigeration, even the ice cream that George buys his daughter (as penance for refusing to take her to the movies) melts away. Martha's lot in life will improve not only because George realizes how much she loves him, but also because he finally recognizes the obsolescence of their own household objects (as they reconcile, he suddenly notices that one of the coffee cups is chipped) and the endless nature of Martha's housework. When Martha makes the happy announcement that she is expecting another child, he makes jubilant plans: "Now we gotta get that washing machine quick there. All that diapers and stuff. We gotta get the washing machine first when the electricity runs up this way." By inference, electricity and new technology may eventually help with George's farming troubles—crop failure, flooding, worms, disease—as well. The play does not suggest an actual solution to dire money problems that face this young couple, nor does it explain how they will finance their planned purchases. But it nonetheless suggests a happy ending where their lives are transformed by the magic of new technology.

Unlike Bond's *We'll Go See the World*, Kubojiri's *Country Pie* does not necessarily see first-generation Japanese as backward or ignorant of progress. Young and old alike embrace change; indeed, it is Okasan who tells her daughter: "You get washing machine first. Number one good. No need break back washing clothes. Save plenty time." But this young Japanese American couple and their growing family must redefine themselves as active participants in an unfolding era of progress. They do so by first breaking with extended Japanese family structures and loyalties, and then by constituting themselves as an independent nuclear unit possessing those things that ensure their "completeness." Through their transformation into happy consumers of labor-saving devices and new domestic goods, George and Martha not only save their marriage, but also live up to their quintessentially American names.

Both plays, however, are preoccupied with how acceptance of "progress" or modernization defines the "character" of Asians and Asian Americans. Both plays affirm that the inevitable process of modernization produces a corresponding need for new "ethnic" identities that can keep up with the changing times. *We'll Go See the World* shows a generation of older "Asian" characters who will ultimately be left behind by the inventions exemplifying the new world; the other presents a family of "Asian American" consumers whose future will rely on the promise of electricity, new products, and new lives. Unlike *We'll Go See the World*, *Country Pie* reads "Asian" as not necessarily incompatible with "progress"; and in so doing, it sets the stage for picturing new "Asian American" identities on the move.

COMEDIES AND TRAGEDIES OF (IM)MOBILITY

The juxtaposing of "old" Asian and "new" Asian American characterizations must be seen in the context of the more general reconfiguration of Hawaiian "multiculturalism" in postwar and Cold War America. In the first half of the twentieth century, the rise of a more progressive and liberal view of race relations, championed by the Chicago school of sociology, took hold of the popular imagination. Within this framework, a more "cultural" and "ethnic" view of difference emerged, one that stressed a process of immigration and inevitable assimilation, and characterized a set of generational differences that would pass away with succeeding generations.[13] It is this shift in attitudes toward race that in fact enables the imagination of the multiracial population of Hawai'i to be considered "American" (or at least "Americans-in-progress").

Significantly, as Henry Yu has pointed out, in the 1920s Hawai'i became one of the prime sites of study for the Chicago sociologists, "the ultimate racial laboratory, a place where the formation of the cultural melting pot they had predicted for the West Coast was already taking place" (2001, 167). This interest in Hawai'i as the "racial frontier" renewed the "island fantasy" already put in place by the white planter class of "a Hawaii supposedly dominated by the old native Hawaiian aloha mentality of hospitality and tolerance" (2001, 168–69). In the vision of the "new" Hawai'i, racial tensions here are downplayed through contrast with racial tensions elsewhere. Commissioned in response to the racially polarizing and highly publicized 1931 Massie case,[14] the U.S. Department of the Interior's tract *Hawaii and Its Race Problem* (1932) relies on narratives of racial harmony and "progress." In his 1932 report, William Atherton Du Puy is concerned that "there is much talk in the continental press of race antagonisms in Hawaii." He continues:

> This talk is based on a lack of understanding of the relations between the races over there. In the States race conflicts and race prejudices are often intense. In the islands they are practically nonexistent. The masses are of a common, lowly, and unpretentious origin. The whites through a century have felt sympathetic toward them. The social question of race has never

been raised. It does not exist. It is never raised except by some outsider who brings his prejudices with him or some continental newspaper which bases its interpretation of events in Hawaii on race prejudices that exist where it is published.

If this outsider had an appreciation of the beauty of the interracial relations of these islands he would hesitate long before taking any step that would interfere with them. Race prejudice is a mad, intense, unreasoning thing, and arousing it where it does not exist is an act as malicious as the introduction of the plague. (129–31)

Of course, the ultimate goal is racial assimilation, which would provide a testimony to the success of "American" ways of life: "It is a part of the beautiful experiment, here in the mid-Pacific, that self-government is to be tried out under conditions and with human material that is new" (130). In his assessment of Hawai'i's racial groups, Du Puy describes at some length "a group of some 23,000 "haoles," "white men, mostly from continental United States, but with a sprinkling of Scotch and English":

It is this group that guides all the rest toward adjusting itself into the American mold of citizenship and government. When it is noted that language, manner of dress, manner of life generally, homes, schools, industries, business establishments, transportation, all of which are admittedly progressive and up to date, are all on the American plan, it must be admitted that this handful of "haoles" gives evidence of having considerable enterprise and ability. (27–28)[15]

Du Puy imagines Hawai'i as led by the haole minority out of what is thought to be a state of isolation and backwardness and into the modern world. The multiracialism of Hawai'i is led by haoles of "enterprise and ability"; members of all other ethnic groups will become successful *as Americans* by emulating haole leaders.

Du Puy's rhetoric quite clearly designates a new role for Hawai'i in the postwar United States, whose victory over enemies clearly marked by openly racist and imperialist policies could be seen as signifying the moral as well as the military superiority of America. As the designated bastion of racial tolerance, in other words, Hawai'i becomes Du Puy's emblem of America's new prominence as guardian of fairness, liberality, and democracy—in contrast to the cruel racism and tyranny of America's wartime enemies, Nazi Germany and Japan. During World War II itself, as well as throughout the "Pacific Rim" era and the drive toward statehood that followed the war, Asian American identity in Hawai'i was necessarily determined by the everyday interactions of Hawai'i's multiracial population as well as by a set of elaborate discursive imagined fantasies that responded to Hawai'i's perceived importance as racial "showcase" (Kent 1983, 122). Hawai'i epitomized the future of "American" racial relations in an idealized, almost mythical way—a way that was untouched by the history of mainland slavery, segregation, and violence. Of course, sustaining this vision of Hawai'i's happy multiculturalism required the suppression of the United States' active participation in colonialism and forced annexation, together with accompanying anti-immigration laws and restrictions, segregation, slavery, and cultural genocide. Postwar policy makers may have recognized that such suppression could be effected, at least in part, through a new kind of attention paid to Asian Americans.

According to Robert Lee, Asian Americans were stereotypically reconfigured during the postwar period as the "model minority": that is, as "a *racial* minority whose apparently successful *ethnic* assimilation was result of stoic patience, political obedience, and self-improvement" (1999, 145). Put another way, this reconfiguration distinguished Asian Americans from other, less "obliging" or "cooperative" minority group—such as African Americans: "The representation of Asian-American communities as self-contained, safe, and politically acquiescent became a powerful example of the success of the American creed in resolving the problems of race" (Lee 1999, 160). Of course, the "model minority" myth necessarily ignored the history of exclusion laws, unfair and oppressive labor conditions, and violent prejudice that affected the lives of Asian Americans; furthermore, the duly sanitized myth constituted a white American appropriation of Asian American history as part of its own "success story." This change in how Asian Americans figured in the public imagination was consistent with U.S. economic interests in the Pacific Rim; the emphasis on an Asian-friendly climate was crucial to attracting (for example) Japanese tourism, investments, and participation in multinational corporate ventures. Most importantly, such a view of Asian Americans fits within the model of assimilation established by white European immigrant groups, thus affirming the ability of the "melting pot" to absorb even the most "alien" in its all-encompassing democratic values.

That Asian American success figures heavily as testimony to this vision of Hawai'i as progressive "melting pot" can be easily traced through particular works from the *College Plays*. Significantly, the "comedic" actions of both *We'll Go See the World* and *Country Pie* rely heavily not only on dismissals of antiquated "Asianness," but also on the refiguring of a new kind of Asian American, one that can be demonstrably incorporated into the American body politic, one that helps substantiate the image of a more liberal postwar United States.

This vision is consistent with a significant number of other characterizations in the *College Plays*. As I have indicated elsewhere,[16] "Asian American success" is a driving theme of such plays as Bessie Toishigawa Inouye's *Reunion* and *Nisei* (Volume II) and Robert Suyeoka's *The Last Refrain* (Volume IV), which portray the Nisei World War II veteran as winning a legitimate "American" identity through his military service and sacrifice. Further, we see preoccupations with "success" pushing student playwrights toward a particular genre: the interracial romance. Indeed, the interracial romance offers clear-cut and predictable responses to "progress" and ethnic identity. Not only do Japanese and Chinese[17] parents oppose their children's interracial unions, the unhappy children rebel in ways that characterize parental resistance to interracial romance as old-fashioned and "backward," effactually ennobling a younger generation of Asian Americans whose insistence on interracial dating and marriage marks their more "modern" attitudes. Moments of Henry Chun's *The Man They Left Behind* (Volume VII), for instance, seem to echo the comic—and "comedic"—depictions of *We'll Go See the World,* as its "Old World" Chinese and Japanese fathers, Mr. Young and Mr. Tananka, bemoan their sons' marriages with "fast" haole women:

> YOUNG. A-ah, *haole* no good. No-o-o good.
> TANAKA. Yah, no gurru. But smart how make machine, doh. Airprane, icebox, car—too much smart.
> YOUNG. A-a-ah, waste tam, dees kahn. Dees kahn airplance no good. *Haole* ony like go mo' fass, mo' fass! Bime by airplane fo' down, ellybody *mahke.* Wen my boy go mainlan', I no lettum go fly airplane. I tellum go on boat, mo safe. An' dees kahn car no good, too. Look how many pippo get kew elly year by automobrew. Dees kahn *haole* like too much hully, hully!
> TANAKA. Yah, ol' time mo' betta. In ol' time, young falla lissen to papa, mama san.

At the end of Chun's play, progress (in the guise of new furniture) is literally thrust upon Mr. Young, who is opposed to change of any kind; the moving man intrusively replaces Young's old Chinese furniture with the new "haole" furniture ordered by his wife ("He lifts him up slightly by the back of the collar, takes away his jade-inlaid black stool, and shoves a shiny, chromium-plated one under him"). This comic moment employs, as do similar moments in many of the plays, a familiar tension between parent and child, "Asian" and "American," "East" and "West," and "traditional" and "modern." Asian American assimilation through interracial union serves as testimony to the liberal racial mixing that is a sign of the future.

For You a Lei and the "Hawaiian Way"

A significant number of the College Plays are preoccupied with the reimagining of "Asian Americans" as successful exemplars of the possibility of cultural hybridity and social mobility. In these plays, these new identities are often defined in relation to both "obsolete" or "traditional" Asians who cling to cultural difference, or to benevolent haoles who represent the intervention of enlightened and progressive attitudes and who most often appear as teachers, social workers (such as Mrs. Wall in We'll Go See the World), and counselors. Upwardly mobile Asians move toward "whiteness" and away from the "backward" status of the racialized "other," a space that is significantly occupied not only by those Asians who are resistant to change, but also by native Hawaiians and members of other, less assimilable Asian ethnic groups.

Yet this is by no means the characteristic mode of representation in the College Plays. Importantly, implicit tensions within even the most "comedic" of the plays—act as important counternarratives to the racialized discourse of "progress." One such example is Wai Chee Chun Yee's For You a Lei (Volume I).[18] Set in a tenement in the slums of Honolulu, this play not only offers a grimly realistic portrayal of Asian American poverty (including what some scholars note as the earliest example of Hawaiian Creole English ["pidgin"] writing), but also inspires an interesting set of questions concerning the social immobility of its characters.

Roger Bell notes the postwar financial success of a number of Chinese Americans in Hawai'i: "As measured in per capita terms, the Chinese had by 1959 replaced haoles as the wealthiest ethnic group." This change "was influenced by two important factors: the immense wealth of a small number of new Chinese millionaire businessmen like Chinn Ho and Hiram Fong, and the influx of large numbers of mainland white wage and salary earners in defense and service industries, especially tourism, which substantially reduced the average per capita income of whites" (Bell 1984, 112). However intriguing these statistics may be, however revealing they are of the immense changes taking place in the situations of Asian Americans after World War II, they cannot be interpreted as indicative of a uniformity of ethnicity or class. As Bell cautions, although the figures suggest "a general correlation between class and ethnicity," they fail to represent "the substantial inequalities which existed within each group" (113). *For You a Lei* not only suggests that all Chinese are not destined to move up the social scale; even more importantly, it draws our attention to the values underscoring the relative nature of both "mobility" and "success."

Mrs. Lee, "a middle-aged woman of slight build," spends days and nights in domestic labor in order to support her five children. Her difficult life is complicated further by the constant rebellion of her eldest daughter, Ah Lan, who plays hooky from school. Confronted by Ah Lan's haole teacher, Miss Carter, Mrs. Lee expresses her wish that her daughter be sent to reform school, only to be told by her son Ah Quon that reform school would seal Ah Lan's fate. Ah Quon decides to buy his sister "one peenk carnation lei" so that she will return to school the next day to participate in the lei program. The end of the play is uncertain—it is not known whether Ah Lan will return to school, whether she will be sent to reform school instead, or whether, in picking flowers for her lei, she has fallen into the river and drowned.

This uncertainty fuels a variety of interpretations. *For You a Lei* suggests the now-familiar opposition between "Asian" backwardness and haole-led progress. Mrs. Lee's rough manner, her inability to deal with her daughter, and her unkempt appearance (she has disheveled hair and is "dressed in a two-piece Chinese costume of plain material"; "as she walks, she drags her ragged slippers along with her") mark her as uneducated, recalcitrant, and unenlightened. Her old-fashioned emphasis on duty, hard work, and family loyalty is juxtaposed with Ah Lan's desires to be with her boyfriend, to spend her money at the movies, to pick flowers in the park, and, at all costs, to escape her mother's stingy and joyless expectations. Married at fifteen and inured to a life of hard work, Mrs. Lee cannot understand her daughter's desire for pleasure: "Me, I wan come Hawaii from China wan only fiteen year old. Me, I marry ole man, get keed, go hana-hana. Why Ah Lan no can?" Mrs. Lee's situation might well exemplify a version of the "old Hawaii" as "a mid-Pacific backwater," to use Noel Kent's phrase (3). The play accentuates Mrs. Lee's exhausting and endless manual labor—she is constantly hanging out clothes, ironing, carrying her baby on her back; there is no promise of labor-saving devices (as there was in *Country Pie*) that would make Mrs. Lee's life easier. She cannot take a part-time job that allows her more time with her family because none pays enough. If she did not spend her nights caring for "boss baby," she would be spending them working in the cannery. Forced to work day and night outside her own home, she in turn imposes her household duties onto her own children, trying to maintain parental control by beating and scolding them.

If Mrs. Lee is associated with the problems created by urban poverty within the older, feudalistic Hawaiian economy (where Chinese were "imported" to become part of white plantation labor forces), then education presents the possibility of individual redemption from the brutalizing effects of the postfeudal environment. Put another way, education is the vehicle of modernization that entails "the introduction of a modernized and 'enlightened' capitalist order." In contrast to Mrs. Lee, the haole teacher Miss Carter is the voice of compassion and reason, telling Mrs. Lee that her daughter is a "good girl" and trying to lift Ah Lan out of the impoverishment of body and spirit that is her mother's life. But Mrs. Lee, who cannot appreciate the value of education, comments that school is "only good for learn how tal lie."

And yet the play does not unequivocally present the "new" order—education, progress, and "haolification"—as a clear, inevitable solution to problems of the "old" life: familial and ethnic isolation, drudgery, and poverty. Instead, the play takes a skeptical view of all possibilities—all conditions that might allow the play's characters to break out of abject poverty. Miss Carter, though well intentioned, is incapable of solving Mrs. Lee's real problems of depression, exhaustion, and severe financial need; moreover, the threat of the reform school acts as a reminder that schools are punitive as well as uplifting. Nor does *For You a Lei* suggest that the problems of the Lee family are transitory or even escapable. Seen clearly, Mrs. Lee's problems have nothing to do with racial backwardness or a refusal to "go with the times"; they have everything to do with social stagnation and with the lack of true social reform.

In short, Yee's play does not promise that modernization will eradicate urban poverty; Yee asserts that the illusion of "progress" only masks deeply entrenched class divisions. If there is any optimism in the play, it is offered through another avenue. The opening dialogue between the ten-year-old Ah Mui and her neighbor friend Leilani hints at another dimension of the play, one that counters an exclusive emphasis on the binary opposition between "haole" progress and "Asian" immobility. Within this Honolulu slum, the colonial oppression of Native Hawaiians is virtually indistinguishable from white subjugation of immigrant workers. Yet, although both these Chinese and Hawaiian families labor for haole profit and live side by side, they do not share the same attitudes toward work and money. Leilani taunts Ah Mui with the fact that her mother has a better job than Mrs. Lee; Leilani's mother "only gotta work day time, and every night she bring poi home." Leilani also indicates that her mother is critical of Mrs. Lee's attitudes toward work and money: "My ole lady say da pake wahine next door lolo for make money, boy. Da kind job she got, she mo' batter no work." She is likewise disapproving of Mrs. Lee's beating of Ah Lan: "She say, waste time wan your ole lady come home. She only good for hit your seester, Ah Lan. Everytime we hear Ah Lan yell, boy. We no stink ear, you know."

Leilani's comments make it clear that Mrs. Lee's problems are rooted less in her "backward" condition than in the fact that she is "lolo" for money. In a money-driven society, Mrs. Lee has sacrificed her will and body as well as family harmony in attempting to meet the "haole" terms of survival, if not success. She no longer sees any possibilities beyond the value system of Western capitalism; she even embraces reform school as a state-sponsored solution to her daughter's problems, seeing it as a means to shift a personal responsibility that is crushing her ("No need lick'em, no need kaukau money"). Mrs. Lee's philosophy of behavior is based purely on monetary relationships. "Ah Mui, you go tal da teacher only reech-kine peepul wear long lei all right . . . long kind, short kind, any-kind all right. Poor peepul go hana-hana, O.K. If no get flowers, no wear, see?" For her, "hana-hana" is the only means of existence.

Thus, what is coded as "Hawaiian" through the play promises some respite from the overwhelming social emphasis on money and work. In particular, the lei becomes the symbol of hope, of escape through a different notion of valuation—where the life or light of indigenous Hawaiian cultural values replaces, however tentatively, the terms of self-improvement through hard work, modernization, and education. The isolated and pleasureless domestic toil of Mrs. Lee is contrasted with the labors of Ah Mui and Leilani, who intersperse their making of leis with playful banter, hulas and rhumbas, and dreams of new dresses. Leilana tells Mrs. Lee that Ah Lan is good for picking flowers, if not for doing housework; she reminds Mrs. Lee that should Ah Lan fall into the river, she "no can make lei for you, too." Significantly, when Mrs. Lee receives a day off her job in order to get ready for lei day, she spends her "vacation" working at home. The allusions to leis, to the natural beauty of the islands, suggest an idyllic life that is almost fully eclipsed in the rest of the play by the scramble to get ahead. Even the play's setting— the bleak tenements with their laundry lines and garbage cans—is a far cry from the romanticized portraits of Hawai'i suggested by the leis.

In a spirit of hope, of determined extravagance, Ah Quon decides to buy his sister a "peenk" carnation lei, believing it will save her from delinquency. The final dialogue of the play—where Ah Quon initially asks his mother for money as a reward for telling his sister to go back to school, and then decides to buy his sister a lei for the school program— presents a figurative transition away from the "old" terms of both "Chinese" familial duty and the "new" economy of "hana-hana" to a third possibility, albeit a highly tentative one. That is, what might redeem Ah Lan (if she is not, as suggested by the ominous siren that sounds later in the play, already lost to the river) is the lei that her brother buys for her as an opulent gesture of brotherly affection.

What might be called the "Hawaiian way" is presented in Yee's *For You a Lei* as an alternative to capitalistic interethnic competition, to "white" or even "Asian" ways of living and knowing. When the play draws attention to the problems of urban poverty, it does not suggest that the resolution to such problems is only in the ethic of hard work, education, assimilation, and competition that distinguishes what will later be labeled the "model minority" variety of Asian American success. In this way, Yee's play questions the values by which communities and individuals are supposed to climb the socioeconomic ladder— industry, discipline, personal and familial sacrifice. The play also questions the ends of the Asian American rise to "whiteness" through competition with the "other." Thus, *For You a Lei* joins other works in Willard Wilson's collection to provide a means of reenvisioning ideal relationships among those of different ethnic identities while reevaluating how the concepts of work and upward mobility reconfigured the real and imagined lives of Asian Americans in prewar and postwar Hawai'i. Together with the other works comprising *College Plays*, Yee's *For You a Lei* helps reveal and explain the tensions, uncertainties, and contradictions within the variety of Asian American identities on the move during the mid–twentieth century.

Notes

1. *College Plays* is one of three overlapping collections. Volumes I–IX of "University of Hawaii Plays 1958–1969" includes plays from the playwriting classes taught by Edward A. Langhans of the Department of Drama. "Theatre Group Plays 1946–1969" includes 14 volumes of plays from the annual University of Hawai'i Theatre Group Playwriting Contest, edited by Edward A. Langhans.

2. Roberta Uno, for instance, calls these student writers "a pioneering generation of Asian American playwrights" and praises Wilson for having "fostered the emergence of a new drama, focusing on the Asian experience in Hawaii, expressed in a uniquely Asian American dialogue" (1993, 5). Also see chapter 1 of my *Performing Asian America: Race and Ethnicity on the Contemporary Stage* (1997). Charlotte Lum's *These Unsaid Things* and Wai Chee Chun Yee's *For You a Lei* appear in *Paké: Writings by Chinese in Hawaii*, edited by Eric Chock (1989). Bessie Toishigawa Inouye's *Reunion* is in *Kumu Kahua Plays*, edited by Dennis Carroll (1983).

3. This by no means constitutes the majority of the plays. Of the 127 plays included in these volumes, only 22 were written by students with obviously Asian surnames.

4. It is not clear who, aside from Wilson and perhaps other students in the class, would have played audience to these works; the majority of them were clearly written as assignments by first-time playwrights, rather than as scripts for professional production. The few that saw any kind of production were only performed in student workshops or one-time amateur productions at the University of Hawai'i. Indexed in "Theatre Group Plays 1946–1969" are those plays that the University of Hawai'i Theatre Group awarded or produced locally. Among those that the University of Hawai'i Theatre Group produced were Bessie Toishigawa's *Reunion* (May 7–10, 1947), Robert Suyeoka's *The Return* (May 13–14, 18–21, 1949), and Clara Kubojiri's *Country Pie* (Jan. 9–10, 15–17, 1953).

5. Although Misha Berson's *Between Worlds* (1990) is often hailed as the first collection of contemporary Asian American plays, it was in fact Dennis Carroll's *Kumu Kuhua Plays* (1983) that was the first widely distributed published collection to include works by Asian American writers from Hawai'i such as Edward Sakamoto and Bessie Toishigawa Inouye.

6. See, for instance, Yuko Kurahashi's *Asian American Culture on Stage: The History of the East West Players* (1999) and Dorinne Kondo's *About Face: Performing Race in Fashion and Theater* (1997), as well as *Performing Asian America* (1997).

7. The 1989 median incomes of ethnic groups in Hawai'i (from 1993 U.S. Census figures) are as follows: Black $27,338; Caucasian $41,878; Chinese $48,518; Filipino $41,955; Hawaiian $37,960; Japanese $52,982; Korean $37,420; Samoan $23,914; Total $43,176 (Okamura 1998, 196).

8. Such concerns are expressed at more length in the articles by Morales (1998) and Fujikane (1994), as well as Houston Wood's *Displacing Natives: The Rhetorical Production of Hawai'i* (1999).

9. One example were the tensions following the landslide win of Democrats in territorial elections in 1954 and subsequent political victories for Democrats later. Although Filipinos as well as Japanese Americans supported the Democratic party, the former did not enjoy the rise in economic status of the latter, but were "regarded as mere junior partners" (Haas 1992, 21).

10. The 1993 U.S. Census figures for the ethnic composition of Hawai'i report the following percentages: African American 2.4%; Caucasian 31.4%; Chinese 6.2%; Filipino 15.2%; Hawaiian 12.2%; Japanese 22.8%; Korean 2.2%; Puerto Rican 2.3%; Samoan 1.4%. The 1994 Hawai'i Health Survey gives a somewhat

different picture: African American 1.5%; Caucasian 24.1%; Chinese 4.7%; Filipino 11.4%; Hawaiian .8%; Japanese 20.4%; Korean 1.1%; Puerto Rican 0.3%; Samoan 0.3%; Mixed part Hawaiian 35.5; "other mixed" 17.5%. Both are cited in the editor's introduction to *Multicultural Hawai'i: The Fabric of a Multiethnic Society* (Haas 1998, 19).

11. Mary L. Dudziak and Robert G. Lee have provided us with some figures: "While overseas investments grew at about 10 percent per annum—twice the growth rate of domestic investment—American investment in the Pacific Rim outside Japan brought a 25.5 percent return on investment, and investment in the Japanese economy brought in 11.3 percent. Between 1951 and 1976, the book value of American investments in the Pacific Rim grew from $16 billion to $80.3 billion" (Dudziak 1998; qtd. in Lee 1999, 156).

12. I have chosen to retain the playwright's spelling, "Okasan," even though the Japanese title for "Mother" is generally rendered as "Okaasan" in current American orthography.

13. For a summary and critique of this model, see Omi and Winant (1994).

14. An upper-class white woman, Thalia Forescu Massie accused five local men, Benny Ahakuelo, Henry Chang, Horace Ida, Joseph Kahahawai, and David Takai of rape and assault. After a deadlocked jury found insufficient evidence to convict these men, Ida was seized on the street and severely beaten, and Kahahawai was killed by Massie's husband, mother, and friend. The subsequent trial of the three murderers resulted in conviction, but they were released after serving just one hour of their sentences in the judge's chambers.

15. Du Puy concludes with the satisfactory progress of "Americanization" of the "oriental races" (1932, 127–28) and argues for the potential self-government of this "new . . . human material" (131).

16. My essay "Asian Americans in Progress: *College Plays 1937–1955*" focuses specifically on interracial romances and plays depicting nisei veterans.

17. I have found only one significant example involving a Korean family, in *Mama's Boy* by Margaret C. Kwon (Volume I). Interestingly enough, here the mother opposes her daughter's marriage to a Chinese man, whom the mother describes as a "foreigner"; the daughter's wish to marry seems directly tied to her desire to leave her alcoholic, abusive mother and their impoverished household: "He's nice, so nice. He dresses swell, he's polite, he has a good job, and—and he likes me. And I want to marry him—even if he's Chinese."

18. *For You a Lei* received its first reading by the Rainbow Interpretation Organization (RIO) at a workshop of "Literary Pioneers" at the *Lucky Come Hawaii: The Chinese in Hawaii* conference held at the East West Center on July 20, 1988 (Chock 1989, 235). Also see Sumida (1986, 312).

Works Cited

Bell, Roger J. 1984. *Last Among Equals: Hawaiian Statehood and American Politics.* Honolulu: University of Hawai'i Press.

Berson, Misha, ed. 1990. *Between Worlds: Contemporary Asian-American Plays.* New York: Theatre Communications Group.

Carroll, Dennis, ed. 1983. *Kumu Kahua Plays*. Honolulu: University of Hawaiʻi Press. Chock, Eric, ed. 1989. *Paké: Writings by Chinese in Hawaii*. Honolulu: Bamboo Ridge Press.

Dudziak, Mary L. 1988. "Desegregation as a Cold War Imperative." *Stanford Law Review* 41 (November): 61–120.

Du Puy, William Atherton. 1932. *Hawaii and Its Race Problem*. Washington: U.S. Government Printing Office.

Fujikane, Candace. 1994. "Between Nationalisms: Hawaii's Local Nation and Its Troubled Racial Paradise." *Critical Mass* 1 (Spring/Summer): 23–57.

———. 2000. "Asian Settler Colonialsim in Hawaiʻi." *Amerasia Journal* 26 (2): xv–xxii.

Haas, Michael. 1992. *Institutional Racism: The Case of Hawaiʻi*. Westport, CT: Praeger.

———. ed. 1998. Introduction. *Multicultural Hawaiʻi: The Fabric of a Multiethnic Society*. New York: Garland.

Kent, Noel J. 1983. *Hawaii: Islands under the Influence*. New York: Monthly Review Press.

Kondo, Dorinne. 1997. *About Face: Performing Race in Fashion and Theater*. New York: Routledge.

Kurahashi, Yuko. 1999. *Asian American Culture on Stage: The History of the East West Players*. New York: Garland.

Lee, Josephine. 1997. *Performing Asian America: Race and Ethnicity on the Contemporary Stage*. Philadelphia: Temple University Press.

———. 2002. "Asian Americans in Progress: *College Plays* 1937–1955." In *Re/collecting Early Asian America: Readings in Cultural History*, ed. Josephine Lee, Imogene Lim, and Yuko Matsukawa. Philadelphia: Temple University Press, pp. 307–325.

Lee, Robert G. 1999. *Orientals: Asian Americans in Popular Culture*. Philadelphia: Temple University Press.

Morales, Rodney. 1998. "Literature." In *Multicultural Hawaiʻi: The Fabric of a Multiethnic Society*, ed. Michael Haas, 107–130. New York: Garland.

Okamura, Jonathan. 1998. "Social Stratification." In *Multicultural Hawaiʻi: The Fabric of a Multiethnic Society*, ed. Michael Haas, 185–204. New York: Garland.

Omi, Michael, and Howard Winant. 1994. *Racial Formation in the United States from the 1960s to the 1990s*. New York: Routledge. (Orig. pub. 1986.)

Sumida, Stephen. 1986. "Waiting for the Big Fish: Recent Research in the Asian American Literature of Hawaiʻi." In *The Best of Bamboo Ridge*, ed. Eric Chock and Darrell H. Y. Lum, 302–321. Honolulu: Bamboo Ridge Press.

———. 1997. "Postcolonialism, Nationalism, and the Emergence of Asian/Pacific American Literatures." In *An Interethnic Companion to Asian American Literature*, ed. King-kok Cheung, 274–88. Cambridge: Cambridge University Press.

Uno, Roberta. 1993. *Unbroken Thread: An Anthology of Plays by Asian American Women*. Amherst: University of Massachusetts Press.

Wilson, Willard, ed. *College Plays, Volumes I–X*. Typescript. University of Hawaiʻi, Manoa.

Wood, Houston. 1999. *Displacing Natives: The Rhetorical Production of Hawai'i.* Lanham, MD: Rowman & Littlefield.

Wright, Theon. 1972. *The Disenchanted Isles: The Story of the Second Revolution in Hawaii.* New York: Dial.

Yu, Henry. 2001. *Thinking Orientals: Migration, Contact, and Exoticism in Modern America.* Oxford: Oxford University Press.

7   Toyo Suyemoto, Ansel Adams, and the Landscape of Justice

JOHN STREAMAS

TOYO SUYEMOTO[1] was born in Oroville, California, in 1916, a time when laws were being passed in West Coast state legislatures forbidding immigrant Japanese, or *Issei*, from owning land. A second-generation Japanese American, or *Nisei*, Suyemoto grew up in Sacramento, in what she calls "a multicultural community, surrounded by numerous nationalities" (Moran 1995, 37). Encouraged by her mother to write poems, she published even as a teenager and became "one of the most prolific and talented of the prewar Nisei poets" (Yogi 1996, 68). She was a young mother in her mid-twenties when the war began; she and her family were among the 120,000 persons of Japanese descent, or *nikkei*, imprisoned in the remote concentration camps that the government called "relocation centers." She continued to write, and her work turned not more private, as one might expect of a writer imprisoned in a remote place, but more public.[2] Susan Schweik calls her "the Japanese American woman poet who gained the broadest possible reading public—though that breadth was extremely limited—outside Nikkei circles in the war years" (1991, 186).

Schweik argues that Suyemoto's work is "so relatively *presentable*" that, even as "resistance and critique" are "embedded within the forms and diction of poems," the poems themselves "appear apolitical" (186). Here I will examine six poems, five of them written during the war years in the Topaz camp in Utah, to argue that, while they remain "presentable" today, their "resistance and critique" were particularly relevant to the imprisoned nikkei community, and that the language of both their presentability and their critique is a simple language of landscape.[3] In these poems landscape is oppression, as in the racial geographies of plantations, reservations, and concentration camps. To stress this point, I will compare the senses of landscape in Suyemoto's poems and in

Ansel Adams's photographs of the Manzanar camp in the California desert.

In 1983 Suyemoto published in *Amerasia Journal* several poems and an autobiographical essay in which she says her wartime poems reflected "the conditions of internment" (1983, 75). Literary work produced in the camps was so subject to the exigencies of imprisonment that a writer could not assume a postwar legacy. More so than fiction, whose composition would have demanded stretches of time and a risky adherence to representational narrative, such short poems as Suyemoto's offer immediacy in verbal snapshots of oppression.[4] Suyemoto's tone is neither angry nor urgent; like her readers—the imprisoned Issei and Nisei—she knew that Japanese American oppression took the form not of torture and extermination but rather—because of the remoteness of the camps and the unknowable duration of the war—of monotony and banality. The embodiment of that monotony was for Suyemoto the Utah desert. For a racial community who had not lived in such a place, who had in fact prospered as farmers in regions of America where rain was relatively plentiful, a sudden and brutal removal to a prison camp in a remote desert was especially oppressive. Merely to describe the parched barrenness of the place would have sufficed to express commiseration and hint at outrage. Drawing upon the English and Japanese poetic traditions she had learned from her teachers and her mother, Suyemoto transformed description into a critique that her fellow inmates must have inferred. All these elements are evident in her poem "Gain," which appeared in 1942 in *Trek,* the Topaz literary magazine:

> I sought to seed the barren earth
> And make wild beauty take
> Firm root, but how could I have known
> The waiting long would shake
>
> Me inwardly, until I dared
> Not say what I would gain
> From such untimely planting, or
> What flower worth the pain?

The tone and sentiments here contrast with those of "Transplanting," which Suyemoto published in *Trek* in 1943:

> No anchorage in shallow dust,
> No searching hold has found
> More than shadows to grasp
> Where hope withers in the ground.

Oh, guard the exposed roots against
Untimely sun and wind;
Some other soil may prove
More flower-wise and kind.

So let a richer earth restore
What once had died in need.
Strong roots will then respond
And bear tomorrow's seed.

Considered chronologically, these poems move progressively away from the personal. "Gain" appeared in the first year of the poet's incarceration, and its speaker feels personally the earth's barrenness. For it is she who "sought to seed the barren earth," she who shook inwardly and finally refused to speculate on the "untimely planting" and "the pain." "Transplanting" was published in the second year of Suyemoto's incarceration, and it develops a biblical trajectory from the first stanza's "shallow dust" and shadows and withering hope to the third stanza's assurance of strong roots bearing "tomorrow's seed." But now the speaker herself appears in none of this—at least not to speak strictly for herself or to lament personal misfortunes. She does not say that it was she who sought anchorage in dust, whose hope withers as she grasps at shadows. Yet it is no generic person who narrates the poem, no Everywoman, either. For the bleakness that the narrator points to in the first stanza is not ubiquitous; somewhere "other soil" is kinder to flowers and "richer earth" restores life. Indeed, such life-sustaining soil could be brought to this desolate place to sustain strong roots and seeds. But it is the narrator's immediate audience, the unnamed "you" inhabiting the first stanza's desolate location, who must "guard the exposed roots" and set the new soil to its restorative work, thereby following the narrator's injunction to transform a wasteland into a paradise. Hope itself is transformed into a certainty that strong roots will "bear tomorrow's seed."

"Topaz," published in mid-1944 in *All Aboard,* the final issue of the Topaz literary magazine, seems at first glance to mimic the tone, bleakness, and two-stanza structure of "Gain":

The parched earth waits for April miracles
Though spring was done so long ago
(As if the summer sun could be
Incentive for the grass to grow!)

The dust is lost upon the careless wind,
Seeds choked in unwatered sand—
How can roots defy the drought
Denied the shelter of the land?[5]

Considered more carefully, however, the apparent tonal and structural resemblance to "Gain" is far less significant than its particular kind of impersonality. As in "Transplanting," the speaker is not evident, and is not a personal presence. But in "Topaz" there is no addressee, no "you" either. The grammatical subjects of all clauses, dependent and independent and absolute, are "earth," "spring," "sun," "dust," "seeds," and "roots"—and yet none of these nouns functions as a subject, for the earth waits impossibly for miracles, the sun is only mockingly a spur to growth, dust is lost, and the roots cannot defy drought. Nature is not an actor but is acted upon, or at least exploited by an extranatural power that enforces barrenness as punishment. The poem's existence depends on the central tension it creates: it disallows a human presence, yet it exhibits a distinctively human voice, speaking without self-reference but in pained sarcasm: "As if the summer sun could be/Incentive for the grass to grow!"

Despite its seemingly conventional structure, "Topaz" is formally looser than most other poems Suyemoto wrote in camp. It is also more strident. It asks a question that is less inquiry than assertion or accusation, pointedly underscoring issues of evacuation and incarceration. It obliquely refers to the uprooting of Nisei from the productive West Coast farms or businesses they managed or owned prior to the war. Nisei—the generation of Suyemoto's peers—could legally own land on reaching adulthood; and for this reason, they represented to racists a greater threat than their immigrant parents. The forced removal of Nisei from their homes and lands was a betrayal of trust and of fundamental rights of citizenship. In fact, while Suyemoto and most of her Topaz neighbors came from cities in the San Francisco Bay area, the majority of them had strong ties to the land: of working Japanese Americans in California, Oregon, and Washington prior to the war, 45 percent labored in the growing of crops or plants and another 18 percent worked in "wholesaling, retailing, and transporting food products" (U.S. Commission on Wartime Relocation and Internment of Civilians 1982, 122).

Yet the poem's reference to "roots" without "land" surely recalls the plight of Issei, who prior to the war were altogether prohibited from owning land. Following the war, both Issei and Nisei faced restricted rights of property ownership. Dillon Myer, who directed the War Relocation Authority (WRA), the civilian agency that managed the camps, referred to Japanese Americans in the title of his memoir as "uprooted,"[6] but western states where the camps were located denied many Japanese Americans the opportunity to take root, even after the war. And all Japanese Americans were forced to meet rigid "re-settlement" rules specifically designed to prevent Japanese American "community-building." In its final line, the poem obliquely addresses the denial of internees' rights to perceive land as "shelter." Instead, sand is their inheritance; and seeds in sand take no sheltering root but, like dust, blow away in the wind. Thus, the poem finally underscores the poignant irony that a people prevented from taking root can hardly be uprooted.

With so much of prewar Japanese America's economic survival dependent on the land and its produce, with nature providing themes and images of traditional Japanese poetry, and with most Issei and Nisei sharing the experience of evacuation and imprisonment in remote and barren places, Suyemoto could afford to use metaphorical shorthand and to risk certain assumptions about the inability of white censors to intuit her political implications. Such metaphors are delivered in ellipsis, in the cultural codes of Japanese America. Suyemoto did not know her parents' language well enough to write in it, but she was well educated in both Japanese and English poetic traditions. She conveys her poetic meaning, therefore, in the modes of both traditions. In *haiku* and *tanka*, barren or desolate surroundings are invariably used to suggest the poet's own physical or spiritual impoverishment or hunger. In traditional English literature, a barren landscape is an unnatural one; and to the non-nikkei reader, "Topaz" is a glimpse of suppressed growth, a glimpse of the American landscape as nature gone unnatural. To the nikkei reader, "Topaz" also encodes the human origins of the unnatural landscape: the equally unnatural and impoverishing forces of human suppression.

In much of its propaganda the WRA referred to the camps as "colonies" and to the inmates as "pioneers" whose mission was to develop and improve a land. Schweik charges that the WRA deliberately located the camps "on desert terrain in order to take advantage of Issei skill at improving soil" (1991, 88), and historian Sandra C. Taylor writes that the government hoped to use Topaz after the war "as a showplace to demonstrate the latest in agricultural methods" (1993, 109). In recent years Topaz has been shown, ironically, not always to have been a barren, desolate place. Utah scholar Leonard J. Arrington writes that native peoples who lived there for hundreds of years named it for an abundance of water, as it once held "a lake formed in Pleistocene times and connected with the Great Salt Lake" (1997, 21). In the nineteenth century white migrants cut canals and irrigation ditches that made a relative garden of the place once "so desolate in aspect," says Arrington, "that many visitors remarked that the site must have been chosen to prevent the inhabitants from maintaining contact with the outer world" (22). Arrington's description recalls Suyemoto's own geographical memories:

> The climate ranges from a boiling 106 degrees in summer to a frigid 30 degrees below zero in winter. The rainfall averages between 7 and 8 inches per year. One characteristic of the area is the wind, which keeps up a seldom interrupted whirl of dust. Another is the non-absorbent soil which, after a rain, is a gummy muck, ideal as a breeding ground for mosquitoes. (22)

To internees who were, like Suyemoto, primarily from "the Bay Area, San Francisco and Oakland" (Taylor 1993, 104), the Topaz desert must have seemed particularly forbidding and discouraging.

Long before the camp was closed, many Topaz inmates had had contact with the world immediately outside the camp, most frequently in seasonal agricultural labor "on sugar beet, fruit, and livestock farms" in west-central Utah (Arrington 1997, 49). Although Topaz itself never achieved any important degree of agricultural self-sufficiency, the WRA purchased water and piped it into camp so that inmates not only grew vegetables and grains but also raised poultry and livestock (38). Suyemoto does not describe or even mention this agricultural labor in her camp poems, yet her imagery alludes to the agricultural facts of Topaz life. Surely the effect of her poems would have been diminished if the only agricultural referent for internees had been the comparatively easy labor they had performed on northern California farmlands. When Suyemoto writes of "hard earth" and "barren ground," of "parched earth" and "shallow dust," she writes from knowledge of and experiences with the soil of the Utah desert—as well as from memories of a very different and much more fertile previous home. Topaz *was* a barren place of alkali soil; and the WRA would not have called it a "colony" if the site had been habitable to the Mormons and others who had tried, says Arrington, to settle it in the previous century (21–22). The low level of agricultural self-sufficiency achieved at Topaz was frustrated by workers' having to devote most of their labor to maintaining and improving residences and public utilities (38). But the physical aspects of life in Topaz—the harsh land and climate, the hard work of building and maintaining—matter only because of the racial geography of the camp.

While Suyemoto wanted her poems to reflect "the conditions of internment," the reader of "Topaz," which is ostensibly about a parched

land's barrenness, must infer those conditions. Apparently the moni-
tors of the WRA did not infer them. If today some readers who share
neither the poet's race nor her wartime experiences can infer her meanings, it is mostly because in the 1960s *Sansei*, or third-generation Japanese
Americans, worked with civil rights movement contemporaries to make
racial awareness a social and cultural imperative. Indeed, it is crucial
to remember that Suyemoto wrote at a time when racism and paranoia
pervaded American culture—and when virtually all Japanese American
discourse was held to be secretly subversive and traitorous. Therefore, it
is between layers of referential connotation and racist overreading that
Suyemoto insinuated her sense of camp life and injustice. Writing about
the poems "Gain" and "In Topaz," Susan Schweik follows Suyemoto
into this inner layer of meaning:

> The packed figure of "barren ground" which links both these poems in-
> vokes, with a sharp political edge, more than the obvious extremity and
> deprivation of the physical conditions of camp life—dust storms, freez-
> ing cold, and blistering heat, sunbaked, unyielding dirt. It is important to
> bring to the *Trek* poems, as Suyemoto's Japanese American readers at the
> time would have brought to them, a sense of a whole politics and mythol-
> ogy of agriculture in Nikkei experience: of an American "promised land"
> which kept revealing itself to immigrants from Japan as a wasteland, pre-
> venting them from owning property in their own names, exploiting their
> labor; . . . of the WRA's deliberate choice to locate camps on desert terrain
> in order to take advantage of Issei skill at improving soil. (1991, 188)

Unfortunately, nikkei literary culture largely disintegrated after the war,
and so those Issei and Nisei readers who comprised Suyemoto's only
sure audience no longer read or sponsored the literary magazines or
critical journals most likely to have published her work. Recognition
and appreciation had to wait for the silence-breaking, canon-expanding
1970s and 1980s.[7]

Japanese Americans' attitudes toward their incarceration did not necessarily follow the trajectory of these three poems, moving from personal
frustrations to communal imperatives and finally to considerations of
exploited nature. Yet the injustice done to them almost dictated such a
development. For after the first losses of personal belongings and following their imprisonment as "enemy aliens," they were thrown into
deserts whose very soils must have seemed a cruel rebuke to their agricultural knowledge, skills, and needs. And then, as they became recon-
ciled to the drabness of their barracks, their surroundings, and their very
lives in camp, they quite naturally would have turned to one another

for emotional stability, forming sustaining alliances and friendships. Finally, as endurance itself became less and less a question, their thoughts might well have turned to issues of injustice and the many disruptions of camp life.

Such disruptions have been well documented: the administration of the so-called "loyalty oath" to all adult internees, the institution of programs for "relocating" younger nikkei to the East and Midwest for work or school, and the enactment at the war's end of federal and state "band-aid" programs that failed to provide adequately for older Issei. Poems like Suyemoto's map the otherwise undocumented responses to the monotonies and disruptions in camp life. Peter T. Suzuki claims that "poetry circles, poetry publications, and poetry contests developed in all the camps" (1977, 244); and, though the tanka he has examined were written in Japanese, many of them echoed Suyemoto's concerns. Violet Kazue de Cristoforo observes that the many wartime *kaiko* (or "freestyle") haiku she translated from Japanese into English expressed "the turmoil and anguish" suffered by their imprisoned writers; these haiku, she insists, comprised "a poetry of resistance to the inhumanity of war" (1996, 16–17). While most WRA administrators were unlikely to have a poetic sensibility or, by 1944, to consider poems as potential agents of subversion, camp literature in English still must have borne some risks—especially work that, like Suyemoto's, was written in accessible language. One might consider, for example, Suyemoto's "In Topaz," published in 1943 in the second issue of *Trek*. The accusatory subtext of this poem is barely concealed:

> Can this hard earth break wide
> The stiff stillness of snow
> And yield me promise that
> This is not always so?
>
> Surely, the warmth of sun
> Can pierce the earth ice-bound,
> Until grass comes to life
> Outwitting barren ground!

Unlike "Topaz" and "Transplanting," this is a winter poem: the earth is barren, to be sure, but it is also "hard" and "ice-bound." Racial and cultural tensions are transformed into a clash between forces of nature. The hard earth may "break wide" the deathly "stiff stillness of snow" and the sun's heat may pierce the ice that, coffin-like, encases it; but until grass "outwits" the ground, the earth remains barren. The certainty of

"Transplanting," in which roots will bear seed, is now only a conditional hope that the sun *may* melt the ice so that "ground-outwitting" grass may grow. But the obvious implication is that, while the sun will melt ice, it probably will not transform barren ground into fertile fields. Like Suyemoto's other camp poems, "In Topaz" asks a question. The answer is cast in vague hopefulness and persistent ironies. That is, "In Topaz" is not a perverse riddle or a monologue of delusion but a common-sense assessment. It asserts that, realistically, the snow and ice merely reinforce the soil's deadening character; and yet it holds out the possibility of resistance, of piercing and outwitting threatened loss.

The last of Suyemoto's wartime poems that I wish to examine is "Growth," written in September 1945, one month after Japan surrendered and one month before Suyemoto and her family left Topaz:

> Have I so changed with time
> That songs I once wrote pall
> By judgment grown mature
> And thus more critical?
>
> The one who sang was then
> So young, not yet aware
> That doubts and questions were
> To be her daily fare.
>
> And now in wonderment
> I ask: how did that child
> Develop so her songs
> And life were reconciled?

Here is a return to the personal, the first person. The speaker looks back on the places and times she has occupied. The poems she once wrote—before the war, before the camps—were songs of innocence. This poem opens and closes on questions; the first of these is answered in the second stanza. The second stanza also suggests an answer to the closing question, as obviously the work of maturing in both life and art depends on a growing awareness of the "doubts and questions" that are "daily fare." Of course, the truest answer to the closing question is that the speaker developed as she and her racial community were removed from their homes and imprisoned in unfamiliar, barren places. She expressed these "doubts and questions" in the poems she wrote while imprisoned; and if here she assumes the luxury of looking back on her progress, it is only because her imprisonment is nearly over. She looks not at parched earth and icy crusts but at the poems she wrote about them.

"Growth" is therefore a crucial proleptic retrospective, a glimpse into a future when the poet might enjoy the detachment that follows deliverance from trauma and precedes wonderment. Yet even six decades later Suyemoto spoke of her life in the desert in the spare language of her camp poems. Surely all imprisoned nikkei had a sense of landscape as oppression, but Suyemoto's poems, merely by describing the desert's harshness, articulated this sense. And surely many sympathetic non-nikkei understood the significance of the camps' locations in isolated, unfamiliar places.

But some did not understand, including Ansel Adams, who wrote these words in his introduction to *Born Free and Equal,* his collection of Manzanar photographs:

> I believe that the arid splendor of the desert, ringed with towering mountains, has strengthened the spirit of the people of Manzanar. I do not say all are conscious of the influence, but I am sure most have responded, in one way or another, to the resonances of their environment. (qtd. in Armor and Wright 1988, xvii)

Underlying Adams's sense of the land's beauty and majesty is a suggestion of its superiority over the internees. The deserts of Manzanar and—by extension, of Topaz—were harsh, according to Adams, only for as long as they were unfamiliar. After a few months' adjustment, then, internees could only be inspired and empowered by the landscape. If in 1942 Adams had traveled to Topaz and read "Gain" in a copy of *Trek,* he might have understood and sympathized with Suyemoto's frustration and despair over "barren earth," "untimely planting," and the waiting that "long would shake/Me inwardly." After all, the desert was new and unfamiliar to the poet, he would say, and soon its beauty would raise her spirits. But in 1943, when Adams first took his cameras to the camp at Manzanar, he might have been surprised to know that the author of "Transplanting" still longed for a home with a "richer earth" and "strong roots" and remained resentful of a desert that gave its imprisoned inhabitants only "shallow dust," "shadows," withering hope, "exposed roots," and "untimely sun and wind." And in 1944, when Adams's photographs were earning the acclaim of New York liberals, "Topaz" still spoke of parched earth waiting vainly for the miracles of a long-overdue spring that might never return. Again, the poem's urgent but disembodied voice seems to blame not nature but man—an outside force that turns the desert into a punishment, a weapon.

Many of Adams's exterior views of Manzanar in 1943 show, in the background, mountains whose size and majesty diminish the desert landscape and the heat's effects.[8] In "Catholic Church" and "High School Recess Period," foregrounded Manzanar streets fill the scenes, and dust bears the imprint of feet and tires. But the dust, though dry, is not hot, as the students and churchgoers wear winter coats and caps and scarves, and the mountains behind the students are partly blanketed by snow. The imprisoned here are busy and social, apparently unharmed by their environment and even inured to its seasonal processes.

Two of Adams's best-known works come from his visits to Manzanar. Of "Winter Sunrise, the Sierra Nevada, from Lone Pine, California, 1944" Jonathan Spaulding writes, "The two-dimensional series of horizontal bands give the image its modernist simplicity and strength, while the vast three-dimensional space and enveloping light give it the romantic grandeur he often sought out in the war years" (1995, 207). And of "Mount Williamson, the Sierra Nevada, from Manzanar, California, 1944" Mary Street Alinder says, "It is ripe with the mystical and holy presence that Ansel believed permeated the area surrounding the camp" (1996, 240). And while Adams himself wrote that it was "the arid splendor of the desert, ringed with towering mountains" that had "strengthened the spirit of the people of Manzanar," he nevertheless sought "romantic grandeur" and "mystical and holy presence" in the mountains, the clouds, and the play of sunlight in distant planes—and not in the camp itself or even the desert surrounding it. Furthermore, Adams documents this "mystical presence" as a free and mobile observer, viewing the camp and its inhabitants close up or from afar; otherwise, he chooses not to view them at all. Therefore, his relationship to the landscape was fundamentally different from that of the Japanese Americans imprisoned in the camp. His Manzanar work represents, says Spaulding, an "attempt to portray the natural landscape in social terms" (1995, 206); and yet, despite his belief in the injustice of the incarceration, he failed to understand that landscape can be a tool of injustice, that even people imprisoned in Eden are not free to appreciate paradise, let alone those imprisoned in hell. Instead, as he took in the far-distant landscape surrounding the camp, he projected his own awe and wonder onto the inmates of Manzanar.

This is not to say that beauty cannot exist in a site of injustice. Nor should Adams necessarily be faulted for attempting to create visions of romantic grandeur and mystical presence through his photographs of the Manzanar internees. But the difference between his and Suyemoto's visions of the landscape—one as inspiring, the other as oppressive—is not merely the consequence of differing experiences. For even if Adams had been imprisoned in the desert, his experience would have remained different from that of all other internees, given that he had not known lifelong racism. Thus, he is simply wrong when he suggests that acts of prejudice are aberrations, merely occasional visitors to peoples of color, and that the incarceration of Japanese American citizens was no more or less than a particularly regrettable aberration of wartime hysteria. His landscapes inhabit a geography that is oblivious to racism, because it exists outside his experience, his known social arena.

A community whose ethnicity or "race" determines the place of its location—or relocation—knows that place (or landscape) itself inhabits or constitutes a racial geography. Adams looks beyond parched earth to towering mountains. Suyemoto is clearly aware of the towering mountains near her own camp in Topaz, but what she nevertheless continues to *see*, even in her third year of imprisonment, is parched earth and choked seeds. To be sure, Japanese Americans adjusted to their prisons, even eking out an agricultural life of sorts. But such "improvements" did not undo the fact that they were imprisoned in the desert. Though they improvised gardens, they still lived among exposed roots, barren earth, and dust "lost upon the careless wind."

In 1944 Adams's photographs traveled to a museum in New York, while Suyemoto and her poems remained imprisoned. The photographs were meant to ennoble and inspire, the poems to reflect "the conditions of internment." Although audience and intention differed for Adams and Suyemoto, landscape was, in both cases, a function of both art and politics. But while Adams's art, through its unexamined politics, reaffirmed mainstream authority and ideals, the surer politics in Suyemoto's poems stirred the inmates. In this crucial way the poems differ from Adams's Manzanar landscapes, which presume to reveal a racial community whose very presence they do not comprehend.

Long before the war, Suyemoto had found her voice in traditional poetic forms. As a "war poet" she had the advantages of a literary education, a literary mother, and artistic maturity; still, she had to learn to fit her voice to the contingencies of war. Earlier I noted Schweik's argument that Suyemoto embeds "resistance and critique" in poems whose forms and diction would seem to discourage politics. Here I will add that this embeddedness is partly a function of time and location. If, sixty years after these poems were composed, readers have little trouble seeing the resistance and critique in Suyemoto's artfully simple declarations and questions about dust and drought and stunted growth, it is largely because the politics of the poems have risen to the surface. Non-nikkei readers in Suyemoto's time—particularly those few, such as WRA readers, who had a chance to see the poems—may well have noticed the critique. But few, if any, would have noted the resistance. The Topaz camp was, after all, in a harsh desert, and so an imprisoned poet steeped in Japanese poetic tradition might reasonably be expected to write harshly about her natural surroundings. But even if she had wanted to, Suyemoto could hardly have admonished her nikkei readers to active revolt; therefore, her resistance is more deeply embedded still—in encouraging the kind of thinking within her readers that will lead to resistance. Not only did the war confine Suyemoto and her community—through an indefinite and unknowable sentence—to a few barren acres of desert sand, it similarly constricted Suyemoto's literary universe to the barbed-wire confines of the Topaz camp. Therefore, the personal and the political in Suyemoto's discourse are implicitly bound together.

In such a closed system, where distinctions blur between public and private, Suyemoto obviously had to write with caution. Still, she could assume that her small pool of readers would understand her referents and (in Frank Chin's phrase) her "Japanese American English."[9] Nevertheless, in her closed world even a hint of political engagement was a step into the public realm. That her camp poems have outlasted the oppression that provoked them indicates not the triumph of a particular resistance but the continuing relevance of fighting oppression in contingent yet historically informed ways.[10] In contrast, Adams's Manzanar landscapes survive as monuments to the natural world and to his vision of that world—but not to nikkei empowerment.

Years after the war Suyemoto would revisit the Utah desert in a poem called "Topaz, Utah." No longer needing to link the harshness of the landscape to racial injustice, Suyemoto recognizes that, for some creatures at least, the desert is home. The poem's final stanza bears quoting for its obvious contrasts—especially in subject and tone—to the wartime poems:

> Stillness is change
> For this abandoned place, where strange
> And foreign tongues had routed peace
> Until the refugees' release
> Restored calm to the wilderness,
> And prairie dogs no longer fear
> Where shadows shift and disappear.

> The crows fly straight through settling dusk,
> The desert like an empty husk,
> Holding the small swift sounds that run
> To cover when the day is done.
>   (transcribed in Yogi 1996, 68)

Here, as in the wartime poems, the desert is "like an empty husk," only now it is empty because the Japanese American internees are no longer part of it. But here too is an awareness that the desert sustains some life. Long before Japanese Americans became prisoners, prairie dogs and crows and other creatures established themselves in a natural world of "stillness" and "calm" and "small swift sounds" that has been restored now that the prison is gone. This awareness of desert life in the postwar poem does not contradict or undo the sense of barrenness and death in the camp poems. Rather, it reinforces the earlier work's descriptions and themes. For the immediate effect of the injustice, an effect that remained at the core of Suyemoto's poetic sensibilities during her three years in Topaz, was the intense and smothering sterility that necessarily defines any racial geography. Suyemoto can see the desert's fullness only long after she has been released from its prison.

During the war, Suyemoto wrote in "Transplanting" that "hope withers in the ground" where hands find nothing more substantial to hold than shadows. Even after the war, in her more generous description of the desert in "Topaz, Utah," Suyemoto perceives the landscape as being hospitable only to flying crows and bold prairie dogs—and she still sees shifting and disappearing shadows. The memory of racial geography forever haunts its old landscapes. In a 1995 review-essay for *The Nation*, poet Lawson Inada quotes the last four lines of "Topaz, Utah" and honors Suyemoto as "our major Camp Poet and Nikkei Poet Laureate" (1995, 206). The slow but steady discovery of Toyo Suyemoto reinforces this view among contemporary readers who can only wonder at the sure and steady courage of her resistance and critique.

Notes

Acknowledgments: I wish to acknowledge the indispensable support of a grant from the Civil Liberties Public Education Fund and the equally indispensable critiques and suggestions of the editors and of my wife Valerie Boydo. Toyo Suyemoto generously shared her poems as well as her insights and information on Japanese American history and culture. I made final revisions after learning of her passing, but still I thank her for her inspirational friendship. I use her poems here with her verbal permission.

1. She was known, and published, under her married name, Toyo Kawakami or Toyo Suyemoto Kawakami. At least one critic uses her married name. But most of the poems I will discuss here were published under the name Toyo Suyemoto, and as she expressed a preference to be known in print by this family name, this is the name by which I refer to her.

2. The biographical material is from sources I cite and my formal interviews and casual conversations with Suyemoto. As will become evident, my reading of her poems draws heavily upon the important study by Susan Schweik, *A Gulf So Deeply Cut* (1991). Schweik's most significant contribution is her insistence that contemporary readers historicize the poems.

3. As my citations indicate, my textual source for "Growth" is the poet's own typescript copy and for "Topaz, Utah" a critical study (Yogi 1996). "In Topaz" was first published in February 1943 in the second issue of *Trek*. As *Trek* and its successor *All Aboard*, though produced by Nisei writers, were officially published by the government—the official publisher is The Projects Reports Division, Central Utah Relocation Center—and as they are available only in historical archives and museums and in some Japanese American family collections, I will note here that "Gain" may be found in Schweik's essay. I have discovered no contemporary, easily accessible reprintings of "Topaz" and "Transplanting." By "war years" I mean not only the time of the exclusion and incarceration of Japanese Americans but also the tense period before Pearl Harbor when war between Japan and the United States seemed imminent and when war had already begun in Europe.

4. Suyemoto told interviewer Grant Din just how quickly she could produce poems for the camp magazine. Asked by Miné Okubo to produce a poem within hours, she eagerly complied:

> I'd finish a poem, write it out neatly, tack it on the door to the barracks, and along about 3 o'clock [in the morning!] I'd hear footsteps on the path, and I could hear Miné's voice talking to her brother, who always accompanied her, and, you know, the door opened, and a few steps, the door closed, and the poem would appear in the new issue of *Trek!* (qtd. in Schweik 1991, 181)

5. In *All Aboard* the second line of the first stanza of "Topaz" was published as "Though spring was done a long ago." In an interview with me, Suyemoto says that the indefinite article "a" in this line should have been "so," and so I provide the correct version of the poem here.

6. His title is *Uprooted Americans*, which is curious not only for its acknowledgment of an uprooting but also for his noun "Americans." His subtitle identifies Japanese Americans, but the main title could easily have been *Uprooted Japanese Americans*. To compound the irony, the book unavoidably discusses noncitizen Issei as well as Nisei who renounced their citizenship.

7. The idea of breaking or shedding silence appears in the titles of several poems, stories, and books by Japanese Americans. For example, an early anthology of Asian American poetry took its title from Janice Mirikitani's poem "Breaking Silence," a poem that also appears, with the title poem and another

called "Prisons of Silence," in Mirikitani's book *Shedding Silence;* and Yasuko I. Takezawa titled her study of the redress campaign *Breaking the Silence.* Silence as an important theme in nikkei literature is examined by King-Kok Cheung's study of the fiction of Joy Kogawa and Hisaye Yamamoto, *Articulate Silences.*

8. Most of Adams's camp photographs may be found in the Armor and Wright book *Manzanar* (1988)."Winter Sunrise" and "Mount Williamson" appear in most collections of Adams's work; I viewed them in the exhibit *In Praise of Nature: Ansel Adams and Photographers of the American West,* mounted by the Dayton Art Institute. Though Adams's Manzanar book *Born Free and Equal* seems to have been badly reproduced in insufficient numbers and soon went out of print, several of its images appear often in books on the incarceration, and in 1978 the Wight Art Gallery at University of California, Los Angeles, mounted the exhibit *Two Views of Manzanar,* offering Adams's work beside the work of nikkei inmate Toyo Miyatake.

9. I borrow the phrase from Frank Chin et al., who wrote in the introduction to their anthology *Aiiieeeee!* that in the camps "a Japanese-American English was developed and the symbols of the Japanese-American experience codified" by writers such as Suyemoto and Hisaye Yamamoto (1974, xxxiv).

10. After the war Suyemoto lived in Ohio, where her studies and work in universities brought her into contact with prominent writers and scholars. Among them, poet Karl Shapiro and critic David Daiches praised her poems—as she told me in my interviews with her.

WORKS CITED

Adams, Ansel. "Mount Williamson, the Sierra Nevada, from Manzanar, California, 1944." *In Praise of Nature: Ansel Adams and Photographers of the American West.* Dayton Art Institute, Dayton. 30 Oct. 1999–2 Jan. 2000.

———. "Winter Sunrise, the Sierra Nevada, from Lone Pine, California, 1944." *In Praise of Nature: Ansel Adams and Photographers of the American West.* Dayton Art Institute, Dayton. 30 Oct. 1999–2 Jan. 2000.

Alinder, Mary Street. 1996. *Ansel Adams: A Biography.* New York: Holt.

Armor, John, and Peter Wright. 1988. *Manzanar. Photographs by Ansel Adams, Commentary by John Hersey.* New York: Vintage.

Arrington, Leonard J. 1997. *The Price of Prejudice.* Delta, UT: Topaz Museum. (Orig. pub. 1962.)

Chin, Frank, Jeffery Paul Chan, Lawson Fusao Inada, and Shawn Wong, eds. 1974. Introduction. *Aiiieeeee! An Anthology of Asian-American Writers.* Washington: Howard University Press.

de Cristoforo, Violet Kazue. 1996. *May Sky: There Is Always Tomorrow. An Anthology of Japanese American Concentration Camp Kaiko Haiku.* Los Angeles: Sun & Moon.

Inada, Lawson Fusao. 1995. "Ghostly Camps, Alien Nation." Review of *Democracy on Trial: The Japanese-American Evacuation and Relocation in World War II,* by Page Smith. *Nation,* Aug. 28, pp. 204–11.

Moran, Virginia. 1995. "Jewel of the Desert." *Aim* (Fall): 37–39.

Schweik, Susan. 1991. *A Gulf So Deeply Cut: American Women Poets and the Second World War.* Madison: University of Wisconsin Press.

Spaulding, Jonathan. 1995. *Ansel Adams and the American Landscape: A Biography.* Berkeley: University of California Press.

Suyemoto, Toyo. 1942. "Gain." *Trek,* December, p. 20.

———. 1943. "Transplanting." *Trek,* June, p. 8.

———. 1944. "Topaz." *All Aboard* (Spring): 53.

———. 1945. "Growth." Typescript. Sept. 12, Poet's papers.

———. 1948. "Transplanting." *Common Ground* 7 (4): 10.

———. 1983. "Writing of Poetry." *Amerasia Journal* 10 (1): 73–79.

———. 1996. "In Topaz." In *Quiet Fire: A Historical Anthology of Asian American Poetry* 1892–1970, ed. Juliana Chang, 54. New York": Asian American Writers' Workshop.

———. 1998. Personal interview by John Streamas. June 9.

———. 2000. Personal interview by John Streamas. Apr. 28.

Suzuki, Peter T. 1977. "Wartime Tanka: Issei and Kibei Contributions to a Literature East and West." *Literature East and West* 21: 242–54.

Taylor, Sandra C.1993. *Jewel of the Desert: Japanese American Internment at Topaz.* Berkeley: University of California Press.

United States Commission on Wartime Relocation and Internment of Civilians. 1982. *Personal Justice Denied.* Washington: U.S. Government Printing Office.

Yogi, Stan. 1996. "Voices from a Generation Found: The Literary Legacy of Nisei Writers." *Forkroads* 5 (Fall: 64–73).

8   Wounded Bodies and the Cold War: Freedom, Materialism, and Revolution in Asian American Literature, 1946–1957

VIET THANH NGUYEN

IF THE Eaton sisters' lives and writing represent a basic template of ethical choices for Asian Americans, the lives and work of Carlos Bulosan and John Okada represent a midcentury update of these choices, framed in the declining moments of a racial equilibrium they shared with the Eatons. The period of the Great Depression through World War II and the Cold War that Bulosan and Okada lived and wrote in was therefore a time marked by both optimism and pessimism for Asian Americans, as new opportunities developed for people of color even as their violent suppression continued. These were conditions that ultimately gave these authors the ability to be moderately more confrontational with American society than the Eaton sisters. Like the Eaton sisters, Bulosan and Okada presented their concerns about racial oppression through gender and sexuality, in this case through the lives of Asian American men who are deeply wounded by the racial violence and discrimination that often worked through emasculation. *America Is in the Heart* (1946) and *No-No Boy* (1957) are Bulosan's and Okada's attempts to recuperate the wounded bodies of Asian American men, speaking to American society in terms that it could understand: freedom and materialism. In *America Is in the Heart*, the narrator, Carlos, presents himself as someone like other Americans during the eve of World War II, concerned with being free, especially as the shadow of fascism looms.[1] Freedom becomes a coded concept in the book for the struggle not only against fascism, which could bind all Americans together, but also against racial discrimination and labor exploitation, which pitted Americans against each other. In *No-No Boy*, Ichiro, the "disloyal" Japanese American who refuses to swear allegiance to the United States during World War II and is subsequently sent to prison, proves on his return that he is a "true"

American by conceding the importance of American wealth—houses, furnishings, cars, and businesses—which has been bestowed upon the "loyal" Japanese Americans.

Bulosan's and Okada's choices, like those of the Eaton sisters, were strategic attempts to be heard in American society as they talked about difficult issues, respectively the exploitation of Filipino Americans and the incarceration of Japanese Americans. While both were forthright about the historical events with which they were concerned, and did not shy away from identifying with their ethnic descent, the rhetorical strategies they chose produced different consequences for their work. In Bulosan's case, the language of freedom and antifascist struggle proved popular amongst American audiences, while in Okada's case, the lack of such outright appeal to an America that was in the heart, an appeal that might offset the horrible events with which he was dealing, meant that *No-No Boy* would disappear almost immediately.

In both cases, however, the recuperated manhood presented at the books' conclusions were compromised or limited by the authors' flexible strategies, their decision to accommodate, even marginally and ironically, the demands of dominant society. In *America Is in the Heart*, hopeful Carlos embraces a feminized America, but he can never embrace a (white) American woman. In *No-No Boy*, Ichiro finds a lover, but his desire to reenter American society with all of its material promise comes at the cost of ignoring the significance found in the broken bodies of dead friends. Seemingly the only way out of the dilemma these authors faced as they confronted a postwar society bent on believing itself to be the bastion of world freedom, even as its own foundations were undermined by racism, was to step outside of that society altogether. This is what Bulosan did in his novel *The Cry and the Dedication* (1995), which can be read as a companion text to *America Is in the Heart*. Set in the Philippines during the Huk rebellion, which lasted from 1946 to 1956, *The Cry and the Dedication* is the consummated romance of revolutionary struggle that *America Is in the Heart* could not be. The manhood that the United States denied to Filipino migrant laborers as an extension of its own racist colonial policies in the Philippines is reclaimed by Bulosan in *The Cry and the Dedication*, both as a requirement of political revolution and its allegory in the novel, sexual fulfillment. Bulosan is able to imagine a revolution, not only of Filipino peasants against Filipino elites but the colonized against their neocolonial masters of the Cold War, the United States. The rhetorical reliance upon the concept of freedom that is the basis of *America Is in the Heart* is gone, suggesting that it was only outside of the political and cultural space of the United States—even in an imagined fashion—that Bulosan could be at his most critical of American imperialism and its related domestic racism.

These three books are signposts of an era in decline, a time of racial equilibrium marked by the racial dictatorship of whites, whose violence in the earlier part of the twentieth century is marked for Asian Americans in literary history by the work of the Eaton sisters. While the Eatons could be considered the origins of Asian American literature in English, Bulosan and Okada, by critical consensus, are the most important Asian American writers of the midcentury.[2] Bulosan and Okada are not panethnic entrepreneurs like Winnifred Eaton, yet their flexible strategies demonstrate that they struggled with the political and cultural regime of the United States as it transformed itself into a superpower whose rule was justified by its own sense of democratic exceptionalism. Their efforts to construct a usable manhood within the confines of this regime are testimony to the limits of a domestic Asian American literature, circumscribed not only by geographical borders but by the ideological borders of an America that was not only in the heart but in the mind as well.

WORLD WAR II AND THE COLD WAR

America Is in the Heart was published in 1946, *No-No Boy* was published in 1957, and *The Cry and the Dedication* was written sometime in the early 1950s. These dates are significant in the history of the Cold War. In 1946, Winston Churchill delivered a speech in Fulton, Missouri, in which he coined the term "the iron curtain" in order to characterize the rule of the Soviet Union over eastern Europe. This speech is the rhetorical commencement of the Cold War, and marks the transformation of the Soviet Union from being an uneasy ally and rival of the United States to becoming its outright enemy. The shifting nature of the Soviet Union's representation in the United States would also mark the changes in American society's perception of Carlos Bulosan. While Bulosan and *America Is in the Heart*, which chronicles the travails of a Filipino migrant laborer in the 1930s and his eventual reconciliation with America, were initially well received in the United States, Bulosan himself would eventually be blacklisted by the FBI and die in poverty and obscurity in 1956.[3] The transitional quality of the year 1946, in which the United States was transformed from an uneasy ally and rival of the Soviet Union into its outright enemy, signals the changing reception of Bulosan's book from its initial reception to its later disappearance.

In the year after Bulosan's death, 1957, two events of the Cold War occurred, one that we remember—the launching of Sputnik—and one that we forget—the death of Senator Joseph McCarthy. The contrast between the two events in terms of historical significance is evidence of a drastic shift in the Cold War's domestic importance for the United States. After 1957, the Cold War was no longer defined primarily in terms of McCarthyism and its attendant atmosphere of demagoguery, hysteria, and persecution. Instead, the Cold War came to be marked by something more insidious and dangerous still: the consolidation of both an internal security state and the military-industrial complex, which were cemented together by a deeply embedded American lifestyle of anticommunism.[4] The launching of Sputnik, which inaugurated the space race, becomes important here because of its status as a major factor in enhancing the feeling of insecurity in the American population that the internal security state and the military-industrial complex were designed to stem. Insecurity and the constant buttressing of security through military spending and domestic surveillance thus became two of the primary agents of action in the Cold War.[5]

It was also in the year 1957 that John Okada's *No-No Boy* was published. *No-No Boy* is a book that is marked by its obsession with disloyalty, insecurity, surveillance, and confession. Like *America Is in the Heart*, one of its central characters is America itself; unlike Bulosan's book, in which America is a contradictory symbol of both democratic pluralism and international socialism, America in *No-No Boy* is an ambivalent icon primarily because of its embodiment of the limits of pluralism, limits that are defined by the dissent that bears the name of disloyalty. In *No-No Boy*, two modes of disloyalty are in operation: the original disloyalty of the no-no boy and the invisible, overarching presence of the communists and other un-American types who presumably infested America at the time of *No-No Boy*'s writing and publication. The promises of American pluralism and the specter of disloyalty are prominent influences in the shaping of a postwar Asian American culture. In some ways, the postwar period witnessed the growth of opportunities for Asian Americans that had been initiated during World War II, as the United States found itself caught in its own contradictions, arguing that it was waging a war to protect freedom and democracy while exercising racial discrimination domestically. This recognition of contradiction compelled the United States to repeal the Chinese Exclusion Act in 1943, finally allowing legal Chinese immigration—at a quota of 105 per year. The repeal of the Chinese Exclusion Act, with its combination of political symbolism and marginal change, is emblematic of the moderate shift in conditions for Asian Americans.[6]

The pattern of progress and setback continued for Asian Americans in the 1950s. The gains in immigration made by Chinese Americans through their status as "American allies" during the war were bittersweet and short-lived: they became the objects of persecution during the McCarthy era, as all Chinese in the United States were tainted by association with Red China. In the case of Japanese Americans, incarceration in concentration camps was countered by the achievements of Japanese American soldiers that eventually altered white American perceptions of Japanese Americans and allowed for the creation of a Japanese American middle class. Korean Americans finally became visible in American society, but only because the Cold War heated up in Korea in 1950. Perhaps the only Asian American group who did not suffer additional negative consequences in the years after World War II were Filipino Americans, who benefited from the white American perception of them as brave allies during the war and afterward.[7] The mixed results and marginal gains in civil rights and domestic opportunities for Asian Americans developed in contrast with the domestic Cold War environment of surveillance and countersubversion, which saw un-Americanness in every act of nonconformity and disloyalty in any un-American act. Therefore, even as World War II created limited political and social opportunities for people of color, the Cold War imposed greater restrictions on Americans as a whole, and American society remained a racial dictatorship. For Asian American men in particular, there was the opportunity to pursue the economic benefits of a patriarchal society massively geared for war while still being worried about the continuing and wounding effects of racism.

MASCULINITY AND THE MATTER OF RACE

Masculinity and heterosexuality become important dimensions of Asian American experiences because of the ways in which the American public sphere has been defined as a masculine and heterosexual place that rules over a feminized and maternalized private sphere.[8] Michael Kimmel describes the transition from manliness to masculinity for the northeastern elite as one from an "essence" to a "performance" of manhood, in which masculinity had to be proven by the acts and appearance of the body, rather than through its restraint (1996, 120). Economic and cultural changes at the end of the century helped to propel "performative" masculinity into dominance by the 1930s. Performative masculinity was in large measure the legacy of Theodore Roosevelt, who had argued earlier in the century that imperialism and warfare were crucial to regenerating masculinity and civilization, insisting that "an effeminate race was a decadent race; and a decadent race was too weak to advance civilization," and that "only by embracing virile racial expansionism could a civilization achieve true manhood." This process, Roosevelt taught, "was the ultimate meaning of imperialism" (as summarized by Kimmel 1996, 190).

In relation to Roosevelt's racial discourse of masculinity and civilization, both Carlos and Ichiro initially occupy positions that might be defined as what R. W. Connell (1995) calls "subordinate" masculinities, which still carry the power of being a competitive threat to hegemonic masculinity. It is not surprising that as men of subordinate masculinities, Carlos and Ichiro wrestle with the roles, privileges, and accomplishments of hegemonic masculinity, which, being denied to them, may seem both desirable and execrable at the same time. Both struggle to attain a more dominant kind of masculinity than has been granted to them. For Ichiro, the sign of dominant masculinity is the ability to own actual things or commodities that represent the owner's access to the economic life of a wealthy American society, and the attendant ability to settle down—to buy a house and start a family. To be a patriarch in the mode of a middle-class white man thus entails economic privilege in *No-No Boy*. For Carlos, the important possession is not so much material things as a public identity, a life in the public sphere of politics and power that was denied to men of color, and a life that for Carlos meant being a poet and political activist. Since the public and private spheres in American society were traditionally gendered, the struggle for Carlos to be a man of the public sphere also entailed a corollary effort to define those women who might supplement him. Metaphorically, this effort is realized in the conclusion of *America Is in the Heart*, with its vision of America as a feminized, embodied land that embraces Carlos.

In both their visions, what becomes clear is that a masculine Asian American body politic is not only a racial subject but always at the least a gendered and sexed subject. The history of the Asian American body politic's regulation and production through exclusionary and discriminatory legislation demonstrates this intertwined history of racial and gendered formation.[9] Domestic American orientalism was put into practice through such legislative acts as the Page Law of 1875, which forbade the immigration of Chinese women as prostitutes on the assumption that all Chinese women immigrants were prostitutes, and in various antimiscegenation statutes that were passed because of fear concerning the depraved sexuality of "Mongolian" and Filipino men.[10] These attempts to regulate the Asian American body politic were clearly designed to control the reproduction of the population, and also to limit the possibilities for and potential of work and mobility.

The Asian American body politic, produced from these discourses of discrimination, is thus a material body (Butler 1993, 9), but it is also deeply embedded in the movement of labor and capital; and its bodily, material shape is partially albeit inevitably determined by work. Labor, meanwhile, being racially determined in the United States, is itself distorted and shaped by the signification of race in the legal code and system that limited and limits the possibilities of Asian American life and existence in the United States.[11] For Japanese and Filipino Americans at this time, their bodies mattered because the exploitation of their labor was inseparable from the construction of their race, gender, and sexuality. Because their labor was inexpensive and their humanity was in question, Filipino Americans' lives were, according to Bulosan, "cheaper than those of dogs" (1946, 143); as beasts, then, their behavior and identity were dehumanized and even criminalized, especially their sexuality.[12]

For Carlos, the awareness of the way Filipino sexuality is perceived in American eyes means that his efforts to claim manhood and the prerogatives of the public sphere must be joined with a disavowal of the "natural" sexual desires that white men take for granted as well as of the "criminal" sexual desires projected onto Filipinos. In contradistinction to the discourse of bestiality that white society uses to demonize Filipinos, Carlos must enact a discourse of revolutionary morality, one that is both politically conscious and sexually chaste. This discourse finds its others in two kinds of women in the United States, those who are chaste or virginal (and who are usually white) and those who are eroticized (and usually of color). As Rachel Lee argues convincingly, eroticized women are associated with the social circumscription and economic exploitation of Filipino men (1999, 23–25). These women—Indians, Mexicans, or poor whites—are the only ones allowed to sexually interact with Filipino men.[13] In repeated incidents throughout *America Is in the Heart*, such women lure men into degraded behavior, maritally entrap them and destroy their futures, or turn one man against the other.[14] Carlos is horrified to discover that the "bestial Filipino" is not simply a white-imposed racist stereotype but an actual condition that he and his fellows seem to be sinking into. After a scene in which one friend has sex with another friend's wife, he says, "I almost died within myself. I died many deaths in these surroundings, where man was indistinguishable from beast. It was only when I had died a hundred times that I acquired a certain degree of immunity to sickening scenes such as . . . this" (*America* 135). Ultimately, Carlos' experiences with degradation (most often through erotic women) "fuel [his] desire for a less hostile and fragmented community that seems possible only by way of excluding [these women's] eroticized presence" (Lee 1999, 206).

Carlos turns to chaste women who represent the opposite of exclusion, exploitation, and degradation, namely inclusion into "American" society and the fulfillment of America's pluralist promises. Rachel Lee lists the women in question—Eileen and Alice Odell, Miss Mary Strandon, Doris Travers, and Marian—who nurture and educate Carlos when he is at his lowest (1999, 31–32).

Eileen is the personification of "the *America* I had wanted to find," "an America [which] was human, good, and real" (235). The sexual unavailability of the chaste white women who embody America is testimony to America's paradoxical qualities in *America Is in the Heart*.[15] Inasmuch as America ostensibly offers democracy and community to immigrants of all backgrounds, the fact that the nation is represented metaphorically through such women demonstrates what the entire text of the book makes clear: that the ideal America is ultimately unreachable for the Filipino immigrant. The famous conclusion of the book makes the representation of America through the figure of a woman explicit:

> It came to me that no man—no one at all—could destroy my faith in America again. It was something that had grown out of my defeats and successes for a place in this vast land . . . something that grew out of our desire to know America, and to become a part of her great tradition, and to contribute something toward her final fulfillment. I knew that no man could destroy my faith in America that had sprung from all our hopes and aspirations, *ever*. (326–27)

The feminization of the land and its representation as a body or a part of the body (the heart) in Bulosan's passage is a common trope in American literature, as Annette Kolodny has demonstrated in her book *The Lay of the Land* (1975). Yet, the metaphor of America as a female body is, for Filipino men, an irony, since this is one "lay" they cannot have, denied to them legally through antimiscegenation laws and the violent hatred of white men for Filipino men and the sexual threat they embodied. The image of the implicitly white, feminized American body with its "huge heart unfolding warmly to receive me" can be suitably contrasted to what Carlos sees as he is being forced by other men to lose his virginity: "I trembled violently, because what I saw was a naked Mexican woman waiting to receive me" (159); the act subsequently leaves him "trembling with a nameless shame" (160) that eventually disappears with the promise of this other embrace that America offers.

For Marilyn Alquizola (1989 and 1991), the ending is ironic in another sense, namely that it flatly contradicts the evidence of the entire book, which has been a litany of racist abuse by whites toward Filipinos. Alquizola argues that Carlos' "hopes and aspirations" are, in the end, meant to be considered as foolish by the astute reader, as they are by Carlos himself, the ironic narrator. E. San Juan Jr. (1995b) and Michael Denning (1997) read the ending of *America Is in the Heart* differently, arguing that it is not so much ironic as strategic. Its celebration of an America with universal potential and its apparent erasure of racist oppression should be understood as expressions of the Communist Party's Popular Front rhetoric. The Popular Front from 1935 to 1947 sought to rearticulate the language of the American Dream and American possibility in the service of anti-Nazi fascism and an alliance between the United States and the Soviet Union during World War II, temporarily submerging or muting the language of international class struggle.[16] Mainstream readership interpreted the celebration of America in Bulosan's book as an act of consent to a deeply mythological vision of the nation. Ironically or strategically, and regardless of the specific interpretation assigned to the conclusion of his novel, Bulosan compromises with American pluralism in the conclusion, exercising a standard rhetorical trope of a feminized America and erasing any sign of erotic desire on his part. The domestic masculinity he constructs for himself is ultimately one that disavows the erotic as a "privilege" too dangerous to claim.

CLASS, CULTURE, AND THE COLD WAR

While American readers initially may have thought of Bulosan's book as an act of consenting to the nation, it was the implicit idea of consent, or consensus, as the political basis of democracy and freedom that ironically undergirded mainstream American anticommunism within only a few years of the publication of *America Is in the Heart*. In the absolute, Manichean vision of Cold War political demonology, communism became associated with not only subversion but also deviance, and hence many categories of noncommunist deviance became politically suspect by association. *No-No Boy*, with its distinctions between "good" Japanese Americans and "bad" Japanese aliens, enacts the central role for minorities and other suspected deviants during the era of the Cold War in which the novel was written—their default status as political demons. The only escape from the closed world of countersubversion was to accept as vociferously as possible its vision of good, which, to quote Robyn Wiegman, is defined by "America," "this nation's most pervasive and contested ideology . . . that rhetoric of nation, narrative of origin, and abstract locus of supposedly equal entitlements" (131).

Japanese Americans, of course, had experienced in the 1940s how abstract the idea of "equal entitlements" actually was. In February 1943, Japanese Americans in concentration camps were asked to prove their loyalty by the federal government through responding to a questionnaire titled "Application for Leave Clearance." Question 27 read: "Are you willing to serve in the armed forces of the United States, wherever ordered?" Question 28 read: "Will you swear unqualified allegiance to the United States of America and faithfully defend the United States from any or all attack by foreign or domestic forces, and forswear any form of allegiance or obedience to the Japanese emperor, to any other foreign government, power or organization?"[17] Ichiro and numerous others answered no to both questions. In the 1950s, with the memory of the internment and the loyalty oath fresh in their minds, Japanese Americans witnessed the creation of a federal employee loyalty program, mandated through Truman's Executive Order 9835, where 13.5 million federal workers, or a total of 1 in 5 American workers, were subject to security checks by 1953; 4,756,705 were actually checked, and the FBI conducted 26,000 field investigations.

While the situation of federal workers and Japanese Americans is far from a perfect comparison, the loyalty program was premised on the same logic of the internment and the loyalty questionnaire to which Japanese Americans were subjected, on the basis of a presumption of guilt. The difference, besides race, was that the federal loyalty program and various other state, municipal, and academic loyalty oaths and investigations subjected the entire American population to the presumption of guilt, which led to what Joel Kovel characterizes as "a time of massive conformism around a resurgent mythology of patriarchy"; society was "united around the patriarchal expulsion of the red devil as well as a around a triumphant consumerism. . . . The fear of nuclear annihilation overshadowed all others . . . fear became omnipresent. It spread to all spheres of personal existence" (Kovel 1994, 106). Domestic anticommunist liberalism was therefore a logical extension of two things, American anxiety over foreign threats and the danger of nuclear war, and a long-standing American xenophobia.

Resulting American anxiety led to increased defense spending, which grew from $13 billion out of a GNP of $285 billion in 1950, or 4.6% of the GNP, to $50 billion of a GNP of $365 billion in 1953, or 13.8% of the GNP (Brands 1993, 39). To a large extent, domestic prosperity was accelerated because of this defense spending, so that by the mid-1950s, while "six percent of the world's population lived in the United States . . . [the US was] producing and consuming over a third of the goods and services of the planet. American industry used half of the world's steel and oil, and three fourths of all the cars and appliances on earth were consumed in the United States. Real gross national product (GNP) increased from $206 billion in 1940 to more than $500 billion in 1960" (Whitfield 1991, 69–70). The reality of this Cold War prosperity filters into *No-No Boy*, where the presence and function of commodities is made explicit: commodities such as cars, televisions, houses, and furnishings are signs of not only prosperity but loyalty. That is, the Nisei veterans and their families live in middle-class luxury, while the disloyal Japanese Americans live in poverty. The reward for loyalty, both during World War II and then implicitly during the Cold War, is the participation in America's bounty.

The ownership of property and commodities, which is the most material sign of assimilation into American culture, is therefore a corollary to the willingness to sacrifice one's life and body for this American culture. This is illustrated most graphically by Kenji, a Nisei veteran who befriends Ichiro. Kenji has lost a leg in the war, and the gangrene that is eating away at the stump eventually kills him. Kenji's reward for his service and his leg is a new Oldsmobile from the government. More importantly, the material wealth is something that his entire family of American loyalists shares in: "Hisa and Toyo are married to fine boys, Hana and Tom have splendid jobs, and Eddie is in college" (Okada 1957, 118). The house is noticeably decorated with "new rugs and furniture and lamps and the big television set with the radio and phonograph all built into one impressive, blond console" (118). The material wealth is mirrored by the happiness of the family, a Japanese American version of the Cleavers or the Nelsons or other happy, well-adjusted middle-class white families that filled the TV screens of the 1950s during the writing of *No-No Boy*. In contrast to Ichiro's fragmented family, where the mad mother rules over an emasculated father, and where Ichiro's younger brother hates him so much he organizes an assault on Ichiro, Kenji's family is depicted as loving, communicative, upwardly mobile, and fecund. Kenji's sacrifice has enabled his family to survive the community-destroying effects of relocation, which Harry Kitano (1991) argues is a process of internal colonization.[18]

Thus, *No-No Boy* demonstrates that for one to belong to America, one must be able to claim the right to own things, the right to have things that belong to oneself. This, like the "crime" of draft resistance and refusal to declare loyalty, are catch-22s: Japanese immigrants could not become citizens, and in some states, noncitizens could not buy property.[19] Perversely, in the eyes of Ichiro and other Americans, the most tangible sign of the Issei's refusal to become American is their refusal (even when they had the chance) to buy property and, short of buying property, of buying the commodities—furniture, decorations, luxuries—that would testify to permanence. Yet, when the Japanese did own property or leased the farm property they worked on, they were perceived by other Americans as an economic threat to American small farmers. Exclusive rights to citizenship and ownership become legal methods justifying an already existing anti-Japanese racism, and Ichiro accepts the law without seriously questioning its hypocrisies and inconsistencies. He is therefore able, without irony, to regard his brother Taro's decision to run away from home and join the army as the one he should have made: Taro will "come out [of the army] and walk the streets of America as if [he] owned them always and forever" (81).

For those suspected of disloyalty like Ichiro, the Cold War accelerated the xenophobia already present in American society. Within this climate, *No-No Boy*'s portrayal of Ichiro takes on added significance. His plight as a suspected traitor, and the consequences he suffers of exclusion, isolation, imprisonment, paranoia, and stigmatization, while a direct product of and reference to the internment camps, can also be read as an implicit commentary on the domestic Cold War. The lesson that the Japanese Americans learned foreshadows the lesson that the majority of Americans learned in the 1950s. This is that being American demanded a submission to a society structured around a state of permanent war, with a commensurate internal security apparatus that operated not so much by visibility as by omnipresence. Thus, while Ichiro rejected the legitimacy of detention in the concentration camps, he eventually consents to the virtual panopticon of American identity.[20] It is the all-seeing model of the panopticon that serves as the structure of countersubversive containment that *No-No Boy* as a Cold War text critiques. The panopticon limits the possibility of resistance, for Ichiro never believes that his no to the draft and to the loyalty oath can be construed positively, as a rejection of the contradictory demands of incarceration and patriotism. Instead, Ichiro, like a good prisoner, must learn to accept his punishment as just, his crime as actually illegal, and his rehabilitation as proscribed. In short, Ichiro must learn to confess, in a manner that reflects Cold War rhetoric, which offered suspected subversives the option of annihilation or therapy (Hinds and Windt 1991, 113–18). As Foucault (1979) might have put it, the Asian American body politic is no longer punished through violent spectacles of abuse, segregation, and persecution but is instead more effectively disciplined through learning to love America.

To fulfill the conditions of loyalty demanded by countersubversion, the alien must find another alien whom he can denounce and against whom he can define his necessary inclusion. Thus, it is because Ichiro cannot systematically understand American society and its racism that he turns inward to the Japanese American society he knows best in order to discover the alien. He is most concerned with his family, demonizing in particular his mother, who stands in for both an essential Japanese racial identity and certain of the forces that emasculate Japanese American men. Accordingly, Ichiro sees his father as an "old woman," a "goddamned, fat, grinning, spineless nobody" who was "neither husband nor father nor Japanese nor American but a diluted mixture of all" (Okada 1957; 6, 12, 116). Indeed, the mother's domination of the father is so complete that Ichiro believes they have effectively traded gendered roles: "[Pa] should have been a woman. He should been Ma and Ma should have been Pa. Things would have worked out differently then. How, I don't know. I just know they would have" (112). Being a "nobody" reflects the negation of the body and the spirit that emasculation entails, as Ichiro acknowledges when he describes himself using this term (76).

Ironically, the sign of being a nobody in *No-No Boy* is having a *whole* body. That is, in the context of the war, physical sacrifice for Nisei soldiers is the tangible sign of being *somebody*, of mattering in the public sphere of American life. In a slightly different but comparable way, militarism becomes a sign of masculinity during the Cold War; to be "soft" on communism, a common partisan political charge, was to be reluctant to use military force (Kovel 1994, 5). In *No-No Boy*, however, war participation had to be physically evident in order to overcome that other physical stigma: racial identity. Ichiro and Kenji's relationship demonstrates this irony of masculine and racial performance. Although Kenji's wound is fatal, Ichiro envies him, and remarks fervently that he would gladly trade places; Kenji, on reflection, agrees with Ichiro's assessment (Okada 1957; 59–65, 73).

Kenji and Ichiro's homosocial relationship becomes a ground for illustrating the performance of masculinity. As Butler (1999) argues, gender is a culturally compelled, reiterative performance; it is the variety of social acts that men undertake, consciously and unconsciously, to prove a concept of masculine identity that is based on the idea of an essence, a definable core of manhood that contradictorily should need no proof. Masculinity becomes a performance in the public sphere to demonstrate a private identity, as Kenji's case demonstrates (Kimmel 1996, 329–35). Kenji's missing leg and visible stump become symbols for the phallus: the missing leg is the physically disempowering price Kenji pays for the symbolic power that remains visible in the stump, so that the phallus is always absent but always present, bestowing power and extracting pain. The phallic and heterosexual dimensions of this missing leg are clear in Ichiro's envious appraisal of it:

> Give me the stump which gives you the right to hold your head high. Give me the eleven inches . . . [which] made it so that you can put your one good foot in the dirt of America and know that the wet coolness of it is yours beyond a single doubt. (Okada 1957, 64)

It is crucial to recognize that the phallic symbolism encodes Ichiro as having power as well, which becomes clear when Kenji, referring to their respective problems, asks, "Whose is bigger?" (64). Kenji answers his own question: "Mine is bigger than yours in a way and, then again, yours is bigger than mine" (65). The narrative demonstrates that masculinity is a wound, whose degree of injury is nevertheless a testament to the amount of power that is present. The ambiguity of Kenji's answer reflects his and Ichiro's inability to assess the nature of each other's sacrifice and damage consistently. The tragedy of the situation is that either choice, Ichiro's or Kenji's, ends with an equally crippling result: the destruction of the spirit or the destruction of the body. Ichiro's fear of spiritual death resonates with the rhetoric of the Cold War that depicted communism as an internal disease or sickness; Ichiro is fearful, then, of being consumed internally by this infection of disloyalty that he must excise (Hinds and Windt 1991, 9).

These attempts at excision manifest themselves in various ways: Ichiro's rebellion against his mother, his search for sexual fulfillment with Emi, the quest for worthwhile work, and the establishment of a masculine bond with Kenji. They are insufficient inasmuch as they are all attempts to enact, to perform, and to prove his loyalty and masculinity (an essence that should not have to be proven) against the seemingly undeniable, visible proof of his identity as Japanese (an essence that cannot be disproven). The only real resolution for Ichiro lies in renouncing the stage for this visibility: the body itself. For Ichiro, the racialized body is taken as the *cause* of racism, when it is in actuality an *effect* of racism. Okada demonstrates his ironic awareness of the difference when he writes in the preface to *No-No Boy* that Japanese Americans, as of December 7, 1941, had *become* "animals of a different breed" (1957, vii).[21] The preface, with its extended examination of the physical features of Japanese Americans that mean one thing before Pearl Harbor and something completely different after Pearl Harbor, testifies to the contingent nature of race: that it is not inherent but mutable, a product of social, political, and economic forces and negotiations that together comprise racial formation. In the course of *No-No Boy*, race is naturalized for Ichiro as an inherently visible property of the bodies of Japanese Americans.

Carlos also recognizes the problem of visibility, and to some extent he recognizes the production of a visible essence through racism. As he memorably noted, "It was a crime to be a Filipino in America. . . . [W]e were stopped each time these vigilant patrolmen saw us driving a car. We were suspect each time we were seen with a white woman" (Bulosan 1946, 121). To be a Filipino was to be continually under surveillance, to live in a police state, with the threat of actual imprisonment and violence always present. Carlos extended this understanding of his virtual imprisonment metaphorically, asking, "Was everybody moving toward a faith strong enough to blast away the walls that imprisoned our life in America?" (280) Even more than this, he understood that the visible mark of his criminal status—his body, rather than the uniform of the prisoner—threatened to become not merely an imposed sign but his actual self. He says, "I was running away from myself, because I was afraid of myself. I was afraid of all that was despairing in that swamp of filth—that dark dungeon of inquisitional terror and fear" (294).

For Ichiro, racial criminality is also present, in both literal and figural senses. Even though he has left prison behind him, he carries its memory with him like any reformed prisoner should, by being condemned to a "prison of forever" (Okada 1957, 40). He wonders why "in my freedom, I feel more imprisoned in the wrongness of myself and the thing I did than when I was in prison? Am I really never to know again what it is to be an American?" (82) For Ichiro, to be an American is to be free; in order to be free, he has to admit to the cryptic crime he has committed. And since his alleged crime has its roots not in an act but in the imposed stigmatization of his skin, absolution can be sought only in the disavowal of his body and its significance. Although this disavowal is not the only choice, but indeed is a choice based on a misrecognition of race as natural rather than social, for Ichiro the narrative of his liberation from his imprisonment is the narrative of forgetting his own body. On his return to Seattle, what he fears most is being seen by other Japanese Americans and being recognized for who he is and what he did. He is constantly aware of the fact that others recognize him for what he has done. Eventually, however, he confesses to the crime he has committed. "I have been guilty of a serious error," he thinks. "I have paid for my crime as prescribed by law. I have been forgiven and it is only right for me to feel this way" (232). His internal acknowledgment of his just imprisonment, his confession to the essence of who he is perceived to be and its link to his performance of ingratitude and rebellion, is immediately rewarded. "There was room for all kinds of people," he thinks. "Possibly even for one like him"; and indeed, this seems to be true, as he walks up to a "cluster of people . . . [who] hardly gave him a glance"(233).

In this penultimate chapter of the text, Ichiro believes that by confessing to his crime and consenting to a particular vision of America, he has been liberated from his body—a liberation that is ultimately put into question by Okada's conclusion. *No-No Boy* ends with Ichiro witnessing a concluding moment of violence, as Freddie, another no-no boy, is killed in a car wreck, while his adversary, a Japanese American veteran named Bull, is reduced to an infantile state, crying "like a baby in loud, gasping, beseeching howls" (250). Throughout the novel, characters' frustration at comprehending their situations has found expression only in incoherent screams like Bull's (12, 40, 68, 176), signifying their inability to articulate a positive answer to their double-bind dilemma—imprisoned at home and forced to prove their loyalty abroad. Thus, Ichiro's final, optimistic thoughts—that there is a "glimmer of hope," a "faint and elusive insinuation of promise" (250–51) in the America he occupies—are as insubstantial as they sound. Yet such thoughts were necessary, because, as Jinqi Ling (1995) argues, Okada was writing at a time in which the Civil Rights movement was just commencing, and he was writing of a time when Civil Rights as a movement did not yet exist, which circumscribed his options. Kandice Chuh agrees, stating that in "voicing . . . uncertainty, Ichiro expresses the unintelligibility of the American nationalist narrative that at once presumed disloyalty and demanded self-sacrifice" (1996, 106). As both Chuh and Ling make clear, Ichiro's confusion about the American narrative, resulting in his concluding optimism, is partially due to his inability to recognize the injustice of the loyalty questions and to imagine anything more than an individual, alienated response.

Both Carlos and Ichiro struggle to articulate masculine, American identities at the conclusion of the respective books. While Carlos shares with readers a more forceful conviction about American possibility than does Ichiro, both men are constrained by the limits placed on their imaginations by the American narrative of possibility. For Carlos, the narrative centers on American pluralism and its promise of inclusion; for Ichiro, it focuses on American law. That is, for Ichiro, it is the law that asks the questions that he cannot answer and to which he cannot demand alternatives. Carlos, in contrast, is trapped in the dilemma of the "American Way," as Sacvan Bercovitch (1993) has defined it. According to Bercovitch, America is unique among nations because it allows for dissent; but such dissent is ultimately limited by an implicit consent to the possibilities allowed (and dictated) by American democratic practice. In other words, the American Way itself is what one must finally consent to as an American, the common ground that enables people to agree to disagree. The American Way is thus an ideological space, and as Terry Eagleton argues, "Seen from within, [ideology] has no outside" (1976, 95) and accordingly defines the horizons of one's vision. In this limited realm of political maneuver, Carlos, as a narrator who is either ironic or strategic, must affirm the ideological basis of American society, its belief in itself as a place where true disagreement is possible. In the end, both Carlos and Ichiro must step outside the American Way, outside the ideological consensus of American society, if they are to articulate a masculinity that is not conflicted by the contradictions of American society relative to race. While neither Carlos nor Ichiro successfully negotiates this challenge in their respective histories, Bulosan imagines in his later novel, *The Cry and the Dedication*, a literal and ideological masculine space outside America.

REVOLUTION AND ROMANCE

While a close analysis of *The Cry and the Dedication* is outside the scope of this essay, a brief consideration of the novel's conclusion is necessary.

The novel is set in the Philippines during the time of the Huk rebellion, which lasted more than ten years, from 1946 until 1956.[22] As the novel unfolds, the group of rebels at its center, led by the heroic Hassim, brings a virginal woman named Mameng into its ranks, ostensibly to "restore" the health of Felix Rivas, with whom they are to rendezvous. Rivas is returning from the United States with money for the revolution. While he was abroad in the United States, Rivas had his testicles crushed by a gang of white Americans. But the rebels decide that Mameng, as a virgin, should not have to confront Rivas uninitiated (although why *any* form of sexual initiation would not be degrading is also not mentioned). Mameng's clear choice for her first lover is Hassim, but he, in turn and without any apparent reason, selects Dante. A stand-in for Bulosan himself, Dante is a writer with a poetic pseudonym who has lived in the United States for fifteen years. His writing involves "tracing our history from the revolutionary viewpoint"; but when he thinks about America, "a land he could not forget," he is torn between seeing it as a place of "bitterness" or of "great beauty" (Bulosan 1995; 5, 25, 18).[23] Dante, who knows "everything about Hassim, all, his political and private life," understands why Hassim has passed the task of sexual initiation to him: Hassim too has been sexually wounded, this time by Filipino government forces (116). Hassim the revolutionary leader and Rivas the revolutionary savior are parallel figures whose sexual damage at the hands of an American-sponsored government and American racism, respectively, are symbolic of the emasculation of poor Filipino men in the American empire. While such emasculation cannot be recuperated in the United States, where sex with white women is outlawed and sex with poor women and women of color is morally degraded, it can be recuperated in the Philippines through the instrument of revolution. The morally conscious Carlos of *America Is in the Heart*, struggling to come to dialectical consciousness, is realized in the figure of Dante, who returns from America as a sexually potent warrior of the revolution capable of initiating Mameng.

The figure of Mameng and the sexual act she must engage in have another symbolic dimension as well, which is represented in the landscape that the revolutionaries must journey through. As Hassim observes, "the land is barren" (52), devastated by war and oppression. It is the revolution that must save the land and make it fertile once more, and it is Mameng who must heal the revolutionaries and be made fertile herself. The embodiment of the land by a woman reflects the parallel personification of the American landscape as feminine in *America Is in the Heart*, but the distinct difference in *The Cry and the Dedication* is that Dante, unlike Carlos, can return the embrace that the woman offers. Bulosan writes that "because it was Dante who had seen other lands and years, it was through him that the expression of the resolution would be realized, then to be poured warmly upon Mameng, who was the denuded landscape" (54–55). She, in her turn, "would inundate with all her fertility the sterility of the world they were remaking, the world of their enemies" (59). While their sexual union figuratively restores the barren land, they themselves are also reborn as individuals from this union, transforming sexual intercourse into a fundamental act of revolution against the oppression of imperialism, capitalism, and racism that destroys humanity.

Bulosan's and Okada's flexible strategies involve an engagement with an ideology of pluralism and consensual dissent that neither author felt they could ignore, and which was deeply implicated in the racial relationships and representations of their moment of racial equilibrium. As long as Bulosan and Okada stayed inside that ideological space, their criticisms were muted, distorted, or marginalized by their readership and, to some extent, by themselves, as they relied on an authorial irony about racial relations and racial identities that many readers did not understand, even though that moment of racial equilibrium was in decline and heading for crisis. Perhaps because they could sense this decline and impending crisis, and because they were never sure that America's promise of inclusion was genuine, Bulosan and Okada failed as ethnic entrepreneurs. They created fictional personas who were not sufficiently "sold" on the American dream, and whose efforts on selling themselves as bona fide Americans were troubled by authorial suspicions about America.[24] Okada's *No-No Boy* is nevertheless the portrait not only of those Japanese Americans who refused, however ambivalently, the United States' call for patriotic duty, but of those in the ascending Japanese American middle class who were forced to pay for their success. Besides being an example of a flexible strategy, then, the novel also demonstrates a flexible strategy on the part of the Nisei generation who went to war fighting for a country that had compromised its ideals and laws.

It is only with *The Cry and the Dedication* that we witness what could be articulated once the author stepped outside of the ideological space of the American Way, and once his characters were situated outside of the geographical borders of the United States. Bulosan is able to articulate concerns that would not be domestically heard by other Asian Americans until the late 1960s. His recuperation of a wounded manhood, healed through a virile sexuality that enables and is enabled by a violent revolution, deploys a romantic model of nationalist revolution that is common to the narratives of an emerging anticolonial third world. In such a model, not only are race, class, and nation foundational to a revolution, but masculinity and heterosexuality themselves. Like the Huk rebellion that it draws from, *The Cry and the Dedication* fails to overturn the dominance of an American neocolonialism but marks a hot spot in the Cold War whose suppression is testimony to the threat that it posed to the American world order.

Notes

1. The narrator of *America Is in the Heart* is generally referred to as Carlos. In the book, the narrator undergoes two name changes, from Allos (in the Philippines) to Carlos (on coming to the United States), and finally to Carl (in a clear reference to Karl Marx) when the narrator undergoes a conversion to Marxism. The critical convention of calling the narrator Carlos refers to Carlos Bulosan, of course—despite the fact that the book is not so much a personal autobiography as a collective autobiography of the Filipino migrant.

2. For critical views of Bulosan in book-length surveys of Asian American literature, see Kim (1982, 43–57) and Wong (1993, 133–36); and for Okada, see Kim (1982, 148–56). The critic E. San Juan Jr. has made it his life's work to expound the importance of Bulosan to Asian American and radical literatures. For a recent selection of his critical work on Bulosan, see San Juan (1992, 1995, 1995a, 1995b). Finally, in his afterword to *No-No Boy*, Frank Chin (1979) describes the historical importance of John Okada's work, at least to Chin and his colleagues. For an account of the literary history of this time period for Asian Americans, and the impact of politics and publishing on *No-No Boy* in particular, see Jinqi Ling (1995, 360–62).

3. For autobiographical information on Bulosan's life, see Evangelista (1985) and Morrante (1984). According to E. San Juan Jr., Bulosan was the most visible of all Filipino American writers during the 1940s. His decline and downfall are illustrated in his death in 1956. He died on the steps of Seattle City Hall after a bout of drinking and pneumonia. By then, he had already been blacklisted as a subversive by the FBI. *America Is in the Heart* would not be reprinted by the University of Washington Press until 1973.

4. For general histories on this time period and the impact of the Cold War domestically, see Leffler (1994, 56–126), Gillon and Kutz (1993, 2–41), and Mason (1996, 8–22).

5. For accounts of the impact of McCarthyist anticommunism, see Albert Fried (1997) and Richard Fried (1990). For accounts of the more entrenched and structural version of anticommunism, see Whitfield (1991), Carmichael (1993), and Kovel (1994).

6. Immigration was relaxed in several ways after the repeal of the Chinese Exclusion Act. Subsequent to the war, the War Brides Act allowed American

servicemen to bring home wives of Asian nationalities. In 1946, Asian Indians were allowed naturalization rights and a small immigration quota. The McCarran-Walter Act of 1952 eliminated the racial restrictions of the 1790 naturalization law and allowed immigration from the "Asian-Pacific Triangle," but with only 100 immigrants from each nation of the triangle allowed. For a fuller account of these changes, see Takaki (1989, 357–418).

7. The Philippines, even after becoming independent from the United States in 1946, remained a critical part of the American strategy in the Pacific in the Cold War years. For detailed information on the changing situations of various Asian American groups in the immediate post–World War II era, see Takaki (1989, 357–405) and Chan (1991, 121–42).

8. For a history of American manhood and its relationship to the construction of public and private spaces, see Rotundo (1993), Kimmel (1996), and Bederman (1995). Rotundo is primarily concerned with pre-twentieth-century middle-class New England manhood; Kimmel with middle-class American manhood from the same period through the twentieth century; and Bederman with late nineteenth- and early twentieth-century American manhood in the imperial context.

9. Asian American studies, however, sometimes treat the Asian American subject as genderless, such that gender only appears in the infamous "women's chapter." Takaki, for example, has been criticized by Elaine Kim (1982) for organizing his history in this way, treating women's appearances as contributions or exceptions to the normative, masculine narrative of Asian American history. See also Okihiro for an argument on "recentering women" and gender in historiographical narratives (1994, 64–92).

10. On the history of the Page Law, see Chan (1991, 54) and Takaki (1989, 40). On antimiscegenation laws and their eventual repeal, see Takaki (1989; 101–102, 330–31, 342, 406, 473) and Chan (1991; 59–61, 116).

11. On the partiality of law in relation to race in general and Asian Americans in particular, see Matsuda (1996; 21–27, 51–59). On the usefulness and limitations of Butler in relationship to the representation of the body in law, see Hyde (1997, 147).

12. Hysteria over the heterosexual desires of Filipino males was crystallized in various antimiscegenation acts. See Takaki (1989; 327–31, 341–43).

13. See Parreñas (1998) for an account of white women's status in the dance halls frequented by Filipino laborers during the 1930s. Ironically, these women were mostly poor or working class who also, Parreñas argues, found some upward social mobility through the pay they received.

14. A list of these incidents in *America* follows: an Indian woman who entraps Carlos' friend into marriage (103); a blonde woman who works in a taxi dance hall (105–110); a girl who is raped (113–15); anonymous women at an orgy (131–32); and a wanton Mexican wife (149–51). White women of the wealthier classes or from more educated backgrounds also pose threats to Carlos and other Filipino men when their sexuality is unchecked: the wealthy woman who displays her naked self to Carlos (141–42); Helen, the agent provocateur and labor organizer who seduces Carlos' brother (202–203); and another labor organizer, Lucia Simpson, who is motivated by sex (290–93).

15. Sheng-mei Ma argues that Carlos' desire for or admiration of white women stems from the legacies of Spanish and American colonialism and the construction within them of the "white" or "fair" woman as an idealized object of desire whose capture is a sign of assimilation. Carlos and other Filipinos engage in "eroticizing America" (1998, 79) in order to "validate their own masculinity" (80). Bulosan's precedent for doing so, Ma argues, is found in the nationalist Filipino classic *Noli Me Tangere* by the national hero José Rizal, which also features a mestiza, fair-skinned heroine named Maria Clara. It is this eroticization, in contradiction to revolutionary class politics in Bulosan's work, that troubles Ma because of the ambivalence toward America it produces.

16. See Denning (1997), Rideout (1992, 241–54), and Foley (1993, 243) for accounts of Popular Front strategy and its impact on the development and history of the proletarian novel in the United States. Bulosan's Marxist sympathies become extremely clear—that is, shorn of the language of American pluralism and celebration—in his journalism, as Evangelista also notes (1985, 213). See also Bulosan (1979).

17. Question 28 was eventually rewritten for the Issei, the immigrant generation, who faced an impossible dilemma with the original phrasing: because they were ineligible for U.S. citizenship, answering yes would render them effectively stateless. The revised question read: "Will you swear to abide by the laws of the United States and to take no action which would in any way interfere with the war effort of the United States?" The information in this endnote comes from Daniels (1971).

18. For other sources on the social and economic effect of relocation on the Japanese American community, see Daniels (1971), Daniels, Taylor, and Kitano (1991), and Weglyn (1976).

19. On various alien land law acts that prevented Asians from owning property in states that included Arizona, Arkansas, California, Idaho, Kansas, Louisiana, Montana, New Mexico, Oregon, Utah, Washington, and Wyoming, see Chan (1991, 47) and Takaki (1989; 203–208, 411–13). For legal restrictions on the Japanese that prevented them from becoming citizens, see Chan (47) and Takaki (207–209).

20. A panopticon is a penal structure built around a central watchtower. The prisoners' cells surround the watchtower and are all visible from the watchtower. Surveillance is thus always a possibility. For an explanation and theoretical account of the panopticon, see Foucault (1979, 170–228).

21. It could be argued that Japanese Americans were already of "a different breed" because of legislative acts like the 1790 Naturalization Law and the 1924 Gentleman's Agreement, acts that prevented Japanese Americans from attaining citizenship and that barred them from immigration. War, internment, and the deprivation of civil rights, however, are a completely different matter, transforming Japanese Americans from undesirable aliens to incarcerated subversives.

22. The subsequent information on the Huk rebellion comes from Kerkvliet (1977), Kessler (1989), and Pomeroy (1992). While their assessments of the Huk rebellion are similar, Pomeroy, as a member of the rebellion himself, is the most sympathetic to their cause and the most critical of U.S. motivations. The date

for the end of the rebellion, 1956, comes from Kerkvliet; there seems to be some disagreement amongst scholars over the exact end of the rebellion, however, as different dates in the second half of the 1950s have been offered. For an extended analysis of *The Cry and the Dedication* please see ch. 2 of my book, *Race and Resistance: Literature and Politics in Asian America*, from which this essay is extracted.

23. According to San Juan, Bulosan—like his character Dante—intended to write a four-novel series tracing a century of Filipino history from the revolutionary viewpoint; *The Cry and the Dedication* was to be one of this series (San Juan 1995a, ix).

24. I use the term "ethnic entrepreneur" rather than "panethnic entrepreneur" because neither Bulosan nor Okada demonstrated any penchant for building an Asian American identity or for using cross-Asian relationships or confusions as Onoto Watanna did.

Works Cited

Alquizola, Marilyn. 1989. "The Fictive Narrator of *America Is in the Heart.*" *Frontiers of Asian American Studies: Writing, Research, and Commentary*, ed. Gail M. Nomura et al, 211–17. Pullman: Washington State University Press.

_____. 1991. "Subversion or Affirmation: The Text and Subtext of *America Is in the Heart.*" In *Asian Americans: Comparative and Global Perspectives*, ed. Shirley Hune et al, 199–210. Pullman: Washington State University Press.

Bederman, Gail. 1995. *Manliness and Civilization: A Cultural History of Race in the United States, 1880–1917*. Chicago: University of Chicago Press.

Bercovitch, Sacvan. 1993. *The Rites of Assent: Transformations in the Symbolic Construction of America*. New York: Routledge.

Brands, H. W. 1993. *The Devil We Knew: Americans and the Cold War*. New York: Oxford University Press.

Bulosan, Carlos. 1973. *America Is in the Heart*. Seattle: University of Washington Press. (Orig. pub. 1946.)

_____. 1979. "Labor and Capital: The Coming Catastrophe." *Amerasia Journal* 6:134.

_____. 1995. *The Cry and the Dedication*. Philadelphia: Temple University Press.

Butler, Judith. 1993. *Bodies That Matter: On the Discursive Limits of "Sex."* New York: Routledge.

_____. 1999. *Gender Trouble: Feminism and the Subversion of Identity*. New York: Routledge. (Orig. pub. 1990.)

Carmichael, Virginia. 1993. *Framing History: The Rosenberg Story and the Cold War*. Minneapolis: University of Minnesota Press.

Chan, Sucheng. 1991. *Asian Americans: An Interpretive History*. Boston: Twayne Publishers.

Chin, Frank. 1979. Afterword. *No-No Boy*. Seattle: University of Washington Press.

Chuh, Kandice. 1996. "Transnationalism and Its Pasts." *Public Culture* 9:93–112.

Connell, R. W. 1995. *Masculinities*. Berkeley: University of California Press.

Daniels, Roger. 1971. *Concentration Camps U.S.A.: Japanese Americans and World War II*. New York: Holt, Rinhart & Winston.

Daniels, Roger, Sandra C. Taylor, and Harry H. L. Kitano, eds. 1991. *Japanese Americans: From Relocation to Redress*. Seattle: University of Washington Press.

Denning, Michael. 1997. *The Cultural Front: The Laboring of American Culture in the Twentieth Century*. London: Verso.

Eagleton, Terry. 1976. *Criticism and Ideology*. London: Verso.

Evangelista, Susan. 1985. *Carlos Bulosan and His Poetry: A Biography and Anthology*. Seattle: University of Washington Press.

Foley, Barbara. 1993. *Radical Representations: Politics and Form in U.S. Proletarian Fiction, 1929–1941*. Durham: Duke University Press.

Foucault, Michel. 1979. *Discipline and Punish: The Birth of the Prison*. New York: Vintage Books.

Fried, Albert, ed. 1997. *McCarthyism, The Great American Red Scare: A Documentary History*. New York: Oxford University Press.

Fried, Richard M. 1990. *Nightmare in Red: The McCarthy Era in Perspective*. New York: Oxford University Press.

Gillon, Steven M., and Diane B. Kutz. 1993. *America during the Cold War*. New York: Harcourt Brace Jovanovich.

Hinds, Lynn Boyd, and Theodore Otto Windt Jr. 1991. *The Cold War as Rhetoric: The Beginnings, 1945–1950*. New York: Praeger.

Hyde, Alan. 1997. *Bodies of Law*. Princeton: Princeton University Press.

Kerkvliet, Benedict J. 1977. *The Huk Rebellion: A Study of the Peasant Revolt in the Philippines*. Berkeley: University of California Press.

Kessler, Richard J. 1989. *Rebellion and Repression in the Philippines*. New Haven: Yale University Press.

Kim, Elaine H. 1982. *Asian American Literature: An Introduction to the Writings and Their Social Context*. Philadelphia: Temple University Press.

Kimmel, Michael. 1996. *Manhood in America: A Cultural History*. New York: Free Press.

Kitano, Harry H. L. 1991. "The Effects of the Evacuation on the Japanese Americans." In *Japanese Americans: from Relocation to Redress*, ed. Roger Daniels, Sandra C. Taylor, and Harry H. L. Kitano, 151–58. Seattle: University of Washington Press.

Kolodny, Annette. 1975. *The Lay of the Land: Metaphor as Experience and History in American Life and Letters*. Chapel Hill: University of North Carolina Press.

Kovel, Joel. 1994. *Red Hunting in the Promised Land: Anticommunism and the Making of America*. New York: Basic Books.

Lee, Rachel. 1999. *The Americas of Asian American Literature*. Princeton: Princeton University Press.

Leffler, Melvyn P. 1994. *The Specter of Communism: The United States and the Origins of the Cold War, 1947–1953*. New York: Hill & Wang.

Ling, Jinqi. 1995. "Race, Power, and Cultural Politics in John Okada's *No-No Boy*." *American Literature* 67 (2): 359–81.

Ma, Sheng-Mei. 1998. *Immigrant Subjectivities in Asian American and Asian Diaspora Literatures*. Albany: State University of New York Press.

Mason, John W. 1996. *The Cold War: 1945–1991*. New York: Routledge.

Matsuda, Mari. 1996. *Where Is Your Body? And Other Essays on Race, Gender, and the Law*. Boston: Beacon Press.

Morrante, P. C. 1984. *Remembering Carlos Bulosan: His Heart Affair with America*. Quezon City: New Day Publishers.

Nguyen, Viet Thanh. 2002. *Race and Resistance: Literature and Politics in Asian America*. New York: Oxford University Press.

Okada, John. 1993. *No-No Boy*. Seattle: University of Washington Press. (Orig. pub. 1957.)

Okihiro, Gary Y. 1994. *Margins and Mainstreams: Asians in American History and Culture*. Seattle: University of Washington Press.

Parreñas, Rhacel Salazar. 1998. "'White Trash' Meets the 'Little Brown Monkeys': The Taxi Dance Hall as a Site of Interracial and Gender Alliances between White Working Class Women and Filipino Immigrant Men in the 1920s and 30s." *Amerasia Journal* 24 (2): 115–34.

Pomeroy, William J. 1992. *The Philippines: Colonialism, Collaboration, and Resistance!* New York: International Publishers.

Rideout, Walter. 1992. *The Radical Novel in the United States 1900–1954*. New York: Columbia University Press. (Orig. pub. 1956.)

Rotundo, E. Anthony. 1993. *American Manhood: Transformations in Masculinity from the Revolution to the Modern Era*. New York: Basic Books.

San Juan, E., Jr. 1992. *Racial Formations/Critical Transformations: Articulations of Power in Ethnic and Racial Studies in the United States*. New Jersey: Humanities Press.

———. 1995. "In Search of Filipino Writing: Reclaiming Whose 'America'?" *The Ethnic Canon: Histories, Institutions, and Interventions*. Ed. David Palumbo-Liu. Minneapolis: University of Minnesota Press.

———, ed. 1995a. Introduction to *The Cry and the Dedication*, by Carlos Bulosan. Philadelphia: Temple University Press.

———, ed. 1995b. Introduction. *On Becoming Filipino: Selected Writings of Carlos Bulosan*. Philadelphia: Temple University Press.

Takaki, Ronald. 1989. *Strangers from a Different Shore: A History of Asian Americans*. Boston: Little, Brown.

Weglyn, Michi. 1976. *Years of Infamy*. New York: William Morrow & Co.

Whitfield, Stephen J. 1991. *The Culture of the Cold War*. Baltimore: Johns Hopkins University Press.

Wong, Sau-ling Cynthia. 1993. *Reading Asian American Literature: From Necessity to Extravagance*. Princeton: Princeton University Press.

9 Suffering Male Bodies: Representations of Dissent and Displacement in the Internment-Themed Narratives of John Okada and Toshio Mori

Suzanne Arakawa

THE CONSTITUTION's blighted promise in John Okada's *No-No Boy* (1957) and in Toshio Mori's camp stories (1940s–1950s) is heightened by the paradoxical measuring of personal or communal freedom through tropes of dissent and displacement. In *No-No Boy*, Okada signifies freedom through the Japanese American who, despite pressures to assimilate, chooses to dissent. By the novel's end, however, the dissenter appears to desire a resolution wherein he shares a unified identity with other Americans. Much like Okada, Mori writes narratives of shame or rebellion, narratives that capture the chaos of wartime and postwar Japanese American bodies and communities. However, in most of Mori's internment camp short stories, the relative displacement or integration of Japanese American bodies inside and outside the camps takes precedence over dissent as a measure of freedom. Thus, while dissent is for Okada a catalyst potentially bringing about "open-ended closure" and often painful renegotiation under the aegis of a kind of assimilation, Mori's character-driven stories posit that Japanese American soldier bodies may eventually be incorporated into both the Japanese American and mainstream narrative consciousness. In showing that a contested identity is the troubling "natural" inheritance of ethnic Americans, Okada's and Mori's internment narratives ultimately inscribe the anxious and sacrificial[1] bodies of internees onto the American cultural and geographical expanse, subversively mapping an evolving Japanese American identity of *becoming* rather than of *being* that nonetheless forestalls its own erasure from the American landscape.

Internment-themed narratives foregrounding the trope of dissent struggle to incorporate both the resisting Japanese American male body and the Japanese American soldier/veteran body. Patricia Chu has emphasized that in *Constituting Americans: Cultural Anxiety and Narrative Form*, Priscilla Wald contrasts "'official narratives' about American national identity with personal ones, concluding that 'national narratives actually shape personal narratives by delineating the cultural practices through which personhood is defined.'" Chu thus concludes that "stories of individual subject formation must fit, or at best challenge, recognized forms, which in turn are negotiated in relation to public accounts defining nation" (2000, 10). On one level, it may be argued, Okada and Mori struggle to connect personal narratives of "individual subject formation" to official narratives concerned with "American national identity"; given the time period in which they lived, both authors were subject to cultural demands that they write "established discourses," or officially sanctioned ones (Chu 2000, 10). Here, if "the untold, 'repressed' stories" delineating the "published narratives' unconsciousness" are to be validated—that is, if the author is to "write and publish a narrative of subject formation"—he or she must "position himself or herself in relation to the 'language' of his or her culture's narrative conventions." Such positioning will determine "his or her survival as an 'author,' a subject known through words" (Chu 2000, 10–11).

One of the "established discourses" of late 1940s and early 1950s America tells the World War II grand narrative of victory over oppression, a victory purchased by the sacrificed bodies of Allied soldiers. According to Elaine Scarry, "War is relentless in taking for its own interior content the interior content of the human body" (1985, 81). Katherine Kinney furthers Scarry's argument when she insists that "the purpose of war . . . is to confer upon ideology the 'incontestable reality of the body,' a reality which is made 'compelling and vivid' through wounding" (2000, 8). However, "the reality marked by wounding has a 'referential instability'; the body may be claimed by either the side for which it suffered or the side that wounded it"; more precisely, the victorious side secures "the right to claim the bodies and their reality conferring power" (2000, 8). In this context, historical details consistent or compatible with the established discourse may be considered "coherent"; those that contradict or jar it are "incoherent." When one applies Kinney's argument to Japanese American World War II internment-themed texts, one recognizes that the Japanese American "yes-yes boys"—the young males who agreed to take up arms for America—are established as coherent bodies; the "no-no boys" (those who refused to show American loyalties), on the other hand, become "incoherent" bodies. Such a paradigm enables

Japanese American as well as mainstream readers to perceive identity formation in the texts.

If readers perceive identity accurately, they will soon recognize that, at least in some texts, there is a Japanese American "trope of dissent" that straddles the line between valorizing and demonizing incoherent and coherent bodies. That is, in some texts the trope of dissent subverts the notion of a coherent Allied victory in World War II, especially a victory over oppression. Even as the war unfolded, the incoherence of American masculinity dictated a corresponding makeover of American "male culture." Most notably, this makeover relied on the separation, containment, and forced dispersal of the Japanese American male body. Understandably, then, both Okada and Mori provide a clearinghouse of male anxieties stemming from enforced stasis as well as rootlessness; both writers use the Japanese American male body to signify personal being or existence and to undermine larger assumptions about established discourse, especially the discourse of war.

John Okada's *No-No Boy* and the Body Logic of Identity Formation

Seattle native John Okada was a sergeant in the U.S. Air Force during World War II. Although his seminal work *No-No Boy* was published in 1957, it "received little attention"[2] and in 1971, Okada died of "of a heart attack, in obscurity." In the 1970s, the novel was "rediscovered by a group of Asian-American writers" and his work acclaimed as "the first authentic Japanese-American novel" (Cheung-Mare 1990, p. 1900). Since its rediscovery, *No-No Boy* has been reissued by the University of Washington Press. Okada's novel depicts the postwar Japanese American community in Seattle already fragmented by Pearl Harbor, the internment, and other sociopolitical consequences of the Pacific War. But following the war's end in 1945 the community is decimated by internal suspicions and dissensions and by the self-hatred inevitably arising from profound humiliation. The novel registers divisive, bitter conflicts among families, relatives, and friends; such conflicts are centered in social displacement, joblessness, alcoholism, cross-generational values, illness, divorce, and death. Ironically, as Japanese Americans tried to dispel their shame by proving their Americanness, they were obliged to accommodate—or even champion—the dominant white culture at the expense of their own.

While virtually all critics agree that the publication of *No-No Boy* marks a crucial milestone in Japanese American literary history, there is little consensus as to the novel's aesthetic or political merits. Some scholars insist that the novel falls victim to assimilationist discourse and dominant cultural concerns; others argue that because central tensions of the novel are left unresolved, its writing finally constitutes little more than an irreconcilable and thus ineffectual registration of anguish. More recent readings have complicated these seminal earlier reactions by focusing on Okada's strategies for negotiating the demands or expectations of his publisher and readers.[3] Although the novel does indeed enact a registration of anguish, where the protagonist himself is an incongruous figure who blindly attempts to work his way through personal "shame" while confused and zealous peers attempt to punish his dissent, *No-No Boy* incisively foregrounds postwar Japanese American shame and self-punishment through its depictions of a suffering community that scapegoats the dissenters in its ranks. Chief among such dissenters were those who challenged the dominant culture by responding negatively to questions 27 and 28 of the so-called loyalty questionnaire—the document ironically was titled "Application for Leave Clearance"—which, in early 1943, was administered by military personnel to all internees seventeen years of age and older.[4]

Ultimately, the questions divided Japanese Americans, as Viet Nguyen emphasizes in the article preceding mine in this volume. But to assert that the two "loyalty questions" themselves were the primary cause of the postwar fragmentation of the Japanese American community would be, at best, an oversimplification. Nevertheless, the questions certainly generated divergent answers; these answers, and the ways in which they were read by other Japanese Americans—both during and following the war, and in the context of the larger internment experience itself—bred intense anxiety, guilt, and strife within individual families and throughout the larger Japanese American community.[5] In its formalized stripping away of constitutional rights, the internment further marginalized Japanese Americans—already defined as enemies by the dominant culture out of fear, economic jealousy, and war hysteria. Of those Japanese Americans who returned to the West Coast after the war ended, few regained the economic standing they had prior to internment. Nevertheless, Japanese American returnees determinedly reconstructed a semblance of community, making costly sacrifices to stimulate a Japanese American economic recovery. Indeed, a modest recovery was achieved in a relatively short period of time, but it exacted a price.

In *No-No Boy*, this price is paid by the community itself, a community torn apart by the need of returnees—and of those who supported their military service—to prove their Americanness. Quite simply, this resulted in the punishment, humiliation, or ostracism of those who failed (or refused) to conform to what the community perceived as the "American national identity." Accordingly, those who were labeled "disloyal Americans"—a group that included the "no-no boys"—were subjugated and ostracized by the larger community. In *No-No Boy*, protagonist and draft resister Ichiro Yamada becomes Okada's depiction of Japanese American identity as objectified by both the dominant culture and the Japanese American community itself.[6] Ichiro feels constant pressure to adhere to conflicting community definitions of an authentic national identity—one American, the other Japanese. Here, "authentic" identity is most often reified through obsessive and distorted readings of the physical—written documentation, human interactions, bodies themselves. At first Ichiro misinterprets physicality to provide evidence of his own guilt. Later, he alters his view of himself as a scapegoat, and he eventually reaches a point where he perceives outside binary constructions of identity and culture, outside East or West, Japanese or American. For fully three-fourths of the novel, however, Ichiro filters his life through a reductive lens, selectively and obsessively collecting and scrutinizing physical evidence for the existence of an authentic American identity. Simultaneously, he points to a single cause of his postwar "incomplete" or "non-American" identity: his Japanese nationalist mother's insistence in 1943 that he side with Japan and answer no to questions 27 and 28 of the "loyalty questionnaire." Ichiro long believes, in other words, that had he not acceded to his mother's fanatic demands, he would be "American" in the present of the novel. The hyper-importance that Ichiro and other characters assign to questionnaire responses, especially as proof of national affiliation or social identity, is enormously problematic. Most obviously, such judgments rest on the assumption that "American" means, in this case, "not Japan" or "not Japanese," establishing the identities as mutually exclusive. As interpreted through a misconstrued vision of national identity as "authentic" (or potentially so), the questionnaire itself becomes irrefutable proof that genuineness can exist—and even that a simple yes or no in answer will establish or create that "authentic identity" (American or Japanese, respectively)—intact and whole.

Such judgments are also inherently monofocal. That is, for Ichiro's mother, identity is solely a matter of "ethnicity" or "blood": Ichiro *is* Japanese despite the fact that he has been born, raised, and educated in America. For Ichiro, on the other hand, identity is a matter of political positioning: if only he had answered yes to questions 27 and 28, he would have secured his identity as authentically "American." Finally, such judgments depend on an obsessive reliance on the empirical—on an inordinate fixation on physical proof. Ichiro looks for justification of the government's stripping him of Constitutional rights. That he *looks like* the enemy is, he believes, a potentially excusable condition; but that—through his questionnaire responses—he has *aligned himself with* the enemy is not.

I would agree with Lisa Lowe (1996) that *No-No Boy's* "anti-developmental"[7] style remains one of its virtues, for it struggles valiantly against narrative conventions; in fact, the fragmented nature of the variegated narrative strategies seems to write against the paradigmatic qualities of the coherent World War II narrative, in content and in style. However, the powerful influence of the World War II narrative compels this text to move toward some form of symbolic coherency, and this coherency on one level manifests in the form of how the male Japanese American bodies confer a reality—the dissenters' bodies seem to have little currency as they do not fit into the domestic or the public spaces, while the living and wounded veterans' bodies appear to have more veracity than characters who enact violence or remain dissembled, and even more clout in the text as makers or producers of a constitutive male Seattle Japanese American body. Thus, the novel both "repeatedly undermines uniperspectivalism" *and* succumbs to a larger coherent World War II narrative that must generate male culture and "the world."

Throughout most of the book, then, as Ichiro weighs everything empirically, he apparently feels that everyone has more right to be on American soil than he. Having returned to society from prison rather than (as is the case for most young men of his age) from the battlefield, Ichiro signifies the resisting Japanese American body unattached to the larger World War II narrative. His literal and emblematic nonconnection to the larger Japanese American and American communities apparently marks him as incoherent and de-masculinized. Pressures on the resisting body are apparently contradictory: on the one hand, that it assert itself by becoming a site of violence; on the other, that it capitulate to the assimilating Japanese American male community and thus to the larger war narrative. For much of the novel, Ichiro's anxiety is for how and when to capitulate, as demonstrated by his obsessive philosophizing about his friend, Kenji Kanno, who, after losing part of a leg during the war, has had frequent additional surgeries in unsuccessful attempts to root out gangrene. While Ichiro admits that Kenji's situation is horrific, he feels that "Kenji could still hope" because "a leg more or less wasn't important when compared with himself, Ichiro, who was strong and perfect but only an empty shell. He would have given both legs to change places with Kenji" (60). Ichiro's absurd reasoning suggests that Kenji's physical loss proves his right to be accepted as "American"[8]; Ichiro's unnatural "stump envy" thus points up the excruciating and self-limiting angst he feels about not belonging to the larger male war narrative. For Ichiro, the veteran's body—perhaps especially if wounded—signifies a "truth-conferring reality" and masculinity essential to the World War II narrative and to "American" identity.

Still, there is a third option beyond the two Ichiro initially considers: rather than being primarily "strong" or "perfect," he can be hopeful. Indeed, even in his rash declaration that he would "give both legs" for what Kenji apparently has, Ichiro implicitly hopes for what he imagines to be wholeness—for what the text bears out as a coherent masculine narrative larger than he is. In a process triggered by his mother's suicide and Kenji's death, Ichiro eventually questions the social construction of identity and belonging; somewhat unluckily, however, his sympathy at Kenji's death and his relief over the death of his own mother underscore his as yet unexamined desire to be connected to the larger World War II narrative: in perceiving Kenji's death as noble and Mrs. Yamada's death as ridding the narrative of a perverse and disruptive masculinized female influence (one that prevents Ichiro's own assimilation or acceptance), Ichiro lulls himself into hoping that he is closer to the larger American narrative than he actually is.

Ichiro's encounter with Gary further problematizes his rootless subject positioning. Gary works at a rehabilitation center as a sign painter during the day; at night, he attempts to reestablish his pre-prison passion for oil painting (224). Gary's self-imposed isolation and his devotion to his art help create a space where he can begin to exist as a subject—thereby escaping white (or communal Japanese) objectification as a hated Japanese American. His nighttime paintings (multifaceted, abstract works that give rise to a variety of meanings and interpretations) become metaphors for his postwar existence as a Japanese American. However, even though his art exemplifies personal construction, it is virtually unknown outside a small circle of friends, and we thus see the futility of his actions. It is not a coincidence that when Ichiro first meets him, Gary is painting the final "i" in the word "Rehabilitation," a sign on a "huge, green van." Gary paints "with deft, sure strokes of the brush"; during the day, he tells Ichiro, "I paint for my keep." But "at night, I paint for myself" (221–22, 224). However, Gary's isolation—self-imposed out of the desire to remain physically and emotionally safe—precludes his ever having an audience. Here we see that while the Japanese American identity itself is a construction in process, the personal Japanese American self who lacks emotional and cultural connections to the larger communal self remains at best ineffectual and incomplete. In selfishly preserving his physical and emotional safety, Gary paradoxically loses his freedom and identity; he also denies his community the reality or truth of his art.

As the novel moves toward its conclusion, Ichiro is at least intellectually persuaded that he has paid for his crime as prescribed by law (232), and is prepared to reach out more frankly and less defensively to his community. He has intuited that existence and identity are connected to but not necessarily driven by ideology, let alone by empirical evidence. At last able to face the expectations of white Americans—and the costs of meeting or not meeting them—Ichiro becomes open to the possibility that he must assert himself as a subject in postwar America. In short, Ichiro realizes he can try to live with ambiguity, especially given that he remains a part of the unspoken or repressed narrative below the surface of the larger myths of war and national identity. The last lines of the novel show Ichiro thinking about the people who have given him hope and understanding and who have enabled him, however tentatively, to name himself as a subject: "He walked along, thinking, searching, thinking and probing, and, in the darkness of the alley of the community that was a tiny bit of America, he chased that faint and elusive insinuation of promise as it continued to take shape in mind and in heart" -(250–51).

Although the bodies of Emi and Mrs. Yamada are crucial in *No-No Boy*, they ultimately exist as secondary catalysts and are situated as such overshadowed by the potency of the pervasive male-centered World War II narrative. While Ichiro comes to understand that his situation is neither his fault nor "the fault of his mother, who was now dead because of a conviction which was only a dream that blew up in her face" (229), such understanding does not fully negate the "mild shiver" of repulsion he feels as he looks down on his mother's body in the bathtub, where she has drowned herself, or his springing from the limousine that would have taken him to watch his mother's cremation (185, 195). Indeed, despite the sympathy for his mother that slowly manifests itself in the final section of the novel, Ichiro's rejection of her cold withered body is maintained through the novel's conclusion. Insofar as her body represents the fallen country of Japan and its perfervid nationalistic ideology—or the now-dead nationalism of first-generation Japanese Americans—the mother's tough, sinewy nature as a die-hard survivor (like Japan itself) is renounced, even demonized. In contrast, and as a conflation of the female body and American national identity, the supple and voluptuous body of Emi underscores, in Ichiro's case, the specter of the assimilation narrative with its complex subconscious yearnings to belong. The virtual impossibility of resisting the grand narrative of assimilation is borne out repeatedly through the collective Japanese American experience in the novel.

However, in contrast with other characters that negotiate material spaces more cautiously, Ichiro does not initially rein in his desire to belong, a desire that seems beyond rational understanding. Late in the novel, after Ichiro intuits from Gary (referred to earlier) and Carrick (a white who harbors neither ethnic nor political animosity toward Ichiro) that he himself owns responsibility for making something of his postwar life, Ichiro apparently recognizes that "belonging" is contingent upon "reaching out," especially to the rejecting other—and in this context, when Ichiro places his hand on Bull's shoulder in the next-to-last paragraph of the novel, the image has particular poignancy. However, this gesture occurs only after fellow no-no boy Freddie's death—and that Freddie's problematic body must be rendered out of the text signals the narrative's push to contain or excise its dissembling males and to ostensibly promote a coherent postwar American male culture. In life, Freddie existed as a rootless gadabout dictated only by his desire for freedom, which he preserved through arguably selfish draft ducking. In death, Freddie is suddenly larger, his body almost emblematically paralleling those of the dead and wounded war veterans. Thus, although Freddie is excised from the narrative, his dead body can be claimed and memorialized by readers, depending on how they position themselves in relation to the larger World War II narrative.

In the end, *No-No Boy* suggests that the production of male culture occurs outside the domestic sphere (or, by extension, outside the community itself) in the comparatively neutral public spaces (for Japanese Americans) of bars, institutions, or hospitals. With deliberate irony, Okada creates the only functional home in the novel—that of Kenji's family—as an almost perfectly "Americanized" one. Compounding the irony of this created "Americanized" space are three other facts. First, it is a domestic space devoid of a mother figure, its harmony and nurture being the products of immigrant male society. Second, Kenji chooses to leave it so that it will not be contaminated by the gangrenous flesh of his decaying body. Finally, it is Kenji's sacrificial Japanese American male body—whose masculinity, despite successive amputations and resultant humiliations, is never questioned—that secures his martyr-like and iconic status within the victorious American World War II narrative. Still, Ichiro remains the protagonist of the novel; its most crucial themes must be assignable to his character and not to Kenji's. Very much in evidence at the novel's conclusion are the communal dissent and disintegration, which predicate the narrative's central tensions. Indeed, only late in the novel does Ichiro seem to understand the unfortunate truth pointed out by Gary: that even the "yes-yes boys" face the impossible challenge of having to "prove that their blood is as red Jones's or Torgerson's or Mayo's or what have you" (227). Nevertheless, insofar as Ichiro is a "representative man," a scapegoat, there is—via his body, his identity as a Japanese American no-no boy—a figurative subsuming of the personal and familial demons behind the larger dissent. Thus, while the end of *No-No Boy* is largely somber, the novel finally embodies the faint hope—through sacrifice—of a (re)negotiated American identity and place.

ROOTLESSNESS/STASIS AND DISSENT/RESISTANCE IN TOSHIO MORI'S CAMP SHORT STORIES

Toshio Mori was born in the Northern California East Bay Area in 1910 and made a living as a nurseryman, operating his family's business. The only time he spent out of the area was during World War II, when he was interned at the Topaz concentration camp near the town of Delta in west-central Utah. In the years prior to the war, Mori applied himself to the task of learning how to craft fiction and studied on his own short stories written by acclaimed masters, one of whom was William Saroyan, "who later became his advocate in literary circles and described him at the outset of his publishing career as 'one of the most important new writers in the country.'"[9]

A prominent motif in Toshio Mori's internment and/post-internment stories, published in various journals from 1940 to 1947, is the sense of disorientation or dislocation inherent in the camp experience. Three of these stories and the short novel *The Brothers Murata* (2000) are the focus of my discussion here; the three stories were reprinted in *The Chau-vinist and Other Stories* (1979). The government-mandated uprooting of Japanese Americans from the familiar security of their West Coast homes and businesses and their subsequent physical containment on stretches of what some internees justifiably perceived as the American waste-land resulted in an extraordinary and virtually unimaginable sense of violation, displacement, and abandonment. Mori notes a strange para-dox in the fundamental character of the internment experience: while there is a sense of stasis, a grim predictability in the stationary confine-ment of the camps, there is also an unquestionable rootlessness, a clear emotional disengagement in the avowed impermanency of the camps themselves. On the one hand, then, Mori catalogues name upon name of characters interned at the scattered camps, stretching from California to Utah. Through these lists, he underscores the stasis, the containment of the camps; accordingly, the camps acquire the grim permanence of memorials, as it were, or of cemeteries. On the other hand, Mori points to rootlessness and impermanence in a story like his autobiographical "The Long Journey and the Short Ride" (1959), where a central flashback tells how a mother and two sons travel from the Topaz, Utah, camp to a nearby train station in Delta to see the younger of the sons off to war. While Mori is not so cynical as to imply that the son leaves from nowhere to go nowhere, he helps us see that the son is not leaving "home"—and, more crucially, that should the son return from war alive, the "home" to which he will return is even more ambiguous.

During their internment, quite predictably, internees dreamed not only of escaping the camps but of overcoming their isolation or dis-location. Such dreams, Mori suggests, took two primary forms, each reflective of the contradictory character of the camps. First, in a nod to stasis and predictability, there was an intense but often unspoken need for familiar security through retracing one's steps westward, through "returning home." In a nod to rootlessness, there was a longing for movement away from the camps and across the American landscape, generally eastward, in quest of personal freedom and work.

Thus, Mori's postwar stories employ motifs virtually identical to those of his camp stories. *Stasis* is manifest through Mori's references to government "resettlement" quotas and paperwork, references that em-phasize the government's continuing scrutiny of Japanese Americans and its continuing restriction of their rights—to the end that "contain-ment" remains a physical and emotional fact of Japanese American life. *Rootlessness*, in contrast, is shown in Mori's lists of the often-solitary inhabitants of small and fragile postwar Japanese American enclaves in eastern Colorado, Kansas City, Chicago, Akron, Philadelphia, and New York. A similar "rootlessness" is developed in such prewar stories as "Confessions of an Unknown Writer" (1936) and "Operator, Operator!" (1938), wherein the respective protagonists pessimistically review the direction and significance of their lives.[10] In each story is the grim possibility that the floundering protagonist (and others he figuratively embodies) may potentially be erased from the collective American memory and landscape.

As suggested by the title of Mori's "The Travelers" (1943), there is a concerted focus on the postwar Japanese American as the displaced or "rootless American." In the story, Nisei are shown being scattered like "seeds in the wind" (Mori 1979, 130). Twenty or thirty of these characters end up on the same bus out of Topaz and then in the same Delta, Utah, train station waiting for the same eastbound train that will take them away from the internment camps of the American West. That their lives intersect for a short period of time speaks to their unique "mobility," a mobility arising from crisis and prefiguring a random, uncertain future. Their time together, while constituting a brief oasis of "community" before a diasporic scattering of their number across the American Midwest and the Atlantic seaboard, is equally random and uncertain. As one character notes, "Ain't it strange we meet here? One hour and we part once and for all. Maybe we'll never meet again, eh?" (131). Such impermanence ironically reinforces a veneer of community in the face of denial and passivity. Despite their warm flirtations and quickly established friendships, even the handful of Japanese American youth in the station—soldiers, young professionals, and coeds—question the "bad fortune" of such fleeting encounters. But when the awaited train arrives, the passengers' fragile ties dissolve: "Once on the train the clan dispersed. Soldiers, bright and friendly, were everywhere. And the Japanese faces were now lost in the crowd as they should be" (132). Here, interestingly (and in contrast to Okada's *No-No Boy*), Mori minimizes Japanese American shame—even attaching a certain optimism to uncertainty and change as he suggests the fortuity of former internees' blending, unnoticed and unmarked, with the larger "American" populace. To an extent, Mori highlights courageous male soldier bodies, especially the one who considers making a connection with a young woman traveling east—but then who unselfishly realizes that there's not enough time.[11] Still, security and stasis are profoundly attractive, and the loss of Japanese American community lingers poignantly. These Japanese American bodies are moving toward the larger World War II narrative of blending into an American national identity.

In "The Long Journey"—to which previous reference was made—there is a similar ambivalence of distinction between "inside-camp" and "outside-camp" demarcations, between stasis and change. That is, the story superficially distinguishes between the situation of the mother and older brother who remain behind in camp—and whose rare excursions beyond camp boundaries are negotiated through a battery of forms, documentation, and permits and through submission to close military surveillance—with the freedom and privileges of the younger brother who becomes a member of the highly decorated 442nd Infantry Regiment. Moreover, the surface narrative of "The Long Journey" reveals a concerted lack of bitterness, even appearing rather cheery in its exemplification of American can-do spirit coupled with Japanese *shikata ga nai* ("it can't be helped") fortitude. Examined more closely, however, the story posits that the central tragedy of internment is not humiliation or restricted freedom but the tearing apart of the familial body—the separation of parents from children, of spouse from spouse, and of sibling from sibling. The story also implies the tremendous cost of grudging postwar acceptance of Japanese Americans by the larger American community: the dead bodies of young Japanese American soldiers, the physically and psychologically wounded bodies of Japanese American veterans, the rejected and humiliated bodies of Japanese Americans left in the camps. Thus, while the "inside vs. outside" motif of Mori's narrative mirrors the inclusionist/exclusionist Japanese American mentality in *No-No Boy*'s Seattle, "The Long Journey" has a much darker subtext: the enormous postwar challenge to displaced Japanese Americans who have no recourse to stasis and no security or Truman "normalcy" to maintain—but who, in the face of rootlessness and uncertainty, must somehow facilitate the physical and emotional healing of themselves and their loved ones, the reconstitution of their families, the establishment of genuine and enduring homes.

In the autobiographical "Unfinished Message" (1947), Mori creates a mother-son relationship that stands in stark contrast to the relationship between Mrs. Yamada and her two sons in *No-No Boy*. In Mori's narrative, two brothers constantly seek their mother's approval, perhaps even worrying about the power she exerts over them; but ultimately they revere her. The central plot of the story is simple: on a cold May desert night at Topaz, a mother can't sleep for worrying about her youngest son on the Italian front. A few days later, she and her older son learn that the younger son was seriously wounded at the very time she couldn't sleep. He is sent home, paralyzed from the waist down. The mother hopes for his fu. recovery. Before her son is finally released from the hospital, however, she dies. One evening following the younger brother's return home, he and the older brother hear taps on a living room window. Finding no cause, they believe that their dead mother has attempted to contact them, once more conveying her love and anxiety. It is little wonder that normality for these characters consists in following the impulse to reconstitute family and home—a post-World War II narrative imperative.

The older son narrates the story, remembering the cold May night that provoked his mother's quiet fears. He remembers that when his injured brother was eventually brought to an army hospital in Colorado, his mother's constant desire was to be near her son and to visit him more often. In a very literal sense, it is the younger son's war wounds that allow the other family members to leave Topaz and return home to San Leandro, California; and the narrator considers how his mother "couldn't get out of the camp soon enough," counting hours until "the next train to California would take us back home." Meanwhile, the younger son has been transferred to a military hospital in Auburn, California; and when the train on which the family is riding makes a brief stop in Auburn, the mother is tempted to disembark to pay a brief visit to her son. She decides against it, however, declaring, "We must make ready our home. It must be in a mess. We must first go home and get busy cleaning the place. Our home must resemble our old home for Kazuo" (138). Here we see that, in order to reconstitute itself, this Japanese American family uses the body of the veteran son as a primary motivation: his wounded soldier's body is, in effect, their claim to a postwar American identity.

In a very real sense, the mother in "Unfinished Message" is created as a soldier herself—a strong woman and psychological warrior who still takes care of two adult sons, a woman who wields devotion, worry, and hope in their defense. In trying to reconstitute a normal life despite her family's forced incarceration and the conscription of her youngest son, the mother reveals her central desire for her son—and her family—to be made whole again. Even in death, her words and spiritual presence linger. Through this story, Mori positively creates the Japanese American matriarch and subtly undermines the stereotype of male-centered, hyperpatriarchal Japanese family life.[12] The story also serves—as does Okada's novel before it—to underscore the uncertainty of Japanese American postwar existence, together with the futility of nostalgically looking back upon a supposedly "secure" Japanese American past. Both writers suggest that nostalgia blinds: in both works, the mother dies, leaving the sons to look ahead and not backward. Thus, the writers suggest, the past must not be used as a guide to or paradigm for the postwar Japanese American future. Yet, the World War II narrative must be dealt with and adhered to no matter the cost to the whole or healthy Japanese American male body.

In *Unfinished Message: Selected Works of Toshio Mori* (2000) there are, along with a number of letters, photographs, and an interview, two short stories that highlight Nisei soldiers and their families at the time of the bombing of Pearl Harbor, "The Garden" and "Slant-Eyed Americans." However, the jewel of this compilation is the novel-length work *The Brothers Murata*, which Mori wrote at Topaz in 1944. The novel centers on a difficult relationship between two fictional brothers at Topaz, Hiro and Frank. The older of the two, Frank, is a "no-no boy" who organizes resistance within the camp against Executive Order 9066; Hiro, in contrast, has determined to enlist in the Army. Both claim to be motivated by a sense of love for or duty to America; their conflicting motivations are represented by their respective memories of the lives and words of their dead father (who, metaphorically, signifies a prewar America that is no more). Hiro, remembering his father's unswerving love for the United States, sees no option but to show his loyalty by fighting; Frank, in reminding Hiro that their father was a peaceful man who dreamed of the time when "there will be harmony among the people of the world someday" (156), argues that war can bring neither personal nor international peace. These tensions are collapsed in the opening paragraph of the novel, where Hiro and his friends are on a train returning to Topaz following their basic training at Fort Douglas near Salt Lake City. The young men are introduced simply as a "typical bunch of young fellows in America"; the collective noun "they" describes them: "They each carried a grip. They were friends" (139). Mori emphasizes their American maleness when he describes a "trio of pretty women" teasingly calling them "future G.I. wolves" (139). Then, in one explanatory sentence, Mori reveals their special context: "They were representative Americans but for their Oriental facial features—they were Nisei from Topaz" (139). This confluence of young American maleness with the historical circumstance of incarceration and military volunteerism sets forth the complicated subtext of the novel.

In *The Brothers Murata*, the "resisting" and "consenting" positions of Okada's *No-No Boy* are very nearly reversed. Here, it is Hiro, the "yes-yes boy," who feels isolated; the text highlights moments of violent conflict between Hiro's allies and the "no-no boys" who persecute and, in gang fashion, ambush them. While Hiro is the protagonist of the novel and the character with whom a reader's sympathies lie, and while Hiro desires to "smash" his brother and the oppositionists (144), Mori finally resists taking sides in the novel, supporting the oppositionist side as well. True enough, Hiro, his mother, his fiancee, and the other yes-yes boys are depicted as persevering and courageous. Yet the resisting bodies in the novel also have relevancy and moral authority; at the very least, as one of the yes-yes boys points out, "These Nisei who are demanding civil rights . . . are helping us regain our status" (150). Interestingly, brute force is employed by the diverse young men on each side to underscore and give veracity to their respective viewpoints and words, thereby stressing the corporal "embodied reality" as the central figure in the emerging civil war within the camp. Thus, the young men talk of forming "a nucleus that will surpass the opposition," of the enemy's using "force" and "brutal tactics" to "wean away our fellow volunteers," of the necessity of "force" and "unity"—the "full support of this body"— as the means to overcoming "disorganization" and achieving victory (150). Above all, Mori's nuanced treatment of Frank's and Hiro's respective positions underscores the objectivity and political evenhandedness of the novel. Hiro cannot seem to get Frank to understand how the "no-no" stance threatens Hiro's personal narratives of family, home, and love—narratives ostensibly upheld by the war itself. Yet Hiro is equally deaf to Frank's argument that "Uncle Sam usually forgets problems that were magnified during wartime, and when the war is over it is too late" because "you'd be buried . . . and deserve no attention" (157)—and to the argument that the sacrificial Nisei soldier body, unlikely to be claimed by the U.S. victors, is devoid of veracity in death, thus affording the living little currency to draw upon. Frank's voice is not merely dissenting but pacifist and rational; it avoids the incoherence typical of dissent through its reliance on logic, its appeals to harmony, and its affirmation of a particular male culture and worldview. Hiro, who apparently occupies the moral high ground early on, has a good heart and is sensitive to a fault. For much of the novel, however, he is focused on imagining the potential of others for violence, particularly his brother. "Intelligent ones like Frank are dangerous," he thinks. "Such a kind ignites wherever he makes an appearance" (153). Yet this focus on others blinds him to his own violent potential, as tragically manifest late in the novel.

The shocking and somewhat ambivalent conclusion to *The Brothers Murata* conflates the chaotic male no-no body with the suffering yes-yes male body in a way that is simultaneously incoherent and coherent. The two most prominent women in the novel act as catalysts in driving the action forward to the conclusion. The first of these is Mrs. Murata, Hiro's mother, who—unlike Mrs. Yamada in *No-No Boy*—supports her son's decision to fight for the United States. Indeed, at a crucial juncture in the novel, Mrs. Murata publicly demands an end to the criticism of her son Hiro for enlisting. Though her son has misgivings prior to her speech, he admires her "gumption" (165) and knows that those who persecute him will have a "come-down" (165) as a result. Declaring that Hiro "does not know Japan" but only "the place where he was born and raised" (167), Mrs. Murata carefully justifies Hiro's love for his country of origin by drawing a parallel with the Issei who speak nostalgically of their own native country—and thus becomes for Hiro the justification of his position, and for the suffering interned male bodies an embodied female voice of reason and courage. Hiro's fiancée Jean plays an even more consequential role in Hiro's transformation, especially in her decision to separate herself from her family so that she may remain with Hiro. Having committed herself to this decision, she places Hiro in her debt. And so when she asks, "Without accomplishments what good are readiness and words?" and then demands that Hiro "do something" about Frank or she "won't stay" with him any longer, Hiro—in his passionate desire for a postwar American life, for domestic comfort—is driven toward the act that ends the novel.

As observed earlier, Okada's *No-No Boy* features a symbolic conciliation where no-no boy Ichiro secures interaction with the male yes-yes population. In *The Brothers Murata*, there is no such reconciliation, and thus the dissenting body (which Hiro perceives as preventing his connection with postwar narratives of the privileged American male) must be purged from the text. Hiro lures his brother to the top floor of one of the tallest buildings in Salt Lake City, the ten-story Alta "skyscraper," under the pretense of a last fraternal moment together before Frank must report for his preinduction physical or risk FBI intervention. One last time, Hiro pleads with his brother to change his political stance. When Frank refuses, Hiro pushes him out of a window and "calmly" walks to the elevator. That the novel ends on this dreadful fratricidal note speaks to Hiro's perverted sense of duty to the larger war narrative—wherein he must insure that, in one way or another, Frank aligns himself with the patriotic community or body. Only pages before this final scene, Hiro has reassured himself that "you are not alone," that "you and another you and another you make colors and variegations. You are of one cloth; you are of one family; you are of one world. You and you must learn to live together" (199). In many cases, this passage would be read as a hopeful take on the essence of American being, where agency and individuality are affirmed along with one's connection to the surrounding community. Within the novel, however, the passage anticipates the fact that Hiro's need to bind together the personal and communal has become so obsessive that he will coldly sacrifice his own brother to the larger American World War II narrative of masculine patriotism and duty.

Unquestionably, Okada's *No-No Boy* and Mori's camp stories survive, on one level at least, as ethnic (or even racialized) projects of the historical moments in which they were published. These were moments shaped and even dictated by wartime and postwar hyperpatriotism, an intense loyalty to the United States that—in addition to sustaining the war and the rebuilding which followed it—corrupted generally held perceptions of Japanese Americans, especially those who, simply because they resisted the draft, were believed to be (at best) Japanese imperialists or (more commonly) traitorously anti-American. In the narratives of both writers, the treatment of ethnicity is informed by postwar materialism and by attention to certain costs to Japanese Americans trying to attain the American Dream. However, as neither Okada nor Mori documents the Japanese American bodies subsumed in the capital of American labor, primary costs of postwar materialism to Japanese Americans are glossed over. That is, in depicting Japanese Americans as unwilling or unable to return to or visit Japan and yet fully able and willing to relocate eastward across the United States in search of employment,[13] Okada and Mori gesture toward such secondary social costs as mistaking the exploitation or abuse of the Japanese American laborer for "opportunity," ignoring or misconstruing the role of Japanese Americans in (re)building postwar America, or disavowing the transnational identity (or laborer status) of many Japanese American workers. Thus, neither writer allows for a full blossoming of the trope of dissent, as the Japanese American male bodies in their respective narratives struggle (on the one hand) merely to endure or persist—or (on the other) to merge with the larger American male narratives of postwar victory and patriotism or postwar reconstruction.

Okada's *No-No Boy*, more specifically, emphasizes the tension be-tween one's desire to assimilate and one's perceived inability to do so. Mori's narratives not only point up the complexity of returning Japanese Americans to a pre–World War II home, but question the advisability of attempting such a venture. Clearly, post–World War II elation fed into the desire of many Americans to "normalize" or universalize the so-called American identity; there was a parallel national impulse to normalize postwar relations with Asia, particularly Japan. Somewhat predictably, both Okada and Mori remain mired in precisely this his-torical context, where the need to assimilate appears far stronger than the need to dissent—to condemn the internment and to seek redress for the stripping away of fundamental Constitutional rights of property ownership, freedom of mobility, and freedom to sustain self and fam-ily through self-selected employment. Subsumed into the World War II narrative in Okada's and Mori's texts, then, are the assimilating and dissenting bodies: those who endured internment camps and military combat and those who used jail cells and sometimes intracamp violence to protest—as citizens of the United States—governmental abuses. Such protest, at heart, was a means of registering anguish while attempting to solve the puzzle of how to fit incoherent Japanese American no-no bod-ies into larger social narratives: the American Dream, American mas-culinity, the war itself.

For both authors, the puzzle is compounded by JA-on-JA dissonance and violence. That both writers explored in their works Japanese Amer-icans turning on themselves did nothing to increase their popularity among Japanese American readers in the late 1940s and the 1950s; in-deed, the theme remains somewhat controversial today. The full and candid textual production will continue to be tentative as long as male bodies coherent with larger American narratives are esteemed more highly for their truth-conferring capacity than are the incoherent bod-ies of male dissenters or women. Despite their perceived incoherence, however, the bodies in Mori's and Okada's internment texts exert at least limited mobility or movement, even if only the erratic movement fol-lowing the forced physical and emotional immobility of the internment. Wartime immobility or dissent is exacerbated by the tropes of suffering and sacrifice. In addition to the physical imprisonment endured by no-no boys, all Japanese American males in the early 1940s suffered the imprisonment of identity and ideology, together with the displacement of gender—given that the camps comprised "feminized" spaces where males, simply through the act of responding to the loyalty questionnaire (and regardless of their particular responses), invoked the subversion of their domestic and social roles within the camps themselves, to say nothing of their positions within the larger American society, thereby casting into high relief their connections to the war and thus to the American male mythos. In an attendant way, sacrifice pointed to the loss of one's family, reputation, former life, and future dreams—especially as tied to the larger community and its social patterns. In the narratives of Okada and Mori, such suffering or sacrifice is mediated only to the extent that the dead or injured bodies of Japanese American soldiers are appropriated by the larger World War II narrative and its concomitant means of conferring "truth"—or of positioning America or Americans in relations to the "truth."

The larger American community now acknowledges the tragic injustice of the internment; the United States Government has acknowledged culpability in internment/resettlement policies and has offered limited reparations; and many Americans (perhaps especially those of Japanese descent) are able to see the "no-no boys" as men of integrity—as heroes—rather than as the unpatriotic or seditious *inu* (dogs) they were once accused of being. Nevertheless, fully six decades later, the wounds of the internment remain open; and for better or for worse, contestations over consent and dissent continue. Indeed, the fundamental conflict between assimilation and ethnicity building remains a flashpoint question for the Japanese American community, especially as the internment continues to be interrogated by writers, activists, artists, politicians, sociologists, and citizens.

NOTES

1. Cornel West, in "Diverse New World," asserts: "To gain a universal perspective, the left must have a moral focus on suffering." Although West is speaking to the larger concerns of needing "to understand but also to assist people trying to forge some kinds of more democratic regimes, which is so thoroughly difficult" (1997, 562), his point is well taken, especially as he clarifies it later in the same passage: "Let's not package the debate in static categories that predetermine the conclusion that reinforces polarization—that's the worst thing that could happen. Polarization paralyzes all of us.... The political challenge is to articulate universality in a way that is not mere smokescreen for someone else's particularity. We must preserve the possibility of universal connection. That's the fundamental challenge. Let's dig deep enough without our heritage to make that connection to others" (562). West's easily stated theories are only with great difficulty implemented. Although there have been narrative, historical, and filmic texts highlighting or examining tensions between the "yes-yes"

and "no-no" internees, the polarization between the two "sides" remains more or less intact today. In light of post-9/11 and the Afghanistan and the Iraq wars, the issue of dissent in this country overall appears to be misunderstood and reviled as "un-American." Why? Because in the national imagination, there is a powerful war narrative imperative that overshadows all other deployed strategies. This narrative is automatically invoked against any who speak out against war, to the end that condemnation of war is made synonymous with condemnation of the living, wounded, and dead soldier bodies that signify the ultimate patriotic duty to and the supreme love and sacrifice for the country.

2. See King Kok Cheung-Mare's biography on John Okada in *The Heath Anthology of American Literature* (1990).

3. See Jinqi Ling's article (1995) and Patricia Chu's monograph (2000), to name just two.

4. See Michi Weglyn's *Years of Infamy: The Untold Story of America's Concentration Camps* (1976). Weglyn states that Japanese American females had to grapple with loyalty questions as well, for they were potentially expected to participate in the war as WACs (Women's Army Corps members).

5. According to Elaine Kim (1990), the internment diaspora—wherein West Coast Japanese American communities were broken up and their members "resettled" in inland camps and communities scattered across midwestern and western states—was deliberately orchestrated by the federal government, for it wanted to break the agricultural and real estate hold of Japanese Americans on the West Coast. However, the internment had still more tragic consequences: it "shattered the physical character" of Japanese American communities and fundamentally changed their "sense of ethnic cohesion" (Hata and Hata 1990, 80), to the end that—in Elaine Kim's words—it caused the "fragmentation and disfiguration" of both family and community (Kim 1990, 148).

6. That Ichiro eventually reaches a point where he can act as social participant, even defining the terms of his interaction with others, illustrates Okada's conviction that Japanese Americans could become "subjects" and not just "objects of history" (this use of "subjects" and "objects" is borrowed from Nancy Hartsock [1990, 30]).

7. According to Lisa Lowe, "Virtually ignored when it was published in 1957 and rejected by the reading public for its uncompromisingly unconventional style, *No-No Boy* was reissued in 1976 by the University of Washington Press after an excerpt of it was featured in the anthology *Aiiieeeee! No-No Boy* may be characterized as a realist narrative to the extent that its action proceeds chronologically. But it is anti-developmental in the sense that its condensed, almost static portrait takes place within the small period of several weeks, and it repeatedly undermines uniperspectivalism by alternating inconsistently between a third-person omniscient narration and despairing, angry, or confused interior monologues. The narrative shifts back and forth between different voices within long, run-on sentences, conveying the confusion and entropy of the protagonist Ichiro on his return to Seattle after two years of internment and two subsequent years in prison for refusing to serve in the U.S. Army, and documenting his bitter confusion, isolation, and shame as he confronts Nisei soldiers and veterans, Nisei women, white Americans, his parents, and other Japanese issei. Ichiro is

a deeply divided subject, antagonistic both to the American government that interned and imprisoned Japanese Americans and to Japanese patriots like his mother who feverishly denies Japan's defeat in the war; in effect, the "no-no boy" not only refuses loyalty to either Japan or the United States but also refuses the "enemy/not-enemy" logic of the choice itself. Just as Ichiro's "no" dramatizes the Asian American subject's refusal to accept the dividing, subordinating terms of assimilation, so the novel's stasis, fragmentation, and discontent refuse the development, synthesis, and reconciliation required by traditional canonical criteria" (1996, 50–51).

8. Borrowed from Walter Benn Michaels (1988).

9. From an online review of *Unfinished Message*. http://www.theindependentreviewssite.org/v2_i3/v2_i3_book_rev.html

10. It should be noted, however, that the tone of "Confessions" is finally much lighter than that of "Operator."

11. Time is a recurring trope in Mori's texts.

12. See Ronald Takaki (1993) and O'Brien and Fugita (1991).

13. According to Michi Weglyn: "Thus the turnabout policy of 'indefinite leaves,' beginning in the fall of 1942, which extended relocation privileges to anyone who could pass a stringent security clearance was, of necessity, accompanied by a WRA promotional campaign not only to mitigate evacuee fears but also to reeducate a paranoiac public to differentiate between the bitterly despised foes across the Pacific and fellow U.S. citizens. . . .

"With a grant of $25, a one-way ticket, and an admonition to 'make yourself inconspicuous,' the evacuee was proffered freedom if assured employment in some hopefully non-hostile community, and if the excruciatingly slow security clearance came through in time. The Japanese American Joint Board, made up of representatives from the WRA, the Provost Marshal General's office, and Army and Navy intelligence, had been established on January 29, 1943, to pass on each applicant's eligibility for departure, which was dependent on a staggering number of considerations. . . . Evacuees suspected of holding strong pro-Japanese sentiments were denied leave clearance.

"Leaves were conditional and revocable, for the military had strongly opposed the WRA decision of October 1 to permit leaves on a more permanent basis. . . . "Director Dillon Myer considered the continued pressure and interference from the Western Defense Command as 'arbitrary' and 'categorical' and the repressive nature of the leave clearance procedure as the greatest deterrent to resettlement. . . . Jobs and educational opportunities were repeatedly lost because of delays involved in the validation of an applicant's loyalty, and evacuees came to doubt the sincerity of the WRA's relocation efforts. . . .

"Undaunted, the WRA intensified its dispersal efforts by setting up a total of nine relocation field offices in principal Eastern and Midwestern cities to help develop job opportunities and to provide a prop for evacuees attempting to reestablish themselves. Again they relied heavily on the goodwill and cooperation of church and service groups, who contributed facilities which provided temporary refuge at low prices.

"In larger Midwestern cities, such as Chicago, Detroit, Cleveland, St. Louis, Cincinnati, Milwaukee, and others where employment was plentiful, relocatees found the climate of acceptance surprisingly favorable. Recommended even then was the procedure of having a son or daughter venture forth first to check out community attitudes and pave the way in the crucial area of housing. For re-settling whole families, acceptance was found to be better in urban rather than in rural communities, leaving the WRA faced with the unnerving problem of what to do with its large residue of horticulturists and fisherfolk, the disproportionate number of orchardists and farm specialists who had once tilled vast acreages, who regarded the idea of punching time clocks or going back to the category of stoop labor as distasteful. Included in this collection of 'unrelocatables' were many single persons—the crop followers—usually old and in unsound health, dependency cases due to internment of the breadwinner, widows with small children unable to work.

"So even when the policy of resettlement began to be aggressively encouraged in 1943 to cut camp expenditures while helping to solve the nation's employment problems, these remained a part of the majority populations whose lives and family structure had been so cataclysmically disarranged that no other option was opened to them but to remain trapped" (1976, 101–102).

Works Cited

Benn Michaels, Walter. 1988. "The Souls of White Folk." In *Literature and the Body : Essays on Populations and Persons*, ed. Elaine Scarry, 185–209. Baltimore: Johns Hopkins University Press.

Cheung-Mare, King Kok. 1990. "John Okada 1923–1971." In *The Heath Anthology of American Literature*, vol. 2, ed. Paul Lauter et al., 1900–01. Massachusetts: D.C. Heath.

Chu, Patricia P. 2000. *Assimilating Asians: Gendered Strategies of Authorship in Asian America*. Durham and London: Duke University Press.

Hartsock, Nancy. 1990. "Rethinking Modernism: Minority vs. Majority Theories." In *The Nature and Context of Minority Discourse*, ed. Abdul R. JanMohamed, 17–36. New York: Oxford University Press.

Hata, Donald Teruo, and Nadine Ishitani Hata. 1990. "Asian-Pacific Angelinos: Model Minorities and Indispensable Scapegoats." In *20th Century Los Angeles: Power, Promotion, and Social Conflict*, ed. Norman M. Klein and Martin J. Schiesl, 61–99. Claremont, CA: Regina.

Ling, Jinqi. 1995. "Race, Power, and Cultural Politics in John Okada's *No-No Boy*." *American Literature* 67 (2): 359–81.

Kim, Elaine. 1990. "Defining Asian American Realities through Literature." In *The Nature and Context of Minority Discourse*, ed. Abdul R. JanMohamed, 146–70. New York: Oxford University Press.

Kinney, Katherine. 2000. *Friendly Fire: American Images of the Vietnam War*. New York: Oxford University Press.

Lowe, Lisa. 1996. *Immigrant Acts: On Asian American Cultural Politics*. Durham and London: Duke University Press.

Mori, Toshio. 1979. *The Chauvinist: And Other Stories*. Los Angeles: Asian American Studies Center, University of California.

———. 2000. *Unfinished Message: Selected Works of Toshio Mori*. Ed. Lawson Fusao Inada.Berkeley: Heyday.

O'Brien, David J., and Stephen S. Fugita. 1991. *The Japanese American Experience*. Bloomington and Indianapolis: Indiana University Press.Okada, John. 1979. *No-No Boy*. Seattle: University of Washington Press. (Orig. pub. 1957.)

Scarry, Elaine. 1985. *The Body in Pain: The Making and Unmaking of the World*. New York: Oxford University Press.

Takaki, Ronald. 1993. *A Different Mirror: A History of Multicultural America*, Canada: Little, Brown.

Weglyn, Michi. 1976. *Years of Infamy: The Untold Story of America's Concentration Camps*. New York: Morrow.

West, Cornel. 1997. "Diverse New World." In *Signs of Life in the USA: Readings on Popular Culture for Writers*, ed. Sonia Maasik and Jack Solomon, 557–62. Boston: Bedford. (Orig. pub. 1991.)

10   Toshio Mori, Richard Kim, and the Masculine Ideal

KEITH LAWRENCE

THE NAMES of Toshio Mori and Richard Kim are probably not the first that most literary critics would associate with the development or expansion of Asian American masculinity. Neither is what might be called a "masculinist writer," even in the broadest sense of the term; and neither focuses insistently on the Asian American male. Indeed, pairing the two writers—in virtually *any* context—may seem strangely imperceptive. It would be difficult to find two Asian American male writers with more divergent literary reputations. Mori is generally recognized as an innovative and gifted short story writer; over the last twenty-five years, his works have become firmly ensconced in the Asian American literary canon. Kim, on the other hand, is perceived as a flash-in-the-pan novelist whose popularity and significance extend little further than the early 1960s, when he wrote a pair of best-selling war stories that were never reprinted. While Mori is featured prominently in anthologies of Asian American literature and criticism, only two of the best known critical anthologies recognize Kim—and even then, with only token nods.[1] The literary anthologies ignore Kim altogether.

Yet in their fiction, both Mori and Kim take perceptive measure of mid-twentieth-century Asian American masculinity, and both do so against an implicit critique of American democracy. Further, both teach crucial lessons to those engaged in studies of Asian American manhood—those who, along with Jachinson Chan, recognize the "need to develop critical tools to navigate competing masculinities," to "articulate a fluid and self-critical sense of masculinity" (1998, 100–101). This is not to say, however, that either Mori or Kim puts forward a "masculine ideal" closely aligned with the predominant male types in contemporary Asian American literature. Despite asserting the importance of "exile" or social withdrawal (at least as a *stage* of masculine development), neither Mori nor Kim endorses the Asian American version of the (post)modernist *über*-male—the "Chinatown cowboy" of Frank Chin, for example, or the down-and-out-and-proud antihero of John Yau or David Wong Louie. Mori and Kim would be put off by the subdued desperation of such characters who, somewhat ironically, mime the angst-ridden loner or *isolato* of traditional white American male fiction—and who, in Yau's terms, are "loners by default," given that they "don't feel quite at home with anyone, even themselves" (1995, 324). Nor do Mori and Kim posit a version of the role-straddling male domestic, as typified by the sensitive yet "dis-oriented" protagonists of Chang-Rae Lee or David Low—and as advocated by Chan when he echoes Michael Kimmel's pleas for "a democratic manhood" and a "politics of inclusion" (1998, 101).

Instead, there is in Mori and Kim a studied indifference to or distrust of full inclusion in the American community. The two writers do not indict American democracy for its failure to make full payment on the ideals it owes its citizens so much as they assert the impossibility of such payment in the first place. That is, regardless of how far-extending the "all" in the vexed phrase concluding the Pledge of Allegiance may be, the "liberty" and "justice" in that same phrase are themselves imprecise and heavily qualified terms. For Mori or Kim, however, such a delimiting reality does not justify isolationism or withdrawal, much less assimilation with or subservience to those wielding more power. Both writers champion Buddhist integrity in facing American democracy— and both suggest that the individual male should no more abdicate his social commitment than he should prostitute himself to it. Integrity is accordingly centered in a necessarily fluid spiritual identity, an identity evolving through deliberate emotional refinement and carefully negotiated ethical decisions to live by or discard specific ideologies or cultural constructs. Genuine integrity is therefore not retained defensively; its perpetuation depends on rigorous self-assessment and close attention to others' needs. Thus defined, integrity is an elusive ideal; yet the Asian American male possessing it is empowered or authorized to establish himself within society in fulfilling and meaningful ways.

TOSHIO MORI AND MASCULINE PLACE

In an important sense, Toshio Mori's short stories constitute allegories of masculine place. Indeed, in making the American city emblematic of something other than Western corruption and despair, Mori's writings comprise a kind of twentieth-century anomaly. While Jack Murray cynically summarizes the modern American city as "the landscape of alienation" (1991, 63), in other words, Mori depicts it as potentially warm, close-knit, and nurturing. On first glance, in fact, Mori's city seems a throwback to the eighteenth- and nineteenth-century American village as defined by Lawrence Buell in *New England Literary Culture*: a "self-contained unit, sheltered from the outside world and organically independent"; a community whose "isolation, cohesiveness, innocence, and unchangingness" render it "ethnically homogeneous and institutionally stable" to the point that "the population stays the same, the houses stay the same color; nobody leaves, nobody even dies" (Buell 1986, 306). On closer examination, however, Mori's "village" is a selective and highly exclusive abstraction. It is perhaps best described as situated within an *internal* geography: an idealized and protective community of mind and ethnic identity that is only superficially dependent upon external physical place. Mori's most complete paradigm of such an internal geography is found in *Yokohama, California* (1949), a loosely knit, semiautobiographical collection of twenty-two short stories[2] over and around which Mori's authorial presence—as shaper and nurturer—broods.

As virtually all of his critics delight in pointing out, Mori's title— *Yokohama, California*—blends East and West in a metaphor for Japanese American culture (see, for example, Inada 1985, xiv–xix; Kim 1982, 163–65; Bedrosian 1988, 47). But the title has deeper implications. In the days before air travel, Yokohama, Japan, was the port city to Tokyo and hence to all of Japan. In carefully creating the lives and values at the core of his fictional Yokohama, Mori transcends physical locality through a geographical metaphor for—and map of—the Japanese American soul. Given (metaphorically) the male soldiers who guarded the original Japanese city and (more literally) Mori's male presence in his text, his short story collection becomes in particular a "port" to Japanese American male identity.

Ostensibly set in Oakland and what was then the San Leandro countryside, *Yokohama, California*, claims a setting that only selectively remembers or sees: Oakland itself is reduced to the area around Seventh Street, the heart of the Japanese American community sometimes known as Little Yokohama; through the prerogatives of fiction, twenty-mile-distant unincorporated rural areas are annexed to this section of downtown Oakland. And excluded from this community (because, finally, they are irrelevant to it) are the thousands of non–Japanese Americans who actually lived in Oakland and San Leandro during the 1930s and 1940s. Thus, Mori creates a community without static boundaries and without basis in reality (at least as others might see it), an abstraction that finally exists only in the minds of its inhabitants as a commonality of spirit and ideals.

While some may argue that Mori's internalization of place seems the fruit of a willful ignorance that undermines principles of both inclusion and autonomy, Mori does not implement this literary device naively or blindly. A former World War II internee, a writer who knew first-hand the capricious racism of American publishing, and a man who knew well the injustices of American society, Mori unquestionably understood the limitations of the American democratic ideal. While Mori does not in his stories overtly reject American democracy, he subtly yet frequently questions its viability, finally turning quietly from its promise. In other words, while Mori's "Yokohama" reifies a community, together with its protective and disciplinary forces, the stories through which the community is revealed are concerned only superficially with the larger American society—and even less with American democracy. Unlike Carlos Bulosan, who posits an America of the heart, Mori—an American citizen—establishes in California's interior a "Japan of the heart" that, like the thin sliding screens of a Japanese home, renders inconsequential or even nonexistent all surrounding business and noise.

In his discursive introduction to the 1985 reprinting of *Yokohama, California*, Lawson Inada establishes what has become the traditional reading of Mori's short fiction. But at least two elements of Inada's introduction are problematic. First, he constructs Mori as a writer with unmistakable roots in both Eastern and Western literary traditions—as a "genuine" Asian American author. Not only does Mori establish his stories on traditional Japanese literary forms, Inada tells us, he also "studied French writers, Russian writers, and like most of his American contemporaries, he was an admirer of Sherwood Anderson" (Inada 1985, xv). Repeating the commonplace that the title of Mori's collection is a nod to Anderson's *Winesburg, Ohio* (1988), Inada nevertheless stresses that *Winesburg*, in its focus on "grotesques," is "only a point of departure" for Mori, who creates a very different community characterized by "warmth and humor" (xv). Inada suggests, then, that Mori's legitimacy depends on both his Western familiarity *and* his Eastern uniqueness. Second, and more significantly, Inada is determined to situate the text as "more than a book" and Mori himself as more than simply a skilled writer. The book, says Inada, is "a monument, a classic of literature," a "legacy," and "the enduring strength, the embodiment of a people"; Mori himself is "a master craftsman," an "authentic original" (v, xvi).

These readings are problematic to the extent that they colonize (or even ghettoize) *Yokohama, California* as a sacrosanct and complete encapsulation of a culture and people—as a kind of Japanese American Ur text—and to the extent that they establish a patrilineal heritage for Japanese American literature. Inada's reading does not configure the text as simply beyond aesthetic or political reproach but as firmly ensconced in the literary tradition of the white American male. Perhaps Inada's desire to connect Mori to the "western familiar" springs from the fear that an "unfamiliar" writer will not be read, even by sophisticated twenty-first-century readers, or that a "non-western" writer is somehow incapable of being "American." Regardless, Inada somehow seems reluctant to emphasize the truly distinctive elements of Mori's "western" or "American" side—at the same time that, somewhat paradoxically, he insists on *le difference* of Mori's "eastern" side, touting Mori's "warmth and humor" as its marvelous consequences. All this wreaks havoc with the masculine perspectives of the stories themselves.

I would argue that *Yokohama, California* is not merely a departure from *Winesburg, Ohio*, but that the two are nearly as different in tone and intention as any texts possibly could be. Anderson's book reveals a fractured society; its interest is the suffering of isolated individuals who are neighbors in terms of physical proximity only, and certainly not in terms of mind or heart. Mori's book, on the other hand, emphasizes and even celebrates community, albeit a selective one. Its focus is not nearly so much on personal experience as on the nature of Japanese American spiritual cohesion—a cohesion largely dependent upon (in Bonnie TuSmith's terms) ethnically inscribed "communal values."[3] This focus is maintained, in part, by Mori's employing what might be called a "transforming" or "floating" narrator, one who is in some stories young and in others old; in some male, in others female; in some astute, in others dull. There is no central character in *Yokohama, California*, no *single* shaping consciousness comparable to George Willard in *Winesburg*.[4] Again, Mori's concern is not so much with individual characters or experiences as with the personality of place, the spiritual dimension of a shared geography and its capacity to empower its inhabitants.

All but five of the selections in *Yokohama* are better described as sketches than short stories, sketches of character that lack traditional plot, conflict, or thematic structure.[5] Mori's reliance on sketches is important: it subverts the much more traditionally plotted narratives of *Winesburg*, where "traditions" of all kinds serve to underscore isolation and emptiness. Mori's own inspiration seems to come, as Inada suggests, from late nineteenth-century Japanese literary standards and genres. What Inada ignores, however, is that the short episodic narratives represented by Japanese *shibai* and *tampen-shishosetsu* are primarily the work of male authors and that the narratives themselves are centered in emotion, not characterization or theme or plot. Further, through sentiment, if not indeed sentimentality, these brief narratives affirm the communal conventions, sensibilities, and values of traditional Japanese society. Clearly concerned with formalist aesthetics, Inada protests more than once in his introduction that Mori is not a sentimental writer— arguably not recognizing Eastern aesthetics of emotion or the Eastern reliance on sentiment to captivate and move.

Yokohama, California is framed by narratives about women. It opens with sketches of two elderly grandmothers who transcend time and locale to become mythic earth mothers. Presumably set in a Japanese internment camp during World War II, "Tomorrow is Coming, Children" is a grandmother's somewhat ironic evening reminiscence with her grandchildren, where she repeats familiar experiences and beliefs—her decision to come to America, her first difficult years in a new world, her mature commitment to her adopted land (evidenced by her wish to die and be buried in California), her faith in her grandchildren's future. As Inada makes clear, the story subtly subverts the white/ethnic hierarchy it seems to espouse: the grandmother is not so much telling a story as she is catechizing her grandchildren in historical facts that will allow them to challenge larger "American" authority as they mature. In Inada's words, "Grandma is actually teaching history, interpretation, survival tactics, strategy" (1985, xxii). In this sense and others, the phrase "Tomorrow is Coming" is a dominant theme of Mori's collection. And what Inada may not duly emphasize is that while the phrase is occasionally a warning, it is generally an expression of hope—evidencing faith in the rising generation and future possibilities.

The narrator of the second sketch, "The Woman Who Makes Swell Doughnuts," describes a no-longer-beautiful woman the entire community knows as Mama; the narrator portrays her home as a peaceful depot on the train track of life, a depot filled with the wonderful smell of her doughnuts and with warm, liberating silence. "I bow humbly," the narrator declares, "that such a house exists in my neighborhood so I may dash in and out when my spirit wanes, when hell is loose. I sing gratefully that such a simple and common experience becomes an event, an event of necessity and growth" (23). Inada argues that "this work of fiction belongs in its own category: *tribute*" (xiii), and connects its subject to the quality of *yasashi[sa]*: kindness, compassion, gentleness, generosity of soul. I would argue that "The Woman Who Makes" and "Tomorrow is Coming" are even more the embodiment of *wa*, a simple word meaning peace or harmony but implying a complex of social ideals, all centered in the image of a circle: cooperation, fairness, compromise, respect; appreciation for group potential; commitment to congenial relationships; determination not to shame others but to allow them to save face. More importantly, however, these sketches constitute the "tribute" of a male narrator to two women who have shaped his character, his understanding of himself, and his world. He himself is defined by *wa*, an encircling, uniting, and empowering mindset or communal view that mediates the "loose hell" of the surrounding society and allows him (even more than do racial distinctions) to identify—and understand—the other inhabitants of "Yokohama."

For the moment, I want to skip over the nineteen narratives comprising the body of *Yokohama, California* to consider the final narrative, "Tomorrow and Today," a bittersweet sketch about a young woman who longs for companionship but will probably never marry, a woman who is a skilled manager, a gifted cook, and the glue that binds her family of origin together. Her routine, declares the narrator, "is familiar and not emphasized," appearing "dull and colorless." But in it, he continues, "there is the breath-taking suspense that is alive and enormous, although the outcome and prospect of it"—that she will never enjoy the romance she desires—"is a pretty obvious thing" (165). The reason for optimism, according to the narrator, is that "while she is moving about day in and day out it is not whether she is brave and courageous or tragic and pathetic that is important about her life, but it is her day that is present and the day that is tomorrow which is her day and which will not be" (166). These puzzling words concluding Mori's book are perhaps more straightforward than they initially seem. They emphasize the importance of separating the reality of today from the illusion of tomorrow, the reality of duty from the illusion of dream, the reality of *gambaru* (endurance, hard work, perseverance) or *shikata ga nai* (a calm acceptance of harsh reality expressed as "It can't be helped," "I have no choice," or "It's just one of those things") from the illusion of escape or unfettered self-fulfillment. Mori's implication, however tentative (and however displeasing to twenty-first-century sensibilities), is that the protagonist of "Tomorrow and Today," a member of the rising generation who is learning duty and endurance, will eventually fill the apparently mundane role of community nurturer established by the grandmothers in the first two sketches, a role that authorizes or makes possible the existence of Yokohama in America.

Inside the frame provided by these three narratives, Mori paints the attributes and experiences that allow hope to be perpetuated; he also shows how optimism and trust may be destroyed. In other words, the protagonists of the collection's framing narratives comprise a standard by which the souls of other characters in the collection are measured and through which hope is defined and passed on. Art, Mori suggests throughout the collection, is a crucial vehicle for hope; and in this sense the body of *Yokohama* coheres around the half dozen artist sketches it incorporates. In "The Seventh Street Philosopher," Mori's narrator tells how an eccentric old man in the community announces that he will give a lecture and then rents a large hall for the occasion. On the night of the lecture, there are eleven people in the audience. The old man, says the narrator in language somewhat reminiscent of Faulkner, avoids becoming ridiculous and pathetic because

> he stood before us and in his beautiful sad way, tried to make us under-
> stand as he understood; tried with every bit of finesse and deep thought
> to reveal to us the beautiful world he could see and marvel at, but which
> we could not see. . . . And as he finished his lecture there was something
> worthwhile for everyone to hear and see, not just for the eleven persons
> in the auditorium but for the people of the earth: that of his voice, his
> gestures, his sadness, his pathethicness, his bravery, which are [the] com-
> mon lot and something the people, the inhabitants of the earth, could
> understand, sympathize [sic] and remember for awhile. (31–32)

Another more obvious "artist sketch" is the semiautobiographi- cal "Akira Yano," which on a fundamental level implies the struggle Japanese American writers once faced in getting their works published. On a deeper level, however, the sketch may also hint at reasons for the fictional protagonist's artistic failure. Significantly, his first book is titled *The Miserable Young Man*; and he declares at one point, "I don't know what's wrong with my prose. I am writing life, life as it is" (67). Despite his affirmed commitment to "life," the protagonist has abandoned his own: he fails the engineering courses in which he is enrolled; he shames his parents by dropping out of the college they have sacrificed to send him to; he abandons his roots and moves to New York, living among strangers. The title of his book is as much a self-judgment, finally, as a self-description.

There is a similar tension in the very brief story called "The Trees," which tells how an elderly man named Fukushima, who has just lost all he owns and who now fears for his sanity, asks his lifelong friend Hashimoto for the secret to his happiness, convinced that it is somehow linked to Hashimoto's mystical perceptions of the grove of pine trees near his home. Demanding that Hashimoto tell him what he sees in his trees, Fukushima is not satisfied when Hashimoto replies simply, "Why, I see the trees" (137). The larger context of the story suggests that Hashimoto's contentment, insofar as it springs from his trees, is the product of his walking among them daily. The implication is that happiness does not reside in theory or abstraction, as Bedrosian makes clear (1988, 54), but in application: the point is that appreciation and understanding—and art and life—subsist in movement and in engagement. This philosophy is crucial to the masculine ideals Mori develops in his collection, especially through his male artists, who are effectual to the extent that they "move"—that they perceive, experience, glean, internalize, and finally record the details of their own lives and the lives of others.

Through a kind of metafictional conceit, where the remaining narratives comprising *Yokohama, California* appear to be as much the creation and property of Yokohama's wordsmiths as of Mori himself, the collection self-reflexively probes and assesses the meaning and power of communal and personal identity. Several narratives, including "The End of the Line," "The Finance Over at Doi's," "The Eggs of the World" (which clearly takes off from Anderson's "The Egg and I"), and "Tomorrow and Today," examine loneliness not simply as the consequence of isolation but of the dissatisfaction, boredom, debilitation, mediocrity, and self-ignorance that any community potentially breeds. "Say It With Flowers" insists on integrity of behavior as well as of art. "The All American Girl" (who is a young, "frail" Japanese American barely five feet tall [91]) posits that if a thing of beauty is to be a joy forever, it must exist as unblemished promise, not as known or experienced reality. This story, more than any other, posits the ephemeral, false nature of the larger American dream: a siren song to the (Asian American) men who will listen. "He Who Has the Laughing Face" is a snapshot of a laundry truck driver who goes to the community park during his breaks and after work, leaving "all the causes of sadness, unhappiness, and sorrows of the earth behind in the laughter and the mute silence of time" (126) as he regains equilibrium in watching people, seeing community in richly colorful movement. "The Six Rows of Pompoms" and "Business at Eleven" suggest, albeit in different ways, that potential for success or failure is determined very early in life and that such potential must be carefully shaped by the adults of a community. Finally, "The Brothers" is a wry parable suggesting that all conflict may be cast in terms of sibling rivalry and that any rivalry, no matter how apparently trivial, has within it the seeds of tragedy and evil.

In the end, the abstracted geography of *Yokohama, California* argues that knowing *who you are* is synonymous with knowing *where you are*. As an entity, its narratives argue that community, with all its failings, should not be merely acknowledged but valued, loved. As a somewhat lonely voice in modernist and early postmodernist American literature, it cautiously espouses hope, selectively embracing America via the soul of the Japanese American community. Or does it? As early twenty-first-century readers, we may feel that the collection's optimism comes at the cost of Mori's abstracting, sentimentalizing, and even colonizing his subject. We will complain of the cultural selectivity of the book, pointing out that whites and the negative inroads of their culture are selectively absent from Mori's Yokohama. We will worry about the book's optimism, not only out of place in modernist America of the 1940s but almost unthinkable in the pre- and post–World War II writings of a Japanese American who was himself interned during the war. And regardless of the literary antecedents of Mori's narratives, we will be bothered by their overriding sentiment, their tendency to provoke primarily emotional rather than intellectual, political, or even aesthetic responses.

These issues are at least partially addressed—and the masculine focus of the collection emphasized—by allowing for a collapsing of polarities in the text: Japan and America, for example, or "Japanese" and "white," or city and country, or youth and age, or (more crucially) male and female, or (most crucially of all) optimism and despair. The most curious sketch in *Yokohama* is the one titled "Toshio Mori," the fifth in the book—and one of four narratives written around the character of Hajime Teruo, the de facto George Willard character in *Yokohama*. The sketch has virtually no plot: Spending a restless afternoon at home, Teruo is determined to "wipe out this ominous feeling of standing alone, walking alone, going alone, without a nod or a smile or caress or better, an understanding from someone" (39); and so he goes out for an evening in the city. He ends up at a popular girl's house, but she is already entertaining two other young men, and he leaves. He goes to another girl's house; she isn't home. He goes to a drugstore and sits at the soda fountain; conversation with old friends there intensifies his loneliness. He enters the Roosevelt Theatre to see a vaudeville production, but a blonde with a "throaty voice" (44) sings sad songs about the Ozarks, and Teruo leaves before the show ends. He returns home late, but can't sleep, "unable to understand and share his state of feeling that was accumulating and had been accumulating since birth" (45).

There is no character in the story named Toshio Mori; nor does such a character ostensibly figure into the story at all. It could be argued that the story's title is meant to connect the character of Teruo to Mori's adolescent self. But most readers would make such a connection anyway; and Mori's using the title solely for such a purpose would not be merely coy but awkward. Instead, Mori the middle-aged author deliberately links himself to an uncertain adolescent whose primary characteristic is loneliness, the need to belong and to be understood. Simultaneously, however, readers are encouraged to distinguish between Mori and Teruo. Because the collection as a whole provides alternatives to loneliness and holds out the promise of engagement and fulfillment, we assume its author has learned not merely survival but contentment. Thus, the story collapses youth and age, suggesting not only that human emotions and needs persist (that adolescence is not so much a *stage of* as a *metaphor for* life) but that such commodities as wisdom and contentment are potentially accessible to all, not just the old. Such an interpretation further implies that one must know loneliness and separation before one can know harmony and unity—and that one must know both loneliness and contentment before one can knowingly write either. And finally, the title provides the means whereby Mori asserts himself as an inhabitant of Yokohama, however tentative the assertion.

The issue of "Mori-as-inhabitant" is more complex than it seems, especially given the floating narrator of the collection. If Mori is Teruo, in other words, he conceivably is Takeo and George and Tsuneo as well—and Grandma and Mama and Hatsuye. Instead of seeing merely a communal portrait in *Yokohama*, the ethnohistorical reader will find paradigmatic significance: *Yokohama* as a personal snapshot, certainly, but also as a personal creed devolving from an expansive yet thoroughly grounded identity. Given its collapsing of "masculine" and "feminine" perspectives into a Taoist paradigm for masculine *being*, Mori's collection apparently takes up Jachinson Chan's challenge more than half a century before Chan issued it: to defy "the rigid binarism of femininity and masculinity" and to engage "the consequent reinvention of sexual identities" (101). Mori's paradigm does not, however, assert what Chan's challenge intends. That is, it asserts not a domesticated masculinity, where "domestic" signifies both "feminized" and "Americanized," but an American masculinity that has been enlarged, given authority, and (for want of a better term) "Asianized."[6] Thus, despite the ironies of Mori's rejecting American democracy and advocating the effectual exile of the Japanese American male to an internal landscape, *Yokohama* nevertheless establishes a masculine paradigm where, through the dismantling or reworking of polarized assumptions and traditions, life is not merely possible but potentially good and edifying.

RICHARD KIM AND MASCULINE POWER

Perhaps Richard Kim's stance on masculine power is best seen in terms of "conscientious inactivism." As allegories of Korean American masculinity, Kim's two novels (like Mori's short stories) do indeed suggest a personal responsibility to effect meaningful social change. But Kim also quite clearly suggests (again as Mori does) that the Asian or Asian American male must first exist apart from the kind of social systems commonly associated with American democracy and must *find* himself through exile. Indeed, Kim posits in his novels Buddhist hierarchies of sociality and spirituality implicitly at odds with the personal or communal arrogance and freewheeling idealism of American society. These hierarchies dictate that until one has established authority through self-goodness, one cannot initiate positive social change; that personal goodness (in turn) is dependent on uncluttered self-knowledge; and that self-understanding comes through separation from the world. Viewed superficially, especially given its emphasis on separation, Kim's aesthetic may seem conducive only to a wry self- and world-awareness, an awareness leading to renunciation—or, at the very least, to the determination to play life close to the vest and to avoid failure by planning that it will happen. Certainly, an easy acquiescence to fatalism and despair is the temptation that Kim's protagonists most conscientiously battle: it stunts personal maturity and inhibits all meaningful contributions one might make to others.

   In his personal life, Kim's modeling of the "separation philosophies" of his novels has undermined his reputation as an Asian American writer. A first-generation Korean American, he has held himself aloof from Korean American (and larger American) politics and from public attention. He calls his relatively brief brush with American fame following the publication of *The Martyred* (1964) "flattering and seductive" but also "scary and unpleasant" (Kim 1997, 184n13). And while many of his generation consider the Korean War to be the single most significant influence on personal and national identity (whether such identity is "Korean," "American," or some mixture of the two), both of his novels—set in Korea during the war—are ambivalent about the conflict itself, including America's role in it. Indeed, to the extent his views appear in his first novel, *The Martyred*, Kim suggests that the war brought Koreans little more than a keen awareness of humanity's "clinging onto the precipice of History" (1964, 308) and that, in a postwar world, Korea (or Korean America) can do little more than seek the "courage to fight despair, to love . . . , to have pity on mortal man" (286). When Kim wrote the long personal essay, "O My Korea!" for the February 1966 issue of the *Atlantic Monthly*, he disparaged Koreans' "pretensions about their glorious historical past (which is ugly and shameful) and brilliant cultural heritage (which is shabby and little)," flatly insisting that "when illusions, delusions, and smug contentions are swept away, what is left is a somber reality that the majority of Koreans are poor, miserable, suffering people, oppressed for centuries by governments and politicians, . . . and wavering on the brink of despair" (1966, 116).

Especially removed from the context of Kim's essay, which emphasizes Korean self-assessment and self-governance, these lines suggest an apparent misanthropy and ethnic self-negation only compounded by Kim's apparently "western" literary underpinnings.[7] Besides being heavily influenced by Camus' style and philosophy, *The Martyred* also bears unmistakable traces of Hemingway's language, characterizations, and tone—and of the "lean humanism" typical of much popular American literature of the mid-1930s through the early 1960s. It is a tightly written, well structured, and thematically complex novel that deserves a much wider present-day audience—despite the fact that when the novel is read superficially, there is, apart from its setting, little about it that seems obviously "eastern" or Korean and virtually nothing that seems distinctively Korean American.[8] However, a closer consideration of both *The Martyred* and of Kim's second novel, *The Innocent* (1968), suggests the opposite is true. Decidedly unexotic, the central characters in both novels are Koreans constructed as American types: they are confident, outspoken individualists who live by democratic principles and who are determined to secure personal and national liberty. (Writing about *The Innocent* in *Best Seller* magazine in late 1968, and clearly oblivious to the implications of his judgment for twenty-first-century readers, R. E. O'Brien professes unqualified admiration for "the clear, hard-headed, natural American descriptive passages and dialogue," gushing that "Kim's Korean officers talk and act like American professional soldiers" [288].) And both *The Martyred* and *The Innocent* test democratic principles—or rather, the capacity of human beings to live up to (or simply endure) the responsibilities such principles invoke.

The central action of *The Martyred* takes place in the long, uncertain months in the middle of the Korean War, sometime after the United Nations (UN)-backed southern forces had retaken Pyongyang from the communist Chinese-backed forces of the North. The novel's protagonist is Captain Lee, director of a division of the Army's Political Intelligence forces. Lee is ordered by his superior to investigate the deaths of twelve of fourteen Christian ministers captured and then killed by invading Chinese forces during the initial takeover of Pyongyang. Of the two surviving ministers, one has gone insane and the other initially refuses to tell what he knows. Meantime, a captured communist officer asserts that the twelve ministers—faithless and disloyal—died "like dogs, whimpering, whining, wailing" (Kim 1964, 141). In actual fact, however, we are never entirely certain how or why the twelve die—or why the remaining two are spared. Shin, the minister who initially refuses to talk, eventually asserts that he himself betrayed the other twelve to save his own life. His declaration of guilt is, quite clearly to the reader, not an entirely true statement. Nevertheless, in its turning the twelve dead ministers into martyrs, Shin's "confession" accords perfectly with the aims of the UN forces, who want to marshal support for the anticommunist resistance through the increasingly influential Christian leaders in Pyongyang. And it frees Shin to confide to Lee that he possesses a "terrible truth": that "when we are gone from this life we will never meet again, we will never see our children again"; that "there is no afterlife" (265). As a minister, however, Shin is determined to preserve the hope of his congregation by never revealing his "maddening truth" to them, but by devoting himself instead to "making them believe that God cares for them and I care for them" (266, 286). When war fills the void that faith once occupied, Kim suggests, there are few options other than despair—especially for those who understand that the unfolding of war is dictated by the harsh economies of power and ambition, and not the grand and constant virtues commonly ascribed it.

In rather curious ways, war becomes in *The Martyred* (and in its sequel, *The Innocent*, published in 1968) a metaphor for American democracy—where anything resembling a unified community of mind and purpose is a grand illusion and where idealists hoping to secure unfettered freedom are doomed to failure. This theme is especially emphatic in *The Innocent*, a fictionalized version of the 1962 military coup d'état that resulted in the expulsion from power of President Syngman Rhee and

the subsequent installation of a military-backed regime. The protagonist of the novel is once again Lee, now elevated to the rank of major. As
engineer of the carefully detailed plan whereby the coup is executed,
Lee is a close friend of the revolutionary at the center of the operation,
Colonel Min. Their friendship is undermined, however, by a crucial
philosophical difference: while Min espouses the Machiavellian conviction that revolution necessitates the efficient executions of those who
oppose it, Lee argues idealistically, even "democratically," that only if
the coup is bloodless will its consequences be beneficial and lasting.
Not until Min is assassinated does Lee finally admit the practical necessity of Min's position—although he will forever question its ethical
legitimacy.

Questions of politics aside, a superficial reading of *The Innocent* yields
little more than the coldly cynical interpretation Elaine Kim assigns to
it: that "soft-hearted emotionalism" is dangerous and that (in the words
of the novel itself) "at times one is forced to do evil deeds in order to
be truly moral" (1997, 161).[9] Indeed, unless we see that Kim quite deliberately frustrates reader expectations, we may worry that the novel
implies a "Korean" incapacity to establish "American" democracy; we
may worry, to use Rey Chow's phrase, that Kim is a "native who has
gone civilized" (1994, 126). True enough, *The Innocent* espouses a number
of darkly universal themes through its presentation of Korean patriots:
that even the closest loyalties are shallow and fleeting; that power inevitably corrupts and destroys; that wars designed to unseat tyrants
generally end in new tyrannies; and that any war exacts enormous personal expenditures from those who carry it out. But Kim's intended
applications are, in the end, insistently personal. Both *The Martyred* and
The Innocent name the causes and consequences of what, in a sweeping
historical and political sense, Kim might refer to as "Korean incertitude";
both implicitly condemn the unknowing or unquestioning individual
Korean male—or, by extension, the Korean American male immigrant.
Kim declared in a 1993 interview that he "wanted to show [in the novel]
that you have to be prepared to die for your cause" and that "when you
destroy others, you have to be prepared to be destroyed yourself." Thus,
the 1962 coup failed because individual military leaders "were not prepared to sacrifice themselves. . . . They could not resist the accouterments
of power" (Kim 1997, 162). Kim opines in "O My Korea!" that "each of the
major regimes" over the past 500 years of Korean history helped "create and . . . encourage the sort of political and social atmosphere which
now seems to have become a permanent part of the Korean mentality,"

an atmosphere of "suspicion, mistrust, pettiness and impotence," of "factional strife, intrigues, regicides, and political murders" (1966, 108). Still, Kim believes, "there is a hope for Korea." The "miracle" will come when "Koreans see themselves as they really are now and not as they were in some fanciful golden age that did not exist" (117).

This faint hope not only holds Kim's political cynicism at bay, it is at the heart of the masculine and decidedly Eastern allegory growing out of Kim's two novels—an allegorical pretext hinted at in Kim's dedication of *The Martyred* to "the memory of Albert Camus," where Kim declares that it was Camus' "insight into 'a strange form of love'" that "overcame for me the nihilism of the trenches and bunkers of Korea" (1964, 5). First of all, Kim's Eastern allegory dictates the necessity of seeing life and self clearly, of "knowing the world's grief" (1964, 316). Second, because the temporal is decidedly unfixed and because it is understood through imperfect human consciousness, the allegory mandates a profound distrust of all temporality—of other people; of popular cultural, political, or religious tradition; and of a personal or communal sense of the past. As "refugees," Kim suggests in *The Martyred*, all humanity are "inclined to remember or imagine many things they have left behind" (1964, 312). Third, Kim's allegory posits that the "authentic" may be known only through separation from the world. Lee says at the end of *The Innocent* that before he can "live and work for others" or "die for others," he "must learn to live with [him]self" (1968, 381). Finally, the allegory demarcates only two predictable kinds of existence for the knowing and noble individual: living in the society of others, which requires the living of a lie to protect them (as Shin does); or withdrawing into the self's own dark company, an act necessarily ending in madness, despair, and effectual suicide—as is Park's lot in *The Martyred*. ("I have been clinging onto the precipice of History," Park writes in his final note to Lee, "but I give up" [1964, 308].) There is a third way for the noble man to act, although it carries grave responsibilities. It is to "join in unison" with other "refugees"—to "live with this world and for this world" (1964, 316; 1968, 382) by telling others the truth, as Lee himself tries to do. But one must tell the truth simply and with deep compassion, trying to insure that the problems of the present are not engaged until the past—as imperfectly apprehended as "that terrifying and tragic reality"(1968, 383) may be—has been squarely confronted.[10]

These are all Buddhist themes and principles—and I believe it is no accident that Colonel Chang, the first character we meet in *The Martyred* outside Lee himself, is described as a "stout man" with "a head as bald and shiny as a Buddhist monk's" (1964, 16). Indeed, the military societies of Kim's novels are types of Buddhist monasteries; Chang and his military colleagues are, most simply, acolytes who resemble one another in their being too busy for women, too intelligent to become caught up in the minutiae of daily living, and (at least initially) too dedicated to noble causes to be swayed by selfishness, exhaustion, or public opinion.

Lee himself most nearly approximates the Buddhist ascetic ideal—in his renunciation of the material world and its trappings; in his determination to live for others according to fixed and timeless principles; and in his following the fourth step of the Eightfold Path, the step of "right behavior" with its specific directives: "Do not kill," "Do not steal," "Do not lie," "Do not be unchaste." Through Lee, Kim measures Western humanism and Buddhist renunciation against each other, rendering each more nearly stark, more poignantly lonely, through the contrast. In a sense, he robs his fiction of the voyeuristic quality suggested by Fredric Jameson's pronouncement that "the visual [or artistic] is essentially pornographic" (1). Rather than encountering a new world in *The Martyred* or *The Innocent*, much less an exotic one, we find our own world reflected dimly, coldly, and thinly back to us, regardless of our ethnicity, homeland, or expectations.

In his postcolonial assessment of Afro-Caribbean culture titled "Cultural Identity and Diaspora," Stuart Hall may be overstating the obvious when he says that "identity is not as transparent or unproblematic as we think"—but his subsequent argument is original and meritorious. He asserts that the "very authority and authenticity" of what we commonly mean by "cultural identity" is challenged by the likelihood that identity is not "an already accomplished fact, which the new cultural practices then represent," but "a 'production,' which is never complete, always in process, and always constituted within, not outside, representation" (1990, 222). Hall then poses two questions that extend to the artistic endeavors of every resettled or transplanted people. Is the appropriate methodology of art, Hall asks, "only a matter of unearthing that which the colonial experience buried and overlaid, bringing to light the hidden continuities it suppressed? Or is a quite different practice entailed—not the rediscovery but the *production* of identity. Not an identity grounded in the archaeology, but in the *re-telling* of the past?" (223–24).

Assuming the validity of the implicit response to Hall's rhetorical questions, what then is the nature of Kim's (re)constructed masculine identity in *The Martyred* and *The Innocent*? The conclusion to the former novel pits two scenes against each other: worshipers singing hymns in a Christian worship service and an informal gathering of refugees on the beach singing patriotic songs. Lee walks away from the "voices of those who had their god and could say 'Amen'"; and, "with a wondrous lightness of heart hitherto unknown" to him, he joins the refugees on the beach (1964, 316). At the end of *The Innocent*, an emotionally much older Lee understands that "there was no room in this world for easy despair—or easy denunciation." He feels a rush of love for the "millions of people" of Seoul—the "rich and poor, good and bad, happy and miserable, just and unjust"—and realizes that the tormented city "lay quiet and peaceful and dear to me." But the feeling comes as he observes Seoul from the window of the transport plane that is taking him, under military escort, to America; and the feeling quickly fades. As the plane turns from his homeland, Lee records that "in deep shame and sorrow, [I] buried my face in my hands, offering my silent dirge for the dead" (1968, 383–84).

Put more directly, the identity posited in Kim's two novels is dependent on separation, particularly a separation from "national" or political identity. As represented by Lee's experiences, such a separation is both gradual and voluntary; his own psychological separation from "a maddening world full of idiots" (1968, 348) occurs over time. He first separates himself from traditional belief, religious and otherwise, then from friends, and finally from his homeland and other political ties. Crucially, he does not replace his native land with America or the West. In fact, he is altogether aloof from the West; his "nostalgia," as he terms it, is reserved entirely for Korea. Lee's survival depends not so much on humanistic stoicism as on the willful act of separation itself, a separation from all things temporal, eventually even from "nostalgia."

To the extent that the experience of the Korean American male immigrant is embedded in his novels, Kim does not concern himself with questions of perception or acceptance. Lee's masculinity, intelligence, and integrity are never an issue; Lee is accepted and respected by all men he encounters, American as well as Korean. The assumption here—admittedly simplistic—is that integrity is invariably met with the deference it deserves. The issue of power is another matter. While Kim argues tersely in a 1993 interview that "power corrupts," he also implies in the same interview the absolute right of males to develop "organizational skills, discipline, and expertise" (Kim 1997, 162). Not an escape artist like Frank Chin's Ulysses Kwan (Chin 1994), and not finally a cocooner like the protagonist of David Wong Louie's "Birthday," Kim's idealized man remains physically within his culture while emotionally or spiritually separating himself from it, silently gathering strength—or power, or authority—to reach out to others. In such fruitful masculine withdrawal, Kim implies, one creates opportunity for self-understanding and personal fulfillment, a fulfillment that (somewhat paradoxically) is eventually realized through reengagement with society, through outward acts and not an inward gaze.

Late in *The Innocent* Lee asserts that there can be "indescribable relief" in traveling "the path of an exile" (359). This, I think, would be Kim's paramount adjuration to the immigrant American male—an adjuration spoken somewhat differently but with equal conviction by Toshio Mori two decades earlier: to become a self-knowing exile whose return is prefigured in his departure. Indeed, insofar as both Mori and Kim advance the notion of the masculine exile, they espouse a perspective in harmony with Gayatri Spivak's warning that we must cease to consider ourselves "saviours of marginality" (1990, 225–26). Rather than diagnosing the nature of Asian American masculinity or "saving" it (in the sense of fixing or preserving it), both Mori and Kim concern themselves with naming its potential and enabling its full emergence. Its manifestation will come, both writers suggest, as Asian American males, man by man, prepare themselves to thrive in American society by deliberately leaving it behind for the company of the (ethnic) self—and as, man by man, they prepare in exile for a triumphant return.

NOTES

1. The first of these is King-Kok Cheung's *An Interethnic Companion to Asian American Literature* (1997), which includes Elaine Kim's chapter, "Korean American Literature" (161–63). The second is a critical anthology only in the broadest sense of the term: Lan Cao and Himilee Novas' *Everything You Need to Know about Asian-American History* (1996; see pp. 275–76).

2. Excepting the first story in the collection, "Tomorrow is Coming, Children," Mori completed the manuscript for *Yokohama, California* in 1940; it was originally submitted to a publisher in 1941 and, with the assistance of William Saroyan, scheduled for publication in 1942. World War II intervened; and as Saroyan writes in his preface to the original 1949 edition, "publication of Toshio Mori's first book was postponed" (1985, 4).

3. See TuSmith (1993, viii). To be fair, Inada implies at least some of what I have just written about "selective community" and "spiritual cohesion" in his introduction, but he connects such observations, it seems to me, to Mori's "eastern" side, the side that values community, warmth, and soul. Inada thus ignores the possibility that Mori's perspective of the American city—real or

potential—was different from Anderson's (or the perspectives of other American writers of the 1930s and 1940s).

4. There are, however, a remarkable number of Japanese American males in *Yokohama* named George: one of Teruo's friends in "Toshio Mori" is named George (43); the antagonist in "The Chessmen" is George Murai (99 ff); George Noda is a central figure in "Nodas in America" (108 ff); and still another George is one of the two title characters in "The Brothers" (155 ff).

5. With the exception of "Lil' Yokohama," which is actually a character sketch of the community itself, the selections in Mori's book can be separated into three categories of narratives: first, those of youth, exploring the emotions of childhood and the transition from adolescence to adulthood; second, those of age, suggestive of the elements of a life well lived as opposed to a life wasted, gently emphatic regarding the crucial communal role of the elderly; and finally, the stories or sketches of middle life, works delineating the crucial role of the generation that bridges youth and age and that is deeply responsible to each.

6. King-Kok Cheung describes an "irresistible Chinese male image" of the *shushen* (poet-scholar) who bears some resemblance to the ideal Japanese American male posited by Mori: possessing "gentle demeanor," "wit," and "refined sensibility," he "prides himself on being indifferent to wealth and political power and seeks women and men who are equals in intelligence and integrity" (1998, 190).

7. Frank Chin (1998) would likely reject Kim's novel as a "Korean American" text on these grounds alone, given that Chin's most important cultural metaphor or type is the "Chinatown Cowboy" and that his most fully developed protagonist is named Ulysses Kwan, each a mythological and cultural blending of East and West to create a distinctive Chinese American male subject. And while she has subsequently broadened her expectations, Elaine Kim's preface to her *Asian American Literature* (1982) implies a standard of Asian American subject matter for authors she designates as "Asian American." She writes, "Although I agree that the complexity of each group's American experience merits a separate study, I am myself interested in what Asians in America share and in how they can be compared within the context of their American experiences" (xii).

8. Somewhat ironically, the highest praise from Kim's contemporaries was reserved for the apparently derivative qualities of his work. For example, in one of the first national reviews of *The Martyred*—appearing in *Time* magazine in February, 1964—the anonymous reviewer praised the book as "a somber and remorseless first novel," declaring that it could "stand with the works of Camus, by whom it was inspired and to whom it is dedicated" (1964, 108).

9. There are also aesthetic problems with *The Innocent*: the book is much longer than it needs to be; its many philosophical discussions become tedious rather than engaging or revealing; and its narrator/protagonist is finally an annoying whiner rather than the stoic and determined idealist that Kim apparently intends. And with very little tinkering, the novel could be about gang warfare in Los Angeles or interracial conflict in the historical South.

10. The difficulty of this task is suggested by the conclusion of *The Innocent*. Lee has decided to leave Korea, apparently for America; and as Seoul becomes "smaller and smaller" beneath the transport plane in which Lee is a passenger,

Lee sobs into his hands in a "dirge for the dead—and for my nostalgia." Then come the final ironic words of the novel, written as two one-paragraph lines:

> But—all this, too, is by the way.
> I was still very young when I left the country. (384)

WORKS CITED

Anderson, Sherwood. 1988. *Winesburg, Ohio*. New York: Penguin.

Bates, H. E. 1988. *The Modern Short Story from 1809–1953*. London: Robert Hale.

Bedrosian, Margaret. 1988. "The Koans of Toshio Mori." *MELUS* 15 (1): 47–55.

Buell, Lawrence. 1986. *New England Literary Culture from Revolution through Renaissance*. New York: Cambridge University Press.

Cao, Lan, and Himilee Novas. 1996. *Everything You Need to Know about Asian-American History*. New York: Plume.

Chan, Jachinson W. 1998. "Contemporary Asian American Men's Issues." In *Teaching Asian America: Diversity and the Problem of Community*, ed. Lane Ryo Hirabayashi, 93–102. Lanham, MD: Rowman & Littlefield.

Cheung, King-Kok. 1998. "Of Men and Men: Reconstructing Chinese American Masculinity." In *Other Sisterhoods: Literary Theory and U.S. Women of Color*, 173–99. Urbana: University of Illinois Press.

Chin, Frank. 1994. *Gunga Din Highway*. Minneapolis: Coffee House.

———. 1998. "Confessions of a Chinatown Cowboy." In *Bulletproof Buddhists and Other Essays*, 63–109. Honolulu: University of Hawai'i Press.

Chow, Rey. 1994. "Where Have All the Natives Gone?" In *Displacements: Cultural Identities in Question*, ed. Angelika Bammer, 125–51. Bloomington: Indiana University Press.

Hall, Stuart. 1990. "Cultural Identity and Diaspora." In *Identity: Community, Culture, Difference*, ed. Jonathan Rutherford, 222–37. London: Lawrence & Wishart.

Inada, Lawson Fusao. 1985. Introduction to *Yokohama, California*, Toshiro Mori. Seattle: University of Washington Press.

Kim, Elaine. 1982. *Asian American Literature: An Introduction to the Writings and Their Social Context*. Philadelphia: Temple University Press.

———. 1997. "Korean American Literature." *An Interethnic Companion to Asian American Literature*, ed. King-Kok Cheung, 156–91. New York: Cambridge University Press.

Kim, Richard E. 1964. *The Martyred*. New York: George Braziller.

———. 1968. *The Innocent*. New York: Houghton.

———. 1966. "O My Korea!" *Atlantic Monthly* 217 (2): 106–17.

Louie, David Wong. 1992. "Birthday." In *Pangs of Love*, 3–17. New York: Plume.

Mori, Toshio. 1985. *Yokohama, California*. Seattle: University of Washington Press.

Murray, Jack. 1991. *The Landscapes of Alienation: Ideological Subversion in Kafka, Celine, and Onetti*. Stanford: Stanford University Press.

O'Brien, R. E. 1968. Review of *The Innocent*, by Richard E. Kim. *Best Seller*, Oct. 15, p. 288.

Saroyan, William. 1985. Preface to the 1947 edition of *Yokohama, California*, by Toshiro Mori. *Yokohama, California*. Seattle: University of Washington Press.

Spivak, Gayatri Chakravorty. 1990. "Poststructuralism, Marginality, Postcoloniality and Value." In *Literary Theory Today*, ed. Peter Collier and Helga Geyer-Ryan, 219–44. Ithaca: Cornell University Press.

Time. 1964. "The Courage to Be." Review of *The Martyred*, by Richard E. Kim. Feb 28, p. 108.

TuSmith, Bonnie. 1993. *All My Relatives: Community in Contemporary Ethnic American Literatures*. Ann Arbor: University of Michigan Press.

Yau, John. 1995. "A Little Memento from the Boys." In *Under Western Eyes: Personal Essays from Asian America*, ed. Garrett Hongo, 321–22. New York: Anchor.

11   Home, Memory, and Narrative
in Monica Sone's *Nisei Daughter*

WARREN D. HOFFMAN

> Most of us failed to mention our experience for close to 40 years because to this
> day our emotions overwhelm us .... We must now expose ourselves so no
> innocent person will be submitted to this crippling experience.
> —Elsie Hashimoto, Commission on Wartime Relocation
> and Internment of Civilians Hearing, August 1981

FORTY YEARS after the internment of Japanese Americans
during World War II, hearings were held by a body of the U.S.
Government, the Commission on Wartime Relocation and Internment of
Civilians, in an attempt to come to terms with and redress this shameful
episode in American history. As evidenced by the Commission's report,
Personal Justice Denied (1982), the fact that the U.S. Government had
imprisoned approximately 110,000 Japanese and Japanese Americans
during World War II still seemed impossible for both internees and ob-
servers to grasp: "It became obvious that a forty-year silence did not
mean that bitter memories had dissipated; they had only been buried in
a shallow grave" (297). The words of internee Elsie Hashimoto prefacing
this article testify to the fact that even four decades after the internment,
internees still found it incredibly difficult to discuss their traumatic
experiences.

If it was difficult for Hashimoto to discuss the internment in 1981, one
can only imagine the challenges in creating a narrative about the internment less than ten years after the experience occurred. In thinking about
the relationship between narration and the internment of Japanese and
Japanese Americans during World War II, I am constantly brought back
to Monica Sone's[1] 1953 autobiography, *Nisei Daughter*, which embodies
this narrative challenge. Sone's text is part ethnic *bildungsroman*, part internment memoir.[2] The largest section of the text—not quite two-thirds

of the whole—recounts Sone's life growing up in "skid row" Seattle, while the remaining third tells of the consequences of Pearl Harbor for Sone's family. Here, Sone narrates her time in the Minidoka and Puyallup internment camps; and then, in two brief final chapters, she explains something of her reintegration into "mainstream" American society. Despite the seeming simplicity with which Sone tells her story, the text has confounded the few critics who have responded to it.[3] At times, Sone's autobiography is jarring and unsettling to contemporary sensibilities, depicting the events of internment in an apparently superficial and "whitewashed" manner. Many readers—especially Asian Americans—have quickly discounted the text as overly simplistic, as autobiography that quite consciously panders to a white audience. It is precisely such criticisms, however, that I wish to engage in this article as I consider Sone's strategies of narration as a means of personally coming to terms with World War II internment.

Critics of *Nisei Daughter* tend to fall into one of two camps: (1) those who chastise Sone for her seeming espousal of white America and her championing of American assimilation; and (2) those who read the text as a subtle yet valiant protest against Americanization, a struggle that subverts a hegemonic understanding of literature, history, and memory.[4] Though there are merits to both sides of this debate, the text is neither so clear-cut as either camp pretends nor can it be fully appreciated in either of these opposing lights. If anything, the nature of the text's acceptance, disavowal, and questioning of Japanese American identity mirrors the confusion and uncertainty produced by the internment itself, and therefore inherently forecloses any solitary ideological reading of the text. Further highlighting this ambiguity, Jinqi Ling argues that

> it is never easy to distinguish ideologically transformative texts from ideologically reinforcing ones, for judgments of a text's meaning are formed not only out of its immediate reading environment but also out of its retrospective use by subsequent interpretive communities. In this sense there are no explicitly "oppositional" or inherently "conservative" texts *but only texts that function in such ways in specific concerns.* (1998, 18; emphasis added)

Applying Ling's comment to Sone's text, we are confronted with the following challenges: How do we as readers and critics of Sone's text fifty years after its publication understand Sone's political agency? In what ways do we attach our own contemporary meanings and significations to this autobiography? Rather than criticizing Sone's text for faults in its depiction of Japanese American subjectivity or for its lackluster engagement with the experience of the internment, one must realize that the text comes from an era in which the possibility of unmediated narrative disclosure vis-à-vis the internment was fraught at best. As Traise Yamamoto reminds us, "Nisei women who assume autobiographical authority must be even more careful to present their stories in 'acceptable' terms" (1999, 106). Sone, far from selling out, needed to mitigate her criticism of the internment as she was writing for a white community that was not ready to face the shame of what they had inflicted on Japanese and Japanese Americans.

In line with Ling's argument, I want to situate *Nisei Daughter* firmly in its historical context and examine how the text interrogates the topic of "home," which, I believe, is Sone's main project in writing her autobiography. The need to create multiple homes via the text, whether as citizens, authors, or homeowners, is especially crucial as Sone and her family are repeatedly forced to abandon physical, emotional, psychic, and political homes and create new ones. In this sense, Sone's text details the search for a tangible and secure personal space. Ostensibly finding such a space, then, is essential to the formation of Japanese American identity. Sone must accordingly negotiate the various forms that home may take: her father's hotel, a family house, the internment camp, the Japanese American community—and the United States itself. Clearly, "home" in *Nisei Daughter* is not only multifaceted but also tenuous and unstable. Only in the shape of the textual narrative, with all of its concomitant unevenness, can Sone attempt to create a home—a unified whole (or the promise thereof) that brings together the disparate parts of her identity.

In his introduction to the 1979 edition of Sone's text, Frank Miyamoto argues that as concerned as the young narrator is with questions of personal identity, she still more fervently seeks "an answer to the question 'What is my place in this world?'" (xiv). Identity is thus inseparably tied to place and home and mediated via narration—especially given that the internment camps, where names and faces were replaced by numbers, forcibly demonstrated to Japanese Americans the reality of displacement and the elusiveness of home. While critics have condemned the textual shifts in narrative style and tone, these features deliberately and skillfully underscore Monica's search for a home. Indeed, the frustrated search for home is parallel to the frustrated effort of many Nisei women writers, Sone included, to tell their stories.[5] We can read the multiple homes as elements of a national allegory of the larger Japanese American community, elements that emphasize displacement[6] and, in the face of prejudice and hatred, the potential of Japanese Americans to establish homes as American citizens.

By emphasizing the connection between home and narration, I hope to complicate the previous analyses of Sone's text that have criticized it for selling out. Jinqi Ling quite astutely argues in *Narrating Nationalisms* that Asian American texts written before the 1980s Asian American literary renaissance need to be viewed within their respective historical contexts, an injunction ignored by most critics of Sone's text. Ling posits that "the articulation of individual Asian American writers at given historical moments in [a] period" is often inaccurately equated "with the actual presence of fully realized Asian American agency" (1998, 10). What critics have not always realized about early Asian American texts such as *Nisei Daughter* is how, in admittedly restricted and often circumscribed ways, they nevertheless bucked contemporary expectations and prejudices and changed perceptions of Asian Americans. Issued by a major American publisher (Little, Brown) less than eight years after the close of the war, *Nisei Daughter* neither renounces nor apologizes for Sone's Japanese heritage, but gives her presumably white readers a candid look at the Japanese American community. Furthermore, Sone creates what could be termed an Asian American or, more specifically, a Japanese American identity approximately twenty years before such a term was widely used. Had Sone published this text before the internment, or, more crucially, had she deleted all references to the internment from its pages, she might justifiably be accused of acting the tour guide to curious white Americans intent on reading Japanese America as an exotic community. Instead, only a relatively short time after the internment, Sone affirms her affiliation with and commitment to the pre- and postwar Japanese American community, thereby subordinating her desire for home to the social responsibility dictated by the new racial identity politics emerging from the internment. In this sense, *Nisei Daughter* is not merely autobiography but a social document challenging the official history's view of Roosevelt administration policy and subsequent actions of the American government.

In discussing the subtle ways in which "home" functions in *Nisei Daughter*, I wish to introduce the term *pseudo-home* as referring to a place—whether physical, emotional, or psychic—that *seems* like home but is in fact not home at all. The pseudo-home may be imposed on its occupants by outside hegemonic forces or it may be self-imposed; in either case (and despite apparent short-term advantages), the pseudo-home finally engenders emotional pain and discomfort. The pseudo-home may be confused with the "genuine" home because—for the ethnic Americans who typically occupy it—it is often the only home available. The pseudo-home appeals to its occupants by creating the illusion that they possess full agency as "homeowners," as members of a community, as American citizens. And whether the pseudo-home is consciously or unconsciously embraced, its inhabitants will eventually see that they dwell in a façade and will be required to repress the pain that such realization occasions. *Nisei Daughter*, in pointing to both explicit and unspoken racism, speaks to the pseudo-homes that Japanese Americans are forced into and suggests that the need for a secure and stable home is often at odds with the knowledge that such stability may be illusory. Sone's goal, like that of other oppressed minorities, is to abandon imposed pseudo-homes and create a lasting home on her own terms. For Sone, I would argue, the most lasting home in her text is ultimately the narrative itself.

Such an assertion may seem paradoxical or even tenuous, given that the narrative constructs postwar American society as rife with anti-Japanese American racism, especially as shown by the sociohistorical literary limitations imposed on Sone herself in the 1950s. The unstable nature of home for Japanese Americans during and following World War II may have in fact belied the efforts of contemporary Japanese American critics to affix a single meaning to Sone's text. Indeed, readers who assert that the text does not entirely achieve its goal of truthfully recording Japanese American life before, during, and after World War II may blame such failure on the apparent rise of the pseudo-home (a form that prefers accommodation to resistance) within (or even *as*) the narrative structure. In the end, however, Sone's text is less accommodating than its time period ostensibly allowed: it is a home that Sone comfortably inhabited by insuring its role in preserving her dignity and integrity intact.

From its opening chapters, which describe the physical environs and community in which Sone and her family live, *Nisei Daughter* underscores Sone's conviction that, in crucial ways, a safe emotional and psychic space is attainable only within a physical home. Sone reports that her family's first home was in the hotel owned by her father. While the hotel's guests are primarily itinerant lodgers, Sone's father refuses to give shelter to "petty thieves, bootleggers, drug peddlers, perverts, alcoholics and fugitives from the law," and thus establishes the hotel as a kind of Japanese American safe haven where the family's own living quarters are protected and secure (9). Furthermore, perhaps especially because they live on "Skid Row," Sone's family works to maintain a high level of decency and self-respect (8). And yet despite the warm memories it evokes for her, Sone's childhood home is a kind of pseudo-home in its constituting a threatened space.

As a child, Sone lives a narrow and provincial life, and she is under the impression that "the whole world consisted of two or three old hotels on every block" (14–15). She rarely leaves her neighborhood because her "street itself was a compact little world, teeming with the bustle of every kind of business in existence in Skidrow" (15). Within this inscribed space, white America appears only as peripheral abstractions and official institutions—churches, schools, and government offices—or as court-enforced racism, such as anti-Japanese legislation. But while Monica and her siblings always feel safe in the isolated environments in which the family finds itself, the outside world slowly encroaches on their space, an encroachment that eventually culminates in the internment. But even in the short run, the encroachment is significant. When Monica is twelve, for example, her sister Sumiko is severely ill with asthma, and the family doctor suggests that the Itois move from the city. As Sone's parents begin looking for a vacation house by the beach, Monica and Sumiko excitedly envision "a little white cottage" with comfortable beds and large breakfasts and lots of time for swimming (111–12). During their search, however, the family is repeatedly turned away without explanation. Monica reflects that "being Oriental had never been an urgent problem to us, living in Skidrow" (113)— where she feels an artificial sense of security—and she cannot fathom that white Americans are prejudiced against Japanese. But when Sone hears the words one white woman utters before closing her door on Sone and her mother—"I'm sorry, but we don't want Japs around here" (114)—Sone feels "raw angry fire flash through my veins, and I simmered" (115). Still, her anger is short-lived, partly because she wants to "learn to be as cheerful as Mother" (who, on arriving home, announces to the other family members that "we didn't find a thing we liked today") and partly because the family locates a small beach apartment shortly thereafter (115).

By playing up the role of her child self/protagonist, Sone is able to couch her criticism in the innocence of a young child who is only partially cognizant of anti–Japanese American racism. After all, "the Japanese American autobiographer," Traise Yamamoto correctly posits, "must...come to terms with the necessary disjunction between the 'I' who writes and the 'I' who is written about" (1999, 102–103). In the subtle, almost imperceptible movement between these subject positions in her text, Sone is able to "mask" (to borrow Yamamoto's terminology) or set aside certain childhood feelings about herself and white America[7] — or the still-raw adult emotions induced by the internment and all that surrounded it—and to create a protected textual home for herself.

Although critic Shirley Lim has argued that the aftermath of Sone's losing her temper represents Sone's rejection of Japanese culture and identity, I would argue that Monica's feelings (not simply her anger but also her quick recovery from it) are quite natural to a twelve-year-old child.[8] While Sone does indeed feel gratitude for the family's small vacation quarters in the Camden Apartments and for an amiable land-lady named Mrs. Olsen who makes "wonderful butter cookies" (116), such feelings hardly constitute a capitulation to the white American world. Indeed, these very feelings are undercut by the series of images with which the chapter concludes: Sone's mother composing melan-choly *tanka* (Japanese poetry) as she stands at the apartment's large bay window; the family's further encounters with racism and ostracism at a nearby resort; and the mixed emotions of a crowd of Japanese Ameri-cans at a send-off party for a young nisei named Dick who has accepted a job offer in Japan (117–24 passim). Thus, the hard realities of the out-side world may recede for the young Monica, but they never disappear for the adult narrator. If anything, this narrative structure allows Sone to have her "butter cookies" and eat them, too.

Though Sone's parents are successful in the hotel business, they want to establish a more permanent—that is, a safer and more typical—home in America. To Monica's surprise and delight, her family changes resi-dences after the long illness she experiences as an older teenager.[9] Her family drives to a "new large brown and yellow two-story frame house," with Sone stating that "this was our new home" (143). Each of the three physical homes occupied by the Itois in the early section of the text (the hotel, the vacation house, and the brown-and-yellow home just men-tioned) is relatively isolated from society at large; and, as previously em-phasized, the Japanese American community demarcates much of Mon-ica's world. One of Sone's earliest memories juxtaposes her "shocking discovery" at age six that she has Japanese blood with an ensuing scene in the Itois' kitchen, a scene that situates Sone's "cozily comfortable" family around the dinner table with everyone "in his place" (4). Many subsequent memories are of family activities—from a trip to Japan to dutiful participation in the *undo-kai*, a sports festival or picnic sponsored by Seattle's Japanese community each year. When the bombing of Pearl Harbor is announced, Sone returns home as quickly as possible, and her family gathers around their sputtering radio listening to the news in an act of unity, support, and mutual comfort-giving. When Japanese men are held by policemen and government agents for questioning, Sone's personal anxieties are subsumed in her collective affiliation with the larger Japanese American community; and instead of detailing her own emotions, she states simply that "the pressure of war moved in on our little community" (149).

In emphasizing the role of the Japanese American community in her life and in defining herself as a member of this community, Sone may appear to sublimate or even erase crucial identity issues relative to hybridity. Though Japanese Americans of Sone's generation might have found such issues foreign, their own identity nevertheless bespeaks an early hybridity that should not be discounted. Sone's hybrid nature is poignantly underscored when U.S. Army troops begin searching Japanese American homes for items indicating disloyalty. When the Japanese American community itself methodically destroys Japanese possessions to avert unwanted suspicion, Sone gathers her "well-worn Japanese language schoolbooks which I had been saving over a period of ten years with the thought that they might come in handy when I wanted to teach Japanese to my own children" (155), and she throws them into the fire. A Japanese doll given to her by her grandmother means so much to her, however, that she refuses to part with it. Though Traise Yamamoto reads these objects as "shallow" and trivial (1999, 137), I would argue their significance in connecting Monica—in ways that are not racially bound—to her Japanese heritage. Sone thus attempts to establish a viable personal space in U.S. society by preserving certain valued cultural artifacts rather than by asserting herself as Japanese (or American)—that is, by emphasizing her *ethnic* (or cultural) identity over her *racial* identity. Sone's attempts are closely tied to the fact that within America's multicultural landscape, at least some elements of Japanese *culture* were allowed to survive even the internment itself; Japanese *racial* identity, on the other hand, was the core of the U.S. Government's impetus for isolating Japanese Americans, for separating them from their homes and property, and for interning them in far-flung camps.

If Sone feels any ambivalence concerning her Japanese heritage, it derives primarily from the stentorian Mr. Ohashi, the principal of Nihon Gakko Japanese school. Mr. Ohashi's face, which "seemed to have been carved out of granite" with its "turned-down mouth and nostrils flaring with disapproval" (20), is evidence of his unbending Japanese character. While this very character teaches Sone and the other Japanese

American children to become obedient and well mannered, it is finally an unsatisfactory model for the construction of Japanese American identity. Indeed, Ohashi is defined in marked contrast to Sone's parents who, despite their similar immigrant status, have learned how to maneuver within American society. Subscribing to her parents' hybridity, Sone says that "gradually I yielded to my double dose of schooling," which gives her two personalities. To an extent, she could switch these personalities on and off: that of a noisy, energetic American and that of a timid, obedient Japanese (22). In arguing for the inclusion of Japanese Americans in the U.S. body politic, Sone suggests that an exclusively Japanese or American affiliation is doomed to fail.

Sone also reveals an early sense of a hybrid national identity, of what we now call transnationalism; she even suggests that, despite one's own national affiliation, the sites comprising transnationalism in any given instance problematize the very idea of the nation-state. In her third chapter, Sone describes how ships from Japan dock in Puget Sound and how the sailors on the ships come into town and look around. The Japanese American community in Seattle seems compelled to act as host to these visitors, trying to make them feel welcome during their stay. Confident guides take the visitors to Seward Park, where the Japanese immigrants had created "a magnificent vermilion torii, a replica of the famous torii at Miya-jima in Japan" (60), and proudly introduce the park (with its bridges, Japanese flora, and stone lanterns) as their own "beautiful Oriental garden, complete with torii" (60). Japanese visitors feign admiration, filling the Japanese Americans with pride. For *issei* Japanese, Seward Park is an "alternative Japan" imagined to be as authentic as parks in their former homeland; for *nisei* or second-generation Japanese Americans who (unlike Sone herself) had never been abroad, an outing at Seward Park is as close as they come to experiencing "real" Japan. For the Japanese sailors, in contrast, the park may be lovely and admirable, but it is clearly not Japan and the *torii* remains an obvious artificiality; their lukewarm reaction to Seward Park ironically undercuts its significance to the Japanese American community.

The relationship between transnationalism and authenticity is further complicated in the text when Sone describes the custom of the "at home," a kind of tea party hosted by the visiting Japanese sailors who entertained members of Seattle's Japanese American community on board their ships (61). Sone participates in many of these "at homes" and says that "to walk up the plank to a boat which had just come from Japan was exciting—like a state fair, an educational tour and a trip to a foreign land all rolled into one" (61). The ship metonymically replaces Japan, decentering and transporting the entire nation intact and "authentic" to Puget Sound Harbor. In effect, then, the "at home" dissociates Japan from its geographical site and reconstructs for Japanese Americans a shared national identity with Japan, primarily through customs and rituals (in this case drinking tea). The boat becomes a transnational diasporic space, similar to Paul Gilroy's "Black Atlantic,"[10] which exists outside of the traditional nation space and which mediates between the United States and Japan. The "at home," which is situated transnationally and accordingly deconstructs the rigid Japan/America binary, thus serves as a model for Japanese American personal identity formation. It allows Sone to detach ethnic identity from the nation space, enabling her to declare her status as a U.S. citizen while preserving her Japanese heritage. Sone subsequently emphasizes her ethnicity via the practice of Japanese customs and rituals that can be practiced anywhere.

While privileging this transnational home, Sone adamantly distances herself from the actual nation-state of Japan, the pseudo-home that white America would like to place her in. Significantly, both before and during World War II, many white Americans were in favor of deporting all Japanese Americans to Japan. Indirectly addressing this concern, Sone's fifth chapter recounts a family trip to Japan, where her purpose in writing is not to laud the country, but precisely the opposite—to demonstrate her family's political solidarity with the United States. Indeed, her description of the visit highlights just how foreign Japan is to Japanese Americans, especially to *nisei*. She implicitly answers the questions frequently posed by white Americans: "Where are you from?" and "Where is your home?" by separating herself from Japan-as-nation. Throughout the chapter, Sone reminds the reader that she is an outsider in a strange country. The chapter title alone—"We Meet Real Japanese"—indirectly emphasizes Sone's American identity. But because she herself makes the distinction between "Japanese *Americans*" and "*real* Japanese," she indicates her own subjective positioning as "inauthentically" Japanese. This chapter, though situated far from the politics and events of World War II, concretely addresses the accusation that Japanese Americans were a foreign threat to U.S. security. David Shih has astutely remarked that the title of Sone's text does not report "the author's position within her own family—à la [Jade Snow Wong's] *Fifth Chinese Daughter*"; instead, "the modifier in *Nisei Daughter* importantly signifies the tenure of her family in America. Hence the 'nisei daughter' is both the child of her parents and of her native land [America]" (Shih 1999, 113).

What is left unspoken until the end of chapter 5 is the real reason for her family's trip to Japan: Sone's grandfather is sick and wants to see his family before he dies. Sone and her siblings try to persuade their grandfather to return to America with them, but he simply replies that he is "too old now" (107). This is ostensibly true, but cloaks a more sinister reason: the Japanese Exclusion Act of 1924 renders his immigration impossible. Although Sone passes over the issue quickly, partly to preserve the believability of her "protagonist self" who, as a child, was altogether ignorant of the Exclusion Act and its consequences, the incident with her grandfather demonstrates what Sumida calls the "historicity of her autobiography" (1992, 227). When she states that "*my* country had passed an Immigration Law which kept all Orientals from immigrating to America" (107; emphasis added), she creates a subversive space that emphasizes her loyalty to America while pointing to its racist politics. Sone uses the "innocence" of her childhood self to soften the critique of racism that haunts the text—a critique that the adult narrator, with the luxury of hindsight, subtly weaves into the narrative.

The child Monica realizes how difficult it would be for her to live permanently in Japan. She finds herself the object of unwanted attention from "real" Japanese who know that she is American and who stare at her "foreign clothes" and make her feel "self-conscious" (91). The adult Sone retrospectively describes Japan as "a strange land of bicycles" (90) and an "exotic island" (108)—and makes it clear that she felt few significant ties to the people. Although her disenchantment with Japan stems in part from her being too young to appreciate its culture, for being more concerned with having "adventures" on her vacation than with receiving a cultural education, it also stems from an adult desire to establish her ties to America. Although she plays the part of the dutiful Japanese daughter who accompanies her father sightseeing, she soon declares that she "had really seen old Japan and had no need to see more" (96). In addition, she bristles at ritualized Japanese behavior. When her brother Kenji refuses to remove his shoes before entering a home, for example, Sone begins to agree with him that perhaps "Japan wasn't going to be much fun" (92).

Ironically, Sone never recounts a personal attack from white children in America. But she emphasizes how, in Japan, her American identity is questioned and even ridiculed by the Japanese children in the neighborhood who yell "American-jin! American-jin![*sic*]" (97). The one place where she and her siblings might have fit in most comfortably because of their racial characteristics proves to be unfriendly. Sone's narrative thus implies the possibility of white American acceptance despite American hostility toward ethnic minorities. In contrast, she suggests, an American—let alone a white American—would never be fully accepted by Japanese society even if she knew the customs or spoke the language. Soon tiring of Japan's seeming homogeneity, phenotypical and otherwise, Sone longs for the familiar and welcome diversity of America, perhaps its most essential feature. Sone and her siblings fight the Japanese children in the area, knowing that "the land where we were born was being put to a test" (98). They do not fight for admission into what they see as a closed society, but rather to defend their identity as Americans. In the process of creating an arguably ethnocentric and decidedly problematic portrait of Japan as pseudo-home, Sone creates a more inclusive picture of her American identity. This moment of textual composition confuses the easy equations of America as home and Japan as not-home. Her family's visit occurs before the internment, but she does not write about this episode until 1953. The moment of composition, then, attests to her simultaneous belief in and skepticism toward the American democratic project. Accordingly, the individual segments comprising the autobiography must be read in the context of the whole; Sone requires her audience to consider the democratic idealism of the United States—and of Sone's youthful self—in light of the internment and to see beyond an idealized, harmonious multiethnicity to a sometimes divisive and even tragic ethnic splintering.

Once back in Seattle, Sone reflects on her time in Japan and highlights America's hybrid and multicultural nature. "We had explored the exotic island of the Japanese," she writes. "I had felt the charm of its people. . . . but I had felt I was an alien among them." Then she declares: "This was home to me, this lovely Puget Sound Harbor stretched out before us. . . . This America, where I was born, surrounded by people of different racial extractions, was still my home" (108). Sone's rhetorical structure relies on juxtaposed paragraphs to position the Japanese as "Other," to construct them as a nation with which she lacks connection. They are "*the* Japanese," not her relatives or her community or—in any profound sense—her people. Though they have been gracious hosts, she categorically implies that she will always be a stranger to Japan; this enables her, both rhetorically and narratively, to assert that her true home is America. To do so, she uses language typically reserved by whites to describe the Asian American other: "exotic," "alien," and "charm[ing]" (108). In thus attending to America's multicultural/multiracial makeup, Sone clearly emphasizes America as a nonhomogenous nation-state.

At the same time, however, Sone's own sense of identity is undercut by the identity imposed on her as a "foreigner" in America. According to Elaine Kim:

> When she hears the executive order for evacuation, Kazuko thinks of herself as a "despised, pathetic, two-headed freak, a Japanese and an American, neither of which seemed to do me any good." It becomes evident that the dual identity had been thrust upon her. She had been careful all her life to make clear distinctions, but now suddenly there was no such thing as Japanese American. She was Japanese in the eyes of other Americans. (1982, 78)

With the onset of the war, this "two-headedness" seems to close in on Sone as her identity is suddenly constructed from without, primarily through white hegemonic discourse that ultimately invokes legalized internment. Sone's wartime "two-headedness" should not be conflated with the hybridity that earlier marks Sone's situation: her former hybridity is marked by a sense of agency, while her later situation is largely an imposed one (and an ontological pseudo-home). Thus, even though Sone strives for a hybrid Japanese American identity, given the experience of internment, a false hybridity deriving from her imposed "foreignness" seems to be her inheritance instead, as is reflected in the text's narrative style that embodies the conflicted and ambiguous nature of pre- and postwar Japanese American hybridity itself.[11]

Of all the homes in the narrative, the one that most problematizes the concept of home is, of course, the internment camp. The Itoi family, once assigned to their small space in the camp's barracks, a room measuring eighteen by twenty feet, does its best to make the space beautiful—or at least livable. Monica's mother wants to preserve the dandelions growing up between the two-by-fours in the floor to retain some sense of beauty, while Sone's father uses scrap lumber to build tables, chairs, and cabinets in order to approximate the features of a "real" home. The internees attempt to reproduce a life in the camps that mirrors their former lives; thus, even at its best, camp life can be nothing more than another pseudo-home. In the camps, the children go to school while the adults work; in their "spare time," internees may choose to participate in a variety of structured programs (195). Despite such "amenities," Sone cannot overlook the facts that "the wire fence was real" and that she does not retain "the right to walk out of it" (177). Ironically, the circumscribed view Sone experienced in her own Japanese American community growing up is paralleled in the sense of isolation pervading the camp. Camp internees "drifted farther and farther away from the American scene," she writes, and "the great struggle in which the world was engaged seemed far away, remote from our insulated way of life" (198). In many ways, the internment simply made more visible the limitations and impositions that had always been placed on Japanese Americans.

Somewhat surprisingly, however, Sone's treatment of the camp experience is comparatively brief (comprising only 50 of the 238 pages of *Nisei Daughter*) and bland. One imagines that Sone's internment was a heart-wrenching experience, yet there are—in the two chapters devoted to the camps—few details of the unseemly aspects of camp life, of Sone's anger, and of her family's humiliation or pain. Instead, in the first chapter, Sone describes an excursion outside the camp; in the second, she focuses on her brother Henry's wedding and the reception following it. That Sone's narrative appears complacent in discussing the internment is consistent with the book's publication date: in the early 1950s, very few internees would have been willing to write publicly and candidly about their experiences, and even if they had, even fewer publishers would have agreed to publish their writings.

And so when Sone's family is moved from the Puyallup Assembly Center (informally called Camp Harmony) to the Minidoka internment camp in Idaho, Sone's description of the train ride that takes them there is unusually cheery in tone. Sone writes that, from the train window, her family "drank in the extravagant beauty in hushed reverence. The country was bathed in the warm gold of the bright sun, turning the clouds into a pearly opalescence against the sapphire summer sky. Mountains reared proudly above us and the tumbling blue river below sparkled with the effervescence of liquid brilliants" (190). Taken out of context, one might think that the Itois were going on vacation; any hint of distress is entirely absent from this paragraph. Stephen Sumida appropriately sees such descriptions as built upon "language that appears accommodationist, the language of a Pollyanna" (1992, 228). And yet psychological readings of the internment note that internees tended to repress negative memories, including knowledge of why they were in the camps in the first place—to the end that "for many children, the evacuation was one of the happiest periods of their lives. For the first time, many had no scarcity of friends to play with and discipline was lax.... Adult interviewees, for example, recalled playing from sunrise until breakfast, going to school, playing until dinner, and then playing to a point of physical exhaustion, only to repeat the pattern every day for three years" (Morishima 1973, 16).

Regardless, Sone's response to the camps is not atypical. The official report of the Commission on Wartime Relocation emphasizes that "despite its painful significance, Japanese American discussions about camp, when they occurred at all, for a long time recounted only the trivial or humorous moments" (1982, 297). This narrative and stylistic disjunction is signified by the split between Sone the young protagonist and Sone the adult narrator. Though she is no longer a little girl, Sone remains invested in the innocence that has pervaded her text thus far—and that has, in real life, allowed her emotionally to endure the internment. This is not to say that the adult writer is unable or unwilling to critique her internment experience. On the contrary, Sone uses memory (as do many ethnic writers) not only as a coping mechanism but as a tool for critique. In Sone's case, memory allows her to construct on her own terms a home that is secure and protective; from this protected place, memory also allows her to safely critique what happened to her during World War II.

Put differently, Sone's memories highlight the discrepancies often contained in "official histories" of wartime America in the 1940s. If history is perceived as the "official story," then memory is an individual's personal relationship to the historical narrative, which may either support or call into question the "official story." History's authority comes from the ways in which it attempts to lodge itself in people's memories by such methods as appealing to nostalgia, erasing "unpleasant" events, or discounting problematic counternarratives that call its "authentic" representation of the past into question. This kind of whitewashed history potentially becomes interchangeable with memory as people *believe* it. Conversely, personal or collective memories that challenge such hegemonic histories may be reinscribed as—or into—history.

According to Amritjit Singh, the desire for a seamless historical narrative may cause "the dominant group in any nation-state . . . [to resort] to nostalgia, to mental or cultural ellipses, and to general forgetfulness in search of meaning and definitions that serve its own ideological needs of the moment" (1996, 5). Returning to questions of home and pseudo-home, "official" history is often a site of the pseudo-home in that it imparts a sense of stability and narrative authority at the expense of the memories of dissenting narratives of minority participants. Consequently, memory plays a crucial and formative role in the sociopolitical emergence of ethnic American groups, especially since ethnic Americans must often rewrite the dominant or "official" history—according to personal and communal memory—if they are to find an

American space to inhabit. In line with this, David Palumbo-Liu argues that memory and truth are associated with the process of "*un*concealing" (1996, 214). That is, as history and memory are juxtaposed, "the question confronting us is not 'What is true?' but 'What *makes it possible* for this or that to be regarded as true?'" (215). Deciding what is believable takes on political significance as one considers the issue of who has the authority to speak. In this context, one realizes that as a post–World War II writer, Sone had to jockey with mainstream writers, most of them white males, for narrative authority and credibility—especially insofar as "authority" referred to a controlling interest in mainstream American historical discourse, which even now prefers to forget that the internment ever happened.

In this context, Sone's memoir is not merely significant but revolutionary.[12] More precisely, Sone was required to mediate between the desire to express painful personal truths and the realization that—if she was to publish—she must deal with the realities of audience acceptance. Lisa Lowe asserts that "Asian American works themselves precisely underscore the tension between unifying American cultural narratives and the heterogeneous, intersecting formations of racialized immigrant subjects that are antagonistic to those narratives" (1996, 45). In this sense, Sone was required to mediate her memories against official history. Charging Sone with "selling out" to white publishers and readers, then, is not particularly valid—especially given that her text can be read as an instantiation of her own repressed memories and of the influence on the tone and content of her narrative of a white audience anxious to erase an ignominious experience from American history. As David Palumbo-Liu has observed, the act of overcoming silence is itself heroic, constituting the inscription of "significance where the dominant history has declared (through omission) that there is none" (1996, 223). At the time Sone was writing *Nisei Daughter*, the internment existed largely, if not *only*, in the memories of former internees; and to remember it publicly (albeit modestly), as Sone does in her memoir, is in itself a courageous act challenging "official" institutionalized history. Even in this qualified way, Sone establishes a textual home where none existed before.

For critics and readers who are uncomfortable with the apparently assimilationist stance of *Nisei Daughter*, its conclusion may be the most problematic segment of the text. The final line—"The Japanese and the American parts of me were now blended into one" (238)—not only ties up the text far too neatly, but also champions a coy hybridity that makes contemporary ethnic Americans wince. As a rule, critics who fault Sone for her ending assume that if she indeed had the agency to write and publish *Nisei Daughter*, she also should have been free to represent herself and other Japanese Americans more honestly. But because Sone's final line is ideologically anomalous in comparison to much of the rest of the text, perhaps we should see—in the oddness of its phrasing—confirmation of Sone's having been left unanchored by the experience of internment and of her reaching out to the official discourse of democracy as she grasps for something stable and potentially enabling to hold on to. In the words of Amy Iwasaki Mass, "Under conditions of domination one common psychological response of the dominated group is identification with the aggressor. The emotional anguish of being a victim is handled by an unconscious process in which the victim identifies with the aggressor by taking on the aggressor's ideas, behavior, and points of view" (1991, 159). Thus, while Sone's conclusion may seem to create of her life experience (and of the text itself) yet another pseudo-home as she reaches out for protection and wholeness, we must remember that in the shadow of the internment, only when hybridity is a forced and inorganic choice does it read as false. The ending might appear specious, in other words; but this fact alone does not invalidate the rest of the text, much less turn it into another pseudo-home.

Acknowledging the unstable "home" and subject position at the text's end, Lisa Lowe defends Sone by arguing that "we can read the declaration of Japanese and American 'blending' as a manner of naming a continuing project of suspicion and survival as the nisei subject narrates the violence of a system that demands assimilation through internment, obligatory patriotism, and military service" (1996, 50). In this sense, the concluding words of the text constitute more a "survival response"—a means to persistence or endurance—than an act of betrayal or easy assimilation. Significantly, it is not until Sone writes the preface to the 1979 edition of *Nisei Daughter* that she takes a firm and deliberate stance against the injustices committed by the federal government against Japanese Americans. In this preface she writes about "unfinished business with the government," "a national mistake," and "a petition for redress from Congress" (xvi). Though perhaps this newfound energy or courage is attributable to her maturation or her distance from the experience, it indicates a more favorable social context for speaking out about the atrocities of America's past. "So that their story will not be forgotten and lost to future generations," Sone writes, "the Nikkeis [sic] are telling the nation about 1942, a time when they became prisoners of their own government, without charges, without trials." She blames "President [Roosevelt] and Congress" for yielding to "the pressures of agricultural and other economic interest groups on the West Coast, which for fifty years had tried to be rid of the Nikkeis"—and the mass media for "molding public opinion to this end." But "most astounding of all," she writes, "the Supreme Court chose not to touch the issue of the Niseis' [sic] civil liberties as American citizens"—noting that Justice Robert Jackson's dissent had argued, in part, that "the Supreme Court for all time has validated the principle of racial discrimination in criminal procedure" (xvi–xvii).

Sone's preface thus supports her larger narrative in delineating the quest for home as an ongoing and evolving process, one dependent on a personal agency not always equivalent for all people at different historical moments. Thus, through her original text and her revised preface, Sone contextualizes her life as part of an emerging Japanese American history—a history inextricably tied to memory and shaped by sociopolitical exigency. Above all, as personal history it creates for its author a home that speaks to and for the early twentieth-century Japanese American experience.

Notes

Acknowledgments: I would like to thank Janet Montelaro, Philippa Kafka, Donald Petesch, and Dvora Weisberg, who provided extensive comments and suggestions on an early draft of this essay; David Palumbo-Liu and Tanya Kam helped me think through the issues of home, history, autobiography, and memory in later drafts. Finally, editors Keith Lawrence and Floyd Cheung provided invaluable comments in helping me polish this chapter.

1. Monica Sone is the name I have chosen to use to refer to the text's author and narrator. Some critics have referred to Sone by her maiden family name "Itoi" (which I use when discussing her family) as well as her Japanese first name "Kazuko."

2. It is difficult to definitively position Sone's text in either the autobiography or memoir genre. Insofar as the text starts with Sone's childhood many years before the internment, it reads like an autobiography. However, insofar as the text's narrative progression ostensibly leads us to the moment of internment, which is also the event that makes the publication of the book possible, it could be read as a memoir of the internment experience.

3. The two primary full-length articles that focus exclusively on Sone's autobiography are Shirley Lim's "Japanese American Women's Life Stories: Maternality in Monica Sone's *Nisei Daughter* and Joy Kogawa's *Obasan*" and Stephen Sumida's "Protest and Accommodation, Self-Satire and Self-Effacement, and Monica Sone's *Nisei Daughter*." Both make interesting claims about the text, but

read the text in specific ways that elide any moments of confusion or uncertainty that the text engenders. Other texts, including Lisa Lowe's *Immigrant Acts* (1996), Traise Yamamoto's *Masking Selves, Making Subjects* (1999), and Elaine Kim's *Asian American Literature* (1982), treat Sone's text as part of a larger discussion of Asian American literature.

4. David Shih's dissertation claims that "though its elements of protest are unmistakable, *Nisei Daughter* is not, finally, a protest book" (122). In a statement such as this, Shih almost seems to be faulting the text for a lack, not recognizing that outright protest would have been virtually impossible in 1953.

5. See chapter 3 in Traise Yamamoto's *Masking Selves, Making Subjects* (1999), for more on the challenges that nisei women faced in writing about their lives.

6. I am indebted to David Palumbo-Liu for this insight.

7. See Yamamoto (1999, 115–22) for more on masking in *Nisei Daughter*.

8. See Shirley Geok-Lin Lim (1990) for a discussion of maternal elements in Sone's text.

9. Sone casually writes that she "found [herself] enrolled at North Pines Sanitarium instead of the University of Washington" after having suffered from "nervous exhaustion" at business school (136). Her nine-month stay at the institution passes in a matter of pages.

10. See Paul Gilroy (1993, 1–40) for more on this term.

11. Feroza Jussawalla writes that because hybridity demands acceptance of the dominant white culture and rejection of the ethnic home or the domicile of origin, the "hybrid" ethnic American ultimately robs herself of ethnic identity. That is, if an ethnic American chooses hybridity, the hegemonic body often sees her as a "foreigner" within the adopted society and attaches her to a native—and foreign—home (Jussawalla 1997, 19). Such individuals are then left "home"-less and are attached to neither space.

12. A short scene from Erica Jong's novel *Inventing Memory* (1997) makes this evident. In Jong's text, 1953 is the year that Salome Wallinsky completes a book about the Holocaust titled *Dancing to America*. Commenting on the fate of Wallinsky's book, the narrator writes, "*Dancing to America*, which Salome considered her most important work, was never published. 'Too ethnic,' said one publisher. 'Too female,' said another. 'We'll be sued,' said a third. 'It's obscene,' said a fourth. 'We'll all go to jail,' said the last of them" (185–86). The antipathy of Wallinsky's potential "publishers"—fictional though they may be—is consistent with the time period and helps explain why Sone's autobiography, which was printed by the mainstream press of Little, Brown in 1953, is part Japantown tour à la *Fifth Chinese Daughter* and part "whitewashing" of anti-Japanese sentiment.

Works Cited

Commission on Wartime Relocation and Internment of Civilians. 1982. *Personal Justice Denied*. Washington, DC: U.S. Government Printing Office.

Gilroy, Paul. 1993. *Black Atlantic: Modernity and Double Consciousness*. Cambridge: Harvard University Press.

Iwasaki Mass, Amy. 1991. "Psychological Effects of the Camps on Japanese Americans." In *Japanese Americans: From Relocation to Redress*, ed. Roger Daniels, Sandra C. Taylor, and Harry H. L. Kitano, 159–62. Seattle: University of Washington Press.

Jong, Erica. 1997. *Inventing Memory*. New York: Harper Collins.

Jussawalla, Feroza. 1997. "South Asian Diaspora Writers in Britain: 'Home' Versus 'Hybridity'." In *Ideas of Home: Literature of Asian Migration*, ed. Geoffrey Kain, 17–37. East Lansing, MI: Michigan State University Press.

Kim, Elaine. 1982. *Asian American Literature: An Introduction to the Writings and Their Social Context*. Philadelphia: Temple University Press.

Lim, Shirley Geok-Lin. 1990. "Japanese American Women's Life Stories: Maternality in Monica Sone's *Nisei Daughter* and Joy Kogawa's *Obasan*." *Feminist Studies* 16 (2): 288–312.

Ling, Jinqi. 1998. *Narrating Nationalisms: Ideology and Form in Asian American Literature*. New York: Oxford University Press.

Lowe, Lisa. 1996. *Immigrant Acts: On Asian American Cultural Politics*. Durham: Duke University Press.

Miyamoto, S. Frank. 1979. Introduction to *Nisei Daughter*, by Monica Sone. Seattle: University of Washington Press.

Morishima, James K. 1973. "The Evacuation: Impact on the Family." *Asian-Americans: Psychological Perspectives*, ed. Stanley Sue and Nathaniel N. Wagner, 13–19. Palo Alto, CA: Science & Behavior.

Palumbo-Liu, David. "The Politics of Memory: Remembering History in Alice Walker and Joy Kogawa." In *Memory and Cultural Politics: New Approaches to American Ethnic Literatures*, ed. Amritjit Singh, Joseph T. Skerrett, and Robert E. Hogan, 211–26. Boston: Northeastern University Press.

Shih, David. 1999. "Representation and Exceptionalism in the Asian American Autobiography." PhD diss., University of Michigan.

1996. *Memory and Cultural Politics: New Approaches to American Ethnic Literatures*. Boston: Northeastern University Press.

Sone, Monica. 1979. *Nisei Daughter*. Seattle: University of Washington Press. (Orig. pub. 1953.)

Sumida, Stephen H. 1992. "Protest and Accommodation, Self-Satire and Self-Effacement, and Monica Sone's *Nisei Daughter*." In *Multicultural Autobiography: American Lives*, ed. James Robert Payne, 207–247. Knoxville: University of Tennessee Press.

Yamamoto, Traise. 1999. *Masking Selves, Making Subjects: Japanese American Women, Identity, and the Body*. Berkeley: University of California Press.

12 The "Pre-History" of an "Asian American" Writer: N.V.M. Gonzalez' Allegory of Decolonization

Augusto Espiritu

> Instead of according the people's lethargy an honored place in his esteem, he turns himself into an awakener of the people.
> —Frantz Fanon, "On National Culture"

A Turbulent Affair: Gonzalez and Asian American Criticism

Over the last three decades, N.V.M. Gonzalez has been a marginal presence in Asian American literary studies. Judging from the limited criticism of his works, his relationship with Asian American writers and scholars has been turbulent. Apparently, Gonzalez himself fired the initial salvos. In the early 1970s, as Kai-yu Hsu and Helen Palubinskas sardonically note, Gonzalez struck a somewhat elitist pose vis-à-vis struggling ethnic writers in the Manilatown area: "[T]he internationally recognized short-story writer N.V.M. Gonzalez has little to say about Manilatown because he, as a visiting celebrity in this country, lectures to a more cosmopolitan audience and is housed in quarters with more cosmopolitan appointments. . . . [Gonzalez] dismisses even the label "Filipino-American literature"[1] (Hsu and Palubinskas 1972; 126, 128). Nonetheless, Hsu and Palubinskas did include the Filipino author in their pioneering anthology *Asian American Authors*. "Nestor V. M. Gonzalez," the editors say, "has won all the major Philippine literary awards" (142), including the Commonwealth Literary Award (1941) and the Republic Cultural Heritage Award (1960). They praise the "quantity and quality of his writing," providing a naturalistic assessment of his heroic characters:

> The best of Gonzalez' stories present the rhythm and pulsation of the Filipinos' lives, particularly of those in the villages and frontiers freshly *wrested from wild nature*. The indomitable, stoic spirit of a pioneer farmer, the indestructible desire of an uneducated maidservant for her share of life and happiness, the tearless sorrow of a young mother who has just lost her infant, the feeling of loss and awe of a rustic settler suddenly plunged into an urban center... all are persuasively portrayed without any frills or fanfare of rhetoric. (142, my emphasis)

Hsu and Palubinskas show little consciousness of the colonial and post-colonial Philippine contexts in which such indomitable spirits and indestructible desires were being discharged, but they do show a marked absence of nativism in including a recent Asian immigrant in a collection of "Asian-American" authors.[2]

Just two years later, however, the publication of *Aiiieeeee!!!* (Chin, Chan and Inada, 1974; see Peñaranda 1974) signaled a different trend and a different reception of Gonzalez, a trend reflecting the shift away from a wider interpretation of "Asian American" in Asian American literary studies, a trend toward "masculinist" authors and texts reflective of the desire for acceptance into a pluralist, but nativist, America.[3] The lead essay on Filipino Americans reflects the tendency of editors Frank Chin et al. to draw a sharp divide between Asia and America, between Asians and Asian Americans, as they seek to establish the borders of a new identity-based literary project. In their essay "An Introduction to Filipino American Literature," Oscar Peñaranda, Serafin Syquia, and Sam Tagatac claim that "no Filipino American ('Flip'-born and/or raised in America) has ever published anything about the Filipino-American experience or any aspects of it" (1974, xlvix). Strangely, while positioning themselves as Filipino Americans, they consider "worthy of note" only "those writings of Filipinos in the Philippines about the Philippines." But they label their own survey of Philippine literature—thus defined—as disappointing, for they do not find in the literature the kind of masculinist, antiracist assurance that would help challenge their "invisibility" in the American mainstream, their fear of "ethnic rejection," and their anxiety about maintaining "ethnic awareness amid the bombardment of other influences" (Campomanes 1993, 49ff; Peñaranda et al. 1974, lix). Instead, Peñaranda et al. (1974) are singularly unimpressed by the "dull fiction" of Philippine novels.

Defining Gonzalez only as "a Filipino in the Philippines writing about the Philippines," Peñaranda et al. give qualified approval to only one aspect of his entire oeuvre: the "love element" in his novels *Winds of April* (1941), *A Season of Grace* (1956), and *The Bamboo Dancers* (1957). This last novel is, according to Peñaranda et al., superior to the other two; but even here they damn with faint praise: "The love in *The Bamboo Dancers* is more sophisticated, but not, unfortunately, more successfully told than in Gonzalez' earlier novels." And while displaying a greater regard for the works of Carlos Bulosan and Bienvenido Santos than for those of Gonzalez, Peñaranda et al. nonetheless condemn Bulosan and Santos for having "Filipino-oriented minds" (lvi, lix). Searching perhaps for masculine role models who stood up to America and to racism, Peñaranda et al. are puzzled to find what appears as an effete, feminized "love" for white people and America, expressed in "praises of America and the American" and in the refrain "America Hallelujah!" (lvi) Confronted by this inexplicable sense of otherness, Peñaranda et al. fall back on a comfortable Orientalism of the Filipino as "mimic" and as ideologically confused colonial; at the same time, they lionize the Filipino American as his clear-sighted superior:

> Although geographically and racially he is Oriental, the Filipino is so influenced by Western ways that many adopt and imitate anything American. The Filipino-American, aware of the contradictions in American society, is thus confused and dismayed when he visits the Philippines and finds brown faces with white minds. It is easier to judge someone who is looking at you from a distorted mirror. The Filipino-American writer is seeing and writing about the myth of the American dream, while the Filipino is drawn by the dream that is perpetuated by the heavy American influences in his country. (lxiii)

In 1972, President Ferdinand Marcos declared martial law and proclaimed the "New Society." Except for a brief visit to the Philippines in 1978, Gonzalez decided to remain in the United States during this period. Intentionally or unintentionally, the "visiting celebrity" had become an immigrant. After the anthologies of the 1970s, Gonzalez disappears for a time from Asian American literary studies. For instance, Elaine Kim's scholarly survey of Asian American literature (1984) bypasses him, as do such collections and texts as Chan and Chin's *The Big Aiiieeeee!* (1991), Sau-ling Cynthia Wong's *Reading Asian American Literature* (1993), and Shawn Wong's *Asian American Literature* (1996). However, in 1988, King-Kok Cheung and Stan Yogi of the University of California, Los Angeles—where Gonzalez had taught two years earlier—completed their groundbreaking *Asian American Literature: An Annotated Bibliography*; in it, there is ample bibliographic information about Gonzalez, much of it provided by the author himself. And in

King-Kok Cheung's *Interethnic Companion to Asian American Literature* (1997), Gonzalez himself is coauthor of the chapter on Filipino American literature.

In 1993, twenty-one years after Hsu and Palubinskas published *Asian American Authors* and four years before the publication of Cheung's *Interethnic Companion*, Oscar Campomanes issued his important essay on Asian American literary studies, "Filipinos in the United States and Their Literature of Exile," which provided a significant discussion of Gonzalez' writings in the context of questioning the grand narrative of immigration in "Asian American" literary studies. Campomanes called attention to what he called the "forgetting" of U.S. imperialism in historiography and literary studies. Instead of a teleology of assimilation into the American mainstream, he notes the presence of a thematic of "reverse telos" in Filipino literature in the United States, a yearning for or pointing toward the Philippine homeland. Campomanes uses Gonzalez's writings as a launching point into an exploration of post-colonial Filipino cultural estrangement, an estrangement resulting from successive waves of colonization and—more recently—from the ubiquitous influences of American pop culture and the importance accorded to the English language. Pointing again to paradigms established by Gonzalez's texts, Campomanes suggests that Filipino estrangement is most poignantly revealed through the vagaries of loss and gain in narratives of travel and homecoming. In the context of Campomanes' argument, the fact that Gonzalez had a "Filipino-oriented" mind had in every way ceased to be problematic. Indeed, rather than insisting on the separate natures and domains of Filipinos and Filipino Americans, Campomanes emphasized the shared perspective of deterritorialization and alienation that characterized the discourses of both bodies across generations, forming a unified "imagined community" (Anderson 1983, 57).

Something had happened to effect the change toward a "diasporic" perspective. Sau-ling Cynthia Wong (1996) outlines precisely such a shift in her summation of what she calls "Asian American cultural criticism," a shift resulting (in Wong's view) from *(1)* phenomenal increases in the number of Asian immigrants to the United States, together with the accompanying transformation of Asian Americans into an overwhelmingly immigrant community focused on Asian as well as American (or Asian American) affairs; *(2)* the rise of East Asian economies over the last two decades of the twentieth century, which shifted American economic investment and professional migration toward the Pacific Rim and instigated a period of heavy Asian investment throughout the Americas;

and *(3)* less and less certainty, especially after the end of the Cold War in 1990, about the nature or breadth of boundaries between Asian and Asian American Studies.[4] Almost overnight, Wong (1996) argues, the discourses of globalization, diaspora, and transnationalism shifted crucial intellectual attention from the American cultural mainstream to the Asia-Pacific region. Wong says little about the role of U.S. neocolonialism or imperialism in what she refers to as "denationalization," although subsequent scholarship—especially the writings of cultural critic Lisa Lowe (1996) and historian Arif Dirlik (1996)—has shown the role to be enormous.

My reading of "Bread of Salt" in the following pages springs from the desire to contribute to the "stretching out" of Asian American literary studies—to explore configurations of race and gender in contexts of nationalist and colonialist discourse. Since "Asian American" literary studies did not formally emerge until the late 1960s—after a more or less universal understanding of the phrase itself had begun to crystallize—I refer to the pre-1960s period as "pre-history." This is certainly not to say that this "pre-history" period is insignificant to the study of Asian American letters. Quite obviously, Asians in America were traveling, immigrating, and writing long before the arrival of a social movement that selfconsciously proclaimed itself "Asian American." Indeed, "pre-history" Asian American writers trouble both the periodization of "Asian American literary studies" and its inherent meanings or implications; such writers do so by both expanding and conflating the imagined geography of "Asian America," thereby forcing the label itself to account for works and themes that contradict or even subvert it or its prevailing paradigms. Gonzalez's writings provide a signal opportunity for exploring the interplay between the present of "Asian America" and the "pre-history" past, between Asia and Asian America, and perhaps even between Asian American and the long maligned "Oriental."

THE COLONIAL INTELLECTUAL IN FANON AND GONZALEZ

N.V.M. Gonzalez's short story "Bread of Salt" was first published in 1958,[5] ten years after the end of formal colonialism and during a period of heightening nationalism in the Philippines. This was the period of the famous tirades of Senator Claro M. Recto against a Philippine foreign policy that helped to perpetuate the postcolonial dependency of the country on the United States. It was also the period of President Garcia's "Filipino First" policy, which attempted to protect nascent

Philippine industrialization (Constantino 1978, 269–302). In 1958, Gonzalez was forty-three years old. He was an assistant professor at the University of the Philippines, where the resurgence of nationalism among students and intellectuals led to the formation of the *Kabataang Makabayan* ("Nationalist Youth") in the mid-1960s (Constantino 1978, 339). Such a political and intellectual climate must have subconsciously influenced Gonzalez as he sought a fictive reconstruction of the events of his childhood—even though Gonzalez has denied any overt connections between his fiction and the "politics" of this period. (In fact, he describes himself as being on the sidelines of any kind of political debate [Gonzalez 1998].) Nevertheless, "Bread of Salt" clearly lends itself to a nationalist reading, which may in part account for its continuing appeal.

The story itself is disarmingly simple. On the surface, it is the story of a sensitive young man who falls in love with a rich man's daughter, who in turn rejects him. In this sense, the story is a "growing up" narrative, a story recounting the classic passage from innocence to experience. Simultaneously, however, "Bread of Salt" embodies the mythic quest for social or economic mobility: its young protagonist aspires to join an elite group; he predictably fails to hit the mark; he is subsequently directed toward another quest altogether, one that validates his modest class origins. An important third reading of "Bread of Salt" is as an allegory of the (post)colonial intellectual's journey—via appropriate formal education—toward an understanding of national culture *and* a sense of self within the context of this culture. This reading is suggested by Gonzalez's literary autobiography, *Kalutang: A Filipino in the World*,[6] which was first published in 1972, fourteen years after "Bread of Salt." In *Kalutang*, Gonzalez describes his own "apprenticeship" under colonial patrons and his growing awareness of both colonialism and nationalism. Referring to himself and his colleagues, the generation of Filipino writers reared under the American colonial dispensation and thus publishing in English, he states, "We were unaware . . . that we were living out a pattern of literary activity that had been known, though perhaps not appreciated, in Africa" (Gonzalez 1990, 22).

Referring to what is now a familiar essay in postcolonial theory, Frantz Fanon's "On National Culture"[7] (1963), Gonzalez suggests that Fanon was one of the first students of the Third World to appreciate the literary/colonial efforts of Filipinos. (Of course, Gonzalez is being imaginative here, for Fanon—the Martinican psychiatrist and theorist of the Algerian Revolution—never said a word about Filipinos in his works, at least not directly.) Nevertheless, Fanon is clearly in accordance with Gonzalez's own political views when he describes the evolution of the colonized intellectual toward a sense of national identity. This evolution, Fanon posits, occurs in three phases or "levels"[8] (Fanon 1963, 222). In the first phase, "the native intellectual gives proof that he has assimilated the culture of the occupying power." In the second phase, "we find the native is disturbed; he decides to remember what he is." But since he is not a part of his people, he only has exterior relations with them. And in the third phase, which Fanon calls the "fighting phase," the native, "after having tried to lose himself in the people and with the people, will on the contrary shake the people." Rather than implicitly respecting the people's right to lethargy, he "turns himself into an *awakener* of the people; hence comes a fighting literature, a revolutionary literature, and a national literature" (222–23, my emphasis).

In his summation in *Kalutang* of the first two phases of Fanon's model, Gonzalez quite accurately paraphrases Fanon and quite fairly captures his spirit. However, the summation of the final phase is vintage Gonzalez: he altogether sidesteps Fanon's revolutionary rhetoric, replacing it with what might be called the injunctions of "individualist socialism" when he writes, "With patience, courage, and imagination, we might then move on to the third stage, which would involve our seeking out our own people for instruction and inspiration, joining our talents with their aspiration and efforts" (Gonzalez 223).

To read "Bread of Salt" in context of the Fanon/Gonzalez model of emergent nationalism requires a more complete precis of the story than that offered previously. The protagonist/narrator is a fourteen-year-old male who relishes the regular performance of a certain chore for his grandmother: going to Progreso Street to buy *pan de sal* (a "bread roll"— or, literally, the "bread of salt"[9] of the story's title). As a child, and while returning to his grandmother with the bread, he holds himself back from eating what she has told him is his share. Instead, he claims as his reward the view he sees while returning to his grandmother: the sea wall where stood the magnificent house of the old Spaniard, Don Esteban. The narrator's grandfather had spent his last thirty years as the overseer of the Spaniard's coconut plantation. As an older child, the narrator wonders, would he too serve this "great house"? (Gonzalez 1993, 96–97).

One day he learns that his classmate Aida is the Spaniard's niece. His doubts about the future disappear as he fantasizes that Aida's "real purpose . . . was to reveal . . . her assent to my desire."[10] The young man does everything to be worthy of her—he starts to play handball and he faithfully attends school. Fascinated by his English teacher, whose forte is declaiming Robert Louis Stevenson's "The Sire de Matetroit's Door" (the story of a gentleman who wins the hand of a lady), the young man is sure that one day he too will succeed in his romantic venture. To this end, he dutifully practices the violin and becomes a skilled musician (97, 98–99). He joins the "Minviluz" band led by twenty-two-year-old Pete Saez, a trombone player who supports his mother. They play for his school's Thanksgiving Day program, although the narrator shows no interest in the principal's speech about America, the Pilgrim Fathers, or the feasting on "turkey." Instead, he thinks of the money and the fame he could earn as a violinist in New York, and of saving money to buy Aida a brooch (99–101).

His aunt has brought a maid from the farm to do the house chores. The narrator says that it would now be "no longer becoming on my part" to buy the *pan de sal* and thanks his aunt for her understanding. Unimpressed, the aunt warns him that "at parties musicians always eat last." Shortly before Christmas, the band plays for the *asalto*, or surprise party, which the Buenavista Women's Club is throwing for Josefina and Alicia, Don Esteban's daughters (100, 101). The narrator greets Aida in English with "Merry Christmas!"—and imagines how much the other girls must envy Aida's "fair cheeks and the bobbed dark brown hair which lineage had denied them." The band plays several pieces throughout the night— "The Poet and the Peasant," "La Paloma," "A Basket of Roses," "The Dance of the Glowworms." Don Esteban's daughters also perform music for the crowd, and the narrator gazes at Aida's "long, flowing white gown" and the "arch of sampaguita flowers on her hair" (102–104).

Boxes of food arrive; the narrator remembers his hunger as the table is laid out: "There was more food before us than I had ever imagined. I searched in my mind for the names of the dishes; and my ignorance appalled me" (105). He discovers something exotic—egg yolks dipped in honey and peppermint—and says, "I allowed my covetousness to have its way and not only stuffed my mouth with this and that confection but also wrapped a quantity of those egg yolk things in several sheets of napkin paper" (105). Suddenly, he is startled by a voice behind him, a voice asking, "Have you eaten?" It is Aida who tells him, "If you wait a little while till they're all gone, I'll wrap up a big package for you." He brings a handkerchief to his mouth. "I might have honored her solicitude adequately," he writes, "and even relieved myself of any embarrassments." His ardor for her vanishes entirely. He walks out to the veranda "where once [his] love had trod on sunbeams" and sees his grandmother's window calling him home. As the party breaks up, he tells Pete that he is hungry. They walk down Progreso Street and wait for the baker. He feels the urge to buy for his grandmother the *pan de sal*, although this time with his own money. He watches "the bakery assistants at work until our bodies grew warm from the oven across the door. But it was not quite five, and the bread was not yet ready" (105–106).

"BREAD OF SALT" AS ALLEGORY OF DECOLONIZATION

One can see in "Bread of Salt" the elements of the Fanon/Gonzalez model of emergent nationalism: assimilation, separation, and cultural adherence. Assimilation is most clearly instanced in the narrator's dream of social climbing. Interestingly, the young man is not poor. We are told that he can afford a private education. He owns a violin and speaks English instead of the vernacular. Meanwhile, his aunt can afford to hire a maid from the "farms." The Spaniard's house, on which he trains his gaze, is separated from the town by a stone fence which makes it appear like a "castle." Images of Spanish (and by extension, American) colonialism are thus evoked. The young man's grandfather was neither a tenant nor a field hand, but the "overseer" of the Spaniard's coconut plantation[11] —thereby calling to mind the "intellectuals" Gonzalez describes in his autobiography: those who were compelled or seduced by colonialism to put themselves at the service of the hegemonic.[12] Quite clearly, the young man's query ("Would he too serve this 'great house'?") is also his wish, an ambition reflective of his grandfather's own desire for "acceptance" into the great house. After all, it is the grandfather who, before his death, slyly suggests that the young man court Aida (97).

The story thus weaves the desire for economic advancement with the desire for cultural assimilation—as embodied in the narrator's infatuation with the Spaniard's niece, Aida. The narrator imagines that his submission to the Spaniard is a fait accompli, and that it would be sweetened by Aida's submission to him. Again, Aida's "real purpose," says the protagonist, "was to reveal ... her assent to my desire" (97). While even the naive protagonist understands that such a submission cannot happen naturally, his vision ends there. He imagines that if he is to "live long to honor her," he must transform his body and mind through physical exertion (handball) and education (particularly the study of English and of British literature). Here, ironically, the colonizer's language and culture supplant indigenous knowledge and values; the colonizer's language is the source of prestige and power, and the colonizer's art is established as the highest cultural standard. One sees the narrator's growing snobbery in his assertion to his aunt that "it is no longer becoming on my part" to buy the *pan de sal*, a duty which he now leaves to the lower-class maid from the "farms" (100).

The narrator foolishly believes that his music will allow him to enter the colonizers' world, and that his entrance will come via the fame and fortune he will attain as an artist in New York, although he professes little interest in America's colonial history or customs (disdaining, for instance, the "Pilgrim Fathers" and "turkey"). In this sense, the narrator's dream is analogous to Gonzalez' own youthful dream of becoming a second Jose Garcia Villa[13] —who, during the 1930s and 1940s, succeeded in "crossing over" from Filipino to American literature as he was embraced by the New York literati. But the mature author of "Bread of Salt" has clearly separated himself from such youthful illusions; and the narrative strongly implies that, given their almost certain attachment to imperialistic and selfish values, youthful dreams, if attained by the dreamer, are invariably fraught with serious consequences.

To begin with, the protagonist's infatuation is figured in hierarchical terms. He imagines that Aida has "fixed" his route to school—which follows the political geography of the town "past the post office, the town plaza and the church, the health center east of the plaza, and at last the school grounds." Thus, he metaphorically arrives as object of cultural assimilation via the institutions of power that Aida's father dominates. The narrator's route is in this sense a ritual of subordination. Moreover, the narrator tells us that it was enough that Aida walk half a block ahead of him and, from a distance, perhaps throw a glance in his direction—and thus "bestow upon my heart a deserved and abundant blessing" (97).

In the second place, the narrator's submission is figured in gendered and racialized terms, for Aida embodies his attraction to Philippine American colonial hegemony itself. The description of Aida leaves little doubt as to the sensual qualities that make her "beautiful" to the narrator. First, she is white and she is well born. As previously noted, other girls envy Aida's "fair cheeks and the bobbed dark brown hair which lineage had denied them" (102). The depiction of Aida stands in stark contrast to the narrator's racist descriptions of himself—as, for example, when he observes that "my short brown arm learned at last to draw the bow [of the violin] with grace" (98). Moreover, Aida is always draped in *white*—in school, for example, she wears a "white middy" and at the party she wears a "long, flowing white gown." Perhaps it is only appropriate that the object of cultural assimilation evinces dubious "local color" through the use of the *sampaguita*, the fragrant and ubiquitous—but *white*—flowers that Aida is wearing in her hair.

The narrator's quest to purchase whiteness comes crashing down during the moment in the narrative demarcating Fanon's second phase, the phase of "separation." The moment in question is the narrator's brief experience at the banquet table—which, significantly, is splendorously laid in the house of the Spaniard, Don Esteban, who occupies the town's de facto seat of colonial power. The banquet table, then, is a hegemonic spectacle: its display of food (ever the symbol of opulence in a poor country) could be matched in no other household in town, either in its abundance or its foreign origins (much of it made, we are told, by Swiss bakers in the colonial capital, Manila). The hegemony's "performance" of food is matched by its cultural performance as the Spaniard's daughters play the harp to great applause, their encore song evoking "snatches of the years gone by" as Don Esteban himself "whisper[s] in his rapture: 'Heavenly. Heavenly" (104)—almost as if he were drawing the deep sentiments created by the women to his person and in the service of his power.[14]

The consumption or ingestion of food, the symbol of opulence, becomes the instrument of the narrator's downfall, and of the hegemony's rejection of the colonized intellectual. The food overwhelms him in a way analogous to the seductive inducements of colonial education and political patronage. But he does not yet posses the knowledge required to order these signs of power: "I searched in my mind for the names of the dishes; and my ignorance appalled me." He allows his naivete, his attraction to the exotic (the "egg yolks dipped in honey and peppermint"), and his "covetousness" to guide his path, which leads him past the line prescribed for the lower-class native.

Soon enough, Aida, the symbol of colonialism's cultural seductiveness, returns, this time as the instrument for restoring order. She figuratively pounces on the young man; the element of surprise (the narrator does not see her coming), the sharpness of her inquiry ("Have you eaten?"), and the power of her gaze ("I could not . . . believe that she had *seen* me") are her sure weapons (105, my emphasis). Aida obviously means to do more than warn. She is determined to put the transgressor squarely in his place by treating him as a misbehaving child and certainly not a potential suitor, by pressing the point of propriety and containment. "If you wait a little while till they've all gone," she pointedly tells him, "I'll wrap a big package for you" (105). No wonder that the narrator's ardor for Aida—and for the dream of cultural assimilation she represents—immediately vanishes. The colonial is denied his dignity, his masculinity, his adulthood—and is deprived even of the chance to excuse himself gracefully from the banquet. He had come in service of the master and as a guest, with the illusion that his place was set at the colonial table; he leaves an othered, affronted, and discounted native subject.

Again, the colonial's recognition of his humiliation is immediate: "I walked away to the nearest door, praying that the damask curtains might hide me in my shame" (105-106). We find in him Fanon's disturbed native, the newly sighted individual who "decides to remember what he is." As he walks out onto the veranda (which, in this beautiful passage, he describes as the place "where once my love had trod on sunbeams"), he catches a glimpse of his grandmother's window and imagines it calling him home. That the narrator is thus "called" or beckoned is ironic; but it is also indicative of his redeemable state, of his awakening interiority. That is, he is not yet the embodiment of Fanon's fully colonized intellectual who, "since he is not a part of his people," is capable only of "exterior relations" with them. While the narrator's realization of this truth of "home"—and of his place within it—is as yet unformed, he understands enough to make a conscious effort to buy the *pan de sal*, this time with his own money.

With the other members of the band, the narrator heads down Progreso Street, an undisguised metaphor for the narrator's moral "progress" itself. Importantly, however, "progress" is rearticulated during the course of the story, at first apparently validating the pursuit of colonial values or power, but at last signaling a "return to the folk"—as represented by the band's journey to the bakery.[15] The *pan de sal* is the most immediate, most recognizable, and most cherished symbol of native culture (of "home") that the young man knows, and the labor of the bakery assistants (his own people) becomes the source of his "warmth" and regeneration. Nevertheless, the story ends on a note of deferral: "It was not quite five, and the bread was not yet ready." The repetition of the "not" in "not quite" and "not yet" thus delays the narrator's sense of self-identification and wholeness. Pointing to the narrator's evolving maturity, the "not" also warns that the temporality, the difference, of the folk must be respected. Still, the final sentence of the story implies that the bread eventually *will* be ready—that the narrator's wholeness will come if he seeks it in the appropriate place. In contrast, the colonial other precludes an assumption of complete identification or assimilation; and in this sense, the "unready bread" serves as a marker of the young man's continuing externality in relation to imperialist culture.[16]

The third phase, which Fanon calls the "fighting phase," is instanced in the narrative itself, which records the memory of the protagonist and the now refracted memory of the experienced colonial. As mentioned earlier, Fanon argues that "the native . . . will . . . shake the people. Instead of according the people's lethargy an honored place in his esteem, he turns himself into an *awakener* of the people." We are led by the story's conclusion back to the story's beginning, where the narrator, now an older man, describes the *pan de sal* in terms that reflect his transformation from colonial shame to ethnic wholeness, a wholeness devolving from his love for—indeed his awe toward—the vital elements of his culture:

> The bread of salt! How did it get that name? From where did its flavor come; through what secret action of flour and yeast? At the risk of being jostled from the counter by other early buyers, I would push my way into the shop so that I might watch the men who, stripped to the waist, worked their long flat wooden spades in and out of the glowing maw of the oven. Why did the bread come nutbrown and the size of my little fist? And why did it have a pair of lips convulsed into a painful frown? In the half-light of the street, and hurrying, the paper bag pressed to my chest, I felt my curiosity a little gratified by the oven-fresh warmth of the bread I was proudly bringing home for breakfast. (96)

Notes

Acknowledgments: This paper is a revised version of "The 'Pre-History' of an Asian American Writer: N.V.M. Gonzalez and U.S. (Neo)Colonialism," a paper presented at the American Literature Association (ALA) Conference for a panel on "History, Subject and Identity in Asian American Literature of the 1940s and 1950s," San Diego, May 29, 1998. My thanks to Keith Lawrence of the Circle for Asian American Literary Studies of the ALA.

1. The editors nonetheless feel that Gonzalez's decision to write in both English *and* Tagalog expresses a nationalism shared by other writers like Samuel Tagatac and Joaquin Legaspi.

2. They republished Gonzalez's short story "The Morning Star," which had been written in 1949, the last time that Gonzalez had visited the United States while studying at Stanford University's Creative Writing Program. See Remoto (1996, 7).

3. See the assessments of King-Kok Cheung (1990) and Oscar Campomanes (1993).

4. Wong, however, goes on in this essay to call for a return to a community orientation to counteract the overattention to diaspora that threatens to erase the position from which Asians in the United States can enunciate political projects.

5. N.V.M. Gonzalez (1989, 126) dates "Bread of Salt" in *Mindoro and Beyond: Stories*. I will use Gonzalez's most recent reprint of the story in *The Bread of Salt and Other Stories* (1993). The time of the action in the story takes place in the late 1920s, when Gonzalez was in his teens, living in Romblon, and during a period when the United States still ruled the Philippines as a colony. There is a strong autobiographical cast to this story, as in many of Gonzalez's works, which is explored in Russell Leong's and Jerome Academia's excellent film on the author. In it, Gonzalez talks about familiar scenes of childhood, such as the Spaniard's house and the bakery in Romblon, which provided the building blocks of the story. Of course, none of these comments are to be construed as advocating a peremptory reduction of the story to a biographical interpretation.

6. According to Gonzalez, *kalutang* is the Hanunoo word for two wooden sticks used by Mindoro people to make songs that "help the soul to know where the body is" (1990, 16).

7. The essay is reprinted in Williams and Chrisman (1994).

8. Fanon then switches to "phase" to describe this evolution. Gonzalez uses both "stage" and "phase." Either way, the use of the words "levels" and "stage" indicates a progressivist, or developmentalist, coloring. There is much in Fanon's works which disputes this view. See the references to Fanon in Williams and Chrisman (1994). As discussed later, Gonzalez's story seems to resist this linearism as well.

9. Gonzalez, and the English-speaking protagonist of the story, has chosen to translate *pan de sal* in a literal manner, which might sound strange to English-language readers. But, within the context of the story and the rich cultural and spiritual meanings that the *pan de sal* comes to symbolize in the story, it probably would have made little sense to translate this into "bread roll" or "roll." "Bread of salt" preserves the syntax of the Spanish/Filipino word and even more importantly conveys its hypnotic effect upon the protagonist—his sense of wonderment, which we are invited to share.

10. The language of Robert Louis Stevenson's "The Sire de Maletroit's Door" (collected in *New Arabian Nights*, 1882) as one finds it in the text.

11. His grandfather's relationship with the "Spaniard" calls to mind the hierarchical patron-client relationships that structured social relationships under Spanish colonial rule, something which U.S. colonialism did not destroy but built upon. See Paredes (1988).

12. Gonzalez uses a psychologistic term to describe the colonial consciousness of his generation, "the Jones Law Syndrome." He states that the Jones Law "promised the granting of Philippine Independence as soon as a 'stable' government had been established in the country. 'Stable' then became the operative word, and many a political mission, financed by contributions of twenty centavos or more from each schoolchild, trooped away to Washington to argue the Filipino cause; as it turned out, [U.S.] economic interests, rather than Philippine national stability, was what decided the issue [of Philippine political

independence from the U.S.]. Since 1916 then, the solicitation of foreign, and generally American, approval has become not only a national habit but an expression, alas, of national character." See "Drumming for the Captain," in Gonzalez's *The Novel of Justice: Selected Essays, 1968–1994* (1996).

13. References to Villa abound in Gonzalez's essays on Philippine literary history (for example, "In the Workshop of Time and Tide" in *Mindoro and Beyond* [1989]).

14. There is something in this passage of Vicente Rafael (1990). Rafael shows how the spectacle of Imelda Marcos' beauty and her repertoire of Tagalog love songs at political rallies served to anaesthetize crowds and "to make the hierarchy between leaders and followers seem thoroughly benign" (284–85, 289).

15. The band, whose name ("Miniviluz") is an acronym for the three major island chains of the Philippines—Mindanao, Visayas, and Luzon—is headed by Pete Saez, a responsible member of the lower class.

16. This admixture of delaying and difference is what French philosopher Jacques Derrida calls "le differance"; for example, "In the history of philosophy, terms with double meanings are the ones that have been used to disqualify writing. For example, for Plato writing is a *pharmakon*, both remedy and poison. For Rousseau it is a *supplement*, both the missing and extra 'piece' of language. All of these terms 'inscribe' *differance* within themselves: they are always different from themselves, they always defer any singular grasp of their meaning" (Derrida 1981, 100).

Works Cited

Anderson, Benedict. 1983. *Imagined Communities: Reflections on the Origin and Spread of Nationalism*. New York: Verso.

Campomanes, Oscar. 1993. "Filipino Americans in the Unted States and Their Literature of Exile." In *Reading the Literatures of Asian America*, ed. Shirley Lim and Amy Ling, 49–78. Philadelphia: Temple University Press.

Chan, Jeffery Paul, Frank Chin, Lawson Fusaao Inada, and Shawn Wong. 1991. *The Big Aiiieeee! An Anthology of Chinese American and Japanese American Literature*. New York: Meridian.

Chin, Frank, Jeffery Paul Chan, and Lawson Fusao Inada. 1974. *Aiiieeeee!: An Anthology of Asian-American Writers. Washington: Howard University Press.*

Cheung, King-Kok. 1997. *An Interethnic Companion to Asian American Literature*. Cambridge: Cambridge University Press.

———. 1990. "The Woman Warrior Versus the Chinaman Pacific." In *Conflicts in Feminism*, ed. Marianne Hirsch and Evelyn Fox Keller, 234–251. New York: Routledge.

Cheung, King-Kok, and Stan Yogi. 1988. *Asian American Literature: An Annotated Bibliography*. New York: Modern Language Association of America.

Constantino, Renato. 1978. *The Continuing Past*. Manila: Foundation for Nationalist Studies.

Derrida, Jacques. 1981. *Positions*. Chicago: University of Chicago Press.

Dirlik, Arif. 1996. "Asians on the Rim: Transnational Capital and Local Community in the Making of Contemporary Asian America." *Amerasia Journal* 22 (3): 1–24.

Fanon, Frantz. 1963. "On National Culture." *Wretched of the Earth*. New York: Grove Press.

Gonzalez, N.V.M. 1989. *Mindoro and Beyond: Stories*. Quezon City: New Day.

———. 1990. *Kalutang: A Filipino in the World*. Manila: Kalikasan Press. (Orig. pub. 1972.)

———. 1993. *The Bread of Salt and Other Stories*. Seattle: U of Washington Press.

———. 1996. *The Novel of Justice: Selected Essays, 1968–1994*. Manila: National Commission for Culture and the Arts.

———. 1998. Personal interview by Augusto Espiritu. 25 Oct. Los Angeles.

Hsu, Kai-Yu, and Helen Palubinskas. 1972. *Asian American Authors*. Palo Alto: Houghton-Mifflin.

Kim, Elaine. 1984. *Asian American Literature: The Works and Their Social Contexts*. Philadelphia: Temple University Press.

Lowe, Lisa. 1996. *Immigrant Acts*. Durham: Duke University Press.

Paredes, Ruby. 1988. Introduction. *Philippine Colonial Democracy*. New Haven: Yale University Southeast Asian Studies.

Peñaranda, Oscar, Serafin Syquia, and Sam Tagatac. 1974. "An Introduction to Filipino American Literature." In *Aiiieee!!! An Anthology of Asian American Writers*, ed. Frank Chin, Jeffery Paul Chan, Lawson Fusao Inada, and Shawn Wong, xlviii-lxiii. Washington, DC: Howard University Press.

Rafael, Vicente. 1990. "Patronage and Pornography: Ideology and Spectatorship in the Early Marcos Years." *Comparative Studies in Society and History* 32 (2): 282–304.

Remoto, Danton. 1996. "N.V.M. Gonzalez: Writing as a Celebration of Life." *Chimera* 1 (1): 7.

Williams, Patrick, and Laura Chrisman, eds. 1994. *Colonial Discourse and Post-Colonial Theory: A Reader*. New York: Columbia University Press.

Wong, Sau-ling Cynthia. 1995. "Denationalization Reconsidered: Asian American Cultural Criticism at a Theoretical Crossroads." *Amerasia Journal* 21 (1–2): 1–27.

———. 1993. *Reading Asian American Literature: From Necessity to Extravagance*. New Jersey: Princeton University Press.

Wong, Shawn. 1996. *Asian American Literature: A Brief Introduction and Anthology*. New York: Harper Collins.

13 Representing Korean American Female Subjects, Negotiating Multiple Americas, and Reading Beyond the Ending in Ronyoung Kim's *Clay Walls*

Pamela Thoma

Ronyoung Kim's *Clay Walls* (1987) is an apparently simple novel, particularly because its resolution seems to lie, like a neat Rodgers and Hammerstein musical, in U.S. victory in World War II, in the American dream for Asian Americans, and in middle-class marriage for second-generation Faye.[1] Because of this seeming simplicity and also because of the predilections of contemporary cultural criticism, both within Asian American Studies and within American Studies more broadly, *Clay Walls* has been somewhat neglected by literary critics.[2] Debates over the politics of literary realism that have deeply implicated realist forms in a discursive practice that interpellates conventionally gendered and bourgeois national subjects certainly have discouraged consideration of *Clay Walls* given its evident connection to the American bildungsroman.[3] Despite an investment in the development of an autonomous subject, the interpretive grid of cultural nationalism, which has had enormous influence in Asian American literary studies even to the point of circumscribing feminist literary critique, also may have found little in *Clay Walls* beyond the exposure of anti-Asian sentiment and racism in the United States, because, as numerous critics have pointed out, cultural nationalist perspectives often construct the Asian American subject as male, American born, and English speaking (Lowe 1991, 30–32).[4] Finally, a postcolonial or transnational critical perspective that locates subjects and cultural texts only outside the geopolitical boundaries of the United States and that neglects the connections between patriarchal nationalisms may have overlooked *Clay Walls*.[5]

My analysis of *Clay Walls*, including its ending, contends that the novel is more complex than it seems, addressing many of the ideological concerns that readers and critics in the field have come to expect of contemporary ethnic literature.[6] Kim both enlists and resists conventions of the female bildungsroman in an attempt to represent Korean American female subjects who exceed the discursive limits of patriarchal bourgeois scripts and official stories of Americanization.[7] Further, my analysis of *Clay Walls* follows more recent calls by Asian Americanists to examine realist works as textual practices that participate in a range of strategies and negotiations, sometimes overlapping with those of nonrealist works, which complicate the cultural and economic hegemony of the United States and the subject formations of Asian Americans. As Jinqi Ling emphasizes, "[R]ecognizing both the difference and the continuity between realist and nonrealist works helps reveal not only the ideological and rhetorical complexities of representation in . . . Asian American writing but also its ongoing relevance as active cultural agent to contemporary cultural formations in Asian American history" (1998, 23). I similarly draw upon critical projects that consider women's representations not as static depictions of national subjects but as dynamic formations that uneasily intersect with national and transnational structures and struggles.

First, I discuss how Kim both deploys generic conventions of the female bildungsroman and protests them through plot interruptions and through insertions of historical material that together destabilize the racial, class, and gender ideologies of the conventional American bildungsroman. Then I discuss Kim's revisions of the genre, suggesting how Kim's narrative strategies in *Clay Walls* help to reveal not only further variations of the female bildungsroman but also the limitation of revisions for Asian American women's national and transnational subject formation. Throughout, I focus on Kim's exploration of gender relations and sexuality in the middle-class-aspiring domestic household as a significant site of Korean American women's subject formation connected to an exclusionary America and an imperialist United States.

Several influential critics have remarked on the significant role of the bildungsroman in the tradition of Asian American literature. In *Immigrant Acts*, Lisa Lowe emphasizes the instrumental role of the bildungsroman in canon formation and its problematic reproduction of the bourgeois national subject: "The novel of formation has a special status among the works selected for a canon, for it elicits the reader's identification with the bildung narrative of ethical formation, itself a narrative of the individual's relinquishing of particularity and difference through identification with an idealized national form of subjectivity"

(Lowe 1996, 98).[8] While acknowledging the problems of the conventional national subjectivity that is typically endorsed in the bildungsroman, other critics build upon the understanding that realist narratives such as the bildungsroman are "site[s] for both the construction and the contestation of cultural meanings" and subjects and "do not necessarily produce 'mimetic' results or intellectually less demanding meaning for readers, nor do they have to be seen for this reason as natural accomplices of bourgeois nationalist totalization" (Wong 1994, 130; Ling 1998, 21).[9] Authors construct Asian American subjects in fiction through the negotiation of multiple discourses, and while official national narratives shape and proscribe Asian American authors' fictions in ways that also form the unconscious of published narratives or the "untold stories," official and unofficial narratives intertwine to produce numerous subject positions in and through a single text (Wald 1995, 4; Chu 2000, 10–11; Lee 1999, 66–69). As Patricia Chu contends, Asian American writers turn to the realist bildungsroman "for a repertoire of representational conventions that purport to transcend . . . political differences while providing an idiom for addressing them indirectly" (2000, 16). Chu argues that "Asian American [bildungsromane] do two complimentary kinds of ideological work: they claim Americanness for Asian American subjects, and they construct accounts of Asian ethnicity that complicate, even as they support, the primary claim of Americanness by representing Asian Americans as grounded in highly specific ethnic histories in America" (4). So, while Asian American authors must contend with the conventional marriage plot in the bildungsroman, they tend to avoid "the utopian 'well-married hero' plot, in which the male or female subject's moral and social progress is figured in terms of romantic choices that culminate in marriage" (18–19).[10]

INTERRUPTING THE PLOT OF THE FEMALE BILDUNGSROMAN

In several significant ways *Clay Walls* fits comfortably into the tradition of American bildung that uses romance in a developmental narrative of subject formation that entails assimilation into a unified national consciousness, that is, into white, heteronormative Americanness. The subject of the female bildungsroman more specifically figures middle-class virtues: she is "articulate, sensitive, ethical" and "an idealized woman with whom readers could identify and who could therefore become the heart of a broader imagined community—a nation—that subsumed class differences."[11] As a trope for the sex-gender system, the well-married heroine plot with its ideology of domestic womanhood advances gender relations that subordinate female subject formation to patriarchal and capitalist interests; for Asian American women it also allegorizes the subject's cultural assimilation into white, Euro-American national subjectivity (DuPlessis 1985, 5). Especially in the beginning of the first part of the novel, written from the perspective of Haesu (Kim) Chun, the third-person narrative is concerned with retelling the story of her courtship and marriage to Youngune Chun (simply called Chun in the novel), its connection to their emigration to the United States in 1920, their financial successes, the different forms of intimacy they both clearly desire in their relationship, and the bond, however troubled, they develop for each other as they raise their children. Part 2, written from the third-person perspective of Chun, focuses on the circumstances that force him to leave the family and lead to his death. Most of part 3 of the novel, narrated in the first-person perspective by their daughter Faye, depicts her social and romantic development and conveniently promises closure for the text since it suggests her future marriage. Faye's developmental narrative is also deployed through the shift in her section to the first-person perspective, which can be read to suggest that Faye, in contrast to her parents, is an autonomous and full subject who can speak for herself and make her own romantic choices.[10] In several scenes in Faye's section, her romantic development clearly overshadows other elements of the narrative, as it does even on the day of Chun's funeral when Faye looks at Aunt Clara's face, which has been disfigured by cosmetic surgery, and vows to "never fall in love with the wrong man" (225).

Finally, Kim emphasizes that Haesu and Chun are held to a decidedly middle-class American construction of heterosexual marriage in which masculinity is defined by wage labor and femininity is defined by domestic unpaid labor and consumption.[11] The initial households represented in the text are important in this sense and become the standard to which Haesu and Chun are compelled to aspire by dominant discourse. Mrs. Randolph's home where Haesu works as a domestic is a mansion with thick Persian carpets and mahogany tables in the Bunker Hill area of Los Angeles, and although no Mr. Randolph appears, Mrs. Randolph is clearly well provided for and reigns over the commodities signifying domestic American bliss. The second image of an American household in the novel is Clara and Yim's "rambling Victorian" with more modest but comfortable linoleum rug, velvet pillows, and sofa;

here, too, the gender roles mirror the script with Yim as the head of the house, treating all others "as he would his children" and Clara taking care of the home, practicing the foxtrot to the tunes of Rudy Vallee, keeping scrapbooks of movie stars, and occasionally shopping as a form of leisure and entertainment. In this way and others, Kim makes use of romantic conventions of the female bildungsroman that combine to reinforce a script of development and mobility for Asian American women, both immigrant and second generation.

Almost immediately, however, Kim comments that behind these households' façades and behind the narrative's invocation of the female bildungsroman lies a different narrative of these ostensibly ideal middle-class households, one that reveals how they shelter certain families at the expense of others as a result of structural power inequities. Mrs. Randolph's position is graphically depicted as enabled by the exploitation of Asian immigrant women such as Haesu who clean her house and by people living in "ghettos" "only a few minutes" away, while Yim must work both for the National Association of Koreans (NAK), a Korean independence organization, and as a dishwasher to support his household (7).

In her negotiation of the female bildungsroman, Kim interrupts the romance plot that begins *Clay Walls*. Most significantly, Haesu and Chun's marriage falls apart in the middle of the text and Faye's marriage is deferred beyond the text's ending. The disintegration of Haesu and Chun's marriage may be read according to generic conventions as the narrative's symbolic disapproval of their marriage and as an endorsement of a decidedly Western conception of romantic love, especially given the detailed retelling of their courtship. Chun's subsequent death similarly may be read as narrative punishment for his adultery. In these readings, the deferral of Faye's marriage makes space for the appropriate courtship and romantic thralldom of the romance plot that is largely absent in *Clay Walls*. Yet I read these plot interruptions as snags that begin to unravel the text's developmental plot since they are linked to historical and material realities. Writing from a relatively strengthened position after the repeal of exclusion acts and the restructuring of immigration policies in 1965, Kim augments the indirect address of Asian American political differences and racial exclusion from narratives of Americanization through plot interruptions with a more direct challenge to the script of immigrant assimilation and the promise of Asian American inclusion (DuPlessis 1985, 4).[12] With a keen sense of irony Kim uses the truth value of history as well as verisimilitude to perform a challenge to a genre that typically relies heavily on a realist aesthetic.[13] Social realities that would encourage Kim to structure disruptions into the romance plot are also themselves explicitly inserted in various ways in the text as historical allusions to policies, attitudes, and beliefs affecting Korean immigration in the 1920s, the exposure of the racialized and gendered labor system, and details of the gendered division of labor in the family.

Kim graphically dramatizes and then frankly voices, through Haesu's disbelief and astonishment, the racist tenor of the 1920s when most white Americans thought that "Koreans were 'oriental,' the same as Chinese, Japanese, or Filipino," which is the first of Kim's many references to the racialized U.S. policies of Haesu's times (7). As Sucheng Chan (1991) writes, Korean immigration to the United States in the first few years of the twentieth century was initially encouraged by white owners and managers of sugar plantations in Hawai'i and U.S. labor agents and missionaries in Korea who were seeking replacements for increasingly militant Japanese American workers and was heavily influenced by U.S. and Japanese imperialism, as well as by the racial and sexual politics of U.S. domestic policy.[14] Korean immigration lasted only a few short years before restrictions began to curb it. Anti-Asian sentiment in the United States in the early twentieth century extended to labor and socioeconomic policies and by the 1920s reached a new level with Alien Land Laws, barred membership from unions, occupational taxes, antimiscegenation laws, and vigilante violence, which all severely limited Asian American access to upward mobility and even a living wage and family formation. As Chan observes in the context of a discussion of early Filipino immigrant employment, "the defenders of Euro-American supremacy had had more than half a century to refine and perfect mechanisms for keeping nonwhites in their place. In short, by the 1920s economic niches such as those the Chinese and Japanese had carved out for themselves were much harder to find" (1991, 39). Most readers would be aware of the general economic instability of the nation in the late 1920s and 30s, and *Clay Walls* is very explicit about the Chun family's specific difficulties, but Kim also dramatizes much of the relevant social history of Korean and Asian Americans, depicting, among other things, the segregation of Asians Americans in education and residentially into "unrestricted areas" in Los Angeles, the need to have citizens buy their houses, and the difficulty of finding work that would support a family. Chun and Haesu are exiled to the United States during the height of anti-Asian racism when, despite official narratives

that disguise exclusionary policies, they would have had to use loop-
holes in policies and Yellow Peril discourse that constructed all Asians as
unassimilable, and the author makes this context resoundingly clear.[15]
In highlighting this context, Kim points to a collective history of Asian
Americans that questions the individualist and capitalist identity formation valorized in the bildung form.

The early scenes in *Clay Walls* detail the racially segregated labor
market that Chun and Haesu encounter when they come to the United
States. They both work as live-in domestics, making five dollars a month
but living apart and seeing each other only once a week. Haesu quits
after two months and starts to clean house on a daily basis living at
the Yim's, while Chun continues to work as a live-in domestic. After a
few weeks, Haesu is fed up again and comes up with the idea to sell
fruit from a cart. They work together pushing the cart up and down the
street, and soon they do well enough for Haesu to "stay home . . . like all
yangbans" (aristocrats) in a gendered division of labor uncharacteristic
of the "small-producer family," which usually demanded the unpaid
production work of the entire family and fused work and family life
(Glenn 1999, 14). It is really only for a brief time, however, in the beginning of part 1 of the text that the Chun family narrative follows the
mythical trajectory of immigrant ascent. It is important that Chun only
becomes financially stable and then successful—achieving middle-class
economic status while Haesu is working as a homemaker—through the
informal economy and a corrupt formal economy; that is, through gambling and political graft. In addition, the very same structures cause
Chun's downfall, and his entrepreneurial efforts reveal that the classic immigrant narrative of the self-made man of humble origins is a
myth, as is the middle-class family narrative with its gendered division of labor in which the male patriarch nobly provides for his domestically virtuous or appropriately feminized wife. Chun is forced to
leave Los Angeles and his family in search of work, which he never
finds.

In exposing the racial and gender biases of immigrant success stories,
Kim focuses on the Chuns' efforts to fit the middle-class model, and in
doing so she represents the household as a site of economic exploitation
and physical violence. Although I risk being misread by focusing on
the conflicts in the Chun household, they are crucial to understanding
Kim's exploration of the usefulness of the conventions of the female
bildungsroman for representing Korean American female subjects. As
Rachel Lee points out, "Reading in terms of the nation frequently leads to

a reduction of the role of the family to that of a resistant ethnic enclave vis a vis dominant U.S. culture. However, if one scrutinizes the dynamics internal to the family itself, one perceives rifts within the household, stemming in part from the renegotiation of gender roles" for immigrants in the process of Americanization (Lee 1999, 13). The conflicts in the household are explicitly connected to racialized and gendered processes of Americanization, and characters in the novel testify to the difficulty of fitting into the narrow gender roles imposed upon them by official discourses.

The struggle to conform to a largely economically defined role of masculinity in their households is often the topic of conversation among male characters. The extent to which Chun tries to fulfill his role in the script of Americanization is perhaps appropriately revealed during the poker game in which he loses everything. In response to Karl's suggestion that the only thing that really matters is actually *yangban* class status, Chun is disturbed: this "struck a nerve. Chun had decided long ago that there was nothing he could do about the state of Korean or American politics. He had taken each day as it came, satisfied he had fulfilled his duty if Haesu and the children were clothed and fed. If Karl was right, all that would add to nothing" (171). At the same time, most of the men in the novel also realize that there are few opportunities for becoming breadwinning middle-class patriarchs. Early in the novel when Haesu objects to Chun's gambling, he asks, "Do you know of any other way to make enough money to buy into a partnership or pay the rent?" (2). Likewise, Gilbert Lyu, the professional gambler, refers to occupational barriers for Asians when he says to the rest of the card players, "We're kidding ourselves, we haven't got a Chinaman's chance in legitimate business. The limits have been set and we can't go beyond them" (173).

Haesu tries just as hard to fulfill her feminine role in supposedly typical middle-class American fashion, buying furniture and decorating her house in imitation of the sets in Hollywood films and Mrs. Randolph's home, dreaming of owning luxury cars, and equipping her children with cultural capital through providing private education and piano lessons. Kim indicates that Haesu finds her location in the private sphere familiar, but Haesu clearly takes her queues for a definition of domesticity that is tied to consumer culture from U.S. films, television, and movie magazines. An argument with Chun over a piano that Haesu relentlessly insists they buy, even after learning that their business is in jeopardy, suggests how deeply she is invested in her gender role of middle-class wife and consumer. The masculine and feminine gender roles within the heterosexual middle-class American family model that are imposed in the process of Americanization are not supported by the racially segregated economy or social structures of the United States, and this contradiction impinges on and threatens the Chun family.

Chun's rape of Haesu twice within the first thirty pages of the book may be read to reinforce racially and culturally retrograde stereotypes of Asians. Alternatively, some readers have attributed the conflicts of the Chuns to the considerable social class differences and ambitions they carry with them from Korea.[16] However, I also read these scenes and other violent demonstrations of patriarchal power in the family as effects of Haesu and Chun's frustration with the middle-class family formation into which they are inscribed by dominant discourse. Both of Chun's assaults are directly connected by both characters to his struggle to provide financially and materially for Haesu. Chun and Haesu realize that his wage-earning ability is circumscribed by structural barriers, but when Haesu encodes this fact in terms of his loyalty as a Korean national subject, it challenges Chun's masculine authority, and he responds with sexual assault and payment, in a violent insistence that he is the patriarch he is supposed to be according to scripts of Americanization and Korean nationalist discourse.[17] Readers may wish Chun and Haesu were more critical of the gender roles of capitalist patriarchal family formations that exploit disempowered groups such as Korean immigrant men and women, but this is the historically accurate model of Americanness that disciplines them in the racially biased and gendered process of assimilation. Kim's narrative indicts this model as a violent process, and the contradictory tension between the romantic plot's script of Americanization invoked by Kim, on the one hand, and historical realities she inserts, on the other, remains unresolved in the first two parts of *Clay Walls*.

The tension that preoccupies the first two parts of the novel is somewhat mitigated by Kim's apparent return in part 3 to the more general tension of women's bildungsroman in Faye's story, which can be reduced to a competition between her quest for independence and achievement and her desire for relationship in the form of a morally sanctioned heterosexual romance (marriage).[18] Kim nevertheless continues to register the conflicting material of the middle of the text, resisting not only the racializing representation of Korean American women as "others" to white Americans but also the feminizing representation of Korean American women subjects as assimilated bourgeois women. Given the exclusionary America the novel reveals, it is hard to imagine that Faye or suddenly conjured Dan can enter the "WASP" lifestyle and full American subjectivity that Dan's Yale medical degree and entrance into New Haven society officially enable, and so a skeptical reading of Faye as a domestic heroine seems more in keeping with the cultural work of the rest of *Clay Walls*.

Kim resists, moreover, resolving Asian American political differences through narrative structure or marriage for Faye when she constructs Faye and Dan's final conversation as a discussion about exclusion of Korean Americans in America and in American literature. In this discussion about how literary representations primarily depict white Americans, Dan acknowledges symbolic annihilation as a kind of isolation: "[U]nless one becomes part of that 'other' world" (298). Faye laughs and responds, "Me? In Yoknapatawpha County, however it's pronounced, or in upstate New York? What would I do there? Marry into a good family to raise children who in turn would marry into good families?" (298). When Dan pushes her and argues that they are intellectually and experiencially "part of this society," Faye disagrees, saying, "I don't know. I could never be one of *them*. I don't know if I would want to be. I really have no need to be" (297–98, original emphasis). Acknowledging the bourgeois subject of canonical literature, Faye relates to Dan's cultural and racial isolation in Connecticut through the exclusion she experiences when reading. Then, Faye's amusement at the thought of including herself in American cultural scripts combines with their mutual recognition that the marriage plot for women also symbolizes bourgeois assimilation into the nation to caution the reader against accepting the pat conclusion, which the reader must know is imminent, since, as a member of the audience for this novel as well as the other literature they allude to, the reader is also part of Dan's cultural pluralist "experiential and intellectual" commonality. This warning is especially clear because Faye cannot follow Dan's line of reasoning and because Faye declares that she could never be, nor would she necessarily want or need to be, "American" as it is constructed for Korean American women in dominant discourse. In layering possibility, desire, and need, Faye seems far more dubious than Dan of even a culturally compromising assimilation from descent into consent.

Instead of paving the way for the expected romantic closure by resolving the material and ideological tensions around Asian American women's subject formation that much of *Clay Walls* interrogates, the discussion between Dan and Faye at the end of the novel actually brings the tensions from the middle of the text back to the surface of the narrative and then suspends them when Faye disavows a possible role in conventional narratives of Americanization. Through this conversation Kim links Korean American assimilation to the interpellation of Korean American subjects in literature and throws the resolution of her own bildungsroman into question. Kim also defends her textual challenges to the bildungsroman by suggesting through this conversation that texts that represent Korean American women might very well take on less recognizable structures than those that employ women marrying into "good families." Finally, Kim encourages a skeptical reading of the ending since no proposal or marriage actually takes place on stage and we are left to our own devices to imagine the finale of the now-highly untenable plot. *Clay Walls* does not completely replace the well-married heroine with an Asian American woman-turned-author, as Chu suggests in her argument about some Asian American women's revisions of the bildungsroman. Instead, the author of the novel seems to hover at the close of the text, advising the reader to question the feminized bourgeois American subjectivity in literary texts and to question her own text's promise to turn Haesu and Faye into American authors, the mother into an author of a political history of Korea and the daughter into an author of love letters to Dan.

Nor does the "husband-wife narrative" prevail. In this alternative written by Asian American female authors, emphasis is placed on a bond between men and women that does not abject Asian women; however, husband-wife narratives ultimately "elevate" Asian American female subjects by reproducing the domestic woman or "the privileging of white, middle-class female subjectivities" and do not subvert the bildungsroman (92, 137). Kim's versions of the husband-wife narrative, whether the Chun/Haesu story line or the emerging story line of Dan/Haesu, either do not illustrate a particularly strong bond or are questioned as ideal relationships. These contingent and tentative alternatives thus seem to play a part in the subversion of the bildungsroman. Kim enlists the female bildungsroman's domestic heroine as a framing device in her narrative since she begins the novel with Haesu as a possible heroine in a husband-wife narrative, interrupts this narrative, and switches to a mother-daughter narrative, but then returns to Faye as a possible heroine in the final pages in another open-ended version of the husband-wife narrative. In the process of this vacillating exploration of alternative bildungs, Kim scrutinizes and resists Korean American female subject formation premised on various aspects of feminized bourgeois subjectivity.

THE MOTHER-DAUGHTER ROMANCE AND FORBIDDEN DESIRES

Where Haesu's and Chun's perspectives give way to Faye's in part 3, Kim considers the mother-daughter narrative as a contemporary alternative to the well-married heroine plot, but then returns to another possible husband-wife narrative through the story of Faye and Dan. As much as Kim's variation on the husband-wife narrative resists the complete reinstallation of the bourgeois female subject into Asian American women's writing, Kim seems still more cautious of the mother-daughter narrative, even as her negotiation is evident in her use of the incongruously optimistic tone of the mother-daughter narrative and her obvious focus on Haesu and Faye's relationship.

Wendy Ho (2000) and Sau-ling Wong (1995) have urged critics to take mother-daughter narratives seriously to understand the pleasure and struggle in relationship and Asian American female readers' pleasure in recognition, as well as to explore the largely invisible experiences of Asian American, especially immigrant, women in the United States.[19] Wong's consideration, however, questions the basis of the appeal of mother-daughter narrative, and she devotes most of her attention to how Asian American matrilineal discourse caters to a white female readership that uses these texts "for the Other's presence as both mirror and differentiator" (Wong 1995, 177). Along these lines, Chu observes that as an alternative female bildungsroman the "mother-daughter romance" leverages heroic individualism for Asian American female subjects who are contrasted to othered Asian women in an appropriation of male authors' Asian American immigrant romance, which traces masculinist American subject formation through the abjection of Asian women (Chu 2000, 143). Wong's and Chu's analyses provide convincing explanations for the popularity of some recent texts by Asian American women writers, and they suggest that a closer consideration of the ideological work of the psychologically based mother-daughter narrative is necessary. As I read *Clay Walls*, Kim conveys through tone and especially through the content in Faye's section precisely the sense of strength and perseverance reminiscent of stories of triumphant individualism in which subjects survive hardship in a process of character-building Americanization. Where she departs from and abandons the heroic template, however, Kim indicates that as an alternative representational route to subject formation for Korean American women, the mother-daughter romance plot is limited because it idealizes the mother-daughter relationship as one of sameness and recognition between decontextualized subjects and it desexualizes Asian American immigrant women. Although *Clay Walls* does not provide a seamless counternarrative of Korean American female subject formation, Kim's narrative practice creates gaps and contradictions in the text where the more deeply repressed narratives of women's subjectivity, including female desire, can be indicated and read.

Heroic individualism is borrowed by Kim for the tone of her novel, but she also contests it by situating Haesu socially, constructing her as a subject with a specific background and historically grounded experiences that contribute to her strength and distinguish her from Faye. Chu argues in her analysis of *The Joy Luck Club* that Amy Tan's mother-daughter romance plot achieves little beyond an interweaving of the classic assimilation narrative with a contemporary mother-daughter narrative since it proposes a pseudofeminist version of dominant discourse in which immigrant Chinese women should be recognizable to the reader and are recognizable to their American-born daughters (stand-ins for the reader) because they are essentially already Americans even before emigrating: they struggle and succeed as individual women of exceptional determination and share with readers and their daughters similar processes of gender socialization (Chu 2000; 142–144). The stories these women tell all contain "clear plots in which heroic young women, undergoing trials by ordeal, arrive at epiphanies of character that carry them through their ordeals and, implicitly or explicitly, to America" (Chu 2000, 151). The immigration of these future mothers to the United States and the transmission of their legacy through narratives (authorship) are then taken as proof of their Americanness, while those women remaining in Asia, either literally or through cultural orientation, become the other of these American subjects. In several significant ways Kim's attention to social context and her inclusion of historical record forecloses a reading of Haesu as a self-made woman who exemplifies a masculinist Americanness.

Perhaps most importantly, Kim does not deploy an orientalist narrative of a "backward" Third World Korea from which women must save themselves by emigrating to a First World America, a pattern Sauling Wong refers to as "the Oriental effect" of temporal distancing and quasi-ethnography (1995, 185–90).[20] This is not to say that Korea is undifferentiated from the United States in *Clay Walls* or to deny that Kim positions herself at times as cultural informant in relation to her reader, but Kim is careful not to exoticize or villainize Korea.[21] Kim also refrains in *Clay Walls* from "historical amnesia" in the representation of both U.S.-Korea relations and of Korean history, which would contribute to the sense of an oppressive Korea that stands in contrast to an empowering United States (Chu 2000). In fact, Kim's references to anti-imperialist struggles in Korea, such as the several allusions to the 1 March 1919 Movement and the Korean independence movement in the United States, have the effect of preventing and remarking upon the willful ignorance of readers.[22] Finally, Kim positions Haesu in a particular social location in Korea that contextualizes her agency in the United States. Haesu's family background is especially important in this regard since her mother is depicted as a strong-willed and resourceful caretaker, and her father, though he appears for only two pages in the novel, is depicted as a gentle and loving patriarch. Throughout the novel, Kim draws attention to how Haesu's social class background informs her sense of political rights or entitlements, which helps her to recognize injustice in U.S. racism and imperialism, Japanese colonialism, and various forms of patriarchal authority.[23] The novel opens with Haesu quitting her job as a domestic and figuring out a different way to make money; she tries to intervene in and protest the ideological apparatus of U.S. schools; she insists on better accommodations for her family on the ship when they travel to Korea; she is involved in the Korean independence movement; and she campaigns government officials to make sure that Korean Americans are not "relocated" along with Japanese Americans.[24] Kim's representation of Haesu as a socially located subject intervenes in the heroic individualism one might expect from a dehistoricized matrilineal discourse that idealizes Asian immigrant women as self-made American heroines who have overcome personal, oppressive domestic situations, picked themselves up by their bootstraps, and marched over to America.

Since Kim arguably challenges the classic immigration myth in *Clay Walls*, both symbolically and literally, there is not much of a foundation on which to build a mother-daughter romance that houses the heroic individualism of classic Americanization narratives. Haesu is not envisioned as a self-made American woman, and this presents problems for the idealized relationship that typifies the mother-daughter romance plot. According to Chu (2000), such narratives focus on individual psychological growth to link the immigrant mothers' life stories with their American-born daughters' own stories. These narratives reject conceptions of American subjectivity that exclude Asian American women as unassimilable others and then construct Asian American women as authors. More specifically, the cultural heritage that is the sign of the daughters' difference and initially embodied by the mothers is partly "domesticated" and is also partly transferred and contained in the narrative through the requisite literal journey by the daughters back to the Asian homeland. In short, mothers and daughters become interchangeable when they realize that despite generational and cultural differences, they are both socialized in ways that they must overcome in the process of subject formation. Subjectivity in these narratives is based on bonds of individual achievement between Asian American women, and conventional American subjectivity largely remains in tact. The most general statement of mother-daughter romance plots, in which the daughter personifies and mediates her immigrant mother's Americanization and becomes her primary focus of desire, and in which the immigrant mother "embodies aspects of Asian ethnicity that [the daughter] seeks to incorporate into a larger narrative of Asian American identity," accurately describes the relationship between Haesu and Faye as one in which they seek to recognize themselves in one another, or in which they seek an affirming mirror (Chu 2000; 22, 142; quotation from 22). Yet Kim's use of the mother-daughter romance ends there, since *Clay Walls* represents the gender socialization of Haesu and Faye as different processes that limit their identification to a less-than-complete recognition.

A central conflict in Haesu and Faye's relationship and one that demands considerable attention in the third part of the novel is the definition of Korean American womanhood. Haesu tries to impress upon Faye what it means to be a *yangban* woman, distinguishing it from more materially defined middle-class domesticity in the United States. For example, she refuses to let Faye work a part-time job so she can buy clothes for herself. Haesu is also concerned that Faye remain sexually chaste, and it becomes clear through the way Haesu treats Willie, insisting on curfews and even cautioning him that Faye has to protect her "reputation," that womanhood means marrying into a "good" family, which is encoded as a "patriotic" *yangban* family but which may also be connected to property and money. Faye questions Haesu's notion of womanhood, appropriating her mother's concept of "patriotism" at one point for her own notion of Korean American womanhood that demanded she be "as glamorous as possible" for Willie and the other "boys" returning from the War (279). Although neither Haesu nor Faye formulates a Korean American womanhood that necessarily subverts the domestic womanhood of capitalist patriarchy, Kim foregrounds this generational and cultural dilemma and their divergent definitions of Korean American womanhood as elements of the formation of Korean American female subjectivities. The mandatory trip back to Korea, which supposedly provides the daughter with the knowledge to truly understand her mother and herself and with an ability to distinguish the unassimiliable aspects of their identities from their shared American self, lends virtually no insight to Faye.[25] Kim's narrative complicates the neat compartmentalization of Haesu's identity into one part that is domesticated as a quintessential American and similar to Faye's and another part that is othered as Korean and contained outside an exclusionary construction of America. Kim refuses the trope of idealized identification between self-made immigrant mothers and their self-made American-born daughters and retains differences that substantially destabilize the incorporation of a Korean American female subjectivity that is premised on the adoption of female versions of the masculinist Horatio Alger myth.

When Kim shifts to Faye's perspective and explores the mother-daughter romance plot, moreover, she highlights the less-than-perfect identification between mother and daughter as part of her effort to challenge the conventional well-married heroine plot of the female bildungsroman and the husband-wife narratives that might substitute for it. Since the mother-daughter relationship is not a sexual alternative to the immigrant romance plot but is instead supposed to serve a compensatory function for the Asian immigrant mother that maintains her heroic individualism, it refers us back on some level to the stories of the mother's romantic disappointments, highlighting what is absent from them but now provided in the relationship with the daughter (Chu 2000, 142). While Haesu finds more emotional support and intimacy with Faye than she did with Chun, and their relationship reveals the shallowness of the script of gendered Americanization, it too is less than entirely fulfilling or pleasurable and is certainly not about the mother's sexual desire. Importantly, then, the compensatory function of the mother-daughter romance depends on, but displaces, other stories about the mother—both those that are narrated as disappointments in conventional romance and presumably those that go untold or are about forbidden sexual desire and pleasure.

The conflicts in Haesu and Chun's relationship, which I identified as symptomatic of various ideological and material incommensurabilites that thus represent interruptions in the conventional marriage plot of the female bildungsroman, are simultaneously fragments of a more complete narrative of the mother's sexuality. The stories that are told about the conflicts in Haesu and Chun's marriage mark the pressure of the untold stories or the gaps in the narrative of the novel, and these certainly still remain after Kim shifts to consider the mother-daughter romance. Further, since the mother-daughter romance plot displaces the full story of the mother, the plot as explored by Kim in *Clay Walls* desexualizes Haesu and buries the untold stories of Haesu's sexual desire and pleasure further into the narrative's unconscious. Kim reveals, through contrasting variations of the female bildungsroman, that the mother-daughter romance has limitations for the representation of Asian American female subjects since it seems in the worst cases to contain sexual desire and pleasure outside the narrative or at best to repress or somehow sublimate the mother's sexual desire in the narrative. A reading practice that is alert to the pressure of the untold stories and the gaps and silences in the narrative can begin to limn the untold stories of Korean American women's desire and sexuality.

Much of Kim's initial representation of Haesu and Chun's marriage establishes that Haesu does not find Chun desirable because she considers him to be beneath her; she had always dreamed of marrying a scholar, and she makes it clear to Chun that she is not attracted to him and is only perfunctorily fulfilling her sexual role as a wife (71). The end of the novel also confirms Haesu's desire for a heterosexual partner from the ruling class when Haesu announces to Faye that scholar-patriot Min is moving in with her. One of the difficulties then in her relationship with Chun is Haesu's unfulfilled desire for the ruling class status and nation-state authority embodied by uniformed Korean men. Kim undercuts her own introduction of Haesu as a sentimental heroine who searches for the marriage that will enable her domestication into middle-class life by sending her on an educational journey that challenges this heteronormative construction of desire, an educational journey quite unlike the conventional sentimental heroine's romantic growth.

Yet, the manifest narrative does not fully explore other possibilities for transgressive sexual desire or pleasure. For instance, while Colonel Leland, the admissions officer of the Edwards Military Academy, infuriates Haesu with his patronizing condescension as he tells her of the school's racist admissions policy, Haesu is still so enchanted with the image of the "handsome [white] cadet" on the billboard that she buys the school uniforms for her sons and has their portrait taken along with Faye (in a blue chiffon party dress) to send to her family in Korea (49). Interestingly, this scene is preceded by Haesu's exclamation to Chun: "I can't understand how Clara can give herself to a . . . foreigner, a white man. It's like giving up everything she is. It's capitulation" (48).

This statement and Haesu's disgust with (disgusting) Leland announce quite clearly but perhaps too emphatically that she has absolutely no attraction for white men. Later, when she discusses Hollywood icons with Elena Fernandes, who "jolted Haesu's sense of propriety," we learn that Haesu can find white men attractive (74). The narrative provides virtually no other commentary on possible desire for white men, except to punish Clara with disfiguring cosmetic surgery for her relationship with Scully and the desire for whiteness it entails.

By contrast, Haesu eventually questions the kinds of patriarchal and national power uniforms symbolize. When traveling back to Korea, Haesu learns more about the abusive power of the Japanese colonial administration and even the power of agents of the Korean independence movement posing as crew members on the ship. "[B]eginning to find uniforms distasteful," Haesu instructs the boys to give their Edwards Military Academy jackets away when they arrive in Korea (99). Kim even suggests that Haesu recognizes how sexual desire is structured through the power of uniforms when Haesu thinks about how "[s]eductive uniforms" shield "duplicity and sedition" (99). Finally, Kim implies that Haesu breaks through the class bias of conventional sexual desire when on the first evening after Chun follows them to Korea, Kim depicts the only sexual encounter in the novel in which Haesu seeks sexual pleasure from Chun, though Haesu will not allow Chun to kiss her, something she considers "an act of utmost intimacy" (76). Kim's narrative is relatively rigorous in commenting on and even deconstructing Haesu's class-defined heterosexual desire, but another part of this narrative is the admittedly politically charged and largely untold story of Korean American women's cross-racial sexual desire that remains repressed and is only faintly registered in discussions of Haesu's desire for non-Korean Asian men.

Haesu's sexual desire and pleasure is perhaps most explicitly addressed during the journey back to Korea when she meets Captain Yamamoto/Park, a Korean "posing" as Japanese. From the first moment she meets him and before she learns that he is Korean, Haesu finds him "tantalizing" (68). Their first meeting is followed by her physical arousal: "She undressed and slipped under the covers. The cold sheets made her shudder. She rubbed her hands gently over her body until a soothing warmth began to spread over her and radiate into the bedding. Her hand glided smoothly over her satin underslip" (71). The narrative makes no comment on this sex act. Then, after Haesu learns that Yamamoto/Park is Korean, she disavows her intrigue because she considers him an unpatriotic traitor. However, throughout her voyage Haesu fantasizes about the captain and finally admits to herself for the first time in the novel that she has sexual desire. Haesu's desire for Yamamoto/Park is in ways consistent with her yearning for authority and prestige that is signified by uniforms, but Kim also implicitly poses questions about desire and intimacy forbidden to Korean American women.

Interestingly, while Haesu is sailing to Korea and exploring her physical desires through imagining sexual encounters in dreams, visualizing Hollywood-inspired fantasies, and having conversations about desirable men with Elena Fernandes, Chun is back in Los Angeles having an affair with Loretta Lyu. Since Chun later loses all of his money to Loretta's husband Gil in a poker game and then dies, the narrative may symbolically suggest punishment for Chun's adultery or be read to confirm classist notions of sexual morality. But Kim's narrative strategies may encourage the reader to question the structuring of sexual desire through gender, as well as class, by representing Chun and Haesu in parallel situations, both desiring forbidden partners who are themselves married, but Haesu only dreaming of kisses and affairs while Chun is actually having one, which the narrative describes in erotic detail. In addition to the manifest narrative's contestation of class-based desire, the gaps in Kim's narrative register transgressive and forbidden desire or women's desire outside of heterosexual marriage with Korean men, tacitly commenting on the containment of Korean American women's sexuality.

Just as *Clay Walls* forestalls the replacement of the sentimental heroine of the female bildungsroman with an Asian American female author, it only briefly offers a mother-daughter romance as a revision of the masculinist immigrant romance plot in Asian American women's writing, suggesting elements of the myth of heroic individualism but ultimately critically analyzing an idealization of Haesu and Faye's relationship and the desexualization of Asian immigrant women, as well as the American subject formation that is supposed to spring forth. After revealing the limitations of the mother-daughter romance plot for the representation of Korean American subjects, Kim rather abruptly returns to her negotiation of the well-married heroine plot of the female bildungsroman at the close of her novel.

"What are we doing here?"[26]

By identifying the interruptions, insertions, vacillations, and silences in *Clay Walls*, my analysis of Kim's exploration of the female bildungsroman and its usefulness for representing Korean American female subject formation has underscored the limits of the discourses of Americanness, official and revised, that Kim negotiates in order to remark upon in her narrative. To more fully appreciate Kim's representation of Korean American female subject formation, one needs to push past her negotiation of exclusionary narratives of Americanization and look toward a critique of Asian American literature which examines gender in ways that "emphasize the continuity between America's racialized domestic policies and its imperialist actions abroad" (Lee 1999, 16). This is perhaps especially true for the consideration of Korean American literature given the specific record of U.S. intervention in Korea, the division of the country, and the Korean diasporic community in the United States. As Elaine Kim has commented, "Of particular interest to today's readers is [Kim's] portrayal of the mother's mostly successful efforts to carve out a self-determined identity in America as a woman and as a Korean nationalist" (1997, 169). I return here, then, to my earlier discussion of the Chun household and explore the ways in which Kim's narrative practice both reveals the power relations disguised in the middle-class family formations idealized in and demanded by narratives of Americanization and remarks on their connection to U.S. imperialism and to a Korean diaspora.

Economic exploitation and gendered violence in the family are linked to a broader geopolitical context in *Clay Walls*. In one of their most heated arguments, Haesu blames Chun for their circumstances when she says, "It's because of you that I'm in this strange country. It's because of you that I suffer the humiliation of cleaning up other people's excrement. . . . We are not even in honorable exile" (29). Chun understands her comment as a reference to his name's mistaken appearance on a list of student protestors and his thus "unpatriotic" exile, yet the reader knows that the answer to Haesu's repeated question, "What are we doing here?" is more complicated than the literal answer conveys. Kim suggests a fuller response when the same question is posed by Mr. Yim, who chastises Clara and Haesu for comparing their "hard" lives in the United States with their "fun" lives in Korea (9). Yim reminds the women that they are in the United States because of Japanese colonization and the persecution of patriots. Through Yim, Kim also reminds the reader that the characters' disempowerment in the United States is related to the political crisis in Korea. The colonial structures leading up to Chun's exile become clearer as the novel unfolds, and it is evident that American international interests as well as the Japanese colonial administration actually combine to force Chun and Haesu together and into exile.

Specifically, it is the missionary Reverend McNeil who is responsible for the mismatch of Haesu and Chun, and McNeil who also arranges for the Chuns' exile to the United States.[27] In these twists of the plot, Kim alludes to the history of Korean emigration to the United States at the turn of the century, actually to Hawaii to work on the sugar plantations, which was essentially orchestrated by American medical missionary Horace N. Allen, his friend and businessman David W. Deshler, and American Methodist and Presbyterian missionaries (Chan 1991, 13–16). According to Sucheng Chan, "[A]s a result of the active role that missionaries played, an estimated 40 percent of the 7,000 emigrants who left the country between December 1902 and May 1905 were converts," as are Haesu and Chun who would have had to enter as political refugees (1991, 15).

U.S. cultural and economic imperialism in the form of U.S. missionaries helping to exploit immigrant labor lie just outside the manifest plot of *Clay Walls* in its treatment of America's racialized domestic policies. For instance, during Haesu's most disturbing realization about the racialization of Asians in the United States, when she tells the Koreans for Progressive Reform (KPR) group about her encounter with Colonel Leland at the Edwards Military Academy, the conversation turns to the question, "What happened to 'America, the land of the free'?" Yang comments, "Before we came the only thing we knew about America was what the missionaries told us. 'Freedom' and 'opportunity' they said. They forgot a few things, but we've been here a few years now, long enough to know what to expect." When another character suggests that perhaps the missionaries were not aware of racial discrimination in the United States against Asians, Lee says, "Don't be a jackass. Where have *you* been?" (54–55, original emphasis). This exchange, as well as the narrative emphasis on the role missionaries played in Chun and Haesu's marriage and emigration, can be read as Kim's complex response to questions concerning the subject location of Koreans in America; that is, how Koreans in America contextualize, define, or shape their positions within the larger culture.

Readers may be diverted into locating the national origins of patriarchal ideologies and hierarchies that structure the Chun family, as if that were entirely possible, but a more productive analysis emphasizes how historically and culturally specific gendered and sexual formations such as the family are connected and organized over a range of political structures by capitalist interests, constituting the sites where power is exercised and contested. Theorists of transnational feminist studies contend that "the intersection of gender and work, where the very definition of work draws upon and reconstructs notions of masculinity, femininity, and sexuality, offers a basis of cross-cultural comparison and analysis which is grounded in the concrete realities of women's lives" and which can illuminate persistent features of capitalist exploitation and domination that can then be resisted (Mohanty 1997, 366).[28] Part of Kim's response to the questions "what are we doing here?" and "where have you been?" includes an analysis of the gendered division of labor in the Chun family and a gendered international division of labor. While I am not claiming that *Clay Walls* is a critique of global economic restructuring, Kim anticipates such critiques by underscoring the continuities between the gendered division of labor in Korean and in U.S. households and by highlighting how capital reproduces and transforms locally specific hierarchies to exploit Asian immigrant women in an international division of labor.

The division of labor in the Chun family, both before and after Chun leaves, involves gendered definitions of work that traverse cultural contexts and are adapted by U.S. capital to exploit immigrants and, increasingly, as numerous studies of globalization have shown, Asian and Latina immigrant women. When Chun dismisses Haesu's concerns about gambling, for example, declaring that "money is man's concern," Haesu rehearses the gendered division of labor that the narrator identifies as Confucian: "As long as a man provided for his family, he was beyond criticism. A woman, on the other hand, was measured by how well she served the men in her family; first her father, then her husband and, finally, her son" (28). Yet the overt context of this conversation, gambling, verifies that the Korean structure largely dovetails with the division of labor in the U.S. middle-class family model, which the Chuns are supposed to emulate but which, to repeat, they can only briefly reproduce through the informal economy.

Kim also highlights how capital reproduces and transforms locally specific hierarchies to exploit Korean immigrant women. Haesu's social class status as a *yangban* woman and the racialized feminization of labor in the United States converge to leave few alternatives for Haesu except homework after Chun leaves. While in Korea, Haesu considers how "Korean seclusion was intended to keep precious possessions hidden. As a young girl, she had been hidden from view, required to cover her face whenever she went outside the walls. As her sexuality increased, the greater was her concealment. The higher the woman's rank, the more she was sequestered, and hers was of the upper class"

(105). This observation is later recalled when Haesu decides that instead of working as a domestic she must work at home to preserve the dignity of her family and to make sure that Faye is raised according to her *yangban* heritage (10). Even though Haesu's employer, Mr. Seligman, has never heard of Korea, he hires Haesu after she claims that she grew up doing embroidery, invoking a definition of women's work that she knows is compatible with the garment industry's use of Asian immigrant women who sew for Paris Fine Embroidered Handkerchiefs at home doing piecework (193).

As planned, while Haesu is sitting at the dining room table sewing handkerchiefs, Faye learns about Haesu's girlhood in Korea. But as Faye starts to resist the gender roles that keep her inside after dark, for instance, she questions her mother, asking, "Momma, are you glad you're a woman?" Haesu responds with "Of course . . . although, if I had been a man, I certainly wouldn't be sitting here sewing" (202). In *Clay Walls*, Kim observes that the gender and class hierarchies attributed to Haesu's home in Sunchoun, Korea, also impinge on her in the United States since the gender socialization that sequesters women from men intersects with a racialized feminization of labor in the garment industry in the United States that exploits homework.

In her portrayal of the gendered division of labor in the Chun household and its reproduction by capital interests in the United States in the form of homework, Kim simultaneously resignifies women's work by revealing women's unpaid labor in the household, linking homework to political work, and recognizing the labor involved in Asian American women's subject formation. As we read of Haesu's years of sewing handkerchiefs and then neckties at the dining room table, Kim marches before us all the other work that Haesu is responsible for but which is unpaid and typically unrecognized in official accounts of production, including the reproductive work of feeding, clothing, and caring for her family. Women's labor is additionally redefined in *Clay Walls* through Kim's association of homework with political work. Because homework is wage labor performed in the employee's home, theorists have typically understood homework in terms of how it dissolves boundaries between home and work and how it can obscure from public recognition women's paid labor. However, in Kim's recognition of the household as a site of labor that matters deeply to the Chun family and is valuable, homework also takes on new meaning. Specifically, the KPR starts to hold its meetings in the Chun home to accommodate Haesu's paid labor. The group also gives up its gendered division of labor in which Haesu was the secretary and cooked for the group. While Haesu's political activism surely wanes as she takes on more and more sewing, it seems important that women's paid labor in the household is linked to political work. Chun belittles Haesu's politics, but her political activities affirm her work in the household as valuable labor in the family and arguably sustain her.

Perhaps most importantly for understanding the subject formation of Korean American women, Kim redefines women's labor by recognizing that subject formation in the context of racialized and gendered processes of Americanization and U.S. imperialism and in the context of the Korean diaspora is another type of valuable labor performed by Korean American women. As Hyun Yi Kang has written of the cultural productions of Myung Mi Kim, Theresa Hak Kyung Cha, and Kim Su Theiler, "This then may be a necessary paradox of Korean immigrant identification—that we can most confidently stake a position in relation to both Korea and the U.S. in drawing out not just dissimilarities but formative connections and continuities and in remembering the terms of such collective displacement through the peculiar trajectories of migration and reculturation wrought by that history. The articulation of such twists and detours is no easy and simple undertaking" (Kang 1998, 251). Haesu and Faye must navigate multiple discourses in self formation; and while Kim does not represent either of them as entirely usurping the well-married heroine as bourgeois authors, she does depict them as Korean American women who struggle to define themselves and who perform valuable political and cultural labor as they negotiate the various discourses and structures that contribute to their articulations of who they are.

The American cultural scripts of immigration and assimilation and the Asian American appropriations that are negotiated by Kim in *Clay Walls* reemerge at the end of the novel in the conventional female bildungsroman's possibility of marriage for Faye. *Clay Walls* devotes most of its attention, however, to an exploration of a representation of Korean American female subject formation that does not easily reproduce either a feminized bourgeois subjectivity through the elevation of Korean American women as sentimental heroines in husband-wife narratives or a masculinist heroic subjectivity through the individualization of Korean American women in the mother-daughter romance plot. Kim's narrative strategies perform a complex and sophisticated understanding of subject formation for Korean American women and explore the role of literature and particularly the female bildungsroman in this process.

NOTES

1. See Mast (1987) for a discussion of the national ideologies of Rodgers and Hammerstein musicals.

2. Published essays focused on *Clay Walls* either exclusively or in relation to other texts include those by Hahn (1999), Kim (1990; 1997), Lim (1993), Lowe (1991), Oh (1993), Phillips (1998), and Yun (1992; 2001).

3. See Wong (1994) and Lowe (1996, esp. 5–30) on the relation between literary realism and cultural nationalism. See also Ling, who discusses antirealism in Asian American Studies and implies that this critical tendency is highly gendered.

4. See also Wong (1994). See Lee (1999, 6–12) for an insightful commentary on nationalist concerns in Asian American critical apparatuses and especially the limiting association between cultural nationalism and gender critique in Asian American Studies.

5. See Grewal and Kaplan (1994, 1–33), for a discussion of the usage of "postcolonial" in the humanities. See also Lee (1999, 10–11) for a discussion of the tendency to drop issues of gender and sexuality in postnational or transnational studies in Asian American cultural critique.

6. One formulation of the cultural work Asian American texts are expected to perform is "to expose anti-Asian sentiment in the United States, to limn the trauma inflicted upon Asians by Western imperialism, to envision better worlds where Asians and Asian Americans will not be construed as foreigners in their own homes, to create a common cultural ground for pan-Asian unity, and (more recently) to apprehend Asian Americans' larger global-economic agendas and cross-border alliances" (Lee 1999, 140).

7. For a discussion of cultural scripts, see DuPlessis (1985, 2); Wald defines "official stories" as "narratives that surface in the rhetoric of nationalist movements and initiatives—legal, political, and literary.... Official stories constitute Americans" (1995, 2). See Chu (2000, 12–18) for an excellent summary of the female bildungsroman; following Ian Watt, Nancy Armstrong, Jane Tompkins, and Rachel Blau DePlessis, Chu describes the bildungsroman as a "genre, unlike that of the epic or historical novel, focused on interiority, voice, thoughts, and emotions, rather than public and heroic acts" (2000, 15).

8. For a discussion of the problematic use of the bildungsroman in establishing Asian American literary tradition, see also Wong (1994), Lowe (1994), and Lowe (1991).

9. Wong succinctly describes the ethnicity paradigm as one that "rests on what is known as 'the immigrant analogy,' an analogy which explains racial conflict by subsuming such conflicts within a universal typology of the different developmental stages characterizing the immigrant's assimilation into American life. This universal typology proceeds without reference to distinctions between voluntary or forced entry into the United States, and is thus able to assign equivalence to the situations of African American and Italian Americans" (1994, 128).

10. Kim suggests that the shift in perspectives places Faye in dialogue with her parents and prevents Faye's identity from being subordinated to her parents' (1997, 169–70).

11. I am indebted to Rachel Lee's note that Stephanie Coontz traces this family formation and its imposition on immigrants to the turn of the century (Lee 1999, 162). See Coontz (1992; 8–14, 139). For the history of the roots of middle-class family ideology, including domesticity, and its distinction from working-class domesticity, see Coontz (1999).

12. This in no way suggests that obstacles no longer exist for Asian immigrants. Racialized domestic policies and a racialized feminization of labor especially are well documented in literature. See Lowe (1996).

13. See Oh (1993) for a discussion of context and textual accessibility.

14. I rely on Chan's excellent study *Asian Americans: An Interpretive History* (1991) for most of the information in this and the following paragraphs. See especially chapter 1, "The International Context of Asian Emigration," and chapter 2, "Immigration and Livelihood, 1840s–1930s." See also Kim and Yu (1996, 366) and Hing (1993, 27–36). After the first few years of the twentieth century, which saw several thousand Korean emigrants, by 1910, when Japan "annexed" Korea, Japan and the United States essentially agreed to stop allowing Korean emigration, although about 1,000 women were able to emigrate using the 1908 Gentleman's Agreement clause allowing wives into the U.S. Between 1910 and 1924, Chan reports, only about 500 Koreans entered the United States as political refugees (Chan 1991, 55). In 1924, the National Origins Act, later augmented by the 1934 Tydings-McDuffie Act, halted virtually all Asian emigration to the United States until 1943 when the Asian exclusion acts finally began to be repealed. Kim and Yu report that between 1925 and 1940, about 300 Korean students were admitted into the United States with Japanese-issued passports (1996, 367).

15. See Palumbo-Liu's chapter "Pacific America: Projection, Introjection, and the Beginnings of Modern Asian America" (1999, 17–42) for a discussion of yellow peril discourse in the United States in the early twentieth century.

16. See especially Oh (1993); see also Yun (2001), Phillips (1998), and Lim (1993).

17. Lim reads Chun's behavior as a function of "traditional Korean patriarchal society," in which "women are commodified as objects of exchange and as sexual creatures to serve male desire" (Lim 1993, 585). While this may accurately describe traditional Korean patriarchal society, my point is that his behavior is also part of the disciplining of immigrants into particular gendered formations where capitalist patriarchal power is exercised as part of a racialized and gendered process of Americanization.

18. See DuPlessis (1985, 1–19).

19. Ho (2000; 35, 54–56). Ho's ideas have important implications for an analysis of *Clay Walls*, since the narrative focuses so intently on the women in the Chun household and especially since, unlike Maxine Hong Kingston's *The Woman Warrior: Memoirs of a Girlhood among Ghosts* (1976) or Amy Tan's *The Joy Luck Club* (1989), Kim's text has not enjoyed mass appeal or even much scholarly attention.

20. Chu makes a parallel point, which similarly builds on Johannes Fabian's concept of "allochronism" and observations by Rey Chow about the U.S. conceptualization of Asia as "other," (2000, 148–49). For more sympathetic readings of *The Joy Luck Club*, see Ho (2000) and Lowe (1996, 78–80).

21. As Kim Hahn, Kim's daughter, recalls, Kim was concerned that her novel, were it to be published (and edited) by a major publisher, would be relegated to a stereotypical "third world" account (Hahn 1999, 533).

22. The scene on the ship, in which Mrs. Compton tells Haesu that she has never met a Korean before, also serves this purpose, since Haesu reminds Captain Yamamoto/Park that Mrs. Compton "should certainly know about Koreans.... There must be many of them working for her husband" (73). Kim additionally makes several allusions to U.S. hypocrisy in ignoring the Japanese colonization of Korea, as well as Korea's long struggle for national sovereignty.

23. I am not suggesting that class privilege typically enables insight into injustice. Differences in social class background among Asian immigrants should be acknowledged in analyses of immigrant narratives, however, and familiarity with notions of international politics and U.S. concepts of political rights would, as would familiarity with English (which Haesu does not have), provide advantages for immigrants.

24. While the characterization of strong Asian women also can be deployed to retrograde effect, to orientalize all Asian women as "guardians of ancient... wisdom" or mythic powers, Kim's representation of strong Korean women refrains from essentializing and exoticizing them as folk heroes, shamans, or even tricksters (Chu 2000, 149).

25. The loss of the land in Qwaksan might act as the narrative deportation of Haesu's difference to a distant and inaccessible Korea, especially since it is a result of her associations with the leftist KPR; but the imperialist role of the United States in the division of Korea, which is alluded to in this plot development, makes it far too familiar (and political) for the containment of Haesu's Korean "Koreanness."

26. Haesu's question seems to provide an interrogative and revealing alternative to the slur "go back home," discussed in Kang (1998).

27. McNeil's role in helping Chun and then Haesu emigrate to the United States and escape possible persecution by the Japanese could also be read in salvific terms, but the conflicts and eventual failure of the marriage does not symbolically support this reading.

28. Mohanty defines "Third World women worker" as "both women from the geographical Third World and immigrant and indigenous women of color in the U.S. and Western Europe" and also discusses the term itself as inadequate but still valuable (1997, 366).

WORKS CITED

Chan, Sucheng. 1991. *Asian Americans: An Interpretive History*. New York: Twayne.

Chu, Patricia P. 2000. *Assimilating Asians: Gendered Strategies of Authorship in Asian America*. Durham and London: Duke University Press.

Coontz, Stephanie. 1992. *The Way We Never Were: American Families and the Nostalgia Trap*. New York: Harper Collins.

———. 1999. "Working-Class Families, 1870-1890." In *American Families: A Multicultural Reader*, ed. Stephanie Coontz, 94–127. New York and London: Routledge.

DuPlessis, Rachel Blau. 1985. *Writing Beyond the Ending*. Bloomington: Indiana University Press.

Glenn, Evelyn Nakano. 1999. "Split Household, Small Producer, and Dual Wage Earner: An Analysis of Chinese-American Family Strategies." In *American Families: A Multicultural Reader*, ed. Stephanie Coontz, 74–93. New York and London: Routledge.

Grewal, Inderpal, and Caren Kaplan. 1994. "Introduction: Transnational Feminist Practices and Questions of Postmodernity." In *Scattered Hegemonies: Postmodernity and Transnational Feminist Practices*, 1–33. Minneapolis: University of Minnesota Press.

Hahn, Kim. 1999. "The Korean American Novel: Kim Ronyoung." In *The Asian Pacific American Heritage: A Companion to Literature and Arts*, ed. George J. Leonard, 527–33. New York and London: Garland.

Hing, Bill Ong. 1993. *Making and Remaking Asian America Through Immigration Policy, 1850–1990*. Stanford: Stanford University Press.

Ho, Wendy. 2000. *In Her Mother's House: The Politics of Asian American Mother-Daughter Writing*. Walnut Creek and Oxford: Altamira Press.

Kang, Hyun Yi. 1998. "Re-membering Home." In *Dangerous Women: Gender and Korean Nationalism*, ed. Elaine H. Kim and Chungmoo Choi, 249–90. New York and London: Routledge.

Kim, Ronyoung. 1989. *Clay Walls*. Seattle: University of Washington Press.

Kim, Elaine. 1990. "'Such Opposite Creatures': Men and Women in Asian American Literature." *Michigan Quarterly Review* (Winter): 68–93.

———. 1997. "Korean American Literature." In *An Interethnic Companion to Asian American Literature*, ed. King-Kok Cheung, 156–91. New York: Cambridge University Press.

Kim, Elaine H., and Eui-Young Yu, eds. 1996. *East to America: Korean American Life Stories*. New York: New Press.

Kingston, Maxine Hong. 1976. *The Woman Warrior: Memoirs of a Girlhood among Ghosts*. New York: Vintage.

Lee, Rachel. 1999. *The Americas of Asian American Literature: Gendered Fictions of Nation and Transnation*. Princeton: Princeton University Press.

Lim, Shirley Geok-lin. 1993. "Ethnic and Feminist Literary Theories in Asian American Literature." *Feminist Studies* 19 (3): 571–95.

Ling, Jinqi. 1998. *Narrating Nationalisms: Ideology and Form in Asian American Literature*. New York and Oxford: Oxford University Press.

Lowe, Lisa. 1991. "Heterogeneity, Hybridity, Multiplicity: Marking Asian American Differences." *Diaspora* 1 (1): 24–44.

———. 1994. "Unfaithful to the Origin: The Subject of *Dictée*." *Writing Self, Writing Nation: A Collection of Essays on Dictée by Theresa Hak Kyun Cha*, ed. Elaine Kim, and Norma Alarcon, 35–69. Berkeley: Third Woman Press.

———. 1996. *Immigrant Acts: On Asian American Cultural Politics*. Durham and London: Duke University Press.

Mast, Gerald. 1987. "As Corny as Kansas in August, As Restless as a Willow in a Windstorm: Richard Rodgers and Oscar Hammerstein II." In *Can't Help Singin': The American Musical on Stage and Screen*, 201–218. Woodstock, NY: Overlook Press.

Mohanty, Chandra Talpade. 1997. "Women Workers and Capitalist Scripts: Ideologies of Domination, Common Interests, and the Politics of Solidarity." In *Feminist Genealogies, Colonial Legacies, Democratic Futures*, ed. M. Jacqui Alexander and Chandra Talpade Mohanty, 3–29. New York: Routledge.

Oh, Seiwoong. 1993. "Cross-Cultural Reading Versus Textual Accessibility in Multicultural Literature. *MELUS* 18 (2): 3–16.

Palumbo-Liu, David. 1999. *Asian/American: Historical Crossings of a Racial Frontier*. Stanford: Stanford University Press.

Phillips, Jane. 1998. "'We'd Be Rich in Korea': Value and Contingency in *Clay Walls* by Ronyoung Kim." *MELUS* 23 (2): 173–87.

Tan, Amy. 1989. *The Joy Luck Club*. New York: Putnam.

Wald, Priscilla. 1995. *Constituting Americans: Cultural Anxiety and Narrative Form*. Durham and London: Duke University Press.

Wong, Shelley Sunn. 1994. "Unnaming the Same: Theresa Hak Kyung Cha's *Dictée*." In *Writing Self, Writing Nation: A Collection of Essays on Dictée by Theresa Hak Kyun Cha*, ed. Elaine Kim and Norma Alarcon, 103–140. Berkeley: Third Woman Press.

Wong, Sau-ling Cynthia. 1995. "'Sugar Sisterhood': Situating the Amy Tan Phenomenon." In *The Ethnic Canon: Histories, Institutions, and Interventions*, ed. David Palumbo-Liu, 174–210. Minneapolis and London: University of Minnesota Press.

Yun, Chung-Hei. 1992. "Beyond *Clay Walls*: Korean American Literature." In *Reading the Literatures of Asian America*, ed. Shirley Geok-lin Lim and Amy Ling, 79–95. Philadelphia: Temple University Press.

———. 2001. "*Clay Walls* by Ronyoung Kim." In *A Resource Guide to Asian American Literature*, ed. Sau-ling Cynthia Wong and Stephen Sumida, 78–84. New York: Modern Language Association of America.

Contributors

Suzanne Arakawa is a doctoral candidate in English at Claremont Graduate University. She has taught writing, literature, film, and graduate level multimedia courses at several colleges and universities. She has made contributions to the *Journal of Popular Film and Television*, the *Continuum Encyclopedia of American Literature*, and the *Encyclopedia of World Literature in the 20th Century*. Currently, she is completing her dissertation as well as working on a full-length original play, having recently received an East-West Players/David Henry Hwang Writers/Institute Playwriting Scholarship.

Floyd Cheung is an assistant professor of English and of American Studies at Smith College. He is the editor of a new edition of H. T. Tsiang's 1937 novel *And China Has Hands* (Ironweed Press, 2003). He has published in journals such as *a/b: Auto/biography Studies, Jouvert: A Journal of Postcolonial Studies*, and *TDR: The Journal of Performance Studies*. Supported by a grant from the Woodrow Wilson National Fellowship Foundation, he has begun a book-length manuscript on Asian American autobiographical writing.

Georgina Dodge publishes and teaches in the areas of immigrant literature, autobiography, and multiracial literatures, focusing on Asian American, African American, Chicano, and Native American literatures. An active member of the Society for the Study of Multi-Ethnic Literature in the U.S. (MELUS), she cofounded the Women of Color Caucus within MELUS. She is currently the director of The Ohio State University's Department of African American and African Studies Community Extension Center.

Augusto Espiritu is an assistant professor of history and of Asian American Studies at the University of Illinois at Urbana–Champaign. He is the author of *Five Faces of Exile: The Nation and Filipino American Intellectuals* (Stanford University Press, forthcoming).

Warren Hoffman received his Ph.D. in American literature from the University of California–Santa Cruz. His research interests include

Jewish American literature, queer theory, ethnic writing, and American theater.

Stephen Knadler is an associate professor of English at Spelman College. He is the author of *The Fugitive Race: Minority Writers Resisting Whiteness* (University Press of Mississippi, 2002). He is currently writing a manuscript on transnationalism and early African American fiction, one chapter of which looks at the relation between black abolitionists and the Indian indentureship in the Caribbean.

Keith Lawrence, associate professor of English at Brigham Young University, has published articles on early American narratives and on contemporary Asian American authors. He was the founding director of the Circle for Asian American Literary Studies (CAALS) and its first president. Currently, he is coediting with David Shih an anthology of late nineteenth- and early twentieth-century fiction, most of it by white Americans, which served to formalize American literary constructions of Asia, Asians, and Asian Americans.

Josephine Lee is an associate professor of English at the University of Minnesota. She is the author of *Performing Asian America: Race and Ethnicity on the Contemporary Stage* (Temple University Press, 1997) and coeditor of *Re/collecting Early Asian America: Essays in Cultural History* (Temple University Press, 2002).

Julia H. Lee is a doctoral candidate in English at the University of California, Los Angeles. Her dissertation examines the relationship between African American and Asian American cultural productions of the early twentieth century.

Viet Thanh Nguyen studied at the University of California, Berkeley, and is an associate professor of English and of Asian American Studies at the University of Southern California. He is the author of *Race and Resistance: Literature and Politics in Asian America* (Oxford University Press, 2002), from which his contribution is drawn.

David Shih is an assistant professor of English at the University of Wisconsin–Eau Claire, where he teaches courses in Asian American literature, American literature, autobiography, and creative writing. His article on Louis Chu appeared in MLA's *Resource Guide to Asian American Literature*, and an article on Sui Sin Far is forthcoming in the collection *Asian American Literature: Form, Confrontation, and Transformation* from the University of Washington Press. Currently, he is editing an anthology of early Asian American autobiographical writing and is coediting an anthology of early American literature about Asians and Asian Americans. Both anthologies are forthcoming from Ironweed Press.

John Streamas was born in Tokyo but immigrated with his mother to the United States when he was ten months old. Today he teaches ethnic studies at Washington State University, and for 2004–5 he has received a postdoctoral fellowship from the Asian American Studies program of the University of Illinois. Aside from papers on race, class, and culture, he writes poems, stories, and plays. He and his wife, Valerie Boydo, knew Toyo Suyemoto for only the last few years of her life, but they were fast and close friends, visiting and calling her frequently; and she was, in turn, a source of inspiration and courage.

Pamela Thoma teaches Asian American Studies courses at Colby College in the American Studies and Women's, Gender, and Sexuality Studies programs. Her scholarship focuses on Asian American women's culture, literature, and politics and has appeared in journals such as *Genders* and *Frontiers*. She is director of Women's, Gender, and Sexuality Studies.

Index

V

Varley, H. Paul, 62, 77 (n4)
Villa, Jose Garcia, 258
violence, 273, 284–285

W

Wald, Alan, 96 (n5)
Wald, Priscilla, 184, 267, 289 (n7)
Wan, Peter, 35
war; and Japan, 56 (n4); as metaphor for democracy, 220–221
Washington, Booker T, 35
Watanna, Onoto; *see* Eaton, Winnifred
Watt, Ian, 289 (n7)
Webster, Jean, 41, 48, 49
Weglyn, Michi, 179 (n18), 203 (n4), 204–205 (n13)
West, Cornell, 202 (n1)
Whitfield, Stephen J., 177 (n5)
whiteness, 46–47, 100–107, 112–113
Whitney, James A., 38 (n14)
Wickersham, George, 102, 106
Wiegman, Robyn, 167
Williams, Patrick; and L. Chisman, 262(n7)
Wilson, Willard; editor, *College Plays* (1937–1955), 18, 120, 123–124, 137 (n4)
Wolfe, Thomas, 107
Womack, Craig, 2
Wong, Jade Snow, 9–11
Wong, Jade Snow, works: *Fifth Chinese Daughter* (1945), 9–11; popularity of, 9; contemporary responses to, 9; as modernist text, 10; as appropriation of John Smith myth, 10–11; manipulating narrator of, 11; role subversion in, 11
Wong, Sau-ling Cynthia, 78 (n10), 177 (n2), 251, 252–253, 262 (n4), 276

Wong, K. Scott, 37 (n4)
Wong, Shawn, 251
Wong, Shelley Sunn, 289 (nn3, 4, 8, 9)
Woo, Merle, 9, 10
Wood, Houston, 137 (n8)
World War II, 265; discourse of, 184–188, and Japanese America, 233, 240–244
Wright, Theon, 122

Y

Yamamoto, Hisaye, viii, 156 (n7, n9)
Yamamoto, Traise, 231, 234, 247 (nn3, 5, 7)
Yanagisako, Sylvia, 37 (n3), 73, 76, 78 (n11)
Yau, John, 208
Yee, Wai Chee Chun, Wo*rks: For You a Lei (College Plays,* ed. Wilson, I), 132–136, 137 (n2), 138 (n18); Asian conservatism in, 133–134; class divisions in, 134–135; materialism in, 135; and the "Hawaiian Way," 135–136
Yellow Peril discourse, 30, 271, 290 (n15)
Yin, Xiao-huang, 37 (n4)
Yogi, Stan, 15, 251
Yu, Henry, 128
Yu, Renqiu, 95 (n1)
Yun, Chung-Hei, 289 (n2), 290 (n16)
Yung, Judy, 32
Yung Wing, xi, 16–17, 37 (n2)
Yung Wing, works: *My Life in China and America* (1909), 24–25, 31–36; authority of social position, 32; and Chinese Self-Strengthening Movement, 33; and the Chinese Education Mission, 33, 34; as rebuttal of Roosevelt, 33–34

Z

Zeno, 100
Zhang, Qingsong, 25